SOCIAL POLICIES
AND POPULATION GROWTH
IN MAURITIUS

Social Policies and Population Growth in Mauritius

Report to the Governor of Mauritius

by

RICHARD M. TITMUSS AND
BRIAN ABEL-SMITH

assisted by

TONY LYNES

LONDON AND NEW YORK

Published in Mauritius by authority
of the Mauritius Legislative Council

Sessional Paper No. 6 of 1960
Port Louis

First published in London by
Routledge
2 Park Square, Milton Park, Abingdon, Oxon, OX14 4RN

711 Third Avenue, New York, NY 10017

Routledge is an imprint of the Taylor & Francis Group, an informa business

First issued in paperback 2016

Transferred to Digital Printing 2006

Publisher's Note
The publisher has gone to great lengths to ensure the quality of this reprint
but points out that some imperfections in the original may be apparent

ISBN: 978-0-415-61254-6 (hbk)
ISBN: 978-1-138-98224-6 (pbk)

Contents

		Page
Letter to His Excellency The Governor of Mauritius		xi
CHAPTER 1 Introduction to the Social Problems of Mauritius.		1
CHAPTER 2 The Present Social Services		16
CHAPTER 3 The Problem of Population		42
CHAPTER 4 The Dilemma of Public Assistance		67
CHAPTER 5 Social Insurance and Pensions		85
CHAPTER 6 Industrial Injuries and Diseases		114
CHAPTER 7 Family Needs		125
CHAPTER 8 A National Assistance Board		145
CHAPTER 9 The Fundamental Problems of Medical Care		161
CHAPTER 10 A National Health Service		184
CHAPTER 11 Institutional Care		205
CHAPTER 12 Social Policies and Population Growth		226
APPENDIX A List of Organisations and Individuals who submitted Evidence, etc.		249
APPENDIX B Population Estimates and Projections, by Edith Adams		251
APPENDIX C Income Tax Statistics, by Tony Lynes		292
APPENDIX D Diet Sheet submitted in Evidence		299
APPENDIX E Official Enquiries into Social Conditions and Problems in Mauritius, 1910-1960		300
APPENDIX F Estimated Cost of Social Insurance, Non-contributory and Welfare Benefits		302

Tables

No.		Page
	CHAPTER 1	
i	Number of outdoor relief cases dealt with by the Public Assistance Department, 1953-59	11
ii	Cost of outdoor relief, 1945-58	14
	CHAPTER 3	
iii	Population growth in Mauritius: 1851-1952	45
iv	Live births and deaths in Mauritius: 1871-1955	46
v	Birth and death rates in Mauritius: 1871-1958.	50
vi	Proportion of married women among all women in the child-bearing ages: 1931, 1944 and 1952 Censuses	51
vii	Marriage rates in Mauritius: 1934-1958	53
viii	Age structure of the population of Mauritius: 1931-1957	54
ix	Summary of assumptions adopted for the population projections	58
x	Projections of the population of Mauritius under different assumptions: 1957-1982	59
xi	Projections of the population by broad age groups: 1957-1982	60
	Population of Mauritius by sex and age:	
xii	Projection A: 1952-1982	64
xiii	Projection B: 1962-1982	65
xiv	Projection C: 1962-1982	66
	APPENDIX B	
B-1	Population by sex and single years of age and percentages surviving from birth: 1952	256
B-2	Calculation of birth under-registration in periods preceding three recent censuses	258
B-3	Calculation of under-enumeration of children aged under 5 years in 1931, 1944 and 1952	259
B-4	Females aged 45 years and over in 1952 corrected for over-statement of age	260
B-5	Adjusted population by sex and age: 1952	261
B-6	Mortality levels implied by recent census data	264
B-7	Mortality levels for 1941-51 implied in finally adjusted census data	265

No	LIST OF TABLES	Page
B-8	Comparison of mortality levels implied by census survival ratios and life table mortality rates for a recent period	267
B-9	Some functions of an abridged life table for Mauritius: 1957	271
B-10	Mortality levels implied by life table mortality rates for Mauritius	272
B-11	Age-specific fertility rates for Mauritius: 1955-58	273
B-12	Age-specific fertility rates for selected countries	274
B-13	Derivation of average age-specific fertility rates for Mauritius: 1956-58	275
B-14	Total and ever-married females 10 years of age and over and number of children born alive to them: Census of 1952	278
B-15	Estimation of age-specific fertility rates from number of children ever born to women enumerated at 1952 Census	279
B-16	Distribution of women at specified ages according to number of children ever born, and calculation of births of the fourth and higher orders	281
B-17	Derivation of age-specific fertility rates on assumption of eliminating births of fourth and higher orders	282
B-18	Correction of 1957 female population for over-statement of age at death	284
B-19	Mortality levels from United Nations Model Life Tables and corresponding survival ratios used in projections A and C for Mauritius	286
B-20	Age-specific fertility rates used in population projections for Mauritius	288
B-21	Estimate of births 1957-62 under assumptions of Projection A	288
B-22	Expectation of life at birth for males and females implied in projections A and C	289
B-23	Crude birth- and death-rates implied in the population projections	289
B-24	Comparisons of various population projections for Mauritius: 1957-82	290 |//
	APPENDIX C	
C-1	Resident taxpayers by gross income groups	292
C-2	Proportion of resident taxpayers claiming allowances, by gross income groups	293

No.	LIST OF TABLES	Page
C-3	Resident taxpayers by chargeable income groups	295
C-4	Proportions of resident taxpayers by chargeable income groups obtaining income from various sources.	296
C-5	Life assurance allowances claimed by resident taxpayers, by chargeable income groups	297

Diagrams

Figure

CHAPTER 3

1	Past and future population trends in Mauritius.	44
2	Trend of birth- and death-rates in Mauritius, 1871-1958	48

APPENDIX B

3 Life-table mortality rates by age groups:
   Mauritius and selected United Nations Models:—

(*a*) Males		268
(*b*) Females		269

To His Excellency The Governor of Mauritius, Sir Colville Montgomery Deverell, K.C.M.G., C.V.O., O.B.E.

LONDON 1960

Your Excellency,

In September 1957 your predecessor appointed a Committee of Ministers to investigate the feasibility of contributory, compulsory and comprehensive social insurance in Mauritius. This committee reported at the end of 1958. In January 1959 your predecessor invited me

> "In the light of the report of the Ministerial Committee, to advise the Government of Mauritius as to the provisions to be made for social security, bearing in mind the resources of the territory and the needs of its people".

I accepted this assignment on 24th February and asked whether the terms of reference could be interpreted widely enough to allow me to consider the whole field of social security, health and welfare in Mauritius. I also asked for the services, in London and Mauritius, of Dr. Brian Abel-Smith and Mr. Tony Lynes. These requests were granted.

During the next few months, I took the opportunity afforded by the visits of several of your Ministers to London to discuss with them my terms of reference and hear in greater detail about the problems facing the island. I also studied the reports of earlier committees and commissions and a variety of other papers which helped me to see these problems against the widest possible background.

I had hoped to be able to visit Mauritius in August 1959 but ill-health made this impossible. Instead, I asked Dr. Abel-Smith and Mr. Lynes to go to Mauritius in my place to undertake initial investigations. Accordingly, my two colleagues arrived in Mauritius on 5th August 1959. Dr. Abel-Smith left on 2nd September 1959, and Mr. Lynes on 17th September 1959.

Soon after my colleagues arrived in Mauritius, an advertisement was inserted in the newspapers asking for written and oral evidence. On 28th August 1959, oral evidence was received from seven persons, whose names are among those listed in Appendix A of this report.

In some cases this evidence was supplemented by written statements. I am grateful for the time and trouble which these witnesses took to come and express their views. A meeting was also arranged at Government House for representatives of the trade unions. Twenty representatives attended this conference and a valuable discussion took place.

My colleagues were particularly anxious to ascertain the views of employers in the sugar industry. Accordingly, Dr. Abel-Smith approached the Sugar Producers' Association and asked whether arrangements could be made for him to visit a number of sugar estates and discuss various questions with the estate managers. Dr. Abel-Smith offered four days on which he would be available to make such visits and expressed the hope that it would be possible to visit two sugar estates on each day. Unfortunately, it only proved possible to arrange visits by Dr. Abel-Smith to three sugar estates. I greatly appreciate the co-operation of the Sugar Producers' Association in making these arrangements and wish to thank the three sugar estate managers concerned for the time and trouble they took to make Dr. Abel-Smith's visits so valuable and to answer his questions. Subsequently, Mr. Lynes was able to visit another estate and to meet various members of the staff, job contractors and labourers.

In addition to the evidence collected in this way, Dr. Abel-Smith and Mr. Lynes held a large number of interviews with Ministers and senior officials of the departments concerned, and made numerous visits of observation and inquiry. In all, they managed to visit three hospitals, fourteen institutions, four social welfare centres and three community centres. Five days were spent on surveys arranged with five different district officers of the Public Assistance Department. They were able to sit in on Public Assistance Committees and on interviews of public assistance applicants. They also went out into the field and met a number of public assistance applicants in their own homes. A meeting was also held at Port Louis to enable officials of the Public Assistance Department to make suggestions about improvements in the provisions for social security. Nearly all the staff of the Public Assistance Department were able to attend this meeting.

My colleagues were also anxious to sound public opinion on these issues. I was, therefore, very glad that Ministers were able to arrange for meetings to be held in five different areas of the island at which local residents were invited to express informally their views about the matters covered by my terms of reference. My colleagues were also able to meet a large number of people quite informally on social and other occasions. They found it particularly helpful to give people lifts in the car provided for them and to pick their brains while taking them towards their destinations. By all these means, it was possible to meet and talk to a large number of people. Thus, for example, the mission had discussions with about a quarter of the large sugar estate managers and a quarter of the doctors in the island.

My colleagues returned to London with voluminous notes and original matter amounting, in all, to about half a million words. I was able to supplement all this information with further talks with Ministers in London during the later months of 1959.

A provisional draft report, setting out the historical facts, was then prepared for discussion with Ministers during our next visit to Mauritius in March 1960. On this visit I had planned to collect additional information which the preparation of our draft had shown to be necessary and to investigate certain questions—in particular the work of the Social Welfare Department—which my colleagues had been unable to complete during their visit in August 1959. After these final investigations and discussions, I planned to complete the report in London and present it towards the end of 1960.

This orderly programme was upset by the dramatic intervention of cyclone Alix on January 19th. A delegation of your Ministers arrived in London in the middle of February to hold discussions with Her Majesty's Government about the effects of the cyclone and I took the opportunity to have further talks with these Ministers. Then came the news that another cyclone (Carol) had ravaged the island, causing more damage and destruction than at any time in this century.

I arrived in Mauritius as planned a few days after Carol accompanied by Dr. Abel-Smith. Mr. Lynes, who had reached the island a week earlier, was able to give some assistance with relief work. We found the island overwhelmed by social and economic problems demanding immediate action. Some of the fundamental issues of social policy which we had already identified were greatly magnified and made more sharply obvious. All this made the completion of our work more urgent. We had therefore to restrict the scope of parts of our report and to restrain our inclination to perfect the quality of the facts and their presentation.

During my stay in Mauritius I had talks with representatives of many sections of the community. Despite the exceptional burden of work which the cyclones had imposed upon them, Ministers, officials, and other leaders of the community found time, often at great personal inconvenience, to read and comment on our drafts or to discuss the issues which fell within my terms of reference. I welcomed the opportunity to meet representatives of the Chamber of Agriculture, the Sugar Producers' Association, the doctors and the trade unions, and leaders of the churches. A second notice was inserted in the press and I received oral and written evidence from a number of corporate bodies and private individuals. I toured the island and visited a variety of institutions such as the Central Prison, hospitals, dispensaries, social welfare centres, and the newly established centres for cyclone refugees. I learnt at close quarters something of the administrative problems, central and local, from participating, at the Government's request, in the establishment of a system of registering the population. Dr. Abel-Smith interrupted his work to assist in the planning of this system.

I mention these facts to explain why the report is not as comprehensive and thorough as I had planned. We say nothing about the work of the Social Welfare Department as our observations in this field have been too limited to justify practical conclusions. Our estimates of cost are not as accurate as I would wish: they may need to be revised if more precise information becomes available. Nevertheless, I believe that the facts here presented are sufficiently adequate to provide a valid basis for the conclusions reached.

The proposals we make for social insurance and allied services will call, if they are accepted, for the setting up of new administrative machinery and the working out of a large number of details of organisation and method. Such detailed matters are not within the compass of my terms of reference. In any event, our report would be delayed and greatly lengthened if we were to consider such questions. The services of an expert on these technical aspects of insurance administration could be requested from either the Ministry of Pensions and National Insurance in London or the International Labour Office.

It remains for me to record our gratitude for the generous hospitality, patience and understanding accorded to us while in

Mauritius, and to thank all those who submitted so cheerfully to our endless questioning. In particular, I should like to thank you, Sir, for the extremely helpful arrangements made for our accommodation and travel.

My task was made easier by the reports of earlier committees on subjects within my terms of reference. I found the Report of the Committee of Ministers on Social Insurance particularly valuable.

I wish to thank those who have undertaken special enquiries at our request. An investigation of the occupants of infirmaries and orphanages was undertaken by the Acting Public Assistance Commissioner and a band of voluntary helpers. The Labour Commissioner kindly arranged for his Labour Inspectors to collect some new information concerning the sugar estate hospitals. The Director of the Central Statistical Office undertook a number of special tabulations for us of the Luce enquiry, of the 1952 census and of the income tax statistics. All these involved an already heavily pressed department in several months of skilled and careful work performed with an excellence fully matching the reputation of this Office.

The names of a number of organisations and individuals who submitted evidence or with whom we had discussions are listed in Appendix A. It is difficult to mention by name all those who helped us in our work; I want particularly to acknowledge the kindly assistance not only of those whose names are listed, but of many members of the public, from those living in the refugee centres and humble homes to those holding positions of responsibility throughout the island.

I am also grateful to many public servants in the following departments for their untiring efforts to explain, inform and undertake special inquiries: the Ministries of Labour, Health, Education and Finance, and the Departments of Income Tax, Public Assistance and Social Welfare.

I was extraordinarily fortunate in being able to secure in November 1959 the services of Miss Edith Adams, who was at the time on study leave from the Population Branch of the United Nations. By good fortune, Miss Adams arrived at the London School of Economics in October to undertake private research in the field of demography. She accepted an invitation from me to construct new population projections for Mauritius. The results of her work are represented by the technical appendix on population attached to this report and by the factual basis of Chapter 3. She bears no responsibility whatever for the interpretations, conclusions or recommendations which are based on the demographic facts and projections which were assembled and analysed with objectivity and precision.

To Dr. Burton Benedict, who has studied many aspects of the cultural life of Mauritius, I and my colleagues wish to extend our gratitude for the various ways in which he helped us to understand the social organisation of the different communities.

Miss Sheila Benson, who acted as our Secretary in London, and who was responsible for organising the typing and duplication of our draft report, never spared herself to get the work completed in time. This she did effectively and accurately.

Mr. Ramyead, our Secretary in Mauritius, discharged his duties with great efficiency. He worked untiringly on our behalf and with a sense of public service to which we wish to pay tribute.

I now submit our report for your Excellency's consideration.

I have the honour to be,

    Sir,

        Your Excellency's obedient servant,

            RICHARD M. TITMUSS.

Note on currency

The Currency of Mauritius consists of the Rupee and the Cent, 100 Cents making one Rupee. The Mauritius Rupee is on a par with the Indian and converts to the Pound Sterling at the rate of Rs. 40 = £3, or R. 1 = 1s. 6d.

CHAPTER 1

Introduction to the Social Problems of Mauritius

NEEDS AND RESOURCES

In making our recommendations, we are asked to bear in mind both the resources of Mauritius and the needs of its people. We have interpreted these in broad terms. The social services which a country requires depend on a variety of factors. They depend on the history of the country insofar as these affect social, economic and cultural determinants. They depend upon the ethnic composition of the country and its social structure. They depend on religious and political factors, the quality of the administration, and on the viability of the economy. We have had not only to take account of the past and present of Mauritius, but to form some view of the future to which the population aspires. Mauritius is in a state of rapid change from a low-income cash economy with a strong and extensive kinship system to a society which aspires to a higher national income per head and to a more westernised way of life.

We have assembled in this Report many facts about the past and present of Mauritius. We wish to set out the main heads in this chapter partly to make clear the assumptions on which we have formulated our proposals, and partly to enable those who are less familiar with the island to appreciate its problems in a broad perspective. If our views are of value to the people of Mauritius, they may also be of value to other countries at a similar stage of development. It is for these reasons that we include information which will be broadly familiar to many of our readers.

In the first part of this chapter we outline some of the essential facts about the people of Mauritius—their origins, their history, their religions, their homes and schools and occupations. In the second part we summarise the social and economic problems which have been emerging since the Second World War and show how these problems were strikingly magnified by the cyclones of 1960. This introduction does no more than exhibit the essential inter-relationships of the themes developed in much greater detail in later chapters.

We are by no means the first to consider these questions though our perspective is no doubt broader than that adopted by other students of Mauritius. In Appendix E, we give a chronological list of the commissions, committees and official investigations into social conditions and social policy since the Royal Commission of 1909. There has been no lack of pertinent enquiries. We trust that our Report will not suffer the fate of many of its predecessors.

THE WIDER BACKGROUND

The island of Mauritius is situated in the Indian Ocean, some 500 miles east of Madagascar. It is about 720 square miles in area and supports a population of over 600,000 people. Although just inside the tropics, Mauritius has a temperate climate which favours the production of sugar. This is by far the most important crop grown on the island. The Government is encouraging the development of other crops such as tea and tobacco, but these at present are largely for the local market. Sugar constitutes almost the total of the island's exports. There is as yet little industrial development.

Mauritius was first colonised by the Dutch in the seventeenth century. They found the island uninhabited and imported slaves from Madagascar. The settlement was not a success and the Dutch abandoned it in 1710. Five years later, France laid claim to the island and gave it the name of Ile de France. It remained in French hands until 1810, when it was occupied by the British during the Napoleonic War. By the Treaty of Paris in 1814, the island was finally ceded to Great Britain, and its name changed again to Mauritius. The French settlers were permitted to retain their language and religion. As a result, French and English are both still spoken on the island. English is used for official purposes. The most commonly heard language, however, is Creole, a colourful language mainly derived from French.

The population of the island rose to nearly 60,000 by 1797, including 50,000 slaves from Madagascar and Africa. Under British rule it continued to expand rapidly, and by 1833 it had reached 100,000—three-quarters of whom were slaves. In 1835, the slaves were freed, and a sum of £2 million was paid to their owners as compensation. This raised problems on the sugar plantations as the newly-freed slaves were not anxious to continue to work on them. The planters responded by importing indentured labourers from India. This immigration gave a new impetus to the growth of the population, which increased from 183,000 to 313,000 between 1851 and 1861. After this the rate of increase slowed down; at the turn of the century the population totalled about 370,000 and in 1944 it was still only about 420,000. Since then, however, there has again been a very rapid increase, caused not by immigration but by the combination of a high birth-rate with a sudden fall in mortality following the eradication of malaria.

As a result of the heavy immigration of the nineteenth century the ethnic composition of the population changed dramatically. From an exploited minority of immigrant labourers, the population of Indian descent has grown until it now accounts for about 67% of the people of Mauritius. Some 29% are classified as "general population", including "Europeans and descendants of Europeans, and people of African and mixed origin". Very few of these would claim to be of "pure" European descent. The remaining 4% of the population are Chinese.

This classification of the population can only be regarded as very approximate. It is becoming less meaningful as the result of intermarriage. It nevertheless broadly reflects the occupational distribution. Ownership of most of the larger sugar estates still remains in the hands of the descendants of the original French owners, from whose number come most of the senior staff on the estates. The labourers on the sugar estates are mainly of Indian origin; as are the 18,000 small planters who own about 16% of the sugar land. The "creoles", people of mixed origin, are more generally to be found in the towns and until recently provided most of the recruits to the higher ranks of commerce and the civil service. They have inherited from the days of slavery a prejudice against agricultural labouring work, though this section of the population does provide a proportion of the more skilled workers on the estates. The Chinese section provides most of the island's shopkeepers. There is a "Chinese" shop in every village, providing nearly all the goods required by the local community. Both Indian and Chinese sections are now making an increasing contribution to the professions and administration.

Religious divisions also follow broadly the lines of the ethnic classification. The "general population" is mainly Catholic, while the Indian section is either Hindu or Muslim. Many of the Chinese are Catholics, while others are Buddhists. The Church of England has some adherents in all sections of the population.

The sugar industry is the largest source of employment. Mr. R. W. Luce estimated that in March 1958 it accounted for 51,000 of the 174,000 employed persons in the island. Other agricultural and similar activities, including fishing, accounted for 23,000. There were 30,000 in service occupations (ranging from professional to domestic service), 23,000 in manufacturing industries, 17,000 in commerce, 12,000 in the building industry, and 9,000 in the transport and communication industries. It is not uncommon for women, including married women, and particularly among the poorer classes, to work; in 1958 they accounted for 26% of all employed persons. Between 1952 and 1958, the proportion of females aged 14 and over who were economically active, including the unemployed, rose from 21% to 33%. There was only a small increase in the proportion of economically active males during the same period despite a large rise in the number of boys leaving school.*

The present system of social services in Mauritius is a product of the history of the island. A variety of provisions were made in the nineteenth century for the protection of the immigrant Indian labourers. Thus, provisions were made under the Poor Law for outdoor and indoor relief. In addition, a system of medical care was evolved, consisting both of hospitals and of dispensaries. We describe these developments in some detail in the chapters dealing with the particular services. In addition to these public services, planters were required by law to provide medical care for some of their employees.† From this legislation there has grown up a system of dispensaries and hospitals on the sugar estates. The terms and conditions of service laid down under the Labour Ordinance for the sugar and other industries have been improved and certain social security provisions have been introduced. Social security has thus developed in two separate streams—on the one hand, provision under the Poor Law, subject to inquiry into means and with requirements that relatives should support the impoverished members of the family; and on the other, legislation which has guaranteed minimum wages and provided to a limited extent housing, sickness, maternity and other benefits for employees of particular industries.

There have been two breaches in the principles of the Poor Law. First, in 1931, provision was made for workmen's compensation. We describe this legislation in Chapter 6. Secondly, in 1950, provision was made for old age pensions. They were first subject to a means test, but this was abandoned in 1957.

Primary education is available to all, free of charge, and although it is not compulsory nearly all children of primary school age attend school. Of the 107,000 primary pupils in January 1960, over 60,000 were enrolled at the 113 Government primary schools. Most of the remainder were at Government-aided denominational schools, of which there are 72 in all, including 49 Catholic and 17 Church of England schools. Secondary education is more limited—there are 107,000 primary school places but only some 18,500 secondary school places. There are three Government secondary schools and eight "approved" secondary schools which receive a Government subsidy. In these, higher standards,

* Luce, R. W., *Report on Employment, Unemployment and Underemployment in the Colony in 1958*, Sessional Paper No. 7 of 1958.
† Cap. 214, s. 82.

both academic and physical, are maintained. However, nearly 80% of secondary pupils attend unaided schools, most of which leave much to be desired. Often they are housed in totally unsuitable premises, where unqualified teachers, themselves products of these schools, impart what little academic knowledge they possess to large and overcrowded classes of children.*

The education provided in both primary and secondary schools is geared to a system of Government scholarships. These heavily determine the values and content of the educational system. There are 128 scholarships giving free tuition in Government or aided secondary schools, free travelling and a grant of Rs. 300 a year. In addition, there are six "English scholarships" each year. The winners of these scholarships are offered a university course in a subject of their choice, either in England or elsewhere. Their passage is paid and they receive a living allowance. Of the 36 laureates who won English scholarships in the six years 1953-58, 21 chose to study medicine. The estimated cost of the English scholarships for the year 1959/60 is Rs. 280,000. We refer to this system again in Chapter 9. Other scholarships (normally five each year) are awarded to Mauritian students by the Government of India.

The educational system as a whole has a pronounced academic rather than a practical slant. Its implied aim is to prepare large numbers of young people for clerical and administrative posts. As long ago as 1909, a Royal Commission commented forcibly on the system:—

> "Although the community is almost entirely an agricultural one, hardly anything is done to give either theoretical or practical instruction in agriculture . . . At present the child of an Indian agricultural labourer or small holder learns, out of school, to speak his Indian mother tongue and the local dialect, founded on French and known as Creole.
>
> "In school, he is taught a certain amount of English and French, which, if he follows his father's calling, he will seldom or never use again. He thus obtains a smattering of four languages and an adequate knowledge of none. The nature of his schooling naturally leads him to aspire to become a clerk or adopt some other calling not entailing manual labour. The field of employment open to such youths is small in a Colony like Mauritius, and the result is that a considerable proportion of them become unemployed loungers, living on the scanty earnings of their parents. It is for these reasons

---

* The statistics in this paragraph were provided by the Ministry of Education and Cultural Affairs, Port Louis. Rodrigues is excluded.

amongst others, that we strongly recommend the introduction of technical and agricultural training."*

The passing of half a century has left the problem virtually unchanged. The competition for non-manual employment, and especially for the security of Government employment, is greater than ever, and there is a large and increasing number of young people whose education has fitted them (in their own eyes at least) for employment of a higher status than is available to them. Apart from the Agricultural College, the only real centre of technical education is the Central Prison. Here excellent training is provided in furniture making, shoe making, tailoring and other trades. Selection for technical education is at present based not on aptitude but delinquency.

The educational system and its implications constitute an important part of the social background to our enquiry. We have therefore given this brief description, although we have not interpreted our terms of reference so widely as to include proposals for the future of education in Mauritius.† It is also necessary to give a brief survey of developments in the field of housing, though here again it is within neither our terms of reference nor our competence to offer suggestions for the future.

The traditional form of housing in Mauritius is a simple "straw hut" built round a timber frame. These huts are easily built and the cost of the timber and other materials is about Rs. 250. They can stand up to normal weather but not to cyclones. The materials of which they are built also make them particularly liable to destruction by fire.

In spite of these risks, most of the rural population still live in huts of this kind. In recent years, however, houses built of more robust materials have appeared in increasing numbers. Many of these are the work of private individuals, financed in many cases by loans from the Mauritius Agricultural Bank and the insurance companies. Others have been built by the sugar estates for their monthly paid workers. These vary from the palatial residences of senior staff to the "camps" of small houses for monthly paid labourers. In their efforts to attract labour, some of the estates have taken considerable trouble to make these camps as attractive as possible, with playing fields and meeting halls. Nevertheless, the unwillingness of workers to live on the estates is understandable because of the loss of freedom involved in being tied to one employer. We were disturbed to find, moreover, that on one of the largest

* Report of the Mauritius Royal Commission, Cmd. 5185, 1910, p. 41.
† A more comprehensive account of the educational system and its problems is given in the Report of the Economic Mission, 1960 (the Meade Report).

estates which we visited it is not regarded as the duty of the estate to provide housing for retired employees, except in a few special cases. The labourer who settles in the estate camp must therefore face the prospect of having to find a new home when he is too old or disabled to work.

The other main supplier of modern housing for workers in the sugar industry is the Sugar Industry Labour Welfare Fund Committee, whose activities in this and other fields we describe in Chapter 2. The Fund spent nearly Rs. 3 million on housing estates between 1954 and the end of 1959, and by then had built 373 houses. After the cyclones of January and February 1960, steps were taken to have the asbestos roofs of the houses replaced by concrete slabs at a cost of about Rs. 750,000. In addition the Fund makes loans for house building.

In the urban areas, the standard of house construction is on the whole higher, but the housing conditions in parts of Port Louis are worse than anything we saw in the villages. Hundreds of people are crowded into tin shacks hardly fit for animals. Not surprisingly, tuberculosis and other diseases are very common in these slums, and a large proportion of the families depend on the help, regular and irregular, of the Public Assistance Department. Urban rents are relatively high and there is a very serious shortage of housing in the towns; a situation made worse by the cyclone damage in 1960.

Since 1950 loans for housing purposes have been made by the Government to the Municipality of Port Louis and the three Town Councils. By the end of 1959 loans amounting to Rs. $10\frac{1}{2}$ million had been issued. However, by no means all of this money was used for the construction of houses for lower-paid workers. Some was devoted to "middle-class" housing, which might have been financed more appropriately from other sources. In general it may be said that housing development, even when financed from public funds, has been largely unplanned and uncoordinated.

The gross national product of Mauritius in 1958 was Rs. 658 million. Exports amounted to Rs. 291 million, of which 98·8% in value consisted of sugar and molasses. Imports totalled Rs. 299 million, the highest ever recorded, of which 36% came from Britain and 33% from other Preferential Tariff countries; leaving a small adverse balance of about Rs. 8 million.

The public revenue of the Colony amounted to Rs. 133 million for the year 1957/58. Of this sum, Rs. 47 million was from income tax and Rs. 58 million from indirect taxation. The recurrent and capital expenditure of the Government amounted to Rs. 154 million or 24% of the gross national product. Expenditure on the social services accounted for 38% of Government expenditure. The Education Department consumed 14½% of Government expenditure. The health services took 10%, public service pensions just under 4%, non-contributory old age pensions 4½% and the other activities of the Public Assistance Department another 4½%. Housing loans to local authorities accounted for less than ½%.

Constitutionally, Mauritius has progressed rapidly towards independence in recent years. The 1947 Constitution gave the vote to nearly 72,000 persons, retaining the property qualification only as an alternative to a requirement of "simple literacy", and giving votes to women for the first time. Another innovation was the fact that a majority of members of the Legislative Council were to be elected. In addition the Executive Council, which had previously consisted of the Governor and a number of *ex officio* and appointed members, was to have four members chosen by the Legislative Council. In July 1957, the ministerial system was introduced, and the Executive Council, formerly an advisory body, became in effect a Council of Ministers, consisting of three officials (the Colonial Secretary, the Attorney-General and the Financial Secretary), the four Legislative Council nominees, and five other appointed Ministers. The Colonial Secretary is the head of the Civil Service, and the Ministerial Secretary to the Treasury exercises some of the functions of a prime minister. There are, of course, reserved powers.

The Constitution was again amended in 1958 in respect to the Legislative Council, enabling the general election of March 1959 to take place on the basis of universal adult suffrage. The electorate numbered over 200,000 voters.

The organs of local government in Mauritius consist of the Municipal Council of Port Louis, the Town Councils of Curepipe, Beau Bassin/Rose Hill and Quatre Bornes, and Village and District Councils in the rural areas. These are all wholly or partially elected bodies. The Municipality dates from 1850, while the Town Councils were set up in 1950 to replace the old Boards of Commissioners. The Village Councils were started experimentally in 1947, and while some have flourished, others have been less successful. They are empowered to raise taxes, but in practice they do not do so, their activities being financed by the central Government. Their functions consist mainly of scavenging work and the maintenance of branch roads, but the more enterprising Councils have undertaken a wide range of activities, from bridge-building to the setting up of a day nursery.

The Municipal and Town Councils have a greater degree of independence. They receive financial assistance from the central Government, but they also raise money themselves by means of local rates. Among their most important functions in recent years has been the provision of houses. They are also responsible for the cleaning, lighting and maintenance of streets, various public health services, the upkeep of public gardens and parks, and a number of other functions.

THE EMERGING CRISIS

It will be clear from this cursory description of the past and present of Mauritius, that the economic and social life of the island is dominated by the sugar industry. Its balance of payments, its budget and the prosperity of its people depend upon the earnings, and the use made of the earnings, of its principal industry.

Before the Second World War the island's economy was exposed to the full brunt of international competition. Its people ate or starved according to the price of sugar. There was no protection. In the world slump the price of sugar fell sharply as did the prices of other staple commodities. The price remained very low throughout the thirties. There were riots and demonstrations which were countered, as is customary, by deportations and commissions of enquiry. Remedial measures were proposed, but little progress was made towards implementing them by 1939.

The war brought relative prosperity to the island. The price of sugar rose and so did the wages of sugar workers. There was a growth of retailing, building and service industries. And after the war the price of sugar was not allowed to return to the vagaries of international markets but was regulated under a variety of agreements. But a stabilised price for sugar did not remove all risks from the Mauritian economy. There remained the weather which did not lend itself to national or international control.

The damage caused by the cyclones of 1945, though it did not reach the dimensions of 1892 or of 1960, reduced sugar output by 30%. In the years that followed, the output of sugar varied considerably and for a variety of reasons. Low yields could be caused by either too much or too little rain.

In 1958 the gross national product of Mauritius (the total value of the output of goods and services) was Rs. 658 million (£49 million), or Rs. 1,000 (£75) per head of the population. This represents a higher standard of living than in, say, India or most of Africa, but it is still far below the standards of Western Europe and North America. The gross national product per head of the population rose little between 1953 and 1958. Owing to the very high birth-rate and declining child mortality, the proportion of the population which is "economically active" has been falling. The value of output per head of the economically active population rose between 1953 and 1958 (although with a setback in 1958 resulting from the poor sugar crop of that year). These figures, however, make no allowance for changes in the value of money. In *real* terms—that is, after allowing for the fall in the purchasing power of the Rupee—output per head of the population fell by 14% between 1953 and 1958. Output per head of the economically active population fell by $6\frac{1}{2}$% over the same period. Even if allowance is made for the poor year in 1958, output per worker has clearly been declining.

One explanation for the declining standard of living must be sought in the probability that work has not been found for the increasing number of persons of working age. Evidence about the extent of unemployment and under-employment in Mauritius is not easy to find at any time, but it seems most unlikely that work opportunities have been expanding relative to the rise in the working population. This is certainly true of the sugar industry. Taking the two years 1946 and 1947, the average number of persons then employed in the sugar industry was about 56,000. The average number of persons employed in the two years 1957 and 1958 was also about 56,000. Between 1947 and 1957 the population of working age rose by 20%. The sugar industry has not been absorbing more labour since the war despite an increase in output, an increase in the area under cultivation and stabilised prices.

Compared with the early post-war years the industry is now employing slightly more adult men and slightly fewer women. The most significant fact, however, is that the number of juveniles employed (under age 19) has fallen from 4,400 to about 2,700, a drop of nearly 40%. During this period the number of juveniles on the island has *increased* by well over a third. Despite unemployment, the industry is not attracting young workers. In consequence, its labour force is ageing.

Evidence for the view that involuntary unemployment has been increasing comes from trends in the number of persons receiving public assistance.

In theory, an able-bodied person with or without family responsibilities can only be granted benefit if destitution is established. As a result, very few payments are made to persons classified as able-bodied unemployed. But the number of men receiving assistance because of sickness other than chronic sickness* was over six times as great in 1959 as in 1953. The number of cases receiving benefit without certificates of sickness little more than doubled during

---

* We have excluded from the figures cases of permanent incapacity and diseases of long duration such as tuberculosis.

the same period. This substantial and disproportionate increase in sickness claims in such a short period of time is remarkable. It would seem most unlikely that changes in morbidity could account for this trend, especially in a period when, in relative terms, Mauritius has experienced its most prosperous decade. With the eradication of malaria and tuberculosis coming under control, mortality rates have fallen sharply. It is also unlikely that rising sickness claims can be explained by changes in the criteria applied by Government medical officers. Some part, if not all, of this increase must be due to the growing difficulties experienced by those of weaker health and physique in finding employment and by other factors which we discuss in later chapters on the health services.

A high proportion of manual labourers suffer from anaemia and a high proportion do not get an adequate diet. The over-worked Government medical officer faced with an applicant who complains of giddiness or headaches or backaches—conditions for which clinical evidence is difficult to find—signs a certificate of sickness. If the physical condition of the applicant is poor, the doctor is obviously hard put to certify that he or she is fit for heavy work. The certificate is therefore signed "fit for light work" and the applicant then receives public assistance. Government medical officers have told us frankly that the primary cause is usually economic and not medical. Applicants have failed to find work which brings in enough money to provide an adequate diet for themselves and their families. Doctors resent the fact that they are forced into a situation of having to administer what they recognise to be a disguised, inefficient, and morally discreditable system of unemployment benefit.

During the last week of March 1958, Mr. R. W. Luce carried out a survey of employment, unemployment and under-employment

Table I. Number of Outdoor Relief Cases dealt with by the Public Assistance Department, 1953-59.

Year	Short-term sickness		Chronic sickness	Non-medical	Total
	Men	Women			
1953	1,840	2,143	1,172	5,377	10,532
1954	2,552	2,195	1,488	6,380	12,615
1955	3,216	2,574	2,141	6,653	14,584
1956	4,199	3,199	2,551	7,684	17,633
1957	6,322	4,181	2,920	9,449	22,872
1958	8,972	6,024	3,549	11,078	29,623
1959	12,127	7,074	3,978	12,024	35,203

SOURCE: 1953-58: *Annual Reports of the Public Assistance Department*.
1959: Information supplied by the Acting Public Assistance Commissioner.

in the Colony.* He found that 31,001 persons, or 15·1% of the economically active population, were unemployed. This figure included 4,256 persons who were disabled and whose employability must remain in doubt. Out of 125,396 households in the Colony, over 24,000 experienced some unemployment in the survey week. Mr. Luce concluded, "the figures indicate unemployment on a very severe scale judged by any standard". This situation must be expected to become much more serious as the high birth-rates of recent years are reflected in an increased demand for employment. As we show in Chapter 3, the number of persons of working age will increase by over 50% by 1972.

Mr. Luce's findings have been assailed from many quarters. In particular, the sugar industry has pointed out that it is frequently short of labour and has concluded from this that unemployment is of a voluntary rather than involuntary character. This interpretation of the situation does however suggest, in the light of the evidence we have collected, that not enough is being done to make work more attractive and satisfying, to develop opportunities for training and promotion, and to set examples of civic and industrial leadership.

We are aware that there are many families who are willing to support their older children in the hope of their achieving work of higher social status than their examination results seem to warrant. Unemployment of this kind is to be found among all sections of the community and represents a worthy if misplaced form of self sacrifice to further the social aspirations of their children. There certainly is a reluctance among many of the younger generation to engage in labouring work on the sugar estates. Little is done by employers to offer training or prospects of promotion except to a small group of privileged employees. And even security of employment is often denied to those who do not wish to occupy service tenancies on the sugar estates.

Some of the reluctance of married women as of men to work on the sugar estates must be due to ill-health. Inadequate nutrition and a high incidence of anaemia limit the number of persons who are able to do physically strenuous work for piece rates in the sugar fields. We have been told by doctors engaged in the dispensaries of patients who have been doing strenuous work despite very low haemoglobin levels. And we have been assured by the Superintendent of the Central Prison that given understanding, good leadership and proper food, the Mauritian prisoner works "as well as anybody anywhere".

On the whole, we are inclined to think that there is a substantial

* Luce, R. W., *op. cit.*

amount of involuntary unemployment in Mauritius, and that some part of it is due to a failure to bring together those who are seeking workers and those who are seeking work. The few employment bureaux that are operating in Mauritius are seldom used by private employers. We believe that the failure of employers to apply to the bureaux has contributed to the present situation.

Unemployment is undoubtedly at its worst in the inter-crop season. Sugar is a seasonal industry. There is a drop of employment during the first six months of the year of over 10,000 persons—about one-sixth of the labour force. But this is not the sum total of seasonal unemployment. The lower level of employment and spending inevitably reacts on secondary industries and services. And this effect is reinforced by the fact that those who are employed by the sugar industry in the inter-crop season are paid at substantially lower rates.

The difference between the employment offered by the sugar industry in the crop and inter-crop seasons has been widening since the war. On average in the years 1946 and 1947 there were about 6,000 less people employed in the inter-crop than in the crop season. In the average of the years 1957 and 1958, there were about 11,000 less people employed in the inter-crop than in the crop season and in 1959 the difference rose to nearly 14,000. The statistics for men alone show the same trend. Seasonal unemployment has been increasing.

We have already mentioned the heavy burden of unwelcome responsibilities which growing unemployment has thrown on the Government Medical Service. This is paralleled by an increasing strain shouldered by the Public Assistance Department. The problems of the latter Department are explained and discussed in detail in Chapter 4. There we show, to put it briefly, that in a community where it is very difficult to establish who is working and who is not, let alone the level of normal earnings, it is impossible to operate an effective means test under the present public assistance system. The Department has been struggling with a continuously growing burden of work and it has not been possible to secure that aid is going where it is needed most.

The cost of public assistance has become a heavy drain on the budget. Despite the introduction of old age pensions in 1950, the cost of outdoor relief has risen dramatically since the war.

Between 1945 and 1948, the cost of outdoor relief varied around Rs. $\frac{1}{2}$ million a year. By 1952 it had risen to over Rs. 1 million and in 1953 it was over Rs. 2 million. By 1958, the cost approached Rs. 7 million. Part of this increase can be attributed to growing population, improved scales of assistance and rising prices, but the increase in disguised unemployment and the problems of administering relief on such a vast scale are major causes of this rising expenditure.

Table II. Cost of Outdoor Relief 1945-58.

Year	No. of Cases	Cost Rs.
1945	7,600	465,496
1946	6,899	481,212
1947	7,284	560,219
1948	7,592	546,241
1949	8,153	622,452
1950	9,389	782,320
1951	8,835	939,081
1952	9,655	1,186,794
1953	10,532	2,025,656
1954	12,615	2,092,673
1955	14,584	2,497,003
1956	17,633	3,062,617
1957	22,872	4,198,898
1958	29,623	6,984,786

SOURCE: *Annual Reports of the Public Assistance Department.*

We may conclude, therefore, by saying that the growth of population and other factors has led to a reduction of living standards among certain sections of the people, to growing unemployment, and to a heavy drain on the budget from a creaking system of not very discriminate aid. In Chapter 3 we show projections of the population up to the end of the century. If nothing is done, and barring a catastrophic rise in mortality, the population will more than double by 1982 and may well reach the alarming figure of close on 3 million by the end of the century. Without drastic action, there will be further reductions in living standards and unemployment on a scale so large that no one in Mauritius will be able to question its existence. The administration of public assistance will break down under the strain and impossible burdens will be thrown on the budget. These are the facts which dominate our Report.

THE CYCLONES OF 1960

The effect of the cyclones has been to magnify the social and economic problems of Mauritius. On the morning after cyclone Carol on 29th February about 80,000 people—one-eighth of the population—had taken shelter in schools, village halls, churches, social welfare centres and other buildings. In addition, a larger number of people took refuge with friends and relations. Well over half the houses on the island were damaged or destroyed and a substantial proportion of the sugar crop was lost.

In the weeks after the cyclone the level of employment, normally low in the month of March, fell much lower still. There was heavy expenditure on relief—on issues of free rice and flour to the refugee centres and on two hastily improvised issues of food vouchers to households who had suffered from the cyclone. Without any system of registration or identity card it was impossible either to restrict aid to those who had suffered in the cyclone or to ensure that each household received only one voucher. In the crisis, aid became openly indiscriminate.

The major casualties of the cyclones were the wood and straw huts. A plan was quickly improvised to build temporary terraces of "family units" in wood and corrugated iron. Within three weeks of the second cyclone some of these units were ready for occupation. At the same time longer-term plans were worked out for cyclone-proof housing.

All these schemes of short-term and long-term aid were a heavy drain on the budget at a time when tax revenue was certain to decline. In addition, the reduction in the sugar crop made it likely that less people would be employed in the crop season. There is a real danger that the system of public assistance already heavily strained before the cyclones will break down under the burden of the claims that may well appear in the future.

In short, it may be said that the cyclones have brought to a head the problems and paradoxes of Mauritius. Their economic implications are analysed in the Meade Report. The sugar industry is unable to get enough workers, and workers are unable to find employment. There is more genuine need and more indiscriminate aid. Greater insecurity has been imposed on those already insecure. And, above all, the disastrous cyclones of 1960 have made abundantly clear the need to control population growth.

CHAPTER 2

The Present Social Services

In Chapter 1 we have outlined some of the background information which we will be taking into account in making our recommendations. In later chapters, we shall discuss each service in turn, sketching in the historical development where appropriate, examining the present arrangements and making proposals for the future. In this chapter, we give a straightforward account of the present social services of Mauritius.

SOCIAL SECURITY

Provisions for social security are needed to some extent by all sections of the population. The risk of being unable to earn owing to old age, sickness, or unemployment is not confined to any class, income or ethnic group. Marriage, death, widowhood and confinement are universal contingencies. The support of children involves costs for all parents, rich and poor.

These needs may be met in whole or in part by a variety of different means—by state schemes of social insurance, by non-contributory benefits paid for by taxation, by public assistance services, by schemes of contributory or non-contributory insurance imposed on employers by the state, imposed on employees by employers or negotiated between workers and management. They may be met by voluntary gifts from relations and friends, by loans from shopkeepers and others, by savings made privately, or by insurance with profit-making or non-profit-making agencies. In addition, the state may assist those who are thought to be in need by tax concessions of various kinds. Those who pay part of their taxes by assessment on their income may be allowed to pay less because they have children or other relatives to support, because they are saving for their old age, or because they have spent money on medical bills. It is just as much a cost to the state to forgo tax revenue as to pay out hard cash.

Any policies in the field of social security must take account of all these different means by which needs may be met. We attempt, therefore, in this chapter a comprehensive account of the means by which different groups of the population meet or have met their social security needs in Mauritius. We shall show that the most generous provisions are made for the highly paid employees of the state and other large employers and that the state forgoes large sums of revenue to help income tax payers to insure themselves, and to provide for their children. With the exception of the aged, the blind, war pensioners and the industrially injured in the first months of their incapacity, the needs of the poor are met by the Public Assistance Department at a level which is substantially below subsistence. Hardly anything is done for those of modest means who are not working for Government, the sugar estates and a few other categories of employer.

First, we describe the services provided by the state and the provisions for social security made in the income tax. We then set out the provisions made on an occupational basis for civil servants and others. Thirdly, we outline the charitable provisions which are assisted by the state. Finally, we discuss the activities of trade unions and friendly societies, the proposal to form credit unions in Mauritius and the informal arrangements for meeting social security needs.

Provisions of the Government

The Government agency mainly responsible for the distribution of cash benefits is the Public Assistance Department. Since 1950, the Department has administered a system of non-contributory old age and blind pensions. Originally these pensions were subject to a means test, but this was abolished in 1957. A pension of Rs. 22 per month is now payable to men over 65, women over 60 and to blind persons over 40. The number of pensioners at the end of 1959 was 26,795; the total cost for 1958 (including pensioners in Rodrigues) was over Rs. 7,800,000. Until 1960 the pensions, when in payment, were not considered to be subject to income tax. The Government now proposes to make them taxable.

The system of compensation for industrial injuries and diseases laid down by the Workmen's Compensation Ordinance, 1931, as amended, can be described as a "state scheme" of social security in the sense that it has statutory authority and that the Government accepts responsibility for its enforcement. It provides for weekly payments by the employer for a period not exceeding 12 months in cases of temporary incapacity and lump sum payments for permanent disablement. The payments are based on the previous earnings of the claimant and the degree of incapacity, the maximum payments for total incapacity being two-thirds of previous earnings or a lump sum of four years' wages, as the case may be. If the injury or disease results in the death of the workman, a lump sum of three years' wages is payable to his dependants.

Certain categories of workers are excluded from the provisions of the Ordinance, notably non-manual workers earning over

Rs. 5,000 a year and domestic servants. During 1958, a total of 6,016 cases were dealt with under the Ordinance and compensation amounting to Rs. 213,570 was paid. Of this amount, Rs. 37,577 was paid in 11 cases where death resulted from the injury.

War disability pensions are paid to Mauritius ex-servicemen at half the rates applicable to United Kingdom war pensioners. The weekly rates for a private are as follows (in shillings and pence):—

Degree of disability	Pension		Addition for wife		Addition for each child under 16	
	s.	d.	s.	d.	s.	d.
100%	42	6	5	0	3	9
90%	38	3	4	6	3	4½
80%	34	0	4	0	3	0
70%	29	9	3	6	2	7½
60%	25	6	3	0	2	3
50%	21	3	2	6	1	10½
40%	17	0	2	0	1	6
30%	12	9	1	6	1	1½
20%	8	6	1	0		9

The basic rate for 100% disability was fixed at 20s. in 1943. It has risen to 42s. 6d. (Rs. 28) as a result of successive increases reflecting changes in the United Kingdom rates. However, between 1943 and 1959, retail prices in Mauritius increased by only about two-thirds. The Mauritian war pensioner has, therefore, enjoyed an increase of one quarter in the purchasing power of his pension since 1943.

These provisions for old age and blind pensions, for war pensioners and workmen's compensation are the only *general* provisions, where the amount paid is not subject to a test of means. Apart from the occupational provisions which we describe below, all other cash needs can only be met by the system of "outdoor relief" administered by the Public Assistance Department. This function of the Department was inherited from the old Poor Law, dating back to the 1830's. There are now public assistance offices in all the towns and larger villages, staffed by 13 district officers and about 70 local officers and cadets. Above them are the adjudicating officers who examine each new or renewed application for relief at the head office of the Department in Port Louis. Before adjudication, each case is considered by the local Public Assistance Advisory Committee, composed of prominent members of the local community. Outdoor relief is not given to the able-bodied unemployed except in extreme cases of destitution. In the great majority of cases the granting of relief is dependent on the applicant obtaining a certificate from a Government medical officer.

The methods of calculating outdoor relief are set out in a departmental memorandum dated September 1953. It is expressly stated that "assistance is by way of part maintenance"; the present basic rates are below subsistence level:—

	Rs. per month
1st adult in household	15
2nd adult in household	13
Children:	
aged 9-12 (boys) } aged 9-14 (girls) }	8
aged 6 to 9	7
aged 3 to 6	6
aged up to 3	5

Additional allowances may be given in cases of one-person households and sickness (especially in cases of tuberculosis). A "wage stop" can be applied, and if there is a child in the household earning more than Rs. 26 per month a part of the excess is deducted from the relief scale; but all allowances from charitable organisations are disregarded. In 1959, outdoor relief was given in 35,203 cases. This total includes some overlapping where the same person had more than one spell on relief during the year. The total cost of outdoor relief in 1958 was about Rs. 7 million.

These are the general provisions for social security for the whole population. Persons whose income is large enough to be subject to income tax have additional provision made for their needs by a system of tax concessions. Allowances for children in 1959/60 were at the following rates:—

		Rs.
Children under 16 or receiving full-time instruction:	1st	800
	2nd	700
	3rd	600
	Others (each)	500
Addition for children studying abroad:	Over 16	3,500
	16 or under	1,000

It should also be pointed out that the life assurance allowance can be used to obtain tax relief on the cost of a child's education by means of an endowment policy, the whole of the premiums being allowed as a deduction from taxable income. The children's allowances are therefore even more generous than they appear from the foregoing schedule.

An additional "personal allowance" of Rs. 2,000 is given in respect of the taxpayer's wife, whether she has an income of her own or not; and an allowance of Rs. 500 can be claimed for a dependent relative or housekeeper, subject to certain conditions.

In Appendix C, we give some rough estimates of the cost of the allowances for children and dependent relatives (including housekeepers) for the year 1957-58, in terms of the actual reduction in income tax payable by individual taxpayers as a result of claiming these allowances:—

	Rs.
Children in Mauritius	1,000,000
Children studying abroad	160,000
Dependent relatives and housekeepers	150,000

We estimate that the cost of the allowances for children studying abroad, which were increased to their present level as from the year 1959-60, is in the region of Rs. 500,000 for that year. These estimates do not include the cost of the allowances given in cases where the liability to tax is reduced to nil—an important omission whose size we have no means of calculating.

Tax allowances are also given in respect of life assurance premiums and contributions to pension schemes and widows' and orphans' funds. The cost of tax concessions on individual contributions to pension schemes was Rs. 160,000 for 1957-58. The greater part of the contributions to pension schemes in Mauritius is, however, paid by employers. Subject to certain conditions, these contributions are allowed in full as a deduction from the profits on which income tax is assessed, and they are not included in the above figure of Rs. 160,000. Pensions paid in Mauritius are subject to income tax, but benefits paid in the form of lump sums are not.* Many pensioners do not pay Mauritian income tax, because nearly all employees from overseas, as well as a considerable number of Mauritians, do not remain in Mauritius after their retirement. Even where the pension is taxed, the rate of tax will almost certainly be lower than that which the employer would have paid on the part of his profits absorbed by the contributions. The amount of tax forgone in this way cannot even be estimated, but is certainly considerable, especially at this stage of the development of occupational pension schemes in Mauritius when the total amount of pensions in payment by these schemes is very small in relation to the contributions flowing into them.

The growth of life assurance business in Mauritius was greatly

---

* Under schemes set up after 29 August 1958, three-quarters of the total benefits must take the form of pensions or annuities if the employer's contributions are to be allowed as a deduction from profits.

encouraged by the introduction of income tax in 1950, as life assurance premiums are allowed *in full* as a deduction from income for tax purposes, up to a limit of one-sixth of chargeable income and 7% of the sum assured. In the United Kingdom only two-fifths of such premiums are allowed, and since the allowance does not apply to sur-tax, the maximum *rate* of allowance is two-fifths of 7s. 9d. in the £, equivalent to $15\frac{1}{2}$% of the premiums. In Mauritius, the maximum rate of allowance is equal to the maximum rate of tax, which is now 70%.

We were informed that the insurance companies operating in Mauritius have as yet had little success in selling life assurance in the villages, and the administrative and commission costs of doing so would certainly be high. Life assurance, therefore, has largely become a device for reducing income tax assessments in Mauritius. This impression is borne out by the analysis of the tax allowances in Appendix C. For the income tax year 1957-58, incomes of individuals liable to tax were reduced by life assurance premiums amounting to over Rs. $2\frac{1}{2}$ million. The cost to the Government in terms of tax lost is estimated at Rs. 1,200,000 for that year.

We may summarise the non-occupational provisions for social security by the Government of Mauritius fairly simply. Nearly Rs. 8 million is spent on non-contributory pensions and about Rs. 7 million (in a "normal" year) on "outdoor relief". The Government forgoes income tax revenue of over Rs. 1·7 million to enable the better-off section of the population to provide for their housekeepers, children and other relatives and over Rs. 1·4 million to allow them to save for their old age and for other reasons.

Occupational provisions for social security

The oldest occupational scheme in Mauritius, as in the United Kingdom, is that which provides pensions for clerical and higher civil servants. This dates from 1859, and as amended gives not only a retirement pension at age 60 (or earlier on compulsory retirement) but also a gratuity on death before retirement. Since 1925 one quarter of the retiring pension may be taken as a tax-free lump sum, and 102 of the 105 officers retiring in 1958-59 took advantage of this option. The maximum pension, payable after $33\frac{1}{3}$ years' service, is two-thirds of final salary, while the maximum death gratuity is 25 months' salary. There are at present about 10,000 pensionable civil servants (including aided school teachers who, although not strictly civil servants, were brought into the scheme in 1952) and 1,473 pensions were in payment at 1st July 1959.

Originally, no comparable provision was made for "non-pensionable" manual workers in the Civil Service. Since 1905, however, broadly similar, though less generous, arrangements have been made for them. These are now contained in the Government Servants (Allowances) Regulations, 1952, as amended. The pensions paid to "non-pensionable" civil servants are given at the Governor's discretion and are for this reason called "compassionate allowances". In practice, however, they are granted automatically except in cases of dismissal on grounds of misconduct. The maximum compassionate allowance is two-thirds of average wages for the last five years, payable after 40 years' service, and the maximum death gratuity is one year's pay. There are about 11,000 "non-pensionable" civil servants, of whom two-thirds are engaged on a permanent basis, but at 1st July 1959 only 1,016 compassionate allowances were in payment.

The cost of Civil Service pensions and compassionate allowances for the year 1958-59 was as follows:—

	Rs. (thousands)
Pensions	4,295
Compassionate allowances	647
Lump sum payments on retirement (in partial commutation of pension)	1,648
Lump sum payments on death	238
	6,828

The lump sum payments in partial commutation of pension covered 104 pensionable civil servants, the average lump sum being about Rs. 15,850.

In 1886, the Widows' and Orphans' Pension Fund was created to enable *pensionable* civil servants to make provision for their widows and orphans (aided school teachers are not included). Membership of the fund is compulsory, and the civil servant contributes approximately 4% of his salary. The Government contributes to the fund by crediting interest at the generous rate of 6%, and makes a further contribution in the form of a cost of living allowance to dependants of civil servants who retired before 1st July 1950. In some cases this is as much as 200% of the basic pension, and it adds about 50% to the total amount of pensions now in payment. Since 1932, the fund has had only a "hypothetical" existence, the Government having repudiated its debt in respect of the accumulated balance, while at the same time accepting responsibility for paying future pensions as they arise. At 31st December 1959, the hypothetical fund amounted to about Rs. 18 million. In calculating the pension payable in each case, the contribution record and the ages of the civil servant and his wife are taken into account. There were 1,442 pensions in payment at the end of 1959, and the total cost for that year (including cost of living allowance) was Rs. 1,121,000.

Pension schemes for certain of the employees of the Town Boards and the Municipality of Port Louis were set up in 1925 and 1929 respectively. They are modelled on the Civil Service scheme, but with some differences. In particular, the maximum pension under the Local Bodies Pensions Ordinance, 1925 (which relates to Town Boards), is two-thirds of *highest* pensionable emoluments though the pension is calculated as a proportion of final emoluments—a pension of two-thirds of final emoluments being reached after $33\frac{1}{3}$ years. The Municipality Pensions Ordinance, 1929, gives a maximum pension of two-thirds of final salary after 35 years' service. The number of employees potentially eligible for pensions under these two Ordinances is about 450. The number of pensions in payment at 1st July 1959 was 116, and the total cost for 1958-59 was Rs. 196,805. In addition, under Government Notice 14 of 1948, compassionate allowances may be paid to non-pensionable officers. However, no such allowances were being paid by the Town Boards in July 1959, and only nine by the Municipality.

Pensionable (non-manual) civil servants are normally entitled to 28 days' sick leave on full pay in each year. A medical certificate, which may be given by a private doctor, is required only when a period of sickness exceeds three days. Sick leave exceeding 28 days in the year, up to six months, can be granted with full pay on the recommendation of the Director of Medical Services, and further leave on half pay may be given on the authority of the Colonial Secretary.

Permanent manual employees in the Government service are entitled to 14 days' sick leave on full pay in each year, subject to producing a doctor's certificate for periods exceeding three days. In cases of prolonged illness an additional 14 days on full pay and 62 days on half pay can be given (making a total of three months). "Prolonged illness" in this context means illness extending over a period of 14 days or more, or any period of illness spent in hospital—a somewhat illogical definition which has caused some dissatisfaction. Thus a man who has exhausted his first 14 days of sick leave and is then absent for a further period of 14 days can receive his full pay, while if he returns to work after 12 days' absence he receives nothing.

Casual manual workers in the Government service are entitled after five years' service to the same amount of sick leave as permanent employees. After one year's service, but less than five years, they are entitled to only 14 days on half pay once they have exhausted their 28 days on full pay.

Apart from the question of defining "prolonged illness" these provisions appear to us to be generous. However, their effectiveness is somewhat reduced by the prevalence of malingering in certain Departments, encouraged by the fact that the first 14 days of sick leave (28 days in the case of pensionable officers) can be taken in periods of three days or less without evidence of sickness being produced. It is difficult to estimate the actual extent of malingering, but from a comparison of sick leave statistics for permanent manual workers in the Public Works Department and the Railway Department, it is clear that in the Railway Department it is normal to take 14 days' sick leave in the year, regardless of actual sickness experience; thus, over 80% of the sick leave taken during 1958 was within the first 14 days' leave on full pay to which each individual is entitled, and 91% of this was taken in periods of three days or less. The tendency to take frequent short spells of sick leave is less marked in the Public Works Department.

Outside the public service, the largest occupational pension scheme is the Sugar Industry Pension Fund, a statutory scheme which was set up in 1956 (replacing an earlier Retiring Fund). It covers all monthly paid workers in the sugar industry. Both employers and workers contribute to the Fund. The employer's contribution varies both with the employee's earnings and his age, while the employee pays approximately 5% of his *basic* salary or wage, regardless of age. The employer's contribution is in general by far the larger of the two, especially for the higher age groups. At the inception of the Fund it was decided that contributions in respect of past service from age 30 should be credited to the members, the money being obtained partly from the old Retiring Fund and the Sugar Industry Labour Welfare Fund, while the responsibility for finding the balance was laid on the employers.

The pension is normally payable from the anniversary of joining the Fund preceding the sixtieth birthday, and the annual amount payable is one-third of the total contributions paid by the employee himself plus an appropriate sum for past service from age 30. A larger pension can be earned if retirement is postponed. Up to two-thirds of the capitalised value of the first five years' pension can be taken as a tax-free lump sum on retirement. Of the 465 members of the Fund who retired in 1959, 348 took advantage of this option.

On withdrawing from the Fund voluntarily before retiring age, the employee has the choice, if he is over 40 and has had 15 years in pensionable employment, of either claiming immediate refund of his own contributions with interest, or receiving a reduced pension at normal retiring age. The latter alternative would appear more attractive in the long run but in some cases immediate needs may be sufficiently pressing to outweigh concern for the future. This may perhaps explain why nearly all employees who leave the Fund under these circumstances choose to claim a refund of their contributions.

At the end of 1959, the numbers of contributing employees were as follows:—

Staff	1,303
Artisans	3,485
Labourers (monthly paid)	3,589
	8,377

The contributions paid (excluding the special contributions for past service and management expenses) were as follows:—

	Rs. (*thousands*)
Staff	1,274
Artisans	806
Labourers (monthly paid)	521
	2,601

Of this total, over Rs. 1,600,000 represents contributions by employers. There were 717 pensions in payment in December 1959, amounting to Rs. 12,991 a month excluding lump sums.

Monthly paid sugar estate workers are entitled, under agreements between the trade unions concerned and the Mauritius Sugar Producers' Association, to up to 45 days' sick leave on half pay in each calendar year. Female labourers resident on the sugar estates are entitled to a maternity benefit of Rs. 10, subject to regular employment and residence on the estate for the preceding six months. This is in addition to the maternity allowance of Rs. 10 payable by the employer to female labourers "employed and resident on the estate" under the Labour Ordinance. The Ordinance also provides for one month's unpaid leave both before and after confinement.

The "end of year bonus" paid to regularly employed sugar estate workers compensates them to some extent for their lower earnings in the inter-crop. It is based on the size of the crop and the price obtained. For a monthly worker it can vary from one-third to two and two-thirds months' pay (one month's pay means, in this context, one-twelfth of the basic wages actually earned during the calendar year by the worker in question). Daily paid workers only receive one-quarter of this amount, and to qualify for it they must be paid directly by the estate at a fixed daily rate, have worked regularly on the same estate for 250 days, and (except in the case of artisans and certain other skilled workers) be resident in the estate camp. There must be relatively few daily paid workers who can satisfy these conditions.

There are numerous pension schemes set up by private employers in the sugar industry and in other industries largely as a result of the generous treatment of pension and superannuation fund contributions under the income tax law which we have mentioned earlier. Most of these schemes provide pensions only for "staff" (i.e. administrative and clerical) employees and/or their dependants, and are financed wholly or mainly by contributions from the employer, part of which is in effect recovered from the Government through the income tax. Part of the benefits can usually be taken in tax-free lump sum form. Since 29th August 1958, the lump sum cannot exceed 25% of the total benefits if contributions to the fund are to be allowed as an expense for tax purposes, but for schemes set up before that date there is no such limitation and the lump sum benefits often exceed 25% of the whole. (As in the United Kingdom, the 25% limit follows the standard set by the Civil Service scheme.) Schemes of this kind are operated by many of the larger employers. In the case of the sugar estates, in addition to the Sugar Industry Pension Fund, private death and disablement benefit schemes, limited to staff employees, have been set up by most of the big estates. A typical sugar estate scheme of which we were given details offers a lump sum, payable on retirement at 60 or on earlier death or disablement, amounting to two months' salary for every year's membership of the scheme, up to a maximum of five years' salary. As this scheme was established before 29th August 1958, the whole of the contributions are deductible from the employer's profits for income tax purposes, although no tax is payable on the lump sum benefits.

We are unable to estimate the total cost of these private schemes, either in terms of contributions or pensions in payment, but we were informed by the manager of a local insurance company which has been responsible for setting up a large proportion of them that the premium income in respect of staff schemes received by this company alone for the year ended 30th April 1959 exceeded Rs. 2 million. Of this sum, only about Rs. 164,000 represented contributions from employees. As far as we are aware, no estimate has been made of the emerging costs of all these private and public pension schemes and tax free benefits to the economy of Mauritius in the future. It would seem that their impact is bound to be very heavy indeed.

Certain other occupational arrangements are described below under the heading "Friendly Society and Trade Union Funds".

Charitable funds

Under this heading we discuss the arrangements made to supplement the statutory provisions, first, for ex-servicemen and, secondly, for the blind.

The Ex-Servicemen's Welfare Fund was formally constituted in 1946 to take over from a committee appointed by the Governor in 1942 the function of providing temporary assistance to ex-servicemen. Its objects are set out in Section 3 of the Ex-Servicemen's Incorporation Ordinance (No. 9 of 1946, as subsequently amended) as follows:—

"3. The objects of the Fund shall be to provide temporary assistance to ex-servicemen after their demobilisation and pending their re-settlement into civil life, to provide medical assistance to them, if necessary, to facilitate the return of ex-servicemen who carried on a trade to their trade by the loan of tools, if necessary, to help those who wish to resume their business to such extent and in such manner as may seem advisable to the Committee constituted under section 6 of this Ordinance (hereafter in this Ordinance referred to as 'the Committee') to facilitate the apprenticeship and training of individual ex-servicemen desirous of learning and qualifying for any trade or art, to incur such expenses and give such undertakings as circumstances may render advisable in the interest and for the benefit of ex-servicemen collectively or individually and generally to do all such acts and things as are incidental or conducive to the attainment of the objects of the Fund;

"Provided that any person who voluntarily enlisted after the 15th August 1945 shall not be eligible for assistance."

The Fund's revenue has been derived partly from the Lotteries Fund and partly from a Government grant. The Lotteries (H.M. Forces) Fund distributes its shares of the profits from eight lotteries a year among a number of funds for the benefit of ex-servicemen and others; in 1959, out of a total sum distributed of Rs. 587,000, more than half went to the Ex-Servicemen's Welfare Fund. Until 1957-58 an annual grant of Rs. 100,000 was paid to the Fund by the Government. Grants for subsequent years have been suspended pending a decision as to the future of the Fund. From time to time the Fund has found itself in financial difficulties. One reason for this was the drain on its resources represented by Montebello Farm, originally intended as a farm training centre for ex-servicemen. After making substantial losses (the trading loss for 1957 was Rs. 72,918) the farm was sold in 1958, having (in the words of the President in his annual report for 1958) "failed in its object". Recently the Fund has been compelled to restrict its operations and sometimes to close its office temporarily, partly as a result of the suspension of the Government grant.

The activities of the Fund are now confined to the payment of cash grants on either a regular or a casual basis. About 175 disabled ex-servicemen are receiving regular pensions from the Fund. Of these, about 20% are cases of tuberculosis, while a further 20% suffer from mental disability of some kind. Only about 10% are disabled as a result of war service, and most of these receive a war pension which is supplemented by the Fund. Of the other 90%, two-fifths receive grants from the Public Assistance Department, although the Public Assistance Commissioner stated in a letter to the supervisor of the Fund dated 14th February 1956, that regular allowances made by the Fund would be considered as part of the recipient's resources in assessing any relief which the Department might pay him. Nearly all those assisted by the Fund, with the exception of those suffering from mental disabilities, are stated to be married, and many have large families to support. Family responsibilities are taken into account both in public assistance grants and in war pensions.

The casual payments are now confined to short term payments to sick ex-servicemen. It is very rare for the Fund to pay for any drugs. While the regular pensions mentioned above are intended to bring the beneficiary up to a level of Rs. 80 per month for himself and his wife plus Rs. 15 for each child, the payments made during sickness as casual grants bring the beneficiary up to a somewhat lower level of living.

The Lotteries (H.M. Forces) Fund makes contributions to a number of funds for the benefit of past and present members of the forces. The following payments were made in 1959:—

	Rs.
Assistance to ex-servicemen (including contributions to Ex-Servicemen's Welfare Fund)	356,000
Clinique Mauricienne	65,000
Royal Pioneer Corps	41,000
Ex-Servicemen Association	34,000
Sailors' Home Society	30,000
British Red Cross Society	20,000
Ex-Service Seamen Welfare Fund	16,000
Mental Health Association	10,000
Mercantile Marine	7,093
Others	8,000
	587,093

Grants totalling Rs. 250,000 (of which the Rs. 65,000 shown above is a part) have been made by the Lotteries Fund to the Clinique Mauricienne, a newly built private clinic, in consideration of an informal agreement to reserve a number of beds for ex-servicemen at a reduced charge.

We have mentioned earlier that under the Old Age Pensions Ordinance, 1951, as amended, blind persons over the age of 40 are entitled to a pension of Rs. 22 per month. An additional allowance is paid by the Welfare of the Blind and Prevention of Blindness Society, Rs. 9 a month for men and Rs. 5 for women. The Society also provides blind men with an opportunity of earning a small income by basket-making at the Loïs Lagesse Residential and Training Centre. The work is somewhat seasonal, but a man can earn up to Rs. 4 a day in the busy season. There is no similar provision for women.

The Society receives a subsidy of Rs. 15,000 a year from the Government, and in 1958-59 it collected about Rs. 11,600 in donations and made a net profit of about Rs. 13,500 on sales of baskets.

Friendly society and trade union funds

We have been unable to estimate the extent of the activities of friendly societies in Mauritius, since registration is not compulsory. Moreover, although 318 associations with a total of 53,404 members (probably including some overlapping memberships) were registered under the Registration of Associations Ordinance (No. 45 of 1949) at 31st December 1958, these may have included "benevolent, educational, literary, scientific, sporting and other associations", and we do not know how many carried on friendly society activities. However, the Annual Report of the Registrar for 1958 does state that funeral benefits amounting to Rs. 246,107 were awarded by 122 associations (83 of the Indo-Mauritian Population and 39 of the General Population) to 2,002 beneficiaries.

The Civil Service Mutual Aid Association was incorporated in 1894, to make loans to civil servants of up to three-quarters of their annual salary or pension in order to meet certain non-recurrent expenses. Loans were to be repaid over a maximum of $4\frac{1}{2}$ years. Members have to hold a certain number of shares in order to be eligible for loans. The Association borrows money by means of bill tenders. Its affairs were examined by the Commission on the Purchasing Power of the Rupee, which found that applications for loans were granted almost automatically. Moreover, loans once made often remained outstanding for many years owing to the practice of "re-casting"—borrowing back every six months the amount repaid. In many cases the outstanding loans had to be written off on the death of the member. The Commission considered that these practices "diminish greatly its efficiency as a first line of defence for the Service in cases of genuine need and hardship", and "contribute to an attitude of irresponsibility", and made a number of proposals designed to enable the Association to perform its original function of making small loans to meet sudden crises, at moderate interest and repayable over a reasonable period.

We were told of the existence of a number of other "Mutual Aid Societies", whose main function is the payment of funeral benefits. The largest of these, according to our informant, has some 5,000 members, and pays the following sums on the death of a member or one of his relatives:—

	Rs.
Member	500
Wife	250
Father, mother or child over 10	125
Child, 5 to 10	75
Child, under 5 (including still-born)	50

Some other societies pay smaller benefits. We understand that the cost of a funeral in Mauritius would normally be over Rs. 200. For most families this is a very considerable outlay, and these societies therefore appear to be performing a useful function.

Some of the trade unions also have burial funds, but only three of them paid out more than Rs. 1,000 in 1958, the largest total payments (Rs. 5,560) being made by the General Port and Harbour Workers' Union. The subscribing membership of these three funds is about 2,100, and the benefit payable on the death of a member varies from Rs. 125 in the General Port and Harbour Workers' Union to Rs. 550 in the Sugar Industry Staff Employees' Association. Smaller benefits are paid on the death of a dependant.

There are a very few instances of trade unions paying sickness and other benefits; notably the Sugar Industry Staff Employees' Association, which provides benefits for maternity, education and unemployment.

Credit unions

The formation of the first credit union in Mauritius had to be postponed owing to the untimely arrival of cyclone "Carol". Nevertheless, we include the subject in this summary of existing social services, since the preliminary work has been completed and the movement is shortly to be inaugurated.

A credit union is "a group of people who pool their savings and lend to each other at low interest"—not more than 1% per month. The proposed rules provide that each member must take up at least five shares of Rs. 10 each; the first Rs. 10 to be paid immediately and the balance by monthly instalments. Dividends will be paid on these shares at an anticipated rate of between 3% and 6% per annum. Loans can be made to members of up to one month's salary, repayable over 12 months. Loans made to a member must not exceed three times the value of his shares (whether paid up or not). By means of a group insurance scheme, any outstanding debt is extinguished on the death of a member. In addition, his dependants receive twice the value of his shares provided that he was not over 55 when they were acquired, and smaller increases for shares acquired between the ages of 55 and 75.

Initially it is proposed that credit unions should be formed by groups of employees. Arrangements will be made with their employers for instalments of capital and debt repayments to be deducted from their salaries. The formation of credit unions for the self-employed and for daily paid and casual workers might be possible at a later stage. The introduction of credit unions in Mauritius is mainly due to the initiative of Mr. Edwin de Robillard, and is worthy of encouragement both as a constructive alternative to the system of money-lending at very high rates of interest which we discuss below, and as a much needed example of voluntary mutual aid.

Informal arrangements

In addition to the resources of the family, on which the individual can usually rely for some degree of assistance and support in times of adversity or dependency, there is in Mauritius a complex system of credit which enables daily needs to be met when normal sources of income are interrupted. We can only mention briefly some of the more important manifestations of this system, which has been described in more detail elsewhere.*

In the villages of Mauritius, most of the necessities of life are purchased from a local shop, usually owned by "the Chinaman", who operates a system known as "roulement". This is merely a current account between shopkeeper and customer, to which weekly purchases are added, and from which weekly payments are deducted, in such a way that there is always a balance owing. Normally this balance would not fluctuate greatly from month to month, but if the customer is unemployed or short of cash for some other reason, "the Chinaman" will often give credit for much larger amounts.

Another frequent source of credit is the employer. In the villages

---

* E.g. Sessional Paper No. 6 of 1959, *Report of the Commission on the Purchasing Power of the Rupee*; and Benedict B., "Cash and Credit in Mauritius", in the *South African Journal of Economics*, Vol. 26, No. 3, September 1958.

this usually means the job contractor or the sirdar, but the practice of making loans to employees on the security of their accrued or future earnings is apparently found in all types of employment, including the Civil Service. In the sugar industry such loans play an important part in tiding the daily-paid labourer over the inter-crop season.

Although these arrangements may sometimes lead to the job contractor or shopkeeper acquiring an undesirable hold over his debtors, they appear to have been beneficial in the absence of social security provisions, and they certainly help the worker and his family to weather some of the common contingencies of sickness and unemployment. There is, however, less to be said in favour of the numerous money-lenders, or "casseurs", who batten on misfortune and improvidence by making loans at fantastically high rates of interest. The activities of the "casseur" are described in the Report of the Commission on the Purchasing Power of the Rupee:—

"The system generally operating is simply described. A man who is short of a small sum of money is introduced by a friend to 'someone who can help him out'; he signs a promissory note for the sum received (or frequently for a larger sum) in favour of a person whose name is sometimes left blank and at a rate of 12 per cent per annum; he agrees however to pay a quite different rate of interest varying from 6 per cent to 20 per cent *per month*. So long as the interest—at the monthly rate—is paid regularly no pressure is put on the borrower to repay the capital (and interest is frequently paid in whole or in part over very long periods); in fact further sums are often lent before the capital of the first loan is repaid. Repayment of the capital is indeed discouraged by insistence on repayment in one lump sum which is almost always beyond the means of the borrower. The day comes when the borrower cannot pay his interest; he is then persuaded (with or without the threat of legal action) to make a fresh promissory note for the outstanding principal sum plus accumulated interest and the sum may be rounded up by a further small cash loan; the rate of interest is then frequently increased. If the threat of legal action has to be implemented the plaint is frequently withdrawn later on the completion of a fresh promissory note which then includes the legal expenses as well as the sums owing. Payment is almost always collected by the usurer himself or his agent; the money-lender never gives any receipt for payments of interest and generally refuses payment by cheque or postal order, taking every precaution to avoid any writing which might be used as evidence of the usurious nature of the transaction."*

* Sessional Paper No. 6 of 1959, p. 20.

The Commission quotes a case in which, according to the evidence of the borrower, he had borrowed Rs. 300 in October 1953, and by March 1958, having repaid Rs. 1,186·50 in capital, interest and legal costs, still owed Rs. 374—i.e. more than the original loan (an interesting detail of this case is the fact that Rs. 200 of the money repaid was provided by the Ex-Servicemen's Welfare Fund).

The Commission also describes two forms of savings club, known as "le cycle" and "la caisse noire", which, while they may provide a useful means of saving, can also be a source of loans at extortionate rates of interest. Attention is also drawn to the activities of unlicensed pawnbrokers and to the extent of indebtedness among civil servants.

This elaborate system of credit would appear to be in large part the result of uncertain and irregular earnings, especially in the sugar industry, and low wages which leave no margin for savings. It should be possible to control the less desirable aspects of the system by means of regulation or the establishment of official pawnshops, but such measures are unlikely to reduce very greatly the activities of the "casseur", who is adept at evading legal restrictions and prepared to give loans without security. The development of credit unions will undoubtedly help, but the fundamental answer must lie with the provision of regular earnings.

HEALTH SERVICES

The health services in Mauritius comprise a Government Medical Service, the medical services provided by the sugar estates under the Labour Ordinance, and the services provided by a number of private institutions and organisations. The Government Service includes public health measures and services for the individual, both preventive and curative. The sugar estates provide both hospitals and dispensaries. Among the services in the private sector are the clinics provided by the Maternity and Child Welfare Society, a number of private general practitioners and pharmacists, and the Mauritius Family Welfare Association.

Public health

The Medical and Health Department is responsible for the enforcement of public hygiene regulations, and it employs 65 Health Inspectors for this purpose. They are concerned, amongst other things, with domestic sanitation, an important factor in the prevention of hookworm. Regular talks and film shows on various aspects of health education are given in Social Welfare Centres and elsewhere.

Hospitals

The public hospital service comprises eight general hospitals, the Princess Margaret Orthopaedic Centre, the Brown Sequard Mental Hospital and the Leper Hospital. These are the responsibility of the Medical and Health Department. At the end of 1959, the number of beds in the public hospitals was 2,266, including the two prison hospitals.

The total number of hospital admissions in 1958 was 34,766, representing about 15·3 patients per bed; a very high rate of turnover compared to England and Wales where the corresponding figure was under 8·2 patients per bed. Commenting on the small fluctuations in the annual hospital admissions between 1953 and 1958, the Annual Report of the Medical and Health Department for 1958 states: "The demands on the available accommodation have since many years reached saturation point." The shortage manifests itself not only in a high rate of turnover, but also in the sharing of beds which occurs in some of the children's wards. The establishment of the Government Medical Service at the end of 1959 included 86 full time doctors, but the actual number of full time doctors in the Service was only 74. Similarly, there were 209 vacancies for nurses (including midwives and students) and 46 for medical auxiliaries, out of total establishments of 1,102 and 332 respectively. Both male and female nurses are employed. It is usual for male patients to be attended by male nurses (known as "dressers"), the female nurses being employed in the women's and children's wards.

Section 68 of the Labour Ordinance requires employers to provide certain amenities for monthly paid labourers (and others entitled to be housed by their employers) and their families residing on estates of 25 acres or more. The requirements include hospital accommodation and equipment, medical attendance and treatment including diets in hospital, and a sufficient supply of medicines of good quality. The estate hospitals serve a relatively small number of workers, the average number of monthly paid workers on the sugar estates in 1957 being under 8,000.

There are 27 estate hospitals with about 560 beds. By contrast with the public hospitals, those on the sugar estates seem to be chronically under-occupied. While some of the buildings are modern and well designed, the equipment and staff tend to be minimal. Serious cases of illness are transferred to the public hospitals. The estate hospitals and dispensaries are served by about 11 doctors, all private practitioners. There is a dresser in attendance at each hospital, and sometimes a midwife.

In addition to the hospitals there are five small private nursing homes, run on a commercial basis. There is also the new Clinique Mauricienne, which will provide surgical hospital services to fee-paying patients, but with scales of charges adjusted to the means of the patients.

General practitioner services

In addition to the out-patient services at the hospitals, the Government Medical Service provides free facilities for examination and treatment at 40 static dispensaries distributed throughout the island (including one in the prisons) and four mobile dispensaries. The dispensaries are staffed by dressers who, besides their main duty of dispensing drugs, supplement the efforts of the medical officers who attend at stated hours to see patients. Much of the time spent by the medical officer at the dispensary is devoted to the examination of public assistance applicants and the signing of certificates for them. This has reached such proportions that some of the medical officers have placed a limit on the number of public assistance cases they are prepared to deal with each week. They argue that it is better that some applicants should be given assistance without a medical certificate than that such certificates should be issued without proper examination. In an effort to reduce the pressure on the doctors employed full-time at the dispensaries five private doctors are paid to attend on a part-time basis.

There are about 57 doctors in private practice. We understand that some of these are in semi-retirement, and after taking into account the private doctors employed part-time in the Government service, the effective number is probably not much more than 40. Although the expense of doctors' fees is one that most Mauritian families cannot easily afford, many people go to a private doctor's surgery in preference to the dispensary. We discuss the reasons for this in Chapters 9 and 10. It is estimated that the total income of private doctors from their practices in 1957-58, as declared for income tax purposes, was about Rs. 1 million. This compares with the total salaries of medical officers in the Government service, which amount to about Rs. $1\frac{1}{2}$ million a year.

The dispensaries carry stocks of the more commonly used pharmaceuticals for which no charge is made. Private doctors' prescriptions are dispensed by the private pharmacists, and it is by no means unknown for a doctor to have a financial interest in a local pharmacy. Prices vary very considerably from one pharmacy to another, even for common drugs like aspirin, and the profit margins on certain lines are extremely high.*

---

* Sessional Paper No. 6 of 1959, *Report of the Commission on the Purchasing Power of the Rupee*, p. 9.

We were informed that dressers and other unqualified persons often carry on medical practices illegally. The giving of injections for a charge is regarded as a normal function of the dresser in his off-duty hours. We return later to the discussion of the problem of professional ethics in Mauritius.

Maternity, child welfare and family planning services

There are 24 maternity and child welfare centres, of which 9 are run by a voluntary body, the Maternity and Child Welfare Society, while the remaining 15 are run by the Social Welfare Department, 13 in centres provided by the Sugar Industry Labour Welfare Fund and two in temporary premises. The work of the Maternity and Child Welfare Society is concentrated in the urban areas, while the Social Welfare Centres supply part of the need for pre-natal and post-natal clinics in the rural areas. In addition, one mobile unit visits districts which do not yet have clinics. The Labour Welfare Fund Committee plans to build another 16 centres by 1965. Each clinic is visited by a doctor once, or in a few cases twice, a week. The staff of the clinics also includes midwives, who provide a 24-hour service in some areas. The clinics are used for the distribution of milk to children under one year old who show signs of undernourishment. The clinics are at present used by only a small proportion of mothers who live within a convenient distance of them.

The Maternity and Child Welfare Society spends about Rs. 160,000 a year on the services it provides. It receives an annual grant of Rs. 118,000 from the Government, other grants from the Town Councils and the De Chazal Fund, and about Rs. 30,000 from confinement fees and sales of milk. The cost of running the 15 Social Welfare Clinics falls largely on the Sugar Industry Labour Welfare Fund. Salaries of midwives, amounting to about Rs. 250,000 a year, are included in the Health Department's estimates.

The maternity and child welfare clinics do not offer any family planning facilities, nor advice or guidance. The only positive step taken towards providing these services was the formation of the Family Planning Association of Mauritius in 1957. The Association, whose name has now been changed to the Family Welfare Association of Mauritius, has been given no official support, and its activities have been limited to discreet propaganda and the distribution of contraceptive foaming tablets on a very limited scale. In 1958 it had an income of only Rs. 1,500.

Health services for school children

The School Health Service is staffed by three Government medical officers, three nurses, and three health workers, with the assistance of the Government dentists, a nutrition and health assistant and an ophthalmologist. All entrants to Government and aided primary schools and Government secondary schools are medically examined, and free medical and dental treatment is provided for primary school children. Further examinations are carried out while the children are at school. In addition, vaccination and mass radiography are carried out.

All primary school children receive a free daily allocation of milk (23 grammes of skimmed milk powder per head), together with iron tablets. In cases of serious undernourishment the milk ration is doubled. This scheme was introduced to replace an experimental school meals service in the Grand Port area, which was abandoned in 1948 on grounds of cost. There has been no subsequent attempt to introduce such a service.

INSTITUTIONAL CARE

There are eleven infirmaries and eleven orphanages in Mauritius, as well as a residential institution for blind men. Other institutions with which we are not directly concerned in this Report include the prisons and industrial school and a private home for old people.

The infirmaries have about 800 residents while the population of the orphanages is about 400. All these institutions are run by the various religious denominations. The Catholic Church provides a majority of the beds. The non-Catholic institutions comprise a Church of England infirmary and orphanage, a Presbyterian infirmary, a Hindu infirmary (for women only) and two Hindu orphanages, and a Muslim infirmary and orphanage. Calebasses Infirmary is Government property but its administration is entrusted to the Catholic Sisters.

These institutions house a varied population. While some of the children in the orphanages are in fact orphans, others have parents who, for social or other reasons, are unable or unwilling to look after them. In the infirmaries, homeless old people are found together with the physically disabled, the mentally deficient, convalescents, unmarried mothers and their children.

The Public Assistance Department pays a grant of Rs. 1·20 per day towards the cost of maintaining each destitute inmate of the infirmaries and orphanages. An additional grant is made for the upkeep of the buildings and assistance is given with clothing and equipment. The Department has the duty of inspecting the institutions supported by it in this way, and ensuring that various regulations are complied with.

The Loïs Lagesse Residential and Training Centre provides

accommodation for about 20 blind men, though part of it is at present occupied by men suffering from disabilities other than blindness. The Centre is supported by a Government subsidy, charitable subscriptions and profits on the sale of baskets which are manufactured by the blind men.

SOCIAL WELFARE

Although, for reasons given in our letter to His Excellency the Governor, we are unable to make recommendations regarding the future development of the Social Welfare Department, this account of the existing social services would not be complete without a brief reference to some of its activities and to those of the Sugar Industry Labour Welfare Fund and a large number of private organisations and individuals in the field of social welfare.

The Social Welfare Department

We have already referred to the maternity and child welfare clinics run by the Social Welfare Department in centres built by the Sugar Industry Labour Welfare Fund. These Social Welfare Centres, staffed by welfare officers, are used for a number of other community activities, both educational and recreational. There are reading and writing classes for children who are unable to attend school, and handicraft classes for girls. The women of the locality are taught needlework, cooking and other domestic arts. For the men, there are talks on nutrition, hygiene and other topics. Demonstration gardens are laid out near the centres, and officers of the Agriculture Department give talks and practical demonstrations on methods of cultivation.

The Social Welfare Centres also provide facilities for indoor and outdoor games, singing and dancing, and they are used by numerous youth organisations for these purposes.

The Centres are financed in part by an annual grant of Rs. 3,600 per centre from the Sugar Industry Labour Welfare Fund. In addition, some revenue is raised by charging for services provided and by various money-raising activities.

The Social Welfare Department has encouraged the growth of Women's Associations, of which there were as many as 65 at the end of 1958. Their activities include needlework and other classes, as well as talks on home management and hygiene by Welfare Officers of the Department. The associations raise their own funds, part of which is sometimes used for the relief of distress caused by fire, illness and death.

The Department and its Welfare Officers cooperate with other organisations in welfare activities of many kinds, and the Social Welfare Centres sometimes serve as local offices of other departments.

The Sugar Industry Labour Welfare Fund

This Fund was set up under the Sugar Industry Reserve Funds Ordinance, 1948, to promote the welfare of workers in the sugar industry. Originally it was intended that nobody outside the sugar industry should benefit from the activities of the Fund, but it was soon realised that such a restriction was unrealistic and that most of the welfare provisions needed by workers in the sugar industry would benefit the whole community in the areas concerned. The way was thus open for the Fund to be devoted to a wide range of welfare schemes, but up until now the annual income of the Fund has greatly exceeded its expenditure.

The Fund is administered by a Committee which includes representatives of Government, employers and workers. Government approval must be obtained for any scheme costing Rs. 50,000 or more.

The income of the Fund is derived mainly from a levy of sixpence a hundredweight on sugar sold to the United Kingdom Government under the Commonwealth Sugar Agreement and from interest on the accumulated investments. The total income for 1959 was about Rs. 2,900,000 and the available funds (investments and current assets) at the end of 1959 totalled about Rs. 25 million.

The Committee has given priority in its programme to the provision of housing. The Fund has built housing estates for sugar industry workers, and has made interest-free loans to enable individuals to build their own houses. The houses built by the Fund are sold to the workers slightly below cost, on "tenant-purchase" terms free of interest. In one instance an interest-free loan of Rs. $1\frac{1}{2}$ million was made to a sugar estate company to enable it to build a model village on the estate for its workers.

We have referred above to the Social Welfare Centres which have been built with money supplied by the Fund. Thirteen Centres have been completed and two more are operating in temporary rented buildings. Sixteen more Centres are planned to be built in the next five years.

The Fund has also allocated money for the following purposes:—

(1) Assistance to victims of fire and flood (about Rs. 100,000 in each of the years 1957 and 1958, and Rs. 117,000 following the floods of 1959).

(2) Provision of 48 football fields.

(3) Provision of tarpaulins and chairs for hire at a nominal charge on social occasions.

(4) Loans to the Co-operative Union and Co-operative Store Societies.

(5) A grant of Rs. 2,500,000 to help in covering the past service liability of the Sugar Industry Pension Fund for monthly paid employees.

Voluntary work

If we mention the work done by voluntary organisations and individuals at the end of this summary of the existing social services of Mauritius, it is not because we under-estimate the contribution they have to make, but because their function must always be to supplement and fill the gaps in the official services. In a country like Mauritius, where for many years to come Government will have to concentrate on providing a minimum standard of social security and welfare, voluntary effort is especially important. Fortunately it is not lacking, though at times it may suffer from a lack of co-ordination and from a patronising approach to social needs.

We have already referred to the work of the Public Assistance Advisory Committees, the Maternity and Child Welfare Society and the Mauritius Family Welfare Association, all of which rely largely on voluntary effort. Among other voluntary organisations the British Red Cross Society is outstanding; its work includes visiting the sick in hospitals, institutions and in their own homes, distributing medical assistance, food and small "comforts", providing transport for the sick by ambulance or private car, and helping the victims of fire, flood and cyclone. First aid and nursing services are also provided by the St. John Ambulance Association. The Society of St. Vincent de Paul operates in many parts of the island, distributing relief to the poor. Other organisations whose objects are more limited but no less worthy include the "Repas des Pauvres", organised by Mr. Loïs Lagesse, and the "Amis du Moulin à Poudre" to which we shall refer again in Chapter 11. We were particularly impressed by the work of Mr. Edwin de Robillard and his "Compagnons Bâtisseurs" who voluntarily devoted many hundreds of hours of manual work to the rebuilding of houses destroyed by the cyclones of 1960. We also learnt of other examples of voluntary manual work on a smaller scale, including the construction of a small dam at Crêve Coeur and the rebuilding of houses destroyed by fire. An opportunity to develop voluntary manual work and self-help schemes is provided by the presence of two members of the International Voluntary Service who arrived in Mauritius in May 1960 to organise and participate in projects of this kind.

Space does not permit a complete list of all the examples of voluntary effort, by village councils, charitable and other bodies and individuals, which came to our notice. Such efforts as these have done much to invigorate the social services, and they will be needed more than ever in the years to come, particularly if they can help to unify the different religious and ethnic groups in the population.

CHAPTER 3

The Problem of Population

The relationship of various social and economic factors to the problems which fall within our terms of reference was outlined in Chapter 1. The importance of these relationships was magnified by the effects of the cyclones of 1960 leaving behind them, more sharply obvious, the problems of unemployment and social insecurity. Above all, these effects emphasised the need to take account of the growing pressure of population on the social and economic life of Mauritius. In this chapter we therefore turn to consider the basic facts of population. Its purposes are, first, to trace the trends in population in the recent past and thus to provide an historical frame of reference for our study of the development of the health and social services. Secondly, to describe some new projections of population growth which were made as a necessary part of our task of formulating social policy recommendations for the future. Thirdly, to draw attention to some of the implications and consequences of probable changes in the size and characteristics of the population of Mauritius. Fourthly, to outline our proposals for an integrated policy of social and family planning measures.

There has not always been a "problem" of population in Mauritius. There is one now. It was judged of such urgency early in the 1950's that a committee was appointed to consider its dimensions and its probable effects on the standard of living of the people. The majority of the committee, reporting in 1955, urged the need for education in family planning, since they concluded that if population growth were not limited by voluntary means it would be compulsorily limited in a few decades by rising mortality.*

At the end of our report, in Chapter 12, we repeat and summarise some of the main facts which result from our re-examination of the problem. We then outline our proposals for the introduction and development of population policies which we see as an integral part of our recommendations in the social policy field.

SOURCES AND METHODS

In bringing together the principal features of past trends in population we have drawn liberally from the work of Mr. H. C.

---

* Sessional Paper No. 4 of 1955, *Report of the Committee on Population* 1953-54.

Brookfield,* from the *Report of the Committee on Population*,† and from the Central Statistical Office's report on *Natality and Fertility in Mauritius*.‡ We have ourselves examined in detail the basic statistical data beginning with the 1931 census and extending to the present, with a view to estimating as accurately as possible fertility and mortality levels and trends, and in order to correct for errors or omissions in the age distribution of the population needed as the base for our new projections. This work is described in detail in Appendix B. Only the less technical aspects of our adjustments to the base data and the methods of projection are described in this chapter.

COMPOSITION OF THE POPULATION

Ethnically the population is divided into three major classes—the Indo-Mauritians, who constituted about two-thirds of the total population at the 1952 census; the General Group, comprising the descendants of African and Malagasy slaves, Europeans and their descendants, and persons of mixed blood; and finally a small group of Chinese immigrants and their descendants. While most of the statistical publications for Mauritius present data separately for the major ethnic groups, these data can be utilised only with the utmost caution, since the criteria of classification have not been the same from census to census.§ Moreover, an individual's classification may differ in the census and in the vital registration system.‖ To compute rates in which the numerator is taken from one source and the denominator from the other may produce results that may well be more misleading than enlightening. Of necessity, then, our projections have not been made separately for the major ethnic groups. In theory, this simplification could have introduced error. Fortunately, the rates of growth for the major groups are not very different at present and, consequently, the ethnic structure of the population is likely to change only slowly. Thus, our projections are not invalidated on this account.

TRENDS IN POPULATION GROWTH

Though today Mauritius has one of the most rapidly growing populations in the world, this upsurge in growth is of very recent

* Brookfield, H. C., "Mauritius: Demographic Upsurge and Prospect", *Population Studies*, Vol. XI, No. 2, November 1957, pp. 102-122.
† *Op. cit.*
‡ Mauritius Central Statistical Office, *Natality and Fertility in Mauritius*, 1825-1955, Port Louis, 1956.
§ Mauritius Central Statistical Office, *Census* 1952, Part I, p. 4.
‖ Brookfield, H. C., *op. cit.*, p. 102.

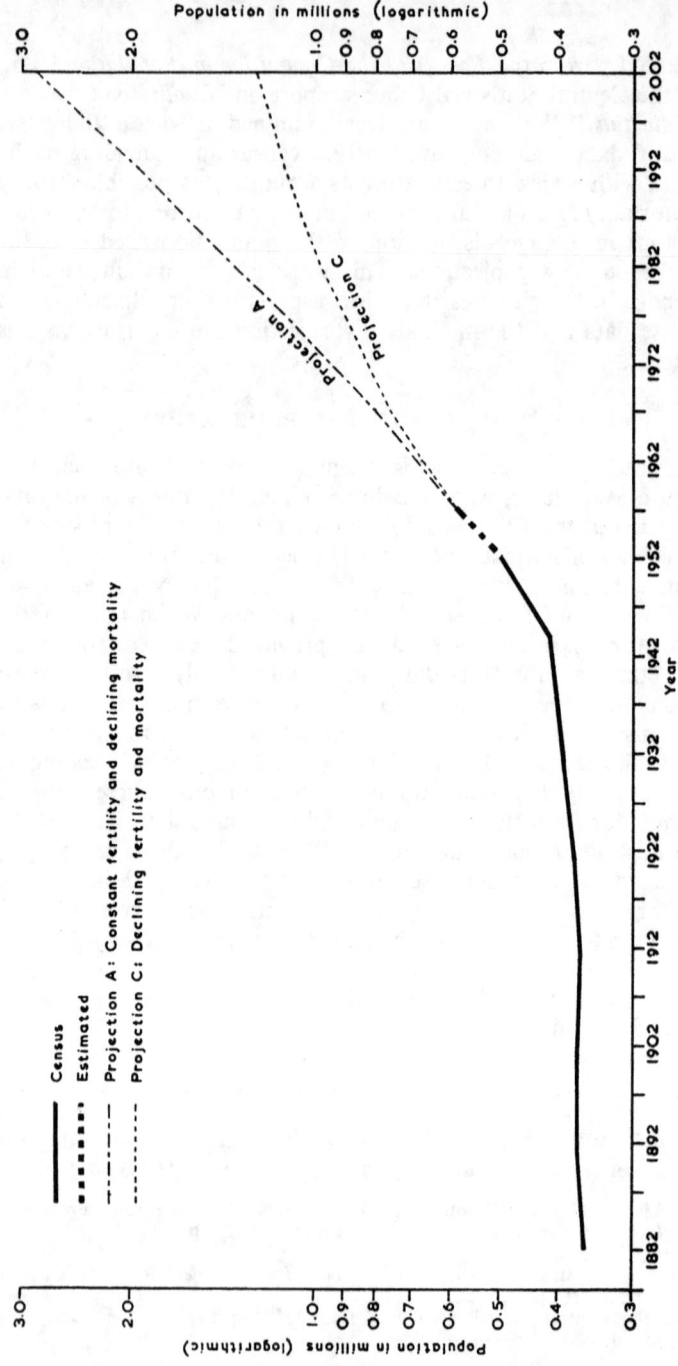

Fig. 1. *Past and Future Population Trends in Mauritius.*

origin. Census records for the island, which date back to the middle of the nineteenth century, show that with the exception of the several decades prior to 1880, when large numbers of indentured labourers were imported from India, the population rose only very gradually from one census enumeration to the next. In fact, the average annual rate of increase amounted to less than half of 1% per annum during each inter-censal interval from 1881 to 1944. (See Table III and Fig. 1.)

Table III. *Population Growth in Mauritius:* 1851-1952.

Date	Population enumerated at census	Average annual rate of increase (%)
20 Nov. 1851	180,823	—
8 Apr. 1861	310,050	5·87
11 Apr. 1871	316,042	0·19
4 Apr. 1881	359,874	1·31
6 Apr. 1891	370,588	0·29
1 Apr. 1901	371,023	0·01
31 Mar. 1911	368,791	—0·06
21 May 1921	376,485	0·21
26 Apr. 1931	393,238	0·44
11 June 1944	419,185	0·49
29 June 1952	501,415	2·26

This low rate of growth was due to unfavourable mortality conditions, which were such that during the first two decades of the present century it was not infrequent for the number of deaths to exceed the number of births annually.

The period of marked demographic growth between 1851 and 1881, when the population doubled, can be almost entirely ascribed to immigration; data on arrivals and departures of Indian migrants during this period show a net immigration of close on 200,000.* This figure exceeded the amount of population increase computed from census comparisons since during the early years of this period mortality took an extremely heavy toll—in part due to the malaria epidemic of 1867-69.

The immigration of Indian labourers ceased to be an important factor in population growth after 1880, although migration of other peoples seems to have been the chief source of growth recorded during the remainder of the nineteenth century.† During the first two decades of the twentieth century there was little change in

* *Report of the Committee on Population,* p. 1.
† Migration records show that there was a net immigration of some 15,000 persons between 1881 and 1901, excluding Indian indentured labourers.

Table IV. Live Births and Deaths in Mauritius: 1871-1955.

Period (a)	Live births	Deaths	Natural increase
1871-75	59,615	46,727	12,888
1876-80	64,221	51,137	13,084
1881-85	66,305	59,678	6,627
1886-90	67,362	59,855	7,507
1891-95	70,190	63,192	6,998
1896-1900	67,258	65,708	1,550
1901-05	68,162	70,163	—2,001
1906-10	66,477	69,504	—3,027
1911-15	71,269	65,069	6,200
1916-20	66,209	72,688 (b)	—6,479
1921-25	74,169	58,789	15,380
1926-30	71,038	58,069	12,969
1931-35	62,448	59,444	3,004
1936-40	68,107	55,786	12,321
1941-45	75,135	59,637	15,498
1946-50	97,974	45,563	52,411
1951-55	115,880	38,504	77,376

NOTES: (a) Figures are five-year totals compiled from various official statistical sources and from Kuczynski, R. R., *Demographic Survey of the British Colonial Empire*, Vol. II, London, 1949.
(b) Including 24,455 deaths in 1919 when the country suffered an influenza epidemic.

population size. Despite a net immigration of almost 9,000 during the first half of this period, the 1911 census recorded a small decline in population as compared with 1901, this being a period when deaths outnumbered births. Thereafter, immigration made no significant contribution to population growth, and in studying recent population trends it can be disregarded. A period of relative prosperity and improved health conditions beginning about 1916 and continuing into the 1920's saw an increase in population growth, but conditions had again worsened by the time the 1931 census was taken. The average annual increment for the decade was then less than half of 1%. A slightly higher rate was registered for the next inter-censal period (1931-1944) which, like its predecessor, was characterised by considerable fluctuations in birth- and death-rates. During the depression years in the 1930's the birth-rate fell to its lowest recorded level, and for three years deaths again exceeded births.

With the dramatic developments of the post-war period, demographic trends entered an entirely new phase in Mauritius. Between the census dates of 1944 and 1952, the annual rate of population growth shot up to an average of 2·2%. The greatest single factor contributing to this rise was the eradication of malaria. Such was the effect of the campaign that the death-rate fell by 32% in one year. Not only did the death-rate fall, but the birth-rate rose during this period. For the ten most recent years (1948-58) the rate of natural increase has averaged 3% per annum. It is this fact, in a situation of already high population density in relation to land and resources, which has focussed so much attention on Mauritius' population problem.

The remarkable rate of population growth which Mauritius has recently experienced is not unique. While the world's population as a whole is estimated to be growing at about 1·6% per annum,* there is a considerable variation in regional rates. High rates of growth have been registered in many countries of Asia, Africa and Latin America. Rapidly falling mortality from very high levels has been the main agent of growth. These changes, substantially brought about by advances in medical science, have not necessarily been associated with improvements in living standards of the people.† A number of countries are known to have rates of natural increase in excess of that of Mauritius—among them El Salvador, Mexico, Venezuela, Taiwan and Malaya.‡ Except for Taiwan, however, none of these countries has a population density approaching that of Mauritius which, today, has more than 300 persons per square kilometre.

TRENDS IN FERTILITY AND MORTALITY

The records of vital statistics, like censuses, go back a long way in Mauritius. At least for the period from 1871 onwards, these data appear to be of a sufficiently satisfactory quality to provide a general picture of the components of population change.§ The trend of the crude birth- and death-rates throughout has been characterised by big annual fluctuations and in the present century by marked cyclical fluctuations as well. (See Fig. 2.)

Rates computed from registered deaths suggest that, following a relatively good decade during the 1870's, when the crude death-rate was about 29, mortality conditions gradually worsened and reached a particularly high level during the first decade of the present century. The crude death-rate then amounted to 38 per 1,000

---

* United Nations, *Report on the World Social Situation*, ST/SOA/33, New York, 1957.
† United Nations, *Population Growth and the Standard of Living in Under-Developed Countries*, ST/SOA/Ser.A/20. New York, 1954, p. 4.
‡ United Nations, *Demographic Yearbook* 1958.
§ Kuczynski noted that birth and death registration was incomplete prior to the 1870's, although he regarded it as having been "fairly complete for many decades" at the time of his study. See Kuczynski, R. R., *Demographic Survey of the British Colonial Empire*, Vol. II, London, 1949.

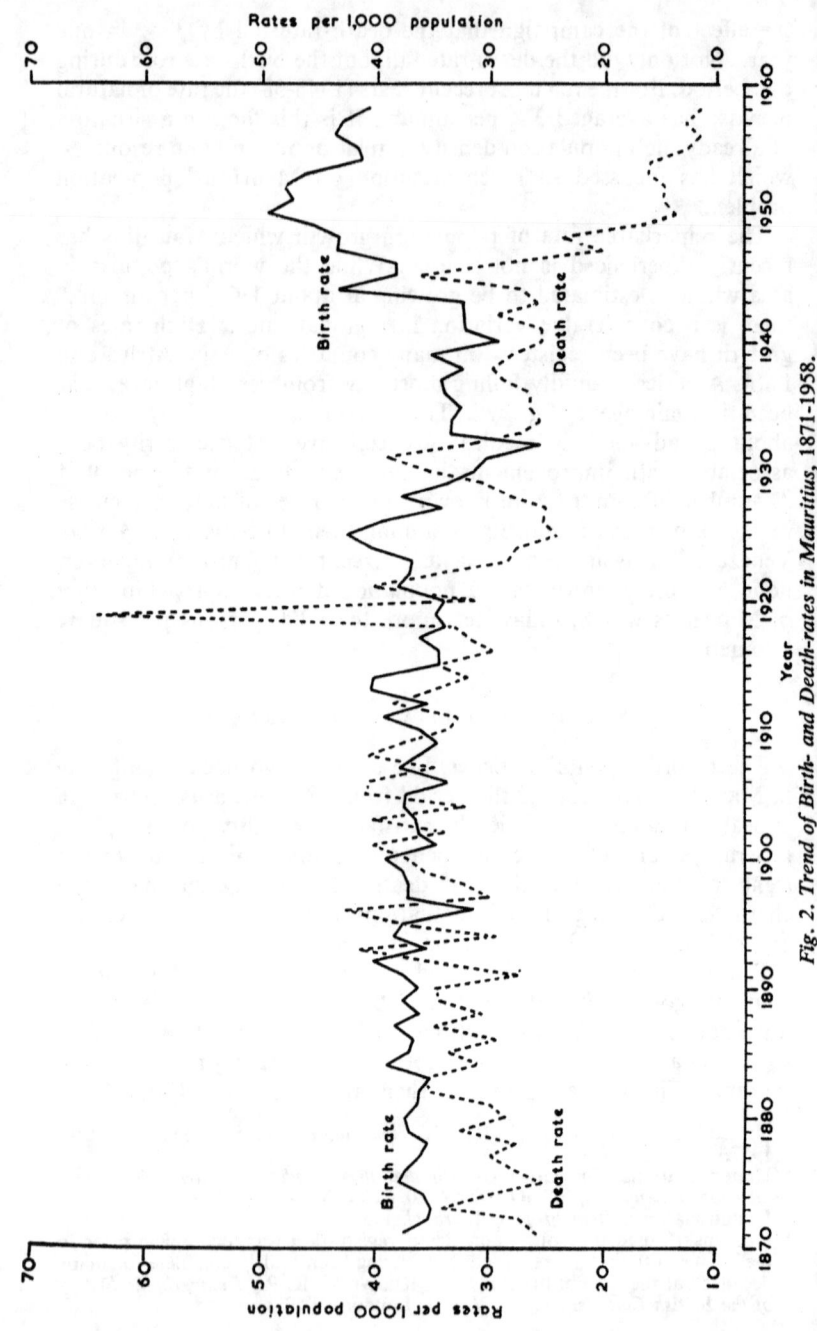

Fig. 2. Trend of Birth- and Death-rates in Mauritius, 1871-1958.

population.* The next decade saw an improvement, except for an exceptionally heavy toll of deaths during the influenza epidemic year, 1919. The years from 1916 to the mid-1920's were relatively prosperous ones for the sugar industry; during this period campaigns against malaria and hookworm were inaugurated and death-rates as low as 24-25 per 1,000 were recorded during a few years. A deterioration in the economic situation quickly restored the familiar pattern of high mortality, however. By the late 1920's employment and wages had already fallen, but the worst period was not reached until the early 1930's when deaths outnumbered births. Undernourishment became an important factor in rising mortality, and malaria and hookworm again assumed prominence, as campaigns against them were largely abandoned.

While an improvement in economic conditions in the early 1940's brought a return to the lower mortality levels which had been achieved in the 1920's, health conditions were still far from satisfactory. A life table constructed from data around 1944 showed that the average expectation of life at birth was only about 32 years for males, and about 34 for females. The first major achievement in controlling mortality had to await the end of the Second World War. Freed from some of the financial stringency of the war period, and with the new modern methods of insecticide spraying which had been developed, the Government was able virtually to eradicate malaria—for long the leading cause of death in the island—within a matter of a few years. The remarkable success of this campaign is demonstrated by the fact that in a period of one year—from 1946 to 1947—the death-rate was cut by nearly one third, from 29·5 to 20·1.† Since 1947 the downward trend in mortality has continued —interrupted only temporarily by occasional fluctuations. The most recent figure available—that for 1958—places the death-rate at 11·8.

While displaying considerable year-to-year fluctuations, the birth-rate, when averaged for quinquennial periods, showed a marked stability up to the second decade of this century. Over the period from 1870 to 1920, the birth-rate stood at around 36-37 per 1,000.

In more recent times, there appears to have been a clear tendency for the birth-rate to rise with favourable economic conditions and to fall during periods of economic hardship. For example, during

---

* Alternatively it might be supposed that there was some improvement in death registration, causing an apparent rise in the death-rate during this period. However, the census results generally lend support to the finding of a rising mortality.

† This spectacular drop in mortality within a year almost precisely duplicated the pattern of post-war mortality control which was brought into effect in Ceylon. There, as in Mauritius, malaria eradication was the principal factor in bringing about a fall in the death-rate from 19·8 to 14·0 in a single year.

Table V. Birth- and Death-rates in Mauritius: 1871-1958.

Period (a)	Birth-rate	Death-rate
1871-75	36·3	28·4
1876-80	36·6	29·2
1881-85	36·7	33·1
1886-90	37·0	32·8
1891-95	37·8	34·0
1896-1900	36·4	35·6
1901-05	36·5	37·6
1906-10	35·9	37·5
1911-15	38·0	34·7
1916-20	34·7	38·1
1921-25	39·0	31·0
1926-30	35·5	28·9
1931-35	31·1	30·3
1936-40	33·1	27·7
1941	32·2	25·6
1942	32·5	29·2
1943	32·6	25·9
1944	43·4	27·1
1945	38·4	36·1
1946	38·4	29·5
1947	43·7	20·1
1948	43·4	23·8
1949	45·6	16·6
1950	49·7	13·9
1951	47·5	14·9
1952	48·1	14·8
1953	46·3	16·1
1954	41·3	16·0
1955	41·8	12·9
1956	43·8	11·8
1957	43·1	13·0
1958	40·8	11·8

NOTE: (a) For dates prior to 1941 the figures are average annual rates.
SOURCE: Rates prior to 1931 from Kuczynski, R. R., *Demographic Survey of the British Colonial Empire*, pp. 862-865. For later years, rates are from the *Yearbook of Statistics* 1957.

the early 1920's the rate reached a level near 40, but fell as low as 26 during the depression of the early 1930's. Such fluctuations, which may appear startling in a population which is not believed to practise family limitation, are nevertheless substantiated by the census data on age structure. Though the census statistics on marital status are far from satisfactory, they do suggest that the reduction of the birth-rate during the depression years was aided by a large-scale postponement of marriages.

Throughout the remainder of the 1930's and well into the 1940's the birth-rate remained at the low level (for Mauritius) of 32-33 per 1,000. No doubt a contributory factor during the latter part of the period was the absence of a significant number of men recruited for the Pioneer Corps. The year 1944 saw a sharp rise in the birth-rate, probably associated with the pattern of recruitment of draftees and the incentive for them to marry which was provided by a dependency grant for their wives.*

Following the end of the war there occurred another marked rise in the rate, and a level near 50 was approached in 1950. In more recent years, it has fallen from this peak level, which reflected to an unknown extent temporary and abnormal influences, such as the "catching-up" of marriages and births which had been postponed during the war. The rate still remains well above the pre-war level, however. It is the fact of continuing high fertility, in combination with the spectacular declines in mortality, which has given rise to the greatest period of population expansion Mauritius has ever known.

Various explanations have been advanced for the recent rise in the birth-rate, among them a higher marriage rate, relatively prosperous conditions in the sugar industry, and the improvement in the health of the population, which has permitted more pregnancies to occur, and more conceptions to result in live-born children.† Whatever the reasons may be, it is important to examine the statistics on marital status for any light they may shed on the possible permanency of these higher fertility levels.

MARITAL STATUS AND MARRIAGE RATES

The proportions of women reported as married according to the census statistics of 1931, 1944 and 1952 are as follows :—

Table VI. Proportion of Married Women (a) among All Women in the Child-bearing Ages: 1931, 1944 *and* 1952 *Censuses.*

Age group	1931	1944	1952
15-19	30·7	35·9	39·9
20-24	62·7	65·5	72·4
25-29	75·0	74·4	83·0
30-34	76·4	76·1	83·8
35-39	75·0	73·9	81·6
40-44	68·1	67·9	76·4

NOTE: (*a*) Including those legally married, married in religious ceremony only, or living in consensual unions.

* Central Statistical Office, *Natality and Fertility* . . . (*op. cit.*), p. 11.
† Brookfield, H. C., *op. cit.*, p. 107; and *Natality and Fertility* . . . (*op. cit.*), pp. 12-13. It has been suggested that the eradication of malaria in an area where its transmission has been perennial rather than seasonal may cause an increase in the birth-rate. See Pampana, E. J., "Effect of Malaria Control on Birth- and Death-rates", United Nations, *Proceedings of the World Population Conference*, E/CONF.13/413, Vol. 1, pp. 497-509, New York, 1955.

According to the census definitions, these data include all women married either legally or religiously, or living in consensual unions. For each age group throughout the child-bearing ages, the proportion of women reported as being married was markedly higher in 1952 than in 1931, or even than in 1944. At the upper ages these differences are partly, but not entirely, explained by a decline in the incidence of widowhood as a result of falling mortality. This decreasing tendency for marriages to be dissolved by the death of the husband while the wife is still of child-bearing age may have contributed to the rise in fertility, particularly among the Hindu population, where presumably the remarriage of widows is not yet very common.

At the younger ages there were reasons, particularly in 1931 owing to the depression, why marriages might have been postponed. It may be significant therefore that the 1921 census data show nearly the same proportions married in the two youngest age groups as were found in 1952.*

Caution must be exercised, however, in drawing any definite conclusions about trends in marriage from the census data because of uncertainty as to whether there were changes in the concept of what constituted "marriage" or in the thoroughness with which the census identified persons belonging to unions not legally recognised. Particularly in a country like Mauritius where marriages taking place outside the civil registration system are common, accurate enumeration of the various categories in a census presents special difficulty. Data available on the different categories of married persons, e.g. those legally married, those married in religious ceremonies only, and those persons living in consensual unions, suggest that there have been some changes in treatment when the various censuses were taken.† Because of this probability we have combined the three classes for purposes of studying trends. This does not, however, mean that we have necessarily removed all the sources of error.

---

* Marriage patterns differ substantially as between the two major ethnic groups in the population. The Indo-Mauritians marry much earlier, and have a much smaller proportion of their group remaining single than does the General Group. Despite their earlier marriage, however, the Indo-Mauritian women do not have significantly larger families than the General Group, according to the 1952 census data on number of children born to women. These data show an average completed size of family of 4·6 for the General Group and 4·8 for the Indo-Mauritians. It seems quite possible that the Indo-Mauritian women, who have a higher mortality rate, may be subject to greater pregnancy wastage; moreover, there may be greater errors of omission in their reporting for a variety of reasons.

† For example: between the 1931 and 1944 censuses there was a sharp decline in the proportion of women recorded as consensually married; some decline in the proportion recorded as legally married; and a marked increase in the proportions classified as married in religious ceremony only.

The official statistics on marriages relate to civil marriages only and exclude the bulk of marriages taking place within the Indo-Mauritian group. Hindus and Moslems generally marry according to the rites of their own religions, and although since 1914 there has been an Ordinance permitting Hindu and Moslem priests to serve as civil status officers for purposes of registering these marriages, such registration does not, we understand, normally take place. Despite these limitations, the data on marriages are useful in giving some indication of recent trends. Exceptionally high marriage rates were recorded in the immediate post-war years, and in fact the rate remained quite high during the early 1950's.

Table VII. Marriage Rates in Mauritius: 1934-1958 (newly married persons of both sexes per 1,000 population).

1934-38	9·5
1946	18·1
1947	17·5
1948	14·7
1949	16·3
1950	13·1
1951	12·7
1952	16·3
1953	13·4
1954	11·7
1955	10·2
1956	10·8
1957	9·9
1958	10·5

SOURCE: Mauritius Central Statistical Office, *Yearbook of Statistics* 1958.

A decline has since occurred, and the present rate is not much above that of the pre-war period. To the extent that the high marriage rates of the post-war period represented the "making up" for previous postponements, we might expect that the present birth-rate (which is lower than that of the early 1950's) would be largely free of this influence and may be stabilised near its present level for some years to come, in the absence of deliberate intervention to reduce family size. However, some of the rise in the post-war marriage rate may have been occasioned by earlier marriage of young people resulting from more favourable economic conditions. Accordingly, present marriage rates may be low because some of the persons who would normally be marrying now have already married and are bearing children. Current birth-rates may still be somewhat inflated by such trends, and it is possible that they may fall to a slightly lower level before stabilising. On the other hand, such earlier marriages occasioned by better economic conditions may continue to influence the trend of fertility.

In general, though, two important facts stand out: the high proportion married among women of child-bearing ages, and the very high proportion of women married at an early age. Barring any changes in attitudes to family planning, both these facts provide a situation in which high fertility rates may well continue to dominate the demographic picture.

THE AGE STRUCTURE OF THE POPULATION

In 1957 nearly 44% of the population consisted of children under 15 years of age. This figure is higher than that shown at recent censuses, owing mainly to the rise in the birth-rate in the years since the Second World War.* The changes in age structure at each census date since 1931 shown in Table VIII reflect very clearly the fluctuations which have occurred in the birth-rate since 1920.

Table VIII. Age Structure of the Population of Mauritius: 1931-1957.

Age group	1931 census (a)	1944 census (a)	1952 census (a)	1957 estimate
	%	%	%	%
Under 15	38·4	35·7	40·8	43·8
15-64	58·7	61·3	56·3	53·4
65 and over	2·9	3·0	2·9	2·9
All ages	100	100	100	100

NOTE: (a) Data have been adjusted to take account of under-enumerations of young children and omissions of men in the military ages who were overseas with the Pioneer Corps.

Although fertility had fallen to a relatively low point just prior to the 1931 census, the large cohort of children born during the early 1920's caused the total percentage under age 15 to be higher at this census (38%) than in 1944 (36%) when the cohorts born during the depression years formed part of this age group. Thereafter, with rising fertility, the proportion of children in the population has continued to increase.

The working age group 15-64 years, on which the economy depends, constitutes at present only about 53% of the population. This figure implies a high ratio of dependants to the working

* Declining infant mortality would also tend to cause an increase in the proportion of children in the population, but the influence of this factor is not as great as that of rising fertility.

population, as is strikingly brought out by comparisons with industrialised countries such as the United Kingdom or the United States, where typically about two-thirds of the population are in the working age group.

A very small proportion of the population—only about 3%—is 65 years of age and over. This proportion has shown no significant change over the period considered in the table.

The difference between the age structure of the population of Mauritius, and that which may be considered as typical of highly industrialised countries, is summarised below:

Age group	Mauritius 1957	Countries of North-West-Central Europe around 1950 (a)
Under 15 years	43·8	24·4
15-64 years	53·4	66·3
65 years and over	2·9	9·2
All ages	100	100

NOTE: (a) Unweighted averages computed from data in the United Nations *Demographic Yearbook*.

THE FUTURE GROWTH OF POPULATION

While a number of population projections have already been made for Mauritius, most of them extending to the year 1982, we decided to make our own projections for purposes of the present study for a number of reasons. At the time the earlier projections were prepared, data on births by age of mother—information which can contribute greatly to our knowledge of fertility trends—were available for only the first six months of 1955: we now have such data extending through the period to 1958 inclusive. Moreover, we could utilise the data on registered births and deaths—which appear to be of a satisfactory quality—for bringing the 1952 census population forward to 1957, which then became the starting point for our new projections. We also thought it desirable to introduce certain adjustments to the 1952 census figures, in view of the under-reporting of young children (a shortcoming common to all censuses), a strong digital preference in the reporting of ages, and a tendency towards an over-statement of age on the part of older women. In addition, it seemed appropriate to adjust the data for the absence overseas of members of the Pioneer Corps, most of whom had in any case returned to the island by 1957. These adjustments are described in detail in Appendix B.*

* Only two of these adjustments necessitated changes in total population size; a figure of 8,300 was added to the group aged under 5 years at the 1952 census to compensate for the under-enumeration of children in the first years of life, and a total of 4,500 was added to the male population in the military ages to account for the Pioneer Corps absences.

The most important reason, however, for our decision to undertake new projections is that none of the previous projections had incorporated what seemed to us, in the light of the data now available, the most realistic combination of assumptions; namely, constant fertility and declining mortality. This combination of assumptions became the basis for our first projection, here referred to as Projection A.*

Strictly speaking, these projections should not be viewed as *predictions* of demographic trends, but rather as calculations of what the outcome would be in terms of future population size and composition if events were to follow one of several alternative courses set out in the assumptions. Even if fertility and mortality did in general follow the assumptions it is not likely that at any particular date the population would, in fact, precisely equal the figure shown in the projections. Fluctuations from year to year are almost certain to continue, and there is no basis whatever for predicting their course. Projections can only hope at best to portray the average pattern of change over some period in the future.

MORTALITY ASSUMPTIONS

As we have already shown, the history of mortality experience in Mauritius had been, until a decade and a half ago, one of great yearly fluctuations in the death-rate, with epidemics periodically taking a heavy toll of lives. Little in the way of a genuine downward trend in mortality could be detected until the mid-1940's. Then, within a short span of years came a tremendous change, as malaria was brought under control. Progress has since continued, though inevitably at a slower pace. The expectation of life at birth for males rose from 32·2 years in 1944 to 49·8 years by 1952. Since 1952 it has risen further to reach 54·0 years in 1957.† The experience of many other countries suggests that mortality will continue to fall, but the period since malaria eradication in Mauritius has been too brief to furnish statistics suitable for projecting a specific rate of decline. In the circumstances, we felt the most reliable estimates of future mortality decline could be derived from the mortality "models" developed by the Population Branch of the United Nations on the basis of the average experience of a sizeable group of countries during the first half of the twentieth century.‡ Thus,

* Details of our three projections are set out in Tables XII-XIV on pages 64-6.
† The 1944 and 1952 figures are from official life tables; the 1957 figure is from an abridged life table computed by us. Comparable gains in life expectancy have been recorded for females.
‡ United Nations, *Methods of Population Projections by Sex and Age*, ST/SOA/Ser.A/25, New York, 1956. See especially p. 28.

we have allowed for an increase of about half a year in life expectancy each year throughout the projection period.*

By this method it is assumed that life expectancy at birth for males might rise to about 65 years by the end of the projection period (1982), a level similar to that of a number of Western countries at present. It is not impossible that a faster improvement might occur, since Mauritius still has relatively high mortality at the middle ages and beyond—particularly among men. Nevertheless, a decline at the so-called "normal" rate, as shown in Projections A and C, is probably neither unduly optimistic nor pessimistic. The future trend of mortality could, of course, be upset if there were a major reversal of economic conditions or a setback in social progress, as a consequence of population pressure. If such a catastrophe were to occur, history suggests that a substantial rise in mortality must be expected. None of our projections assumes an increase in mortality, but in Projection B, as an alternative, we have assumed mortality to remain constant at 1957 levels.

FERTILITY ASSUMPTIONS

The birth-rate, which, except for cyclical rises and falls, had generally averaged about 36-37 per 1,000, rose sharply after the Second World War. While some part of the rise appears to have been a temporary phenomenon reflecting a sudden spurt in the number of marriages, fertility levels still remain high as compared with pre-war "normal" periods. To the extent that the present level reflects such factors as the improved health of mothers, a decline in the incidence of widowhood, and the like, it seems justifiable to assume that fertility rates will continue to be experienced at about the present level. This is our assumption in Projection A. If, however, the present rates are influenced to any great extent by abnormally inflated marriage rates in recent years, they may still be somewhat transitional in nature, and one possibility is that there may be some decline in fertility, though hardly to the pre-war level. For the sake of comparison we have assumed in Projection B that by 1967 the rates will return to the average levels existing over a long period prior to 1952, as reflected in the 1952 census data on numbers of children born to women.†

There is some reason to believe that the fertility levels estimated for the pre-1952 period actually under-state the so-called "normal" levels of the past, since they are based on data which include the

---

* See Appendix B for the exact method of deriving the survival ratios for each sex-age group.
† The age-specific birth-rates derived from these data are shown in Appendix B.

experience of the depression years and, moreover, are subject to errors in memory which tend to give a downward bias. The fertility assumption of Projection B can therefore be taken to represent the lowest level to which fertility might conceivably fall *without* the adoption of voluntary methods of family limitation by a significant proportion of the population.

While the assumptions underlying Projection A have been selected with a view to presenting trends which reasonably might be expected to follow on the basis of past experience, Projection C has been designed to illustrate the effects on population trends of a conscious effort on the part of the whole population sharply to limit family size. More specifically, we have chosen to demonstrate what would happen to population trends if the concept of the three-child family (discussed in Chapter 12) were to be accepted by the population as a whole and put into practice with complete effectiveness by 1972.* This would entail drastic and nation-wide changes in present attitudes toward family size and in reproductive behaviour.

Table IX. Summary of Assumptions adopted for the Population Projections.

Mortality	Fertility	Migration
Projection A: Mortality assumed to decline at a "normal" rate, implying an annual gain of about one-half year in life expectancy at birth.	Age-specific fertility rates assumed to remain constant at 1956-58 levels.	None
Projection B: Mortality assumed to remain constant at the levels estimated for the period 1957-62.	Age-specific fertility rates assumed to decline from 1956-58 levels to reach average pre-1952 levels by 1967. No further reduction assumed after 1967.	None
Projection C: Same as Projection A.	Age-specific fertility rates assumed to decline rapidly from 1956-58 levels to reach, by 1972, levels calculated on the assumption of eliminating all births in excess of three for each woman. No further reduction assumed after 1972.	None

* In estimating the fertility rates for use in Projection C, we first computed age-specific rates from 1952 census data on numbers of children born to women, and then eliminated from these rates the proportion due to births of the fourth and higher orders. For a more detailed explanation of the derivation of these rates, see Appendix B.

Projection C shows that even if so marked a decline were to occur in fertility during the next 12 years, population pressure would not be greatly alleviated *in the short run;* it makes equally clear the vital necessity of bringing about a decline in fertility with all possible speed, so as to ensure the benefits of a lower rate of population growth in the long run. These conclusions are further elaborated upon in the following section, which summarises the results of the three projections. A summary of the assumptions underlying the three projections is given in Table IX.

NEW PROJECTIONS OF POPULATION GROWTH

Projection A—based on assumptions of constant fertility and declining mortality—shows the population growing from its estimated total of 594,000 at mid-year 1957* to 1,365,000 by mid-year 1982.

Over the 25-year period, the average annual rate of increase under Projection A shows a gradual rise from about 3·0% during 1957-62 to 3·8% per annum during 1977-82. At this rate of growth, the population would double in 20·8 years.

Table X. Projections of the Population of Mauritius under different Assumptions: 1957-1982.

	Projection A—constant fertility, declining mortality	Projection B—declining fertility, constant mortality	Projection C—rapidly declining fertility, declining mortality
	(Figures in thousands)		
1957	594·3	594·3	594·3
1962	690·2	683·8	678·9
1967	805·3	773·6	757·2
1972	950·9	876·3	829·6
1977	1,135·9	999·9	902·3
1982	1,365·5	1,142·4	983·3
	Average annual % increase		
1957-82	3·38	2·65	2·03

Given these trends, the proportion of the population under 15 years of age would rise to 47% of the total by 1982,† a figure implying

* Our estimate is higher than official estimates because of the adjustment introduced for under-enumeration of children in the census base figure.

† The rise in the proportion of the population under 15 years of age from 44% in 1957 to 47% in 1982 is due to the fact that the group aged 10-14 in 1957 was somewhat smaller in size, representing the survivors of a cohort born before the recent rise in fertility. In addition, the assumptions of declining infant and childhood mortality have the effect of raising the size of the group under 15 years in relation to the total population.

an extraordinarily heavy burden of child dependants. In fact, the number of children under 15 years of age in 1982 (641,000) would exceed the size of the total population in 1957.

Table XI. *Projections of the Population by Broad Age Groups:* 1957-1982.

Age group	1957	1962	1967	1972	1977	1982
	(Figures in thousands)					
Projection A—						
Under 15	260·1	315·7	364·1	430·4	522·8	641·3
15-64	317·1	354·8	418·3	493·7	581·8	686·8
65 and over	17·1	19·7	22·9	26·8	31·3	37·4
All ages	594·3	690·2	805·3	950·9	1,135·9	1,365·5
Projection B—						
Under 15	260·1	309·3	334·5	362·5	407·6	472·1
15-64	317·1	354·8	416·7	488·4	564·0	638·1
65 and over	17·1	19·7	22·4	25·4	28·3	32·2
All ages	594·3	683·8	773·6	876·3	999·9	1,142·4
Projection C—						
Under 15	260·1	304·4	316·0	309·1	300·3	306·4
15-64	317·1	354·8	418·3	493·7	570·7	639·5
65 and over	17·1	19·7	22·9	26·8	31·3	37·4
All ages	594·3	678·9	757·2	829·6	902·3	983·3

Of these, children aged 5-14 years—the group for whom educational facilities must be provided—would increase from a little more than 150,000 to a total of about 380,000.

In absolute numbers, there would be a large increase in the working ages—about 370,000—but the percentage increase among this group would not be so great as among the child population. In fact, the ratio of child dependants per 100 persons of working age would rise from 82 in 1957 to 93 by 1982. The number of persons aged 65 years and over would grow from about 17,000 to 37,000.

If fertility were to return to the lower levels prevailing before 1952 and mortality were to remain constant—the assumptions of Projection B—the population could be expected to reach a figure of about 1,140,000 by 1982. This is about 200,000 fewer than the total shown by Projection A. The average annual rate of increase over the 25 years on this basis would amount to 2·65%, as compared with the more rapid average annual rate of growth of 3·38% shown by Projection A. The assumption of some decline in fertility and no further decline in infant and childhood mortality has the effect of lowering the proportion of children in the population, and correspondingly raising the proportion in the working ages. For 1982, these two percentages work out at 41% and 56% respectively.

The population 25 years of age and over in 1982 would number about 447,000, as compared with 468,000 in Projection A. This difference is due entirely to the change in the mortality assumption, since all of these persons had already been born by 1957. The major part of the difference in total population between Projections A and B, however, stems from the assumed fall in fertility in the latter. This shows up mainly in the lower projected figure for the population under 15 years—472,000 in 1982 as compared with 641,000 under Projection A. The fertility assumptions underlying Projection B entail a fall in the crude birth-rate to about 35 per 1,000 by 1967.

It is noteworthy that, even given a drastic decline in fertility such as that set out in Projection C, the population would nevertheless not fall far short of a million by 1982. The actual projected figure is 983,000. This means that the potential for a large population expansion is already inherent in the age structure of the present population, owing to the large cohorts born between 1947 and 1957 who, during the projection period, move into the child-bearing ages. Moreover, since it would have been completely unrealistic to assume an immediate changeover to the small-size family pattern, Projection C has allowed for a steady decline in rates, with the goal of eliminating births in excess of three for each woman to be reached only by 1972.* Thus, the total numbers of births shown to occur during the early years of the projection period are not greatly reduced.

The advantages of adopting the course of action depicted by Projection C are, nevertheless, demonstrably impressive. Not only would the total population be nearly 400,000 less in 1982 than if present fertility levels remained unchanged, but a more balanced age structure would result. Table I shows that with rapidly falling fertility only about 31% of the population would be under 15 years of age in 1982, and 65% would be in the working ages. Such a development would bring to Mauritius a population structure not unlike that now existing in the industrialised countries of the West. The numbers in the working ages would not of course be reduced significantly by 1982, since the bulk of this group has already been born.

The really striking contrast between Projections A and C is that relating to the child population. Under the latter, the number of children below age 15 is less than half that shown in Projection A.

---

* We recognise that this assumption of "eliminating births in excess of three" is an over-simplification. It has been adopted for statistical convenience, and is not intended to imply that no individual woman would ever have more than this number of children.

Instead of more than doubling in the next 25 years (as implied in Projection A) the number of children would increase from 260,000 in 1957 to only a little over 300,000 by 1982. Of these, the school-age group would number less than 200,000.

Thus, while a rapid reduction in fertility could begin to stem population growth by the end of the period to which our projections relate, and could most certainly relieve the burden placed upon the working population to provide educational and other needs for numerous child dependants, perhaps its most important contribution would be to create a population structure with a low potential for future expansion.

To illustrate the effectiveness of such a course of action in the long run, we have carried Projections A and C forward to the end of the century.* While projections so far into the future are not worth considering in any detail, it is of interest to see that by the end of the century the population according to Projection A is more than double that of Projection C. In fact, by this date Projection C shows a population of under 1,300,000, or less than would be obtained by 1982 under the assumption of Projection A. The projected total population for the year 2002, on the basis of Projection A, is 2,869,000. (See Fig. 1.)

Even with the adoption of the very low fertility rates assumed in Projection C, the population would, in fact, continue to grow in absolute numbers, though the rate of growth would be greatly curtailed. This projection implies a fall in the crude birth-rate to about 24 per 1,000 by 1972, and a reduction in average family size to about 2·3 children per woman—similar to that in many Western countries today. In reducing their fertility to such levels, these Western countries took a long time—in typical cases five or six decades—as compared with the 15 years allowed for under Projection C.

In the face of the most urgent need, however, a few countries have recently achieved quite significant fertility declines within a short period of time. Japan is, of course, the most notable example, though the methods by which the birth-rate was reduced in this country may be regarded as harsh and unacceptable to the people of Mauritius. The social and family planning policies that we propose

---

* According to our original assumption mortality would fall to a quite low level by 1982, with a life expectation at birth approximately that of a number of industrialised countries at present. Therefore, in projecting the population to the year 2002, no further declines in mortality have been assumed. For Projection A, fertility rates were held constant at 1957 levels, and for Projection C the low rates reached in 1972 were assumed to remain constant throughout the period.

in this Report, and which are brought together in Chapter 12, are so designed as to avoid these painful experiences.

The conclusions we draw from this analysis are unavoidable. No alternative presents itself but action, immediate and sustained, to develop policies on as broad a scale as possible designed to slow down the rate of population growth. The answers must be found within Mauritius; to hope for emigration as a solution is to invite catastrophe.

Families must be limited in size. The rate at which children are born must be voluntarily brought under control. All married couples in the island must be provided with the knowledge and the means, consistent with their consciences and their faith, to limit their families. In Chapter 10 we outline a series of measures to inaugurate a nation-wide campaign of family planning. Such a campaign involves the provision of facilities and information to all those requiring assistance. These should be provided as an integral part of the health and welfare services.

In evidence we have received from doctors, chemists, nurses, midwives, probation officers, social welfare workers and members of the public, and from investigations we and others have made, we believe that there is a substantial number of parents in all classes of the community who wish to avoid the birth of further children. Various harmful and illegal measures are being resorted to at present. The rate of abortion may be quite substantial, particularly among some poorer families. We were informed that there is something like a standard charge throughout the island for the termination of pregnancies under one month of Rs. 20 and Rs. 25-30 for over one month. For poor families the charge is less; for middle-class families, Rs. 50 and over. No estimate can be made of the harm done to the health of mothers as a result of these and other practices.

This is a health problem as well as a social and economic problem. The relatively high rate of mortality among the women of Mauritius aged 20-45 (see Appendix B) probably reflects excessive and continuous child-bearing and these harmful practices to which we draw attention. They should be dealt with frankly and openly through the ordinary day-to-day work of the health and welfare services. Hence, in our recommendations in Chapter 10 for the development and expansion of these services, we have so framed our proposals to give as much priority to the health needs of wives and mothers as to the health needs of husbands and fathers. In the circumstances of Mauritius today, dominated by the menace of over-population, it would be a grave error in social policy to

Table XII. Population of Mauritius by Sex and Age: 1952 to 1982.
PROJECTION A: CONSTANT FERTILITY, DECLINING MORTALITY

Age group	1952	1957	1962	1967	1972	1977	1982
Males							
0- 4	48,024	53,888	61,747	71,896	87,777	108,246	131,610
5- 9	31,685	45,937	52,907	60,926	71,235	87,215	107,748
10-14	25,705	31,356	45,648	52,637	60,701	71,050	87,058
15-19	24,259	25,511	31,130	45,379	52,400	60,507	70,887
20-24	22,120	23,992	25,238	30,859	45,084	52,154	60,295
25-29	23,004	21,777	23,687	24,981	30,624	44,832	51,930
30-34	17,892	22,566	21,429	23,370	24,709	30,367	44,541
35-39	16,147	17,360	22,024	20,983	22,954	24,336	29,984
40-44	13,503	15,427	16,714	21,299	20,377	22,371	23,798
45-49	11,418	12,637	14,514	15,823	20,283	19,511	21,514
50-54	9,239	10,271	11,452	13,280	14,598	18,851	18,260
55-59	6,857	7,906	8,899	10,050	11,789	13,087	17,051
60-64	5,039	5,554	6,414	7,341	8,417	10,007	11,238
65-69	3,136	3,711	4,085	4,819	5,623	6,564	7,930
70-74	1,450	2,035	2,409	2,721	3,287	3,920	4,671
75 and over	1,126	1,103	1,414	1,774	2,144	2,657	3,294
All ages	260,604	301,031	349,711	408,138	482,002	575,675	691,809
Females							
0- 4	47,194	52,940	59,477	69,232	84,647	104,683	127,517
5- 9	31,594	44,825	51,516	58,234	68,152	83,733	103,898
10-14	25,480	31,176	44,440	51,166	57,931	67,893	83,499
15-19	23,529	25,181	30,883	44,107	50,864	57,676	67,669
20-24	21,156	23,113	24,773	30,466	43,626	50,427	57,301
25-29	20,957	20,657	22,584	24,295	29,975	43,054	49,903
30-34	15,900	20,413	20,153	22,114	23,872	29,549	42,555
35-39	14,385	15,429	19,880	19,704	21,696	23,495	29,159
40-44	11,828	13,846	14,918	19,303	19,209	21,225	23,058
45-49	10,448	11,241	13,300	14,396	18,707	18,685	20,713
50-54	8,842	9,797	10,608	12,626	13,738	17,938	17,996
55-59	7,271	8,047	9,064	9,885	11,839	12,959	17,009
60-64	5,775	6,372	7,129	8,111	8,926	10,778	11,890
65-69	4,218	4,682	5,319	6,030	6,942	7,724	9,423
70-74	2,668	3,080	3,548	4,101	4,723	5,518	6,225
75 and over	2,152	2,460	2,892	3,434	4,099	4,887	5,863
All ages	253,397	293,259	340,484	397,204	468,946	560,224	673,678
Both sexes	514,001	594,290	690,195	805,342	950,948	1,135,899	1,365,487

NOTE: These figures are unrounded, and the last two digits of each number have little value; they are included to avoid the introduction of unnecessary rounding errors in cases where the figures are used as a base for further calculations. In each column the figures above the dotted line represent population as yet unborn at the base date and hence are of a lower order of reliability than are the figures below the dotted line, which represent the survivors of existing population.

Table XIII. Population of Mauritius by Sex and Age: 1962 to 1982.

PROJECTION B: MODERATELY DECLINING FERTILITY, CONSTANT MORTALITY

Age group	1962	1967	1972	1977	1982
Males					
0- 4	58,470	60,423	68,829	81,685	93,827
5- 9	52,907	57,406	59,323	67,576	80,198
10-14	45,648	52,574	57,044	58,949	67,150
15-19	31,130	45,319	52,195	56,633	58,525
20-24	25,238	30,797	44,834	51,637	56,027
25-29	23,687	24,917	30,406	44,265	50,981
30-34	21,429	23,308	24,518	29,920	43,557
35-39	22,024	20,915	22,749	23,930	29,202
40-44	16,714	21,205	20,137	21,903	23,040
45-49	14,514	15,725	19,950	18,945	20,606
50-54	11,452	13,153	14,250	18,079	17,168
55-69	8,899	9,922	11,396	12,346	15,664
60-64	6,414	7,220	8,050	9,246	10,016
65-69	4,085	4,717	5,310	5,921	6,800
70-74	2,409	2,652	3,062	3,447	3,844
75 and over	1,414	1,723	1,971	2,268	2,575
All ages	346,434	391,976	444,024	506,750	579,180
Females					
0- 4	56,322	58,202	66,299	78,683	90,378
5- 9	51,516	54,807	56,636	64,516	76,566
10-14	44,440	51,073	54,336	56,149	63,961
15-19	30,883	44,022	50,593	53,825	55,621
20-24	24,773	30,383	43,309	49,773	52,953
25-29	22,584	24,206	29,687	42,317	48,633
30-34	20,153	22,033	23,615	28,963	41,284
35-39	19,880	19,627	21,458	22,999	28,207
40-44	14,918	19,222	18,977	20,748	22,238
45-49	13,300	14,330	18,465	18,229	19,931
50-54	10,608	12,551	13,523	17,425	17,203
55-59	9,064	9,815	11,612	12,511	16,122
60-64	7,129	8,030	8,695	10,287	11,083
65-69	5,319	5,951	6,703	7,259	8,588
70-74	3,548	4,031	4,510	5,080	5,501
75 and over	2,892	3,362	3,859	4,369	4,932
All ages	337,329	381,645	432,277	493,133	563,201
Both sexes	683,763	773,621	876,301	999,883	1,142,381

See note to Table XII.

concentrate scarce health service resources on the needs of male workers alone.

The policies we propose are not, however, limited to the provision of medical care, birth-control facilities and information. In Chapter 7 on *Family Needs* we make a series of proposals designed to popularise the ideal of the three-child family in Mauritius. We recommend the introduction as a matter of urgency of non-contributory family benefits, marriage grants, maternity benefits and other measures designed to encourage later marriage and child-bearing and the spacing of births, and to support the growth of healthy three-child families among all classes in the community. The appeal is to a healthy and more secure family life. These proposals are backed by other recommendations in Chapters 5 and 6 aimed at more security for the family in times of unemployment, sickness and disablement.

At the end of this Report, in Chapter 12, we bring together all our major recommendations and show how they are connected with one another, and with the basic issues of population pressure and the standard of living. Finally, we outline the methods that should be advocated and provided to enable parents to limit the size of their families and so contribute to the future welfare of their country.

Table XIV. Population of Mauritius by Sex and Age: 1962 to 1982.
PROJECTION C: RAPIDLY DECLINING FERTILITY, DECLINING MORTALITY

Age group	1962	1967	1972	1977	1982
Males					
0- 4	55,972	53,059	50,231	50,809	55,590
5- 9		55,228	52,571	49,910	50,575
10-14			55,024	52,434	49,820
15-19				54,848	52,313
20-24					54,656
...					
All ages	343,936	383,603	420,115	456,658	497,165
Females					
0- 4	53,916	51,094	48,440	49,137	53,860
5- 9		52,789	50,297	47,917	48,768
10-14			52,514	50,106	47,783
15-19				52,283	49,941
20-24					51,943
...					
All ages	334,923	373,621	409,467	445,682	486,089
Both sexes	678,859	757,224	829,582	902,340	983,254

NOTE: Figures for age groups not shown are the same as in Projection A. See also note to Table XII on the rounding of figures.

CHAPTER 4

The Dilemma of Public Assistance

The Public Assistance Department is responsible for the payment of "outdoor relief" and old age pensions, for the care of residents in orphanages and infirmaries, and for various subsidiary functions. The Department inherited most of these functions from the old Poor Law. The main statute governing its activities is still the Poor Law Ordinance of 1902, though the title of the Ordinance was changed from "Poor Law" to "Public Assistance" in 1947. This chapter is concerned only with the "outdoor relief" functions of the Department; we discuss institutional care in Chapter 11. Although we shall use the term "outdoor relief" in describing the historical development of the Department, we would urge that in the future the term "public assistance" should be used in place of "outdoor relief".

THE HISTORICAL BACKGROUND

In the nineteenth century, poor relief was administered on a local "parish" basis, just as it was under the English Poor Law. With the growing numbers of paupers and the obvious limitations of the parish system, centralisation became necessary, and the Protector of Immigrants added poor relief to his other responsibilities.* The Poor Law Ordinance of 1902, however, created a separate Poor Law Department with the Labour Commissioner at its head. His duties were to:

"(i) direct and control the administration of relief to the poor;

(ii) establish, with the approval of the Governor, almshouses, workhouses, infirmaries and other asylums for the poor, and direct the management of such institutions;

(iii) receive and disburse, according to the rules herein prescribed, the amount voted annually by the Council of Government."

Outdoor relief could be granted either on a permanent or temporary basis. The conditions for the granting of permanent relief were set out in section 6 of the Ordinance:

"All persons who through advanced or tender age, or infirmity of mind or body, are incapable of working for their own livelihood, and have no relatives liable and able to support them, shall be considered as paupers and shall be entitled to relief."

* *Annual Report of the Labour Department*, 1944, p. 9.

However, permanent outdoor relief could only be granted if "it would be seriously detrimental to the pauper to be removed to an asylum". If he refused to be so removed, or "to perform the work he is directed to do and for which he is deemed fit by any medical officer appointed to examine him", he forfeited any right to permanent relief.

The conditions for temporary relief were not quite so stringent; Section 8 provided that "all persons becoming temporarily destitute through sickness, accident, or other causes may receive temporary relief from the Poor Law Officers". Thus, not only the sick and disabled but also the able-bodied unemployed were eligible for relief. This was the first departure from the rule that casual relief could only be paid to those incapable of working for their livelihood.* The Ordinance provided for the recovery of temporary poor relief from the employer (if any) of the person relieved, or from "any relative liable and able to support him". The "workhouse test" did not apply in the case of temporary relief, which could not therefore be forfeited by refusal to be "removed to an asylum". There was, however, a work test, as there was for permanent relief.

The Poor Law Ordinance made specific provision for the relief of deserted wives "found temporarily or permanently destitute", subject to recovery of the amount expended from the husband, who was liable to be fined or imprisoned.

The Mauritius Royal Commission of 1909 was critical of the way in which it found this system operating. While the Poor Law Commissioner (as he was still called) exercised immediate control over the payment of outdoor relief in Port Louis, the Poor Law officers responsible for the payment of relief in the country districts were with one exception Government medical officers.* Most of the cases were dealt with at the dispensaries, where in addition to money, medicines and food were distributed.† The dispensary was "a kind of soup-kitchen".‡ Indeed, outdoor relief in the country districts consisted mainly of rice with "a pittance of money", varying in amount with the size of the family.§ In Port Louis all relief was in the form of cash, varying from Rs. 1·50 to Rs. 7·50 a month.§

The Royal Commission found that Poor Law expenditure had shown "an alarming increase".* The number of payments of outdoor relief (including relief given at the dispensaries) had risen from

---

* *Report of Mauritius Royal Commission*, 1909, Cmd. 5185, 1910, p. 42.

† *Mauritius Royal Commission*, 1909, Minutes of Evidence, Cmd. 5186, 1910, p. 124.

‡ *Ibid.*, p. 124.

§ *Ibid.*, p. 128.

48,906 in 1907 to 63,321 in the following year,* while the expenditure of the Poor Law Department had increased from Rs. 200,000 in 1905-6 to Rs. 227,000 in 1906-7, and Rs. 259,000 in 1907-8.† The Commissioners regarded this expenditure as excessive and attributed it not to the economic and social conditions of the Colony but to administrative defects, aggravated by "the generally indolent character of the coloured creoles who are the main recipients of casual relief". Despite the conditions laid down by the law, "little appears to be done towards making relatives contribute, and persons in receipt of casual relief are not required to perform any work in consideration of the assistance given them or as a test of their need of relief".‡

Even if no attempt was made to offer work to applicants for temporary relief, the evidence given to the Royal Commission by the Poor Law Commissioner does not suggest that relief was willingly given to the able-bodied:

'... If there is a breadwinner for the family ... when he is in good health and he does not work I give him nothing. I say, "Go and find work; there is plenty to be had." '

'Would you leave him to starve?'—'He will not starve.'

'What about his wife and his children?'—'If his wife is in good health she can find work; she can go out as a servant or something of that sort.'

'What about the children?'—'With regard to the children, if he is the kind of man who cannot find work I may relieve the children.'§

The Royal Commission recommended a scheme of land settlement for the unemployed and their families, by means of Government work stations where "all should be put to work according to their capacities, in return for rations on a reasonable scale". They believed that unemployment was due to the indolence of the unemployed rather than economic conditions. Settlers were to be "punished as recalcitrant workhouse inmates are in England in the event of their failing to work properly". ‖

The Commissioners recommended that the Protector of Immigrants should take over once more the functions of the Poor Law Department. The work was to be decentralised. Local committees were to be set up in the country districts "composed of the Poor

---

* *Mauritius Royal Commission*, 1909, Minutes of Evidence, Cmd. 5186, 1910, p. 124.
† *Ibid.*, p. 126.
‡ *Report of Mauritius Royal Commission*, 1909, Cmd. 5185, 1910, p. 42.
§ *Mauritius Royal Commission*, 1909, Minutes of Evidence, Cmd. 5186, 1910, p. 130.
‖ *Report of Mauritius Royal Commission*, 1909, Cmd. 5185, 1910, p. 43.

Law medical officer and from two to four private persons who would be ready voluntarily to devote some of their time to the investigation of the circumstances of applicants for relief".* However, one member of the Commission, Sir Edward O'Malley, dissented from this recommendation. He did not think that money "provided out of the general revenue of the Colony should be administered locally by bodies composed mainly of unofficial and irresponsible persons", though he conceded that such local committees might usefully assist the central administration in the work of investigating "the condition of the poor about them" and "the circumstances and needs of applicants for public assistance".†

The recommendations of the 1909 Commission seem to have had little practical effect. The office of Poor Law Commissioner was amalgamated with that of Protector of Immigrants but the work of the combined Department continued to be centrally administered, no local committees being instituted.

The next official investigation of the Poor Law was carried out by the Poor Relief Enquiry Commission, which was appointed in 1929 and reported in 1931.‡ The cost of outdoor relief had risen steeply from Rs. 96,000 in 1920-21 to Rs. 295,000 in 1927-28. The Commission ascribed this increase partly to "the increase of pauperism" and partly to insufficiency of control. There had been little change in the system of outdoor relief since 1910. The Poor Law Commissioner still dealt with all cases in Port Louis after enquiries carried out by his inspectors. In the country districts the enquiry work was done by Poor Law clerks. These clerks were generally dispensers employed full-time by the Medical Department, who conducted their enquiries in their off-duty hours. The dispenser reported on each case to the Government medical officer of the district, who was also the Poor Law officer. The final decision on each case remained in the hands of the Commissioner. He was assisted by an Advisory Relief Board, set up in 1927, to which the Roman Catholic and Anglican Bishops each nominated two members, while two other members were appointed to represent the Indian community.

The Commission found little to complain of in the administration of poor relief in Port Louis. For the country districts, however, they suggested that control could be exercised more efficiently either by entrusting the enquiry work to full-time officers under the supervision of the medical officer (thus eliminating the Poor Law clerk-dispensers), or by employing a larger number of dispensers under

---

* *Report of Mauritius Royal Commission*, 1909, *Cmd.* 5185, 1910, p. 43.
† *Ibid.*, p. 58.
‡ The Report of this Commission was not published. A copy was made available to us by Mr. G. Atchia, a member of the Commission.

district officers who would be directly responsible to the Poor Law Commissioner in Port Louis (thus eliminating the Poor Law medical officers, except in cases of sickness). The latter suggestion was adopted in part. All district dispensers were appointed Poor Law visiting officers, with a special duty allowance; but the medical officers retained their Poor Law functions.

One member of the 1931 Commission, Mr. G. Atchia, submitted a dissenting memorandum. He criticised the policy of compelling "paupers who could have been satisfied with a small money grant to accept admission into an Institution as a condition without which relief is refused". While endorsing the views of the majority that there was a serious lack of control in the country districts, he was by no means satisfied with the control exercised in Port Louis. He complained, moreover, that the Poor Law Commissioner had taken no steps to bring to light cases of fraud brought to his notice by members of the Advisory Relief Board.

The Poor Law Administration was again subjected to critical examination by the Commission on the Financial Situation of Mauritius whose report was published in 1932. Despite the rapidly rising cost of outdoor relief, they found no evidence of extravagance apart from the "indiscriminate grant of free coffins for funerals of the poor".* Most of the recipients of outdoor relief at this time were either widows with young children or cases of physical disability.† There was no serious unemployment problem, and therefore no need of assistance to the "able-bodied labouring classes". However, work was provided for some of the women with children in the sewing workshop and laundry maintained by the Poor Law Department in Port Louis. The Commission also noted an increasing tendency, as a result of reduced wage rates, "for the sick and aged poor to apply for some supplement of the scanty contribution which their relatives are able to make for their support".‡

The increase in the number of claims for relief continued without interruption up to 1935. By that year the proportion of "cases relieved" (both outdoor and indoor) to the total population, which in 1926 had been only 8·7 per thousand, had risen to over 36 per thousand,§ a figure which remained practically constant up to the outbreak of war in 1939.

The depressed state of the sugar industry led to a considerable amount of unemployment, especially among the more skilled workers. Owing to the strain imposed on the Poor Law Department

---
* *Report of Commission on the Financial Situation of Mauritius*, Cmd. 4034, 1932, p. 157.
† *Ibid.*, p. 156.
‡ *Ibid.*, p. 157.
§ *Annual Report of the Poor Law Commissioner*, 1935, p. 8.

by the need to make detailed enquiries before giving relief in cases of unemployment, it was decided in 1935 to obtain the assistance of the police. The unemployed artisan was referred to the nearest Police Station for enquiries to ascertain that he had a trade and was in fact "in distress" through unemployment. He was then offered relief work by the Public Works Department, and only if such work was not available within two weeks was he paid "a part maintenance in favour of his children". Such cases were reconsidered at the end of each month.*

The Royal Commission of 1909 had mentioned the problem of the young man who, having received some education, was unwilling to do manual work. "The field of employment open to such youths", the Commission stated, "is small in a Colony like Mauritius, and the result is that a considerable proportion of them become unemployed loungers, living on the scanty earnings of their parents."† Part of the burden of this "intellectual unemployment" seems to have fallen on the Poor Law Department. The Director of Labour reported that in 1938 "the serious unemployment in the Colony is among persons of the clerical class and of the classes which are not accustomed to perform manual labour or are not physically fit for it. . . . The [Labour] Department was able to secure temporary work for some of these persons and others received Poor Relief if circumstances warranted it".‡ In his Annual Report for 1938, the Poor Law Commissioner commented on the rising expenditure on outdoor relief, which he attributed to unemployment and insufficiency of earnings, and added: "In many cases the quantum originally allowed had to be increased and, when other persons belonging to the intellectual class began to turn to the Poor Law Department for assistance, a higher quantum had to be given".§ Similarly, in a report published in 1941, we read that "The practice has . . . been to take the applicants' previous station in life into account. If a man has been used to wearing boots, provision is made accordingly". ||

Owing to adverse weather conditions, unemployment in the sugar industry was unusually severe in 1939, and a substantial programme of relief work was organised by the Government, including agricultural work, road-making and anti-malarial work. In 1940, there was unemployment in Port Louis which led to some disturbances. As this occurred in the crop season, work was found for the unemployed on the sugar estates. This experiment, however, was not

---

* *Annual Report of the Poor Law Commissioner*, 1935, pp. 13-14.
† *Report of Mauritius Royal Commission*, 1909, Cmd. 5185, 1910, p. 41.
‡ *Annual Report of the Labour Department*, 1938, p. 10.
§ *Annual Report of the Poor Law Commissioner*, 1938, p. 13.
|| Ridley, S., *Report on the Condition of Indians in Mauritius*, New Delhi, 1941, p. 32.

a success. The men proved "unsuitable for agricultural work".

In 1941, therefore, relief works were again organised, paid for under the provisions of the Poor Law Ordinance. But from 1942 until the end of the war, the problem of the unemployed was taken out of the hands of the Poor Law administration by the creation of the Mauritius Labour Corps to which unemployed men were conscripted.*

Meanwhile, important administrative changes had taken place. In 1935, the distribution of relief in the form of food, which had been entrusted to the Saint Vincent de Paul Society, was finally abandoned as a result of public criticism. The following year a start was made towards relieving the Government medical officers and dispensers of their duties as Poor Law officers and visiting officers. With the increase in the number of applicants for relief, the duties devolving on these officers had become more and more onerous. The medical officers were no longer able to exercise effective control over the dispensers, who in their turn found it impossible to make adequate enquiries in each case. As a first step, six full-time visiting officers were appointed for the Plaines Wilhems district, under the supervision of a full-time Poor Law officer. By the beginning of 1938, this system had been extended to cover the whole island, and from then onwards the functions of the Government medical officers in the administration of the Poor Law were limited to the certification of sickness and the provision of medical care.† The Advisory Relief Board was abolished in 1938.

Following the enactment of the Labour Ordinance of 1938, the Labour Department was created, and in 1939 the title of Protector of Immigrants and Poor Law Commissioner was changed to that of Director of Labour. However, the Poor Law Department was a separate part of the Labour Department. From 1946, the Annual Reports of the Department were signed not by the Director of Labour but by Mr. K. Hazareesingh, first as Poor Law Supervisor and later as Assistant Commissioner. In 1950, the two Departments became separate in form as well as in fact with the appointment of Miss M. Darlow as Public Assistance Commissioner and Social Welfare Adviser.

An important development dating from the war years was the setting up of local Public Assistance Advisory Committees. These Committees, which now consider all new applications for outdoor relief and make recommendations to the Commissioner, grew out of informal groups of interested persons known as "Friends of the Poor". They were officially constituted in 1945 as Local Poor Law

---
* See Annual Reports of the Labour Department, 1939-45.
† See Annual Reports of the Poor Law Commissioner, 1935-38.

Boards, whose object was that of "stimulating local interest in the work of the Poor Law and in social service generally".* By the end of 1946, nearly every village had its own Poor Law Board and the present system of referring applications to them had been introduced. This was an attempt to bring a measure of decentralisation into the administration of relief, on the lines proposed by the 1909 Royal Commission. It was hoped that there would thus be less delay in disposing of cases. At the same time, the Poor Law officers were relieved of their local duties and transferred to Port Louis, where they combined the duties of "adjudicating" cases referred from the local Committees with a programme of surprise visits to the local offices. The visiting officers were thus left in charge of their areas and were empowered to make immediate payments of casual relief.†

At first the local Committees were handicapped by the lack of any exact criteria either for awarding relief or for deciding the amount to be given. The Poor Law officers had presumably evolved their own working rules, which must have left many questions of detail to be decided as and when they arose. It was clearly necessary to provide the local Committees with detailed regulations on which to base their decisions. A Central Poor Law Board was therefore appointed to "draw up plans for the improvement of the Poor Law System in Mauritius".‡ We have been unable to trace any report by this Board, but the task of laying down a fixed scale of relief and the conditions under which it should be granted was eventually carried out by the Outdoor Relief Committee, under Miss Darlow's chairmanship, which issued its first report in 1952. The system now in operation, which is described in detail below, is based on the recommendations of this Committee.

Meanwhile the local Committees had to cope with the existing system, and many difficulties resulted. The expenditure on outdoor relief rose from Rs. 418,212 in 1946 to Rs. 560,219 in 1947, and the Committees were blamed for "a natural tendency . . . to show the utmost generosity to old people and others who applied to them for help".§ In 1947, therefore, a limit was put on the total expenditure of each Committee. This naturally led to complaints by the Committees, whose members felt that they were being deprived of the wide discretion which they needed in order to function effectively. It even became necessary to create an Arbitration Board to resolve disputes between "senior officers of the Department and those committees that did not agree with the official view". ‖ The following year, one

---
* *Annual Report of the Labour Department*, 1945, p. 13.
† *Annual Report of the Poor Law Department*, 1946, pp. 1-3.
‡ *Ibid.*, p. 2.
§ *Annual Report of the Public Assistance Department*, 1947, p. 1.
‖ *Ibid.*, p. 3.

local Committee, some of whose recommendations had been rejected, went on strike and refused to co-operate with the Department. In general, however, the Committees seem to have become resigned to the limitations laid upon them. Whether their activities resulted in any reduction of the delay in giving relief is open to question. The Commissioner, in her Annual Report for 1951, stated that "given the Advisory Committee procedure it is difficult to put an allowance into pay within a month of the receipt of application".*

The final step in establishing the present general pattern of administration took place in 1951 when, following the appointment of a number of inexperienced visiting officers, it was decided to appoint eight district officers to supervise their work, thus relieving the adjudicating officers of the supervisory functions which they had in fact been unable to perform.†

In 1951 a start was made on what was to have been a long-term building programme for the Department. It was hoped to provide not only more suitable offices but also living accommodation to enable local assistance officers to reside in the area in which they worked. Unfortunately, the programme was abandoned after the completion of only one building, and the Department was left with the unsuitable and inadequate premises, most of which it still occupies. The current five-year plan makes provision for a number of new buildings for the Department, but so far none has been built.

As mentioned in Chapter 1, expenditure on outdoor relief has grown continuously since the war. From an expenditure of about Rs. $\frac{1}{2}$ million in the early post-war years, the cost increased to Rs. 1 million in 1952, Rs. 2 million in 1953 and by 1958 had approached Rs. 7 million. This increase occurred despite the system of re-examining claims by a formidable hierarchy of officials. Part of the increase was due to the introduction of higher scales to meet the rising level of prices. But the growth in the number of claims was substantial—particularly from those claiming to be sick.

THE PRESENT SYSTEM

For the purpose of administering public assistance, the island is divided into 11 districts, with a "district officer" in charge of each. Within the districts there are 29 offices and 21 sub-offices, staffed by about 70 "local officers" (including cadets). Each new application for assistance, in addition to being considered by the local officer and the district officer, comes before the local Public Assistance Advisory Committee. There are 39 such Committees, whose members are prominent local residents selected by the Minister. In urgent cases

* *Annual Report of the Public Assistance Department*, 1951, p. 8.
† *Ibid.*, p. 5.

an immediate payment can be made without the approval of the Advisory Committee, and applications for renewal of a grant need not be submitted to the Committee unless the monthly rate of assistance is to be raised or lowered by more than Rs. 5.

At the head office of the Department in Port Louis, the recommendations of the Advisory Committees are checked by ten adjudicating officers. Above them in the departmental hierarchy is the Supervisor and, finally, the Commissioner and his two deputies (the post of Acting Commissioner is at present held by one of the Deputy Commissioners, resulting in corresponding "acting" appointments at lower levels). Only in exceptionally difficult cases, or where influence is brought to bear from political or other quarters, are individual applications considered at a higher level than that of the adjudicating officers.

If a person calls at his local office asking for assistance, particulars of his circumstances are noted by the local officer and he is given a registration card as evidence of the application. Within a few days the local officer visits the applicant's home in order to verify, as far as possible, the statements made by him. The local officer can make an immediate payment of up to Rs. 5. Next the applicant is summoned to the local office to be interviewed again, this time by the district officer, in an attempt to elicit any information that may have been concealed from the local officer. The district officer calculates the amount of assistance payable in accordance with the Darlow scale, or checks the local officer's calculation. He may authorise an immediate payment of more than Rs. 5. The claim is then brought before the Advisory Committee by the local officer. The applicant may be required, or may himself request, to appear before the Committee. If there are no special circumstances the Committee merely endorses the scaling already prepared by the district officer. The Committee may, however, adjust the assessment either up or down. This is done in cases of long-term sickness, suspected underdeclaration of earnings or where other special circumstances are present. The recommendation of the local Committee is examined by the district officer who records his agreement or dissent before submitting the case to head office for adjudication. The adjudicating officer may return the papers to the local office with a request for additional information. When he is satisfied that all the relevant facts have been disclosed, he decides how much assistance, if any, should be paid, and payment is then made on the next monthly pay day. There are 130 pay points on the island, and payment is made by a pay clerk assisted by two other officers (in practice, owing to shortage of staff, there is sometimes only one officer present in addition to the pay clerk).

An assessment for public assistance is made by comparing the needs and resources of the applicant and his or her family. The only relatives included in the "family" in assessing needs for this purpose are the applicant's spouse and children who are neither married nor earning. Even these are included only if they are living in the same household as the applicant. A household is defined in terms of shared cooking arrangements, but in practice a group of persons paying a single rent, or living rent-free in premises owned by one of them, are assumed to constitute one household.

The present scale of relief was developed in 1952 after an enquiry to ascertain the minimum sum upon which families could live.* On the basis of this enquiry it was reckoned that "the cost of food, fuel and lighting at present prices for a single recipient cannot be less than Rs. 20 per month (exclusive of rent and clothing . . .)". The basic rate for an adult was put at Rs. 12 per month in view of "the probable existence of hidden resources".

The scale has been increased since 1952 because of rises in prices. At present, it is as follows:—

	Rs. per month
First adult	15
Second adult (including the eldest child of a widower)	13
Third adult	12
Other adults	11
Child aged 6-9	7
Child aged 3-6	6
Child up to age 3	5

A number of special cases must be noted:—

 (i) The children of widows, unmarried women and women whose husbands are bedridden or absent—that is to say, all children whose mothers have no husband to support them—are scaled at Rs. 8 per month, regardless of their age.

 (ii) If either of the parents is earning, the eldest dependent child is omitted from the assessment.

 (iii) Normally only children up to the ages of 12 and 14, for boys and girls respectively, are included in the assessment. Older children attending school and sick children over 12 (including girls) may be included as additional adults. Other children of working age who are not earning may be included in cases of sudden destitution.

---

* The first report of the Outdoor Relief Committee (Darlow Report). The calculation of needs was based largely on a survey of public assistance cases, including the household budgets of 20 families living on public assistance.

In addition to this scale, half the rent is paid up to a maximum of Rs. 12 a month. In cases of prolonged illness the proportion can be increased to 75% with no maximum.

Although these rates were not intended to be adequate for full maintenance, they can in certain circumstances compare favourably with wage levels. A couple with two children over 9, three other children aged 5, 7 and 8, and a rent of Rs. 12 could receive Rs. 70 per month; and a widow with eight children could receive Rs. 79 exclusive of rent. Sums as large as this are in fact paid, in spite of the "wage stop" principle laid down in somewhat indefinite terms in the Darlow Report:

> "It is normally undesirable to pay, except for an emergency period, a sum equal to or greater than the earning power of the household, that is, the sum of the normal earnings of earning members."

In practice, the scale rate seldom exceeds the minimum wages of a labourer working full time in the sugar industry, though it may well exceed the amount earned by a particular worker in a particular month. As the Darlow Report gives no indication as to how "normal earnings" are to be assessed or on what period they are to be based, it is virtually impossible to apply the "wage stop" except in rare cases where a man who has been employed at a fixed monthly wage ceases to be so employed and applies for assistance. For a widow, the scale rate would only exceed a woman's "normal earnings" if there are several children, and a widow with several children is unlikely to have had any earnings in the recent past. Thus in the case of widows, the question of a wage stop seldom, if ever, arises.

It cannot, therefore, be said that at present the wage stop is of much importance in reducing the temptation to live on public assistance instead of looking for work. This is done more effectively by the system of disregarded earnings, or "concessions", which enables the members of the household to earn up to a certain limit without such earnings being deducted from the assistance payable. As the Darlow Report explained, "if all earnings are deducted from the allowance proposed, the recipient: (i) loses the impetus to earn, and (ii) is more tempted than ever not to make a declaration of his full earnings". The "concessions" for each member of the household are as follows:—

	Rs. per month
First adult	8
Second adult	10
Third adult	11
Other adults	12
Dependent child over 9	6

	Rs. per month
Child aged 6-9	5
Child aged 3-6	4
Child up to age 3	3

If the eldest dependent child has been omitted from the assessment of needs because one of the parents is earning, the "concession" in respect of that child is doubled. These concessions are intended to ensure that no deduction is made from the assistance payable unless the total income of the household (earnings plus assistance) exceeds the minimum sum necessary for subsistence. As soon as that level is reached, the earnings of the applicant and his wife (if any) are aggregated and any earnings in excess of the total concessions are deducted in full from the assistance given.

As in the case of the wage stop, the earnings so deducted are not actual but "normal" earnings. These may be arrived at by taking the actual verified earnings of a period previous to the application for assistance. More often, however, a figure of "normal earnings" is *assumed* on the basis of current wage rates. If the person concerned is in fact working full time, his earnings may well exceed the assumed figure. If, however, he is able-bodied but unable to find full-time work, the same amount of assumed earnings will still be set against the assistance payable. Since assistance is not normally given to the able-bodied unemployed except in cases of extreme destitution, the alternative to this method of deducting assumed earnings would be to exclude the unemployed person from the assessment entirely. It may therefore happen that an unemployed applicant is assumed to be earning in order that some assistance, however small, may be given. Two other methods are sometimes adopted for dealing with unverified earnings, in cases where the applicant has declared a figure of earnings which is suspected to be lower than his actual "normal" earnings. The first is to halve the concessions allowed. The second is for the local Advisory Committee to recommend an "adjustment" to take account of undisclosed earnings.

Another point at which the discretion of the Advisory Committee is exercised is in the assessment of earnings from "light work". This arises from the practice of medical officers certifying applicants as "fit for light work". We have described this in Chapter 1 as a disguised system of unemployment benefit. Light work is not normally available, especially in the rural areas, but once the applicant has been certified fit for light work an adjustment must be made for assumed earnings from such work. The amount deducted is often only a few rupees a month, but it can nevertheless constitute a hardship. If the applicant admits to having earnings from light work, the amount declared can be treated in the same way as other earnings and deducted in full subject to the usual concessions.

We have said above that only the applicant's spouse (if any) and children who are neither married nor earning are included in the "family" for the purpose of assessing needs. If, however, there are unmarried children who are earning and living in the household, a small deduction is made from the assistance payable to allow for their contribution to the household budget over and above the cost of their own maintenance. The amount deducted is seldom more than Rs. 10 or Rs. 15 a month, since a larger deduction would be an incentive for the earning child to leave the household.

The Public Assistance Ordinance lays a liability on brothers and sisters and all relatives in direct line of ascent or descent to assist the applicant, subject to their means being sufficient. This provision is seldom enforced, and only contributions actually made by relatives, whether living in the same household or not, are taken into account—and then only if they are disclosed.

OUR OWN VIEWS

Before we comment on the present scales of public assistance it is necessary to draw some conclusions from the historical working of the system in Mauritius. We have included a lengthy account in this chapter because we thought it important to show that the problems of the public assistance system are by no means new and that they are growing in scale. Every expedient has been tried to make the system work with justice and economy. None of them has been successful.

The fundamental problem in Mauritius as in other countries is how to give aid to those who are genuinely unemployed without extending it to those who are unwilling to work and to those who actually are working for at least some part of a week. At various times in the past, assistance was given to the unemployed subject to tests of work. But no system of labour camp or work test seems to have stood for very long. At other times assistance has been refused to the unemployed but this has led to heavy burdens of work falling upon Government medical officers and dressers once the volume of genuine unemployment became large. To obtain assistance, many of the unemployed claimed relief on account of sickness. The Government medical officers have thus functioned in a sense and at much public expense as relieving officers. Nor has this fundamental problem of distinguishing the sick from the well and the genuinely unemployed from those who are voluntarily idle been solved by establishing a large hierarchy of officials to investigate the circumstances of every applicant.

In the period since the Second World War, the theory of public assistance has been to deny regular help to the able-bodied unemployed except in cases where there are heavy family responsibilities. The result has been to achieve the worst of all possible worlds. Some of the unemployed feign sickness. Some no doubt are on the border of ill-health because of the widespread incidence of anaemia and other disabling diseases. All these demands, falling on an overworked Medical Service, tend to lower the standard of medical care which can be provided for the genuinely sick, waste national resources and increase the possibilities and incentives for abuse.

We shall show in Chapter 9 that the number of doctors in Mauritius is inadequate to meet the needs of the genuinely sick. For this reason alone it is unfortunate that any part of their time should be spent in examining the able-bodied unemployed. And the healthier the applicant for public assistance, the more of the time of the Government Medical Service is likely to be consumed. It one doctor refuses a sickness certificate, the applicant is likely to go from doctor to doctor until he finds one who is so busy or so credulous that the application is granted. Nor does the waste always stop at the dispensary or the "casualty" department of the hospital. The conscientious doctor faced with a patient complaining of backache will refer him for an expensive X-ray. And even if no displaced disc is found, this does not prove that the patient is malingering.

The persistent applicant is likely in these circumstances to get his sickness certificate. In saying this, we cast no discredit on the skill or integrity of the Government medical officers. Not all illness can be ascertained by clinical examination of the human body. Nor can a doctor disregard evidence of malnutrition, however "normal" it may be in the community in which he is operating. But the effect of inflated demands for certification must be to reduce the time which can be devoted to genuine medical needs, to make it easier for malingering to go undetected and thus to encourage further applications for certificates and further deterioration in standards. The need to protect the Government Medical Service is in itself an important reason for providing explicit aid for the unemployed.

A system which drives the unemployed to apply for sickness certificates has another disadvantage. Once unemployment becomes disguised as sickness it is impossible to distinguish between voluntary and involuntary unemployment. The systematic use of a work test is essential to the efficient administration of unemployment relief. By acquiring a sickness certificate the unemployed man is able to avoid any work test and is even able to supplement assistance with earnings.

By economising on relief for the genuinely unemployed, the Government has fostered a costly form of indiscriminate aid which penalises the honest, encourages disrespect for Government, lowers the morale of the Government Medical Service, spreads corruption, creates waste of scarce medical resources, and imposes a heavy strain on the budget.

These are some of the reasons which have led to continuous criticism of the work of the Public Assistance Department not only by applicants but also by Members of the Legislative Council, by senior civil servants and by the general public. We listened to much evidence of people who obtained assistance and in the informant's opinion ought not to have done so. On the other hand, we received evidence of severe hardships suffered by applicants who had been refused assistance.

What we have written should not be read as a condemnation either of those who devised the present principles of public assistance or of the loyal officials who have tried to operate them in extraordinarily difficult circumstances. We consider that relief should be given to the able-bodied unemployed, but this does not mean that any permanent solution to the fundamental problems of identifying and meeting need in Mauritius can be found by any simple amendment to the public assistance regulations. It is not enough to grant relief to the unemployed subject to a work test. History has shown that this would provide no real answer. It might well create as many new abuses as it prevented. If the solution were so simple it would certainly have been introduced long ago.

For a work test to be effective it must be frequent. This is only another way of saying that there must be enough jobs to offer whether those jobs arise from economic expansion or are deliberately created by government action. But despite the important recommendations of the Meade Report to secure more employment opportunities as soon as practicable, it may be no more than wishful thinking to assume that the situation will be quickly remedied. Moreover, the country has to face the fact of at least another fifteen years of rapid growth in the population of working age. This fact cannot now be avoided. Demands for work and demands for unemployment relief will inevitably increase.

But whatever can now be done to introduce an effective work test, other steps can also be taken which will remove some though not all of the present abuses and hardships of public assistance. At present there is no really effective means of preventing a person receiving assistance while at the same time earning a not insubstantial income which is not disclosed. Some system of work record needs to be introduced. If it were possible to secure that a record card was "lodged" with the employer during any period of employment, the withdrawal of this card and its lodgment with the department responsible during the period when financial assistance was being provided would at least prevent employment under a contract of service.

Ideally, what seems to be required is the issue to each economically active person of an individual record card. As periods of employment in Mauritius can be as short as one day, this card would need a space for each working day in the year. In this space it would be the duty of the employer to record the fact that the individual concerned had been working for him on that day. If such a record were kept accurately it would be possible to pay out money to the unemployed with some confidence that the money was reaching only those for whom it was intended.

We considered the possibility of introducing a card of this type. Eventually we rejected this proposal largely because we doubted whether employers—particularly small employers and illiterate employers—would maintain them with accuracy and thoroughness. There was also the possibility that entries might be made on the cards which were incorrect. Thus, casual services performed for part of a day might lead to an entry in good faith of a whole day's work. Also, it was possible that a friend or relative would be prepared to make entries with the sole purpose of assisting the applicant to receive aid at public expense. In short, there seemed a risk of the whole system breaking down because the records were incorrectly kept.

It seemed to us that a carefully devised scheme of social insurance would provide a more efficient system of work records than could be obtained in any other way. There are many other arguments for social insurance as we shall explain in the next chapter. But the critical advantage of having a work record was the chief reason which forced us to recommend social insurance for Mauritius. Paradoxically, the establishment of social insurance is needed to limit the abuse of public assistance.

The establishment of a work test and a scheme of social insurance are not the only measures needed to improve the social security services. There are further reasons for being dissatisfied with the existing system of public assistance. At present it is possible for a household with a number of dependent children to obtain from public assistance an income which is very close to that which would be obtained if the breadwinner was at work. Indeed, if there are also undisclosed earnings, such a family may be better off on public assistance than other poor families where the breadwinner is at work and no assistance is being received. The present system entirely fails to preserve any incentive to return to work in cases where there are large numbers of children.

The allowances for children provided only to public assistance recipients have a further grave disadvantage. They provide a positive incentive for the poor to increase the size of their families, as the amount of assistance granted depends, among other considerations, on the size of the family. As the number of families receiving public assistance in one form or another has grown rapidly in recent years, the extent of this incentive has also been growing. It is clearly undesirable, to put it mildly, that such a situation should persist in Mauritius which faces the disaster of overpopulation.

To abolish children's allowances from public assistance scales and make no alternative provision for children would be intolerable. It would mean abandoning all responsibility for the children of the poor; for the children already born. The only solution, as has been recognised elsewhere, is to pay a benefit for the family which will be received both by those at work and by those whose earnings are interrupted. In the special circumstances of Mauritius, such a benefit should be devised to give no encouragement to the birth of children in excess of three. Such is the purpose of the family benefit we recommend in Chapter 7.

We have tried to show in this chapter why the needs of the poor can no longer be met by the present system of public assistance. If no action is taken, the cost of assistance will continue its upward spiral and the system of administration may well dissolve into chaos under an intolerable strain. The solutions we propose are set out at length in Chapters 5, 6 and 7. In Chapter 8, we make special recommendations for the organisation and regulation of a new assistance department with smaller and more manageable functions.

CHAPTER 5

Social Insurance and Pensions

EARLIER ENQUIRIES

The earliest proposal for social insurance which we have been able to trace in the official literature of Mauritius comes from the report of a Commission of Enquiry in 1937. "In general we are in favour of old age pensions and sickness insurance ... Such schemes must obviously apply to all sections of the population and not merely to persons employed in the sugar industry."*

In January 1940, the Governor appointed a committee with the Director of Labour, Mr. (now Lord) Twining, as Chairman "to report on the need for social insurance and the prospects of successfully and economically promoting such measures in the Colony". The Committee presented a majority report in January 1941 and a minority report signed by Dr. Millien six months later.† There were reservations to the majority report from Mr. Raymond Hein, the representative of the employers and the Chamber of Agriculture, and from Mr. Marc de Chazal, who had been nominated by the Central Committee of Estate Managers.

The majority of the committee thought that "in Mauritius, where the majority of the labouring classes are engaged in agricultural pursuits, and many do work of a casual nature, unemployment insurance is ... impracticable except perhaps in the case of certain industries of a non-agricultural nature in which casual labour is not normally employed". They therefore suggested that the possibility of a limited scheme for such industries should be investigated.

In the case of provision for old age, the majority were of the opinion that the system of support of old people by the family was breaking down. It would be "inequitable that the full responsibility of providing for the aged should be transferred entirely from the family to the taxpayer. The breakdown of the old system demands that it should be replaced by a new one based on the principle of 'self-help' and the most practicable means of ensuring this is a contributory pension scheme".

---

* *Report of Commission on Unrest on Sugar Estates in Mauritius*, 1938, p. 168.
† The Report of the Social Insurance Committee was not published, and we were unable to trace a copy of it in Mauritius. A copy was eventually made available to us by the Colonial Office, together with Dr. Millien's dissenting memoir.

Accordingly, they recommended a scheme of compulsory insurance to provide old age pensions, widows' pensions and orphans' pensions. Apart from a number of exceptions, the scheme was to be confined to persons with an annual cash income of Rs. 600 per annum or under. A voluntary scheme was envisaged for persons with earnings above this limit. Contributions were to be paid by employed persons, by employers and by the Government. In the case of the adult insured person, the contribution was to be two cents per day. The contributions were to be collected by a system of cards and stamps, each card lasting possibly for a period of three months.

Old age pensions were to be granted at the age of 56. The rate of pension was to depend on the number of contributions which had been paid with a minimum of Rs. 3 per month. The maximum pension would be Rs. 25·50 per month which would be received by a male joining the scheme at the age of 14 and contributing on 300 days per annum at half-rate until he had reached the age of 18, and then at full-rate until his 56th birthday. The majority report expected that the average pension earned by a male would be about Rs. 12 per month. It was estimated that the scheme would cover 70,000 adult wage earners, and that the Government would as a maximum have to contribute Rs. 350,000.

In their note of dissent, Mr. Hein and Mr. de Chazal feared that the whole cost of the social insurance scheme might eventually fall on the sugar industry.

Dr. Millien, in a lengthy minority report, said that the enquiry had not been sufficiently thorough. He felt that the working people of Mauritius were so poor that they could not afford to pay contributions: "no material contribution could be exacted from our workmen for a pension". The rate of contribution which had been fixed was "a mere guess to suit the financial necessities of the Scheme". He accused the Committee of trying to shift the cost of supporting the old people from the taxpayer on to working people in the form of contributions. Moreover, he objected to the income limit on the insured population which he felt was much too low.

Dr. Millien's own proposal for a system of social insurance was to levy a system of licence fees from employed persons at a rate which varied progressively with income from R. 1 per year at the lowest level to Rs. 50 per year at the highest level. Employers were to pay weekly contributions of 20 c. per week for low-paid employees and at the same rate as the employee in the case of the highly paid. The level of pensions was to vary in such a way that the lower paid got more than they were strictly entitled to from their contributions while the higher paid were to get less.

In forwarding the Report of this Committee to the Secretary of State for the Colonies, the Governor said that he was thinking of trying to develop a simple system of unemployment insurance operating in as many industries as possible. He would, however, require those who received relief to engage in some kind of public work of an extraordinary character. He had in mind the construction of new roads, the cleaning and terracing of Government land, the reclamation of swamps as sanitary measures, the digging of canals and the building of reservoir dams.

The Governor hoped to proceed with a scheme of old age pensions at an early date. He wanted the proposals of the Committee examined by an actuary. The Secretary of State agreed that actuarial enquiries should be made into the old age pension scheme but suggested that the Governor should "defer to a later date the consideration of the possibilities of introducing unemployment and health insurance schemes".*

The Report of the Committee was submitted to the Government Actuary in Britain who reported on it in October 1943. He tentatively suggested the possibility of some system of non-contributory pensions for those already over pension age as it would be some years before the scheme proposed by the Committee would come into effect. He also had in mind the possibility of "blanketing-in" late entrants to the contributory scheme. If this were done there would need to be some Government contribution to the scheme as a whole to assist late entrants. The Actuary also suggested that there might be lower contributions for the lower paid and higher contributions from the higher paid.† No action was, however, taken by the Government.

In 1945 a private Bill was introduced by the sugar interests for the payment of retirement benefits to the senior staff on the sugar estates. The Retiring Fund Ordinance covered only the senior staff and the more highly-paid artisans. There were objections to the Ordinance from the Technical Workers' Union on the grounds that their members could not afford the deductions and that the benefits promised were inadequate. It was suggested that the deductions were being levied for the sole purpose of depriving the artisan of his ability to pay union fees.‡ Despite these objections the Ordinance was passed. The Retiring Fund remained in existence until 1956 when it was superceded by the Sugar Industry Pension Fund (see Chapter 2).

---

* *Social Insurance Schemes in Mauritius:* correspondence exchanged between the Government of Mauritius and the Colonial Office, 1948, p. 1.
† *Ibid.*, pp. 8-11.
‡ *Annual Report of the Labour Department*, 1945, p. 8.

In March 1945 the Governor referred to the subject of social insurance in his address at the inaugural meeting of the Central Development and Welfare Committee. "It would be unfortunate if we attempted to apply to this Colony some one or other of the precise plans now being discussed elsewhere without first examining the essential nature of social security at various stages of development, considering how needs change in the process of evolution and finally arriving at provisional conclusions as to the possibilities of Government action in a colony of this type, always remembering that finance must be the limiting factor, that is that policy must be limited by the funds which can be made available from the aggregate income of the community and by the extent to which the wealthier members of the community can be expected to contribute towards the maintenance of those who fall below an ascertained minimum standard, after provision has been made for the maintenance of law and order, defence and other administrative and developmental services, which in their turn should aim at raising the standard of living . . . Social security has the more limited aim of distributing the income actually available to particular communities without depriving individual initiative of all reward or discouraging enterprise, without which we cannot hope for the steady improvement in economic and social conditions at which we are aiming and that, I happen to know, is the view of His Majesty's Government . . . There are no short cuts to the local solution of a problem which has occupied the best brains of the civilized world over a number of years and we should be deceiving ourselves if we thought that we could launch grandiose schemes of social security in this island before we had examined the implications of the problem . . ."*

In 1950, there still being no system of contributory pensions, a non-contributory pension was introduced, subject to a means test and administered by the Public Assistance Department. At first it gave a maximum pension of Rs. 15 per month to all persons aged 65 and over, and to blind persons aged 40 and over. The pension was reduced by the full amount of any income received from other sources. The first payments were made at the end of September 1950, but they included arrears from the beginning of July. It was reported from Souillac that "St. Joseph a des bougies jusqu'au cou".

The means test was the cause of much misunderstanding and resentment. The applicants had not appreciated that the term "income" included wages, and they were therefore extremely surprised when the earnings they had declared on the application

* *Inaugural Meeting of the Central Development and Welfare Committee*, 1945, pp. 9-10.

form were deducted from their pensions. Moreover, whereas it had been intended to make some concessions in the direction of disregarding casual earnings, the amounts declared were such as to make it impossible to disregard them.

There were loud complaints and accusations of sharp practice from those who had been awarded reduced pensions or whose applications had been rejected. In December 1950, therefore, the income ceiling was raised to Rs. 30, resulting in another substantial payment of arrears. However, the administration of the means test continued to present difficulties. It was impossible to apply it rigidly, since exact earnings could not be ascertained and checked. Since it was based on the month's income, many pensions were withdrawn during the crop season. In the case of a "couple, whether married or not, living as husband and wife, in the same house", the joint income had to be divided equally between them for the purposes of the means test, and detailed and extremely personal enquiries were made in order to prove that the couple were living as husband and wife if they said they were not.

In 1953, the means test was placed on a yearly basis, which put an end to fluctuations in the pension from month to month. At the same time, the maximum pension was raised to Rs. 20 a month, and the income ceiling to Rs. 35 (Rs. 420 a year), while the qualifying age for women was reduced to 60. As a result of this last provision, the number of pensioners rose from 12,427 at the end of 1952 to 17,747 at the end of 1953. The means test was finally removed in 1957 and the pension raised again to its present level of Rs. 22 a month. The abolition of the means test added another 8,597 to the number of pensioners, which at the end of 1959 stood at 26,795. Where necessary, an additional grant may be made by the Public Assistance Department to bring the income of a pensioner up to the assistance scale.

In September 1957, the Governor appointed a Committee of Ministers to investigate the feasibility of contributory, compulsory and comprehensive social insurance in Mauritius. The Committee came to the conclusion that a system of social insurance was feasible and recommended that the following benefits should be paid: sickness benefit, old age pension, widows' benefit, orphans' benefit, unemployment benefit and industrial injuries benefit. The scheme was to cover insured persons other than those who were employed by or under the Crown or by other recognised organisations under conditions of service which entitled them to similar or equivalent benefits to those laid down in the scheme.

The total contributions were to be at the rate of Rs. 1·50 per week for men aged 16 to 65, Rs. 1·05 for women aged 18 to 60 and

Rs. 0·36 for boys aged 14 to 18 and Rs. 0·24 for girls aged 14 to 18. One-third of these contributions was to be paid by the insured person, the employer and the State. The contributions might vary between crop and inter-crop in order to limit the variation of income which occurs during the year and thus lighten the burden of the contribution on the worker.

The rates of benefit which the Committee recommended were intended to be as high as could be afforded but low enough "not to encourage malingering, refusal of employment and other abuses". The rate of industrial injury benefit was to be Rs. 10 per week for a single person and Rs. 13 per week when there was a dependent spouse. In the case of other benefits, the level was to be Rs. 9 per week for a single man, Rs. 6·25 for a single woman and Rs. 12 for a man supporting a wife. In the case of the widows' pension, an allowance of R. 1 per week was recommended for each child below the age of 14, up to a maximum of three children. An orphans' benefit of Rs. 2·25 was recommended.

The Committee estimated that the total cost of the whole scheme (including the medical benefits, described in Chapter 9) might amount to Rs. 30 million, while the total income from contributions would only be about Rs. 11 million. The Committee thought that it might be useful to make a start with the implementation of the scheme excluding unemployment benefit "because of the complexity of setting up an unemployment insurance machine". If unemployment benefit were excluded the scheme would only cost Rs. 18 million. Adding to the contribution income the savings which might accrue to the Public Assistance and other Departments, estimated at Rs. 5·64 million, a deficit would remain (if unemployment benefits were excluded) of Rs. 1½ million. This deficit might be covered by Rs. 1 million from a State Lottery, and by a contribution of Rs. 1 million from the Sugar Industry Labour Welfare Fund.

SICKNESS AND UNEMPLOYMENT BENEFITS

We have outlined in Chapter 4 the present provisions made for the sick and unemployed by the Public Assistance Department. Prolonged sickness of the breadwinner or breadwinners creates grave economic problems for the households concerned. Although public assistance officers are legally able to exercise discretion and grant supplements to the standard scales of benefit, and although help is often generous from the wider family circle, there are many cases in which the breadwinner has to return to work before he has regained full health and working capacity.

We have indicated in Chapter 1 that, despite the difficulties of definition, there does seem to be a large and growing problem of unemployment in Mauritius. Much of it may be due to special social factors such as unwillingness or inability to do manual work —particularly hard and physically exhausting work in the sugar industry. There are, undoubtedly, many young people whose families are prepared to maintain them without work in the hope that they will achieve a better paid and more socially respected job in the future.* Unemployment in the crop season may chiefly take these forms and not be very large at present, but despite the energetic efforts which are being made by the Government to find new outlets for employment, the sharp increase in the population may lead to a much more serious problem of general unemployment in the coming months and years. But whatever the present character and future level of general unemployment may be, there undoubtedly is each year a growing problem of seasonal unemployment in the inter-crop season. The sugar industry is a seasonal industry. Its major rôle in the Mauritian economy causes directly and indirectly a great slackening of economic activity in the inter-crop season.

We take the view that the emphasis in public policy should be on the prevention of sickness and unemployment, rather than on alleviation through social welfare provisions. We will be outlining in Chapter 9 the developments which are planned for further preventive action in the health field and for minimising periods of incapacity. The whole question of employment opportunities has been considered by the Economic Mission which has recently visited the island, and we are confident that valuable suggestions will be made to reinforce those measures which are already being taken by the Government.

We mentioned in the last chapter that at present the Public Assistance Department does not normally give assistance in cases of unemployment. If, after searching tests, destitution is established, some temporary aid will be provided but there is no regular system of grants to the unemployed man. One consequence of this is that the only way in which a worker can obtain something like a regular income other than from work in the inter-crop season (as well as at other times) is by establishing that he is sick. In other words, the absence of regular provisions for unemployment assistance imposes an unnecessary strain on the Government medical officers. It also encourages a wrong attitude to drugs and medical care. We will be showing in Chapter 9 that there is an acute shortage of doctors, and we are most anxious that the limited medical staff should be able to devote themselves to those activities which are of

* See Benedict, B., "Education without Opportunity", published in *Human Relations*, Vol. XI, No. 4, November 1958.

the greatest importance to the people of Mauritius. It is therefore undesirable that people with trivial complaints or, indeed, with contrived complaints should take up the time of the Government medical officers. This is one reason why more must be done to help the unemployed.

Assistance is now available for those who are sick, though it takes the form of a grant often of considerable duration based upon a medical assessment of incapacity. The sick are not required to abandon work for the duration of their illness or incapacity, nor are those certified as fit for "light work" given a full rate of benefit if such work is not available for them. In most cases it is not. Thus, the popular notion that assistance is of the nature of a "pension" is not far from the truth.

We considered in Chapter 4 whether the needs of the sick and unemployed might not be best met and wholly met by some reform of public assistance. There are, however, powerful reasons of principle against this course and these reasons are supported by the considerations of cost and administrative expediency mentioned in the last chapter. In principle, it seems preferable that there should be some system of benefit as of right (i.e. without any test of means) such as operates under the conditions of service of Government employees and of certain categories of other workers. It is also important in our view to improve the conditions of service and status of manual workers in the sugar industry upon whose efforts so much of the economy of Mauritius depends. The establishment, even on a limited basis initially, of a social insurance scheme would contribute in this direction. Secondly, we consider that the present heavy borrowing by the sick and unemployed from shopkeepers, job contractors and others leads to undesirable dependency relationships, creates unmanageably large debts for poor families, and hampers the growth of effective trade unions and efficient retailing. Thirdly, the Public Assistance Department enjoys neither the confidence of the public nor of the Legislative Council. This, of course, is no reflection on the present staff of an over-burdened Department. They have been asked to do the impossible. It is essential in our view that public confidence in the work of this Department should be built up. For this to come about it is necessary to reduce the burden of its responsibilities.

The reason we have described as "administrative expediency" means, in the context of public assistance, the need to establish a system of work records which can be properly maintained. Such records would make it possible to ascertain more accurately the earnings of persons receiving assistance. In the context of social insurance, work records are needed to ensure that benefit is only paid to persons who are normally employed, and also to ensure, by temporary withdrawal of the insurance card, that persons cannot legally take employment under a contract of service whilst receiving insurance benefit.

The need for social insurance contributions

We concluded in Chapter 4 that it was more likely that correct records would be kept if the record took the form of registering some contribution payable by employer and employee for each period of employment. Although certain employees might be short-sighted enough to attempt to evade the payment of their own contribution, they would in time appreciate that the loss of the employer's contribution was against their own best interest. And as the benefits of an insurance scheme would only be available to those who had paid an adequate amount in contributions, at least the fund would not be grossly defrauded by fictitious or erroneous records.

Theoretically, it would be possible to put the whole weight of contributions on the employer and rely on the self-interest of the employee to see that the contributions were paid. Such a proposal would of course raise questions of the ability of some employers to find the money. But in addition to these considerations there were other reasons which made us favour a contribution from the employee. First, a heavy employers' contribution would discourage the employment of labour. This is an important consideration in the present circumstances of unemployment in Mauritius. Secondly, employers might demand control over the monies raised solely from employers' contributions. Thirdly, there might develop a demand for benefit to be subject to a test of means. This would certainly be unpopular and, in any event, it is by no means easy to operate in Mauritius a means test which is fair and does not cost too much to administer. Past experience, both in respect to old age pensions and public assistance, made us wish to confine as narrowly as possible the area in which means tests operate in the future.

In addition, there seemed to us a social value in having an employee's contribution. We were told that "government" tended to be regarded as an extraneous body and that there was thus little restraint in all classes from deliberately defrauding government agencies. Democratic identification with government is difficult to achieve in any country but it is more common and understandable for a country with long experience of external control and colonial administration to lack identification of this kind. Progress not only in social security but in many other fields will depend upon the people of Mauritius becoming fully conscious that people who defraud the Government defraud themselves. If employees are required to contribute to a separate fund, they may come to appreciate that they have an interest in preventing the improper use of the social security system.

There are two further reasons for our recommending employees' contribution. When it becomes known that benefit is linked to contributions, there may be a greater incentive for regular work attendance. Secondly, we think it would be in the interests of workers in the sugar, building and other industries for pressures to develop for longer and more regular contracts of service.

Coverage of a social insurance scheme

For all these reasons, we propose the immediate introduction of social insurance to cover the risks of sickness and unemployment. We discuss the question of industrial injuries in the next chapter. Before outlining detailed proposals, a word should be said about the coverage of the scheme.

We recognise that the economic and social consequences of illness and lack of work (or income) are not restricted to employees but extend also to those working on their own account. Moreover, there are many of the latter whose economic position is no better than that of employed persons. Nevertheless, we are unable to recommend any system of indemnity against sickness and unemployment for self-employed persons. For obvious reasons it is much harder in the case of the self-employed to establish the income loss due to illness and to prove whether lack of work is voluntary or involuntary. The creation of a scheme of social insurance for employed persons will make heavy demands on the administrative skill of Government and we feel that not until all these problems have been resolved and the scheme is working satisfactorily should any attempt be made to insure self-employed persons. We would mention, moreover, that neither in the United Kingdom nor in any other country are self-employed persons entitled to any form of unemployment benefit. The self-employed will have to make their own arrangements for saving and the Post Office Savings Bank is already available for this purpose. The recommendations we make in Chapter 7 for non-contributory benefits should, however, be extended to include the self-employed.

The contributions and benefits of sickness and unemployment insurance should, therefore, be confined to "employed persons"— to persons employed under a contract of service. This will include over 200,000 persons in Mauritius. The term "contract of service" will need careful definition. We think it may prove practicable to include certain categories of fishermen within the definition. As a considerable amount of movement takes place during the year and from year to year between the self-employed group and the employed population, it will be administratively necessary to issue cards to virtually the whole population of working age.

Flat rate or wage related contributions

The contribution levied for social insurance could be either flat rate or wage related. If it were flat rate, it would have to be within the ability of all employees to pay. Earnings vary widely in Mauritius between different employees and between different times of the year. Theoretically, it would be possible to levy a higher flat rate contribution in the crop season than in the inter-crop season as suggested by the Ministerial Committee. This would, however, be inappropriate to many occupations. If the same rate were charged for all employees all the year round, the rate would have to be extremely low to prevent it being too heavy a burden on the worker with low earnings in the inter-crop season. It would thus be difficult to obtain sufficient funds to pay even a modest level of benefit. The calculations of the Ministerial Committee are evidence of this. There could, of course, be some system of grading by which lower contributions were paid by juveniles and by women than by adult male employees. But this would not solve the problem posed by the fact that, over the year as a whole, the spread of earnings is relatively large among adult male workers. Our conclusion, therefore, is to recommend a system of wage related contributions by employers and employees.

These considerations were reinforced when we investigated the administrative difficulties of collecting flat rate contributions. If such a contribution were collected by means of a "flat rate" stamp, the stamp would have to be a daily stamp and not a weekly stamp as in the United Kingdom. We do not think that the practice of requiring the first employer in the week to pay the weekly contribution would work equitably and without hardship in Mauritius. This administrative burden was noted by the Government Actuary of Great Britain in his Report of 19th August 1943. He wrote: "A daily assessment of contribution must lead to much more work for everybody concerned, and multiply the amount of record-keeping required at every stage up to pension age; this is so even though, in cases of regular employment by one employer, a multiple stamp for a week or longer interval is adopted. It is not known how this plan would be worked out in detail, but it is inferred that the necessity for a daily rate of contribution implies the necessity for a daily stamp. If this is so a 3-monthly contribution card would presumably have to have about 91 spaces, duly dated

for each successive day of the quarter—a truly formidable card".*
The alternative of a wage related contribution has one obvious advantage. If the contribution were a straight proportion of earnings, it would be adjusted to ability to pay. Thus, more revenue for the scheme could be obtained without casting an excessive burden on the lower paid. We envisage that the contribution would only need to be deducted at the time at which payment is made. For example, those who were paid monthly would only need to pay a monthly contribution. As most of the "daily paid" are in fact paid weekly only one deduction would normally be required. We recognise, of course, that there would be cases where an employee works for one employer for part of the week and for another employer for another part of the week. Indeed, it is possible in some cases that three or more employers might be involved in one week. This would not, however, be a frequent occurrence and it would not be necessary for the cards to have a space for a period shorter than a week although room might have to be provided on the back of the card for additional periods of work of short duration.

We were anxious to keep the system as simple as practicable. We wanted, if it were possible, to avoid the complexities and cost of stamps. Theoretically, it would be possible for the employer to deduct the required percentage from the remuneration of the employee, to calculate his own contribution, and to pay over the total sum required at the end of each quarter or year (as in the United States). After careful enquiries and tests, we came to the conclusion that such a task would not be beyond the literacy of small employers and job contractors, bearing in mind that help with such tasks is already obtained from relatives and friends. The major difficulty in a system of this kind is to find some means of ensuring that the amount recorded on the employee's card as having been paid by both parties actually reaches the public authority responsible for the scheme. It would seem necessary to require every employer to keep, in addition to the employee's record card, a further individual insurance record for every employee who had been with him during the year. On this record would be entered the employer's and employee's contributions for each period of employment. At the end of the year the employer would hand over all these records with a payment representing the money shown by the cards to be due. This system of insurance records would be in addition to the entries made on the employees' cards showing the contributions paid by both employee and employer. Thus, the records office would be able to marry the employee's card, when it

---

* *Social Insurance Schemes in Mauritius:* correspondence exchanged between the Government of Mauritius and the Colonial Office, 1948, p. 12.

was exchanged at the end of the year for a new one, with the records handed in by the employer or employers with whom the employee had been working during the year. Although this would place quite a heavy clerical burden on employers it would at least make it possible for the authorities to follow up and correct divergencies between the employee's work record card and the record slips handed in by the employer at the end of the year.

There is, however, an alternative to this proposal which seems to have merits and to avoid a lot of clerical work though it does involve the printing, circulation, purchase and affixing of special stamps. The employer would be required to affix on the employee's card a stamp representing the joint contribution. This would automatically ensure that the amount entered on the card by means of the stamp did actually reach the appropriate public authority. Normally only one stamp would be required for the week and it would not be necessary to record the days on which the employee reported for work. The card would therefore be simpler than one designed for a daily flat rate contribution.

There should be heavy fines on employers who fail to comply, but there may still be undetected cases where a lower contribution has been charged than was appropriate. At least no-one would be able to draw benefit without contributions actually having been paid by him or on his behalf. The difficulty with this proposal is the large number of stamps of different denominations required if a strictly proportionate contribution were charged. This difficulty could be avoided by introducing ranges of remuneration over which the same contribution would be paid. Thus with about ten different denominations of stamp, the principle of a wage related contribution could be broadly preserved. Moreover, there would be less danger of inadvertent failures in arithmetic as the contributions could be ascertained by looking at a simple table showing the ranges of income and the values of the stamps appropriate to them. This solution seems to us to have most advantages from the point of view of introducing a social insurance scheme with wage related contributions in the particular circumstances of Mauritius.

Widespread publicity by every means would be needed to explain to all concerned their obligations and rights under the scheme. It should be explained throughout that benefit depends upon the payment of contributions and every step should be taken to ensure that all employers are made aware of their responsibilities. There will inevitably be a problem of securing 100% compliance in the early years, but every country launching a social security system has had to face this problem and we are convinced that in Mauritius, given good will on all sides, it can be overcome.

Flat rate or wage related benefits

Sickness and unemployment lead to sharp falls in living standards in Mauritius. We have indicated earlier that, in our opinion, the standards of about half the households of Mauritius are beneath any reasonable subsistence level. While a short though substantial fall in living standards may be endured by an adult in good health without permanent damage, a similar fall for a child can do lasting harm. For this reason alone the benefit available in sickness and unemployment needs to be as close as possible to normal wages.

We have already mentioned that earnings in the sugar industry vary widely between the crop and the inter-crop seasons. Indeed, a manual worker who has enjoyed substantial earnings in the crop season may earn very little in the inter-crop season. The average earnings of "petite bande" labourers in the sugar industry in 1959 were Rs. 23·33 in the crop season and Rs. 19·98 in the inter-crop season. The minimum rate for a full week's work is Rs. 15·48 for a man and Rs. 12·48 for a woman. If these rates had been earned for five days a week throughout the month the earnings would be only about Rs. 52 to Rs. 59 for a man or Rs. 42 to Rs. 48 for a woman. The amount of unemployment and sickness benefit must be below this level to preserve the incentive to work.

In theory it would be possible to pay a higher level of unemployment and sickness benefit in the crop season than in the inter-crop season without the levels of benefit being too close to the lowest wages. While this might be appropriate for the sugar industry it would not be so for other workers. Moreover, it would be undesirable for the social insurance scheme itself to reinforce the tendency for lower wages and less employment in the inter-crop than in the crop season. In our view, therefore, the benefits available from the social insurance scheme should be at the same level throughout the year. Hence they need to be lower, all the year round, than minimum earnings in the inter-crop season. This indicates a benefit of about Rs. 30 a month as the maximum for any manual worker, man or woman. This is in line with the recommendations of the Committee of Ministers.

If this has to be the maximum for a manual worker who has achieved high earnings during the crop season it would seem harsh to recommend anything less than this for the worker with a lower level of earnings, but who is fully entitled to sickness or unemployment benefit.

This consideration, reinforced by other arguments, led us eventually to reject the principle of wage related benefits for sickness and unemployment. For a number of reasons we favoured such an approach but found ourselves in the end compelled to recognise the force of the arguments against it in the early stages of launching an insurance scheme.

In our view the most important requirement of social policy in Mauritius at the present time is to make better provision for the poorest workers. Wage related benefits, based on either a straight percentage of average earnings or some system of grades or classes, might lead to a quite inadequate level of benefit for the large group of daily engaged labourers subject to unpredictable fluctuations in earnings due to seasonal factors, changes in demand for different kinds of labouring jobs, and other factors. Wage related benefits might also run counter to the need to encourage rural workers to grow their own produce, keep cows and chickens, and improve their diet. Such developments are to be welcomed rather than occasional cash earnings from casual and irregular secondary employments.

In our investigations we did not find much evidence of a serious problem of poverty arising from sickness and unemployment among middle-class and skilled workers. In general, their needs appear to be at least partially met by the larger employers—Government, local authorities, banks and other commercial institutions. We did, however, receive some evidence of a need for wage related pensions —a question discussed later in this chapter.

In the absence, therefore, of any substantial need for higher sickness and unemployment benefits for such workers we were led to question the desirability of relatively small and fluctuating (from year to year) benefits for lower paid workers. They hardly seemed to justify at the present time the additional administrative complications that would be involved. The principal one we had in mind was the greater possibility of abuse in the payment of wage related benefits. In dealing with claims, each applicant's average earnings for the preceding contribution year would have to be calculated (an average of at least 52 entries); allowance might also have to be made for weeks of certified sickness and unemployment, and a check made to see that the qualifying conditions, waiting periods and other requirements had been satisfied. A payment voucher would then have to be completed, the amount of the weekly benefit being written in by the clerk. It is at this point that the possibility of abuse presents itself; it could take a number of forms, particularly in a situation where many applicants will not find it at all easy to check the calculations. Also, the detection of small abuses (or errors) by supervisors might well involve heavy administrative costs. The advantages of vouchers with the amount of benefit printed in are obvious. There is also much to be said for a benefit which the applicant knows he is entitled to by virtue of satisfying the contribution conditions.

For all these reasons we conclude, therefore, that the scheme should be launched on the basis of flat rate benefits. If, after further experience, a case emerges for higher benefits for higher paid workers and the administrative problems can be solved then we suggest that the question of wage related benefits should be reviewed.

The standard rate of benefit which we recommend is as close to the general level of wages as seems safe. There are, however, certain cases of sickness—for example, tuberculosis and deficiency diseases—where a high level of nutrition is essential to recovery. When such cases are diagnosed by medical officers we would like to see a higher level of benefit paid (Rs. 45 a month). This higher level of benefit would depend upon the specific recommendation of a Government medical officer and would be subject to review by the insurance medical officer. In such cases, considerations of the incentive to work are much less relevant and are anyway secondary to the need to restore working capacity.

We do not recommend any allowance for the dependants of the sick and unemployed as the rate of benefit is already as close to minimum wages as can be justified. The standard rate of benefit will of course be available to sick or unemployed married women who are normally at work. Thus, where both husband and wife are unemployed, the total benefit will be Rs. 60.

These rates of benefit are not and, indeed, are not intended to be adequate for the subsistence needs of a family. They provide little more than the beneficiary needs to purchase a barely adequate diet for himself or herself alone. Total insurance benefits must in general be less than minimum wages. They cannot provide subsistence in an economy where minimum wages are below that level. We would hope, however, that as minimum earnings are raised the level of benefits would also be raised. To these benefits will, however, be added the non-contributory family benefits recommended in Chapter 7.

Qualifying conditions

In our recommendations about qualifying conditions we have been influenced by a number of considerations. First, we have sought to keep to a minimum the certification work that will fall upon the Government Medical Service. Secondly, we have tried to limit the strain on the employment bureaux as this service is still at an early stage of development, and it will prove difficult to develop an efficient and acceptable work test—particularly for women. Thirdly, we have tried to limit the charge on the fund. It is, however, impossible to estimate with any exactness the extent and duration of sickness and unemployment claims which would qualify for benefit under any scheme we could devise.

For these three reasons we propose rather strict qualifying conditions for benefits. We are convinced that, although needs will be inadequately met at first, this is in the long-term interest of beneficiaries. An excessive strain on the Government Medical Service, a breakdown of the employment bureau service, or an unexpectedly heavy financial burden could all lead to the withdrawal of the scheme and to the conclusion being (perhaps incorrectly) drawn that the operation of social insurance is impossible in Mauritius. If a modest start is made, the scheme could be extended as experience is gained. We would not like our stringent qualifying conditions to be retained beyond the time when they are reasonably required for administrative or financial reasons.

We recommend that sickness and unemployment benefit should only be available to those who have worked for a minimum of 20 weeks during the previous year. A week of work should be defined as a week during which some minimum contribution has been paid. The figure should be chosen so that a man or woman working for five full days for the minimum wages that can be paid in the sugar industry during the crop season qualifies for benefit. To avoid all the complications of several minima, we recommend that minimum wages for women in the sugar industry should be the basis of this qualifying condition. We do not recommend at this stage for sickness and unemployment benefits any system of credits for weeks during which the employee was sick or unemployed, nor do we recommend any system by which rights acquired in earlier years can be carried forward. The rights to sickness benefit or unemployment benefit should depend solely upon the contribution record of the preceding contribution year.

The scale of contributions should be fixed to yield on average $1\frac{1}{4}\%$ of earnings from employees and $1\frac{1}{2}\%$ from employers. The latter figure is higher to include the costs of industrial injury which should fall wholly on the employer.

We are aware that these proposals seem to favour the higher paid who would be able to acquire the minimum weekly contribution in two or three days of work. We are aware too that the younger male adult employees will find it easier to establish right to benefit than older workers, juveniles and women. The alternative of requiring a minimum number of days of work to qualify for benefit would require a separate system of records which might not be accurately kept. Moreover, we want to encourage regular work attendance and the provision of regular contracts by employers.

It should not be forgotten, however, that although higher paid and fitter employees will find it easier to gain a qualifying week of contribution, the level of benefit takes no account of higher levels of earnings.

Thus we recommend the same minimum contribution conditions both for sickness and unemployment benefit. Our proposals concerning the "waiting period" and the duration of benefit are different for the two benefits as there are quite different administrative and other considerations involved. In the case of sickness benefit our primary aim is to help the long-term sick and disabled and make it possible for them to get something approaching an adequate diet while they are struggling to regain health and working capacity. Our second aim is to prevent an excessive strain on the Government Medical Service and the distortion of its work from prevention and rehabilitation to the treatment of relatively minor afflictions. In the case of unemployment benefit we aim to provide some limited support for those who are not at work. We are aware that a really efficient and acceptable form of "work test" cannot be quickly brought into operation. As it is not going to be easy to establish that unemployment is in every case involuntary, the benefit we propose does not wholly take the character of insurance but is partly a provident benefit. In other words, compulsory savings made in the crop season are drawn out in the inter-crop season. Much the same may apply to workers in other industries whose earnings vary substantially over the year.

We recommend a waiting period of over two weeks for sickness benefit. No benefit should be paid until the third Monday following the first visit to the medical service. The applicant should be required to hand over his or her contribution card to the employment bureau at the beginning of the waiting period. If the applicant is admitted to hospital, half the benefit should be paid to the applicant's spouse in cases where there are one or more dependent children. The benefit should be of unlimited duration.

Sickness benefit should only be received by those who accept the treatment prescribed for them, and there should be a limit on the earnings from self-employment allowed to those who are receiving sickness or unemployment benefits. There should be appropriate penalties if illicit earnings are discovered.

The duration of unemployment benefit should vary according to the number of weeks during which the minimum contribution has been paid. The minimum qualifying condition of 20 weeks should give title to 15 weeks of benefit. Each extra two weeks of contribution should give title to a further week of benefit up to a maximum of

26 weeks in one year. In the case of the first application for unemployment benefit in the contribution year, there should be a waiting period of one week. This is to enable detailed investigation to be made about the last occupation of the applicant and the reason for leaving work and to give time for an appropriate work test to be arranged.* If the applicant is found to be entitled to benefit it should be paid retrospectively for five out of the seven days. If the applicant remains unemployed for less than seven days no retrospective payment should be made.

In the case of subsequent applications in the contribution year, there should be a two-day waiting period. Thus, applicants become entitled to benefit on the third working day after the day on which they apply and "lodge" their contribution card. Benefit should be paid weekly and calculated at the rate of R. 1 per day with an additional rupee for those who have been unemployed from Monday to Saturday. To remain eligible for benefit applicants should be required to report to the employment bureau daily at a time notified on the previous day. Thus, an application on a Monday will lead to a payment of Rs. 4 on the next Saturday and Rs. 7 on the following Saturday, providing the applicant has reported on each working day. After any day or days of work the applicant would be required to "wait" again before he or she becomes once more entitled to benefit. The waiting period prevents those who have failed to go to work from receiving benefit for that day and gives the employment bureau the opportunity to arrange an offer of work.

We recognise that the waiting period for sickness benefit is rather harsh. We believe, however, that the traditional means of support are able to prevent undue hardship—the family, and credit from the local shopkeeper. The shortage of doctors is the only reason why we have advocated a longer waiting period for sickness than for unemployment. In some cases the applicant will be able to receive unemployment benefit while he or she is waiting for the sickness benefit to mature. This is likely to apply mostly to those who are of low priority in the application of the work test (see p. 106).

Unemployment benefit should be available to all those who have not refused "suitable" employment. We have given much thought to the meaning which should be applied to the term "suitable" employment in the circumstances of Mauritius. We are well aware that there is not enough appropriate work for those who have achieved some secondary education. This is a fact which must be

---

* Special regulations will be needed to prevent school teachers who are laid off for the school holidays from claiming benefit and for similar circumstances in other occupations.

taken into account in drafting the regulations about "suitable" employment. Thus, for example, it would be wrong to pay unemployment benefit for a period of 26 weeks to someone who had previously been employed as an unqualified teacher while the employment bureau attempted to find a teacher's job. We consider that in cases of this kind benefit might be provided for up to four weeks without applying a work test in a field other than the one from which the employee has been made redundant. After the period of four weeks we think that everyone must be prepared to take on any sort of work that he is physically or mentally capable of doing if benefit is still to be paid.

We recognise that we are challenging here strongly held attitudes of many people in Mauritius. It is entirely a private matter for a parent to support a child in the hope that he or she will acquire a job in Government or in some white-collar occupation outside Government. It would, however, be improper in the circumstances of Mauritius today for the social insurance fund to be used in a similar way. We recognise that there will be strong pressure on Government to allow benefit to be paid for the full period without offering work in an occupation of a lower status than that which the applicant has just vacated. Such pressure must be resisted. Indeed, the viability of the whole scheme may well depend on resolute action in this matter.

We turn next to the difficult problem of organising the work test. An island-wide employment bureau service handling a considerable number of offers of employment is a prerequisite of a really effective scheme of unemployment benefit.

The present employment bureau service is relatively small, has been handicapped in the past by insufficient funds for adequate staffing, and chiefly handles applications for work in Government departments. The number of offices must be rapidly expanded and additional staff of a high calibre should be employed. The work of the bureaux should also be disassociated from law enforcement functions of the Ministry of Labour. But these changes will not in themselves ensure that demands for workers will be channelled through the Service. It would be possible to require by law that all offers of employment should be sent to the Employment Service, but there are serious disadvantages to this proposal. It is unlikely that a newly expanded service could handle with even a minimum of efficiency such a heavy burden of work. And such a step would be strongly resisted by employers and job contractors.

The notification of all vacancies—all unmet needs for workers—would certainly help in reducing involuntary unemployment but would not of itself solve the problem. It might ensure that a man registering as unemployed had a reasonable chance of receiving an offer of work but it would not create more jobs. Nor are we confident that in the coming years a sufficient demand for labour will emerge as a result of economic expansion. It is nevertheless preferable both economically and socially that a man should work for a wage rather than subsist on a dole. More jobs must be created. Private employers should be asked to co-operate by making available as much work as possible. In addition, an expansion of public works will certainly be required. This could take the form of a considerable extension in the normal public works programme up to the estimated need for jobs or of a programme of absorbing on a daily basis in public works all those registering as unemployed. We outline below the advantages and disadvantages of each policy.

The second policy is probably the most efficient means of reducing the number of claims for unemployment benefit, as benefit would only be paid on days when it had proved impracticable to provide sufficient work. Essentially the proposal involves collecting up the unemployed in lorries, calling at different points on the island and taking them to places where work can be provided. There are, however, many difficulties with this proposal. In equity it would seem right that such workers should be paid the normal daily rates for such work. The trade unions might insist on this. There would then be, however, two groups of P.W.D. workers—one group with free transport, the other without. This would be resented by the regular P.W.D. workers who would feel that their status was being challenged and that inefficient and inexperienced workers were being paid as much as themselves. Nor would the system be economical. Inevitably, the unemployed would include those with physical and other handicaps and they might not work well at jobs they had not chosen to apply for. It would, moreover, be hard to find initially good foremen to supervise the work.

Public works organised in this way might easily degenerate into an unpleasant sort of forced labour. Alternatively, such employment might be regarded as a soft and remunerative option to work on the sugar estates. If this occurred the estates would be short of labour. The answer to this might be to allow the job contractors first choice of any labour available on each day. If a man refused to work on the sugar estates he would be denied the right to work in the P.W.D. scheme or to any benefit for a period of (say) a month. In short, the employment bureau would be assisting what might be called the "cattle market" recruitment of labour for the sugar estates. Such a policy would be extremely unpopular.

The alternative of expanding the normal work of the P.W.D. avoids many of these difficulties. It would, however, create a pool of labour which would resent dismissal from the Department when other jobs became available. And it would not of itself be as effective in reducing claims for unemployment benefit. If carried too far it could create a serious shortage of labour for the sugar estates. It is more likely, however, that it would not be carried far enough to prevent there being a considerable number of workers receiving benefit—particularly in the inter-crop season.

In such circumstances, two measures are essential. The first is to insist that those receiving benefit report more than once a day at a designated office as a means of preventing "the unemployed" from undertaking subsidiary occupations. The second is to establish a system of social priorities for the application of the work test. We suggest tentatively that the priorities for offers of work should be as follows:—

(a) able-bodied men aged 14-55 with and without dependent children;

(b) able-bodied women aged 14-55 with no dependent children;

(c) wives aged under 55 of able-bodied men with dependent children;

(d) all men and women over the age of 55 excluding groups (e) and (f).

(e) wives of sick and disabled husbands with dependent children;

(f) widows and deserted wives with dependent children.

So far we have confined our discussion of social insurance to sickness and unemployment benefits. We now wish to recommend that the system created to provide these benefits should be extended, first, to provide a fire disaster benefit and, secondly, after the system has been efficiently established, a supplementary wage related pension.

FIRE DISASTER BENEFIT

A particularly serious risk which faces the Mauritian family is the destruction of its home by fire. This is due to the fact that so many houses are constructed of wood and straw. We recommend, therefore, that the social insurance fund should pay a benefit in cases where fire has led to the destruction of the property occupied by the insured person.

We suggest that the qualifying condition for this benefit should be six months' minimum contribution during the previous contribution year to the credit of either husband or wife or both. If a house which is owned and occupied by the insured person or the insured person's spouse is destroyed or damaged, we suggest that a benefit of Rs. 100 or the value of the damage if it is less than Rs. 100 should be paid to the insured person. In cases where the house is not owned, we suggest that the value of the furniture, clothing and equipment destroyed should be paid up to a maximum of Rs. 50. No benefit of less than Rs. 20 should be paid.

THE DEVELOPMENT OF PENSION PROVISION

Some account has already been given of the history of the present non-contributory old age pension of Rs. 22 a month. In 1950, when this scheme was introduced, there were good reasons for paying the pension, subject to a test of means, without any contribution being required. It was intended to help the poorest sections of the community, who could least afford contributions, and to help them immediately without the delay that the collection of contributions would have involved. Moreover, the administrative costs of collection for this purpose alone would have been relatively high. Since, however, contributions are now to be collected for unemployment, sickness and fire disaster benefits, and since the pension of Rs. 22 is now available to rich and poor alike without any test of means, it seems to us appropriate that any further development of pension provision should be on a contributory basis for all employed persons.

In proposing the introduction of a wage related system of contributory pensions we considered the possibility of also offering some recompense in their old age to those who had limited the size of their families to not more than three children. By so doing, these parents will have made a contribution towards resolving the fundamental problem of unrestrained population growth which faces all sections of Mauritian society today. It would not seem unreasonable, therefore, if society, in due time, recognised in practical form the virtues of self-discipline in family-building habits.

What we had in mind, therefore, was that a "Small Family Pension Benefit" of, say, Rs. 15 a month should be paid to all women still married at age 65 as a supplement to the basic pension on certain conditions. These might include:—

(i) that the woman was civilly married before the age of 45;

(ii) that the woman had never received or qualified for a three-child family benefit; or

(iii) that the woman had given birth in this and/or any previous marriage to fewer than three live-born children;

(iv) that the husband had also attained the age of 65.

We would think it proper that this benefit should be paid to the wife without test of means when she attains the age of 65 although it is provided for husband and wife jointly. She will have had a limited rôle as a mother and, consequently, will have not more than two children to help to support her in her old age. The opportunities of employment for elderly women in Mauritius are extremely limited and are not likely to expand in the future because of the growth of population. If the wife is widowed at age 65 or thereafter the benefit should be reduced by one-half.

We do not recommend the introduction of this benefit immediately. Not only are there certain administrative problems of identifying and verifying claimants but, more important still, it would not seem equitable to start awarding "Small Family Pension Benefits" until the system of family benefits which we propose in Chapter 7 has been in operation for some years. We therefore put forward this proposal for later consideration by the Government. It might well be reviewed in five years time as part of a continual process of extending and developing a long-term family planning policy. Meanwhile, we hope that this and our other proposals for both limiting family size and extending family benefits will be openly and vigorously discussed by all sections of Mauritian society.

WAGE RELATED PENSIONS

We turn now to consider the introduction, on top of the basic pension, of a contributory scheme of wage related pensions for all employed persons above a specified level of yearly earnings.

We think the time is approaching for a start to be made with such a scheme in Mauritius. Although public and private employers have made pension and superannuation provision for some of their employees, especially in the higher paid ranks, there are various groups of employed persons who have become accustomed to a somewhat better standard of living but who, in their old age, have to rely on the present basic pension. Many no doubt get generous help from their families but this pension alone is inadequate to maintain a reasonable standard, especially in the urban areas where rents may absorb most if not all of the pension. These workers are among the most deserving sections of the community; teachers in private schools, clerks, skilled workers, and certain categories of employees of hotels, shops, and various industries. We received evidence of considerable hardship among this section of the population.

Not only is there a need for additional provision for these employees but we are also anxious to establish a scheme which will in the future allow all workers, manual and non-manual, to earn for themselves higher old age pensions. To the extent that the economy becomes more diversified, and the number of workers in clerical and skilled occupations grows, this need for improved pensions will undoubtedly develop. Once a social insurance scheme is established, we think it would be unsound to meet this need by raising the present non-contributory benefit. Additional savings to help to finance capital investment in new undertakings will also become more urgent, and contributions to a pension scheme could be invested in this way. We are therefore led to propose the introduction of a wage and salary related pension scheme.

We limit ourselves in this Report to recommending only the main outlines of such a scheme. Further actuarial investigations are needed before the details can be worked out. Moreover, we think it would be wise to launch first the insurance scheme for sickness and unemployment benefits. Not only will useful administrative lessons be learnt from this operation but additional information will be collected on the occupations and earnings of the population. We suggest that the Government Actuary for Great Britain should be asked to advise the Minister of Labour and Social Security on the data required for detailed planning and to assist with the actuarial inquiries required.

Our main proposals are as follows:—

Contributions and coverage

Contributions would be payable from the start of working life until age 65 for both men and women. They would be a proportion of earnings (including overtime pay and bonuses as well as earnings additional to fixed salary). They should be levied on all earnings up to a maximum of Rs. 25,000 per year. Credits should be given for spells of sickness, industrial injury or unemployment for which benefit is paid.

The contribution should be shared between employers and employees, the Government bearing all the costs of administration and management of the Social Insurance Fund into which would be paid all receipts from contributions in respect to sickness, unemployment, fire disaster, industrial injury and wage related pension benefits.

All employed persons earning more than Rs. 100 a month would contribute to the scheme. This suggested minimum would need to be reviewed after further actuarial data have been collected. We emphasise later that for national reasons this scheme should be as comprehensive as possible. Except for the poorest group of workers, those below the minimum who cannot now afford additional contributions, no contracting-out should be allowed.

Public and private employers with their own pension schemes will have to make whatever adjustments are necessary to such schemes to take account of the level of contributions and benefits payable in respect to all our social insurance proposals.

We think there is a strong case for eventually extending this scheme to self-employed persons with earnings above the minimum. There are probably many who would welcome the opportunity of saving for their old age in a national scheme if the administrative problems could be solved. We suggest that this question should be further examined by the Minister in the light of actuarial advice and experience of the working of our social security proposals.

Benefits

Benefit should be drawn at any age from 65 onwards at the wish of the pensioner. It would vary according to the contributions, and therefore the past earnings, of the pensioner. The relationship between contributions and benefit should not, however, be the same at all income levels. The scheme should be designed to aid the lower paid worker more than the higher paid. We recommend, therefore, that the lower-paid workers should be treated more generously than other contributors and should receive rather more than they would be entitled to on a strict actuarial basis. Taking account of need in this way is one of the major distinguishing differences between social and private insurance. As the scheme develops we consider that the minimum proposed should be progressively lowered so as to bring into the scheme more of the poorer paid workers.

The scheme should be designed to provide all contributors with a total pension at age 65 (including the present non-contributory basic pension) of at least one-third of the average earnings upon which contributions have been charged. As the scheme develops, the period during which contributions have been paid will lengthen until eventually the pension is based on earnings throughout working life. The question whether, in the early years of the scheme, there should be a measure of "blanketing-in" for older workers is one which the Government will have to decide in the light of full actuarial data and other considerations.

All women, whether married or single, insured under the scheme should be given equal rights with men, and they should accept equal obligations. Widows and widowers would be paid a pension at or after age 65 assessed on (*a*) their own entitlement before marriage, (*b*) half the joint entitlement or all their own entitlement, if higher, for years of marriage, (*c*) their own entitlement after widowhood or widowerhood, including periods for which contributions have been credited. For many years, however, the data for these assessments will not be available. Until they are, the general principle should be that the survivor will receive one-half of the joint pension benefit entitlement.

In addition to our proposals for non-contributory benefits, we recommend that when a wage-related pension scheme is started, some provision should be made for widows at age 55 if their husbands had contributed to the scheme. Similar provision should be made for certain categories of widowers, especially disabled or infirm men formerly dependent on their wives' earnings.

In the absence of essential actuarial data, it is not possible at this stage to provide even tentative estimates of costs and rates of contribution. These must await the results of the inquiries we have suggested should be put in hand by the Minister of Labour and Social Security. We envisage, however, that the income and expenditure for a wage related pension scheme would form part of the operations of a Social Insurance Fund which we recommend should be established. The objective would be eventually to maintain the whole social insurance scheme broadly on a "pay-as-you-go" basis, bearing in mind the need to build up in the early years, after the pension scheme is started, a moderate working balance in the Fund. The costs of the present non-contributory pension should continue to be borne on general taxation.

SOCIAL INSURANCE AND OCCUPATIONAL PROVISION

The proposals we have now made for sickness and unemployment benefits, a wage related pension scheme and fire disaster cover represent, in total, a heavy responsibility for the Government to shoulder. The development of an efficient administration will take time and will call for understanding and co-operation from employers and employees alike. In our view, the whole scheme will have to be introduced in stages. Priority should be given to the introduction of benefits for sickness, unemployment and fire disaster cover which comprise the most urgent needs in this area of social policy. When the insurance scheme has been effectively launched measures should be taken to introduce the proposed wage related pension benefits. This will allow time for this particular proposal to be worked out in more detail than has been possible for us owing to the necessity to present our Report as quickly as possible. After these schemes have been in operation for some years, we suggest that further consideration should be given to the question of a "Small Family Pension Benefit".

At an early stage, and especially when a wage related pension scheme is formulated in detail, consideration will have to be given to the question of relating these proposals to existing occupational provisions for the Civil Service, monthly paid workers in the sugar industry and other employees.

We outlined in Chapter 2 the present occupational provisions for social security in Mauritius. Civil servants are entitled to generous pensions and sick pay and have little risk of unemployment. Monthly paid sugar workers also have rights to payment in sickness, a statutory pension scheme and considerable security of tenure. Administrative and clerical employees are even more generously treated. There will inevitably be a demand from all those who already enjoy rights to sickness and old age benefits which are superior to those we have suggested to "contract out" of the national scheme. The demand will be strongest from civil servants and others whose benefits are non-contributory.

We strongly recommend that no requests for "contracting-out" should be entertained. Social insurance must be truly national—particularly in a country such as Mauritius where every step must be taken to foster a sense of unity. Every member of the community —rich and poor, black and white, protectors and protected—must have a stake in social insurance. The participation of those with high social status in the community will also enlist their interest and co-operation in the effective administration of the scheme.

Our objections to " contracting-out " are not solely based on these strong arguments of principle. Any scheme for "contracting-out" would involve the Government in complicated problems of administration as workers moved from one category to another. It would also affect the finances of the scheme as it would be the "good risks" who would be outside the national scheme—those who are less likely to be unemployed and enjoy good health. Social insurance becomes viable by a pooling of risks. The strong must help the weak.

It does not follow from what we have said that civil servants and others who do not at present pay contributions must accept the loss of income created by the introduction of contributions. Representatives of employees will, of course, be free to raise this change in circumstances before the appropriate negotiating machinery and press for compensating adjustments in remuneration.

These are our proposals for sickness, unemployment, old age pensions and fire disaster insurance. In the next chapter we consider the problem of workmen's compensation. Other needs of the family —marriage, maternity, bereavement and the question of provision for children—are separately discussed in Chapter 7 as our recommendations under these heads take the form of non-contributory benefits. All these proposals are summarised in Chapter 12 where we consider their economic and financial implications.

CHAPTER 6

Industrial Injuries and Diseases

HISTORICAL DEVELOPMENT AND EXISTING LEGISLATION

Mauritius introduced workmen's compensation legislation in 1931. It was one of the first British colonies to do so. The Workmen's Compensation Ordinance repealed two earlier statutes, one of which provided for the payment of "fair and reasonable compensation" to workers injured by aloe fibre machinery, while the other, enacted as early as 1888, made similar provision for the victims of boiler explosions, whether employed or not. The Secretary of State, Lord Passfield, was so impressed with the Workmen's Compensation Bill that he dispatched copies to other colonies in 1930 with the suggestion that they use it as a model in drafting their own workmen's compensation laws. Experience both in Mauritius and elsewhere showed that the Ordinance was not without defects, and in 1937 a new Model Ordinance was drawn up.* However, the Mauritius Workmen's Compensation Ordinance of 1931, although frequently amended, remains in force to this day, with most of its defects unaltered.

The Ordinance deals not only with industrial injuries, but also (since 1952) with certain occupational diseases which are listed in Schedule II of the Ordinance. A workman is defined as "any person who has entered into or works under a contract of service or apprenticeship with an employer, whether by way of manual labour, clerical work or otherwise . . . and whether the remuneration is calculated by time or by work done", but the following classes of workers are specifically excluded:—

(*a*) non-manual workers earning more than Rs. 5,000 a year;

(*b*) casual workers (unless the work is connected with the employer's trade or business or the person is engaged by a club for the purpose of a game or recreation);

(*c*) "outworkers";

(*d*) members of the employer's family living in his house;

(*e*) the police force;

(*f*) domestic servants (unless employed in connection with power-driven machinery);

---

* The Workmen's Compensation (East and West Africa) Model Ordinance, 1937

(g) labour contractors and sub-contractors;

(h) persons plying for hire with any vehicle or vessel obtained under a contract of deposit, agency, loan or hire;

(i) the Armed Forces;

(j) civil servants engaged outside the Colony, not employed in the " Government of the Colony".

The basic principle of the Workmen's Compensation Ordinance is that the liability of the employer is not limited to cases where it can be shown that he has been guilty of negligence. It is enough that the accident which caused the injury arose "out of and in the course of the employment". The injured employee is entitled to compensation even though he may have been entirely to blame, as long as the accident was not due to his "serious and wilful misconduct".

In the case of disablement or death resulting from an occupational disease, it need only be shown that "the disease is due to the nature of any employment in which the workman was employed at any time within the twelve months previous to the disablement or death". The employee retains his right to sue the employer for damages under the Civil Code; but once he has exercised this right, he is debarred from claiming compensation under the Workmen's Compensation Ordinance. Similarly, he cannot sue for damages once he has claimed such compensation.

The compensation payable under the Ordinance takes the form of weekly payments for a period not exceeding 12 months in cases of temporary incapacity lasting over three days, and a lump sum payment on death or permanent incapacity. If the period of incapacity does not exceed three days, no compensation need be paid. The amounts payable are now as follows:—

(i) *Temporary total incapacity:* weekly payments not exceeding two-thirds of the workman's "average weekly wages from the employer before the accident", with a maximum of Rs. 60 a week.

(ii) *Temporary partial incapacity:* weekly payments not exceeding one-half of the workman's loss of earnings (i.e. the difference between his average weekly wages before the accident and the wages he is able to earn in "some suitable form of employment or business" after the accident), with a maximum of Rs. 60 a week. (Under the Ordinance as originally enacted, the weekly payments could not exceed one-half of wages, with a maximum of Rs. 30. The proportion was increased to two-thirds in 1947, and the maximum was doubled in 1952.)

(iii) *Permanent total incapacity:* a lump sum payment not

exceeding four years' wages at the rate of the workman's average weekly wages before the accident (until 1952 the lump sum could not exceed three years' wages).

(iv) *Permanent partial incapacity:* a lump sum payment being a percentage of the compensation payable for permanent total incapacity, proportionate to the loss of earning capacity caused by the injury. For certain specified injuries, the percentage to be taken is laid down in Schedule I of the Ordinance. It can never exceed 70% of four years' wages, except in the case of a workman under 21 years of age whose compensation may be increased within certain limits to take account of his loss of future earning capacity.

(v) *Death:* a lump sum payment to the workman's dependants not exceeding three years' wages at the workman's average weekly rate before the accident. If there are persons who were partially dependent on the workman's wages, the maximum compensation payable to them is three times the annual benefit which such dependants received, or would have received, from the deceased. If there are no dependants, compensation is limited to the cost of medical attendance and burial, not exceeding Rs. 500. If the workman has already received any payment as compensation for temporary or permanent incapacity, but subsequently dies from the injury, his dependants cannot claim more than the difference between the lump sum payable in respect of the death and the amounts already paid.

(vi) In addition to the above, reasonable hospital and medical expenses up to Rs. 300 can be claimed.

Compensation for permanent incapacity and death invariably takes the form of a single lump sum payment. But lump sum settlements are not confined to these cases, since the Ordinance allows the redemption of weekly payments by a lump sum at any time.

The Ordinance permits the fixing of the compensation payable either by order of the Court or by agreement between the parties. The workman's interests are protected by the requirement that employers must notify accidents to the Labour Commissioner within three days and by the power of the Court—under Section 19 (2)—to vary an agreed settlement if the amount agreed is grossly inadequate or excessive or the agreement was arrived at through fraud or ignorance. We understand that all claims arising from serious accidents are followed up by the Labour Department to ensure that adequate compensation is paid.

The workman is required to give notice of the accident as soon as practicable, and the application for compensation must normally be made within six months. Medical examination must be arranged at the employer's expense, and the workman must submit to examination by a doctor engaged by the employer, though he can arrange for his own doctor to be present (at his own expense). In case of disagreement, the matter may be referred by the Court to a medical referee, who in practice is a Government Medical Officer. Certification of occupational diseases is carried out by a "certifying surgeon" appointed by the Governor, also in practice a Government Medical Officer.

PROPOSALS FOR THE FUTURE

Historically, the objectives of workmen's compensation have been threefold:—

(1) to maintain income during periods of interruption caused by injury or occupational disease;

(2) to encourage measures for the prevention of occupational injury and disease by imposing the liability for compensation on the employer;

(3) to provide for the rehabilitation of the injured workman.

Of these three objectives, the first is the most immediate. The method by which it is achieved, however, will be strongly influenced by the provisions directed towards the other two objectives.

In many countries, workmen's compensation systems have developed independently of other social security arrangements. There are a number of reasons for this. Firstly, workmen's compensation laws merely modified a liability which already existed. Long before special legislation was considered, employers had a general "common law" liability for injuries to their employees. In some countries, this liability was more clearly defined by employers' liability laws. The only new principle introduced by special workmen's compensation legislation is that the liability of the employer is no longer dependent on his negligence or fault. The reasoning behind such legislation is that any injury or disease "arising out of and in the course of employment" is a cost of running the employer's business. It therefore follows that this cost should be borne by the employer. It was argued, moreover, that workmen who accepted employment in particularly dangerous trades were entitled to some special compensation for the extra risks they ran. As a result of this argument, which might properly have led to higher wages in such trades, workmen's compensation programmes in a number of countries were at first limited to certain dangerous occupations. Secondly, and reinforcing these arguments, workmen's compensation could be introduced without the setting up of an extensive administrative machinery by the Government. While other branches of social security generally involved centralised administration by government agencies, workmen's compensation could be left in the hands of the employers, with the Courts intervening in cases of dispute. Lastly, it was hoped in Britain and other countries that the introduction of workmen's compensation schemes would lead to a reduction in the administrative, financial and legal complexities of employers' liability legislation, and in particular to a reduction in the volume and cost of litigation.

In practice, however, as the experience of many countries has shown, the separation of workmen's compensation from other social security provisions leads to a variety of difficulties and anomalies. The needs of a workman and his dependants, if his earnings are interrupted by injury or disease, are neither greater nor less if such injury or disease is a result of his employment than if it is incurred outside his employment. Looked at in terms of needs, therefore, there is a strong argument for providing the same benefits in both cases. There is often great difficulty, medically and legally, in deciding whether in fact a particular injury or disease arose out of the employment or not, and a vast body of case-law has accumulated in many countries on this question. The costs of maintaining this case-law are heavy. Anomalies also arise where, as in Mauritius, certain categories of employment are excluded from workmen's compensation. It may be that the risks inherent in such employments are relatively small, but this is no comfort to the workman who incurs an injury in such employment.

The argument that the individual employer ought to be made responsible for bearing the cost of injuries to his employees has some force. On the other hand, it is clearly undesirable that each claim for compensation should be fought out between employer and workman. The employer, or his insurance company, always has a great advantage in such negotiations. We understand that in Mauritius the Labour Department does a great deal to ensure that workmen receive the compensation to which they are entitled. Nevertheless, we consider that the present system does not encourage employers to make fair and reasonable settlements. Nor is the Workmen's Compensation Ordinance the only incentive which can be applied to employers to ensure the safety of their workmen. This can probably be done as effectively by the enforcement of safety regulations, and by the fact that employers are liable under the Civil Code in cases of negligence.

It seems, moreover, that most employers in Mauritius insure against their liability for workmen's compensation. To the extent that this results in a pooling of risks, it reduces the incentive for the individual employer to keep accidents to a minimum. Moreover, experience in other countries has shown that the administrative costs of workmen's compensation insurance are extremely high. The Beveridge Report showed that for the United Kingdom in the two years 1938 and 1939, the proportion of administrative expenses to premiums paid to commercial insurance companies for this kind of insurance was as high as 46·5%.* In the case of mutual insurance companies it was 21·6%, but as far as we are aware there are no such companies operating in Mauritius. Even this latter figure is very high compared with the cost of administering a State insurance scheme.

One of the least satisfactory aspects of the present Workmen's Compensation Ordinance is the fact that compensation for permanent incapacity or death takes the form of a lump sum payment. This, together with the limitation of weekly payments for temporary incapacity to a period of 12 months (compared to the limit of four or five years which is usual in other Colonies), and the fact that such weekly payments can be computed for a lump sum, largely prevents the Ordinance from effectively fulfilling its main objective of providing a regular income during lengthy periods of incapacity. In theory, it is true that a lump sum can be used to purchase an annuity, and may thus be converted into a regular income for life. In practice, however, it is unlikely that this is done in many cases. In countries where compensation takes the form of lump sums, it is almost invariably found that difficulties arise through exhaustion of the lump sum before the end of the period of incapacity. Indeed, in cases of permanent incapacity this is bound to happen unless the lump sum is sufficient to provide an adequate income for the rest of the lifetime of the beneficiary. This clearly is not the case in Mauritius, where the maximum lump sum is only four years' wages.

Payment of once-for-all lump sum benefits also conflicts with the aim of rehabilitation. It is based on the assumption that the incapacity will in fact be permanent. Moreover, in the negotiations leading up to the payment of compensation, the gravity of the injury will almost inevitably have been exaggerated by those negotiating for the workman. As a result, he may himself become convinced of the hopelessness of his case, and the task of rehabilitation is thus rendered more difficult.

It is arguable that a lump sum may be more useful to the workman than a weekly pension of equivalent capital value, which would in any case be insufficient for him to live on. This, however, is simply to admit the inadequacy of the compensation. It cannot be

* Cmd. 6404, November 1942, p. 280.

made more adequate simply by paying it in a different form. There is perhaps more substance to the argument that the payment of a weekly pension may encourage malingering. This, however, cannot apply in cases of permanent incapacity or death, and in cases of temporary incapacity the Workmen's Compensation Ordinance already provides for weekly payments.

We therefore reach the conclusion that there is an overwhelming case for the abolition of lump sum compensation. Accordingly, we recommend that all payments should be made on a weekly or monthly basis. It remains to decide, firstly, what changes are required in the rates of compensation, and secondly, for what periods they should be payable.

Here, as in the case of other benefits, we are confronted with the problem of choosing between flat rate and wage related benefits. In the last chapter, we came to the conclusion that for sickness, flat rate benefits were the right answer for Mauritius at the present time. Our preference, therefore, since we wish to assimilate sickness and industrial injury benefits as far as possible, would be to recommend flat rate benefits here also. However, the benefits under the existing Ordinance are expressed as a percentage of average earnings. It is therefore necessary to consider whether the advantages of wage related benefits are sufficient to justify retaining them in this instance. Before doing so, it should be pointed out that the present system does not, in reality, give purely wage related benefits. In the case of temporary incapacity, weekly payments of up to two-thirds of average wages are made, but these are subject to a maximum of Rs. 60 a week, which has remained unchanged since 1952 despite subsequent rises in wage rates. The effect of this is that for temporary total incapacity, compensation is related to wages only for those earning Rs. 90 a week or less, though it is true that few workers to whom the Ordinance applies earn more than this. So far as compensation for permanent incapacity and death is concerned, the fact that the lump sum compensation is based on average wages is totally irrelevant, since the maximum payment, three or four years' wages, is quite arbitrary and bears no relation to real needs.

Wage related benefits can be defended on two grounds:—

(1) they reflect the actual loss of earning capacity due to the injury;

(2) they provide an income related to the standard of life to which the beneficiary was accustomed before the injury.

The first of these points is certainly logical if it is considered that the main object is to compensate the workman for his loss through the injury. However, we are of the opinion that the more important object is to provide for his needs and those of his dependants after the injury, rather than to attempt to estimate a loss between two points in time. A serious injury inevitably results in considerable changes in the way of life of the injured person. It is at least arguable that his needs after the injury will be related more closely to the needs of other persons similarly injured than to his needs before the injury. If this is the case, then the second argument in favour of wage related benefits is considerably weakened. It should be noted that at present in Mauritius the maximum length of time during which weekly payments of compensation are made is 12 months. The picture would look rather different if, as we would propose, such payments were to take the form of a life pension in cases of permanent incapacity. It could then happen, if wage related benefits were given, that two men who had received identical injuries 20 or 30 years previously would be receiving very different amounts of compensation, because their earnings at that time were different. Such a state of affairs would not be easy to justify.

Wage related benefits in Mauritius can also be criticised on the grounds that pre-injury earnings may bear no relationship to family needs. What is of primary importance in our view is the actual need, after an injury, of the worker and his or her family.

We have discussed in Chapter 5 the administrative complications resulting from a system of wage related benefits. The difficult problem of defining, and still more of identifying, "average wages" is avoided entirely if flat rate benefits are given. The amount of compensation payable is dependent solely on the fact and nature of the injury or disease and the needs of the applicant.

We conclude, therefore, that the case for flat rate benefits is as strong for industrial injuries as for sickness and unemployment. Accordingly, we recommend a change from the existing system to a system of flat rate benefits based entirely on the degree of disability. They should not be limited to a fixed number of weeks, but should continue as long as the period of incapacity continues. At pensionable age, the benefit should be reduced by the amount of the pension. An old age pension is intended to compensate for loss of earning capacity and it would involve double compensation to pay both pension and benefit at full rates concurrently.

For the reasons we have already stated, the rates of benefit should be the same as in the case of sickness and unemployment benefits—Rs. 30 a month. The only exception we would make is in the case of permanent total incapacity. Here we feel that a "constant attendance allowance" of Rs. 15 per month could be given in cases of total incapacity where constant attendance on the disabled person is needed.

We are aware that flat rate benefits will involve lower rates of compensation for some categories of workers than they are entitled to under the present legislation. Temporary incapacity can lead now to a payment as high as Rs. 60 *per week* while we are recommending Rs. 30 *per month* (plus family benefits where there are three or more dependent children). We hope that our proposals will be viewed as a whole. There can be no dispute that we are offering the worker much more valuable "social insurance cover" than he has at present. He will be able to claim a benefit *of unlimited duration* whatever the cause of his incapacity for work.

In the light of our proposals in Chapter 7 for survivors' benefits, in which we have taken account of the needs of dependants, where death results from industrial injury or disease special provision is no longer necessary under industrial injuries legislation. The needs of dependants consequent upon death resulting from an industrial accident or disease are no different from their needs when death results from other causes.

The cost of these disability benefits (including the family benefit and notional sums for widows' benefit, rehabilitation services and medical care provided by the Government Medical Service) should continue to be borne by employers, but we recommend that they should be administered through the social insurance scheme, an appropriate addition being made to the employers' contributions. Industrial injuries insurance will thus replace "workmen's compensation". We are led to this conclusion by a number of considerations:—

(1) the arguments against separation of workmen's compensation from other benefits which we have set out above;

(2) the relatively high administrative costs of commercial insurance; and

(3) the fact that no system which lays the liability for compensation on the individual employer can give an absolute guarantee that the workman will receive the compensation he is entitled to, particularly in the case of long-term benefits.

The coverage should be the same as for sickness benefit, that is to say, all employed persons should be covered, including domestic servants (in accordance with the I.L.O. Convention on Workmen's Compensation) and non-manual employees. The payment of benefits should not, however, be dependent on the previous contribution record.

We have recommended a waiting period of over two weeks for sickness benefit, with the intention that this should be reduced as soon as the number of doctors and other administrative factors permit. In the case of industrial injuries, however, the waiting period for workmen's compensation is at present only three days. If a longer period were now to be laid down for the new industrial injuries scheme, the old scheme would have to remain in operation during this extended waiting period. The injured worker would thus receive no benefit for the first three days, compensation under the old Ordinance for the next two weeks (approximately), and insurance benefit thereafter. To avoid the confusion which would inevitably result from this arrangement, we propose that the new industrial injuries insurance benefit should be payable as from the fourth day of incapacity, as under the present system, no benefit being paid in respect of the three waiting days.

Because of this shorter waiting period, and because the right to benefit will not be dependent on the previous contribution record, it is necessary to define clearly the circumstances in which industrial injury benefit rather than sickness benefit can be claimed. The legal complications which have grown up around this question in the United Kingdom and elsewhere are such that we can do no more than point out certain deficiencies in the Workmen's Compensation Ordinance. The task of remedying these deficiencies is one which requires expert legal advice. Some of them, we understand, will be dealt with in the Workmen's Compensation (Amendment) Bill which is to be introduced in the present session of the Legislative Council.

Broadly speaking, we would recommend that the conditions should be similar to those laid down in the U.K. National Insurance (Industrial Injuries) Act, 1948. The particular points which, we suggest, require attention are:—

(1) Accidents arising "in the course of" an insured person's employment should be deemed to have arisen "out of" that employment. This provision was adopted in the U.K. to avoid some of the legal and other difficulties inherent in the phrase "arising out of and in the course of the employment".

(2) An action of an insured person in contravention of any law, regulation or order should not be regarded as misconduct such as to deprive him of the right to benefit, provided that such action was taken "for the purposes of and in connection with the employer's trade or business".

(3) We recommend the adoption of the provisions of Section 10 of the U.K. Act: "Any accident happening to an insured person in or about any premises at which he is for the time being employed for the purposes of his employer's trade or business shall be deemed to arise out of and in the course of his employment if

it happens while he is taking steps, on an actual or supposed emergency at those premises, to rescue, succour or protect persons who are, or are thought to be or possibly to be, injured or imperilled, or to avert or minimise serious damage to property."

We can see no justification for denying the injured employee the right to claim both industrial injuries benefit and civil damages from his employer. We suggest, therefore, that the two remedies should no longer be mutually exclusive. Any benefit payable should be taken into account in full by the Court in determining the amount of any damages (in the U.K. only one-half of the benefit is taken into account, the other half being attributable to the employee's contribution; but no apportionment of this kind will be necessary in Mauritius if, as we propose, there is no contribution by the employee).

We believe that our proposals will assist the process of rehabilitating the injured workman, by removing much of the strain and anxiety which the inadequate benefits of the existing system must produce, by reducing the risks of ineligibility for benefit, and by eliminating some of the lengthy negotiations and litigation which are characteristic of workmen's compensation schemes. In addition, we regard the development of positive rehabilitative services as an urgent need, especially in the circumstances of Mauritius where "light work" is not readily available for the disabled manual worker. The question of institutional care of the disabled is discussed in Chapter 11. There must, however, be many partially disabled persons for whom residential care is not necessary. We therefore recommend that consideration be given to the extension of non-residential training facilities for the disabled on the lines of the Orthopaedic Workshop. We would add, however, that before any steps of this kind are taken, a survey should be carried out as soon as practicable to ascertain the real size and nature of the problem of the disabled in Mauritius, including not only the victims of industrial accidents and diseases, but also those who have suffered non-industrial injuries, polio victims and others. Immediately this information is available it will be possible to draw up a realistic programme of rehabilitation services designed to make the best and most economical use of all resources.

CHAPTER 7

Family Needs

In Chapter 5 we made proposals for a scheme of social insurance to provide sickness, unemployment and fire disaster benefits and wage related pensions. In Chapter 6 we recommended that the existing provisions for workmen's compensation should be replaced by a scheme for industrial injuries and diseases integrated with our main social insurance proposals. Here we consider what provisions should be made for marriage, maternity, children, bereavement, and for orphans and other victims of broken family life. We deal with proposals for both benefits in cash and services in kind.

HISTORICAL BACKGROUND

We have summarised, in Chapter 5, the proposals of the committees of 1941 and 1958 for widows' and orphans' benefits. The earlier of these committees ignored the question of family allowances. The Ministerial Committee stated that it had deliberately limited the basic benefits for children and avoided recommending family allowances, maternity benefits, or extension of children's benefits beyond the age of 14 years. The Committee adopted this attitude "mainly because the demographic tendency in Mauritius is such that any attempt at the present time to introduce such measures would involve such vast expense it could not be contemplated without bringing literal ruin to the island by the diversion of economic resources to consumer expenditure rather than to development expenditure".

The Committee did not apparently consider the extent to which existing provisions for children under public assistance and income tax entailed substantial expense and encouraged population growth. We have had to take these factors into account and to develop positive rather than purely negative policies concerning the fundamentally related questions of family planning and family poverty.

As regards the provision of services in kind for children, the history of the school meals and milk service essentially dates from 1945. In that year an experimental school meals service was started in the Grand Port area. About 1,600 children were given a cooked midday meal, prepared at a school meals centre in Mahébourg. In 1948, a "snack" meal was introduced, consisting of a milk drink, wheatmeal biscuits and yeast tablets, which it was hoped would be cheap enough to be extended to all school children. The children were medically examined, weighed and measured, together with another group of children who were not receiving school meals. It was found that the full meal benefited the children considerably, while the "snack" had less effect because the children receiving it had less to eat at home. However, in 1949 it was decided to abandon the experiment on grounds of cost; the full meal cost 23 cents per head per day, while the "snack" cost 8·7 cents. Efforts to exact a contribution from parents towards the cost apparently met with little success.

In place of the experimental meals service, a scheme was introduced in 1950 for distributing free milk to all primary school children. At first, owing to prejudice against the use of skimmed milk, dried whole milk was given. In 1953, it was replaced by a larger quantity of dried skimmed milk, which provided three times more of the nutrients (calcium and animal protein) which were thought likely to be deficient in the children's home diet. Since 1958, iron tablets have been issued with the milk. A double ration of milk is given in cases where there is evidence of undernourishment.

A study of the height and weight records of school children carried out in 1959 by Miss E. L. Dantier, an officer of the Education Department, showed that while average heights had increased between 1955 and 1958, there had not been corresponding increases in weight; the children were in fact thinner in 1958 than in 1955. This, Miss Dantier suggested, might have been due to the use of skimmed milk, which does not supply calories in proportion to its calcium and protein content; it might be better to revert to the use of dried whole milk or to re-enrich the skimmed milk. Miss Dantier also made proposals for a school meals service, starting experimentally in a few schools, providing meals planned to make good deficiencies in the home diet, and with no charge to poor children. She estimated the cost, including overheads, at 35 cents a day per head.

OUR OWN VIEWS

The needs we are considering in this chapter are all related directly or indirectly to the welfare of the family unit—its formation, its dissolution, its reproduction. Our recommendations are dominated by the population policies we outline elsewhere in this Report. We wish to see reversed the present policies which have built into them an incentive, explicit or implicit, for the procreation of large families. In their place, we propose the substitution of policies designed to popularise the three-child family and to provide a social and psychological brake to the rearing of more children. To have any hope of success in the time left before the pressure of population becomes unbearable this brake must be applied to as many parts of the social and economic system as possible. We therefore want to encourage later marriage, to raise the status of women, to provide incentives for the longer spacing of births, to provide for safer motherhood, and to discourage the birth of more than three children to each couple.

We do not believe that these objectives can be incorporated in social policy unless measures are simultaneously taken to help those families who are suffering from poverty and ill-health. Hence we recommend that the proposals we make in this chapter should be non-contributory, and that the assistance provided should be concentrated on the poorer sections of the community. As we wish to avoid all the administrative complications of a series of tests of means we propose, as a simple solution, the criterion of income tax payments. The cash benefits we recommend in this chapter should therefore be restricted to all families where the head of the household was not, in the preceding year, assessed to pay tax. Marginal cases will have to be dealt with by regulations providing for proportionate payments.

SURVIVOR'S BENEFIT

Only one category of needs of the family has not direct demographic implications—the needs which arise from the death of a parent. We consider these needs first.

Between about 15-20% of married women in Mauritius go out to work. From the census report and additional data supplied by the Central Statistical Office, we find that the proportions of married women of different ages at work in 1952 were:—

Age	%
20-24	11·5
25-29	13·8
30-34	16·3
35-39	18·1
40-44	19·1
45-49	20·7
50-54	20·4
55-59	20·6
60+	12·0

Although we have no firm evidence, we understand that the proportion of widows at the younger ages who are in employment is higher. In view of this and for other reasons we do not consider it necessary for a benefit of unlimited duration to be paid to all women whose husbands die, irrespective of their age and family circumstances. We recognise that the death of a husband will normally reduce the standard of living of his widow. It would, however, be unjust to provide a younger widow without family responsibilities with a higher standard of living than a single woman of the same age.

Nevertheless, we think it appropriate to recommend a benefit to enable a widow without dependent children to readjust herself to the situation of being a "single" woman again. She may have to move house or find lodgers. She may also have difficulty in finding work. For these reasons, we recommend that a benefit should be paid to a widow aged over 21 (married or unmarried) for a period of three months following the death of her husband. Such a benefit should be at the rate of Rs. 20 per month.

It may well be asked why such a benefit should not be paid to a husband left without dependent children on the death of his wife. The reason we would give for this is that in nearly all cases a man earns more than a woman. A man is also less likely to have to change his mode of living on the death of his wife.

Thus, we recommend a short-term benefit payable only to a widow for a period of three months in cases where there are no dependent children. Where there are dependent children, we consider that a benefit should be paid until the last child reaches the age of 14, providing that no new union has been formed. The purpose of the benefit we propose is to compensate the survivor for the contribution to the upkeep of the family which the deceased partner would have made, be it in cash or in kind. Our recommendation is that a monthly allowance should be paid at the rate of Rs. 20 per month to a husband on the death of his wife and at the rate of Rs. 30 per month to a wife on the death of her husband. It seems justifiable to pay a higher benefit to a widow because the husband almost certainly made the larger contribution to the upkeep of the children. In the case of the widower, we consider it justifiable to pay an allowance, though at a lower rate, because he is unlikely to be able to undertake the care of the children without assistance from relatives or neighbours.

This benefit should be paid to all widows and widowers whether the death "arose out of and in the course of the employment " or not. It should be paid to the widows of the self-employed and of those who for one reason or another have had a bad contribution record in the social insurance scheme. The main purpose of this benefit is to safeguard the welfare of the children and it would be wrong for children to be penalised for the bad work attendance of their parent before death. Hence the survivors' benefit should be non-contributory on the lines of the present old age pension.

No benefits should be paid to widows and widowers who were, in the preceding year, assessed to pay income tax (as widows or widowers), except in cases where death arose "out of and in the course of the employment".

No benefits of any kind under this section should be paid to widows or widowers while they are still under the age of 21.

In addition to these proposals we gave serious consideration to the problem of the older widow without dependent children. We had in mind particularly the age group 50-59. These women will be ineligible (or no longer eligible) for the benefits we propose for widowed mothers and their children.

From various calculations we have made we estimate that at present there are about 5,000 widows in this age group. Of these, perhaps 500 still have children under 14; they will qualify (at least for a time) for the benefits we have already recommended. To provide a benefit of, say, Rs. 20 a month for widows aged 50-59 without dependent children under 14 (in addition to the short-term benefit) would cost very approximately Rs. 1·2 million a year. This would add considerably to the total cost of our social security proposals.

We hesitate to put this recommendation firmly until more facts are available about the circumstances of the older widow. We do not know what proportion in this age range are at work or how many are rendering service to and are being maintained by a related family group. What is important, therefore, is to ascertain the standard of living of these older widows. Some of the severest cases of hardship may be found among these widows; particularly as we believe that it may be difficult for many of them to find work owing to ill-health and other reasons.

We suggest, therefore, that the Government should put in hand a survey of the means and circumstances of older widows. With additional staff, the Central Statistical Office is admirably equipped to undertake such an enquiry. When the facts are available we would urge the Government to examine the possibility of providing a non-contributory benefit for these older widows without dependent children. For women who lose their husbands after reaching the age of 50, this would in effect mean continuing the three-monthly benefit until the widow reaches the age of 60 and qualifies for an old age pension. Those eligible for such a benefit might include the whole age group or only certain categories; for example, widows with permanent disabilities or suffering from chronic ill-health and ineligible for sickness benefit.

MARRIAGE BENEFIT

The marriage of a daughter involves her family in heavy expenditure. "For poorer families it represents one of the major expenses during the lifetime of the parents".* This expenditure is often financed by borrowing at exorbitant rates of interest. There is therefore in our view a case for a benefit in such circumstances. Moreover, the population problem requires, as a matter of social policy, the encouragement of later marriages. We therefore recommend that a benefit of Rs. 50 should be paid to the father (or mother in the case of a widow or separated wife) on the marriage of his daughter, provided:—

(a) that it is a civil marriage;
(b) that the girl and her future husband are aged 21 or over at the time of marriage;
(c) that the girl has borne no children from any previous union of any kind;
(d) that the father (or widow or separated wife) was not in the preceding year assessed to pay income tax.

We recommend that this benefit should be non-contributory. We want to encourage later marriage among the whole population —not just among insured workers.

MATERNITY BENEFIT

The purpose of a maternity benefit is to make it easier for a pregnant woman to leave her employment a reasonable time before her confinement and to stay away from work until she is really fit again. The payment of a maternity benefit should also make it possible for a mother to be better fed before and after her confinement. It should therefore make some contribution towards the improvement of the health of the mother and her baby.

While a maternity benefit is desirable for the reasons stated, it can be criticised on the grounds that it eases the burden of parenthood. It may be said to conflict with a policy of reducing the birthrate. We therefore recommend that a maternity benefit should be available only if five stringent conditions are satisfied. First, we

* Benedict, B., *Indians in a Plural Society: A Report on Mauritius* (unpublished MS., 1960, p. 159).

recommend that no benefit should be payable to any woman who has given birth to a child, live or dead, during a period of 24 months before the expected date of the birth for which she is claiming. If parents spaced the birth of their children at two-year intervals, it would make a substantial contribution to the reduction of the birth-rate in Mauritius. Secondly, no benefit should be paid to any woman under the age of 21. Thirdly, the benefit should only be paid to a woman who has attended an ante-natal clinic, provided there is one in her area, has marked a form stating that she has been informed of family planning facilities, and has lodged her card with the insurance office for the period for which she is drawing benefit. Fourthly, no benefit should be paid to any woman who already has three living children, and, fifthly, no benefits at all should be paid to any woman whose husband was, in the preceding year, assessed to pay income tax.

If all these conditions are satisfied, we recommend that a non-contributory benefit of Rs. 20 a month should be paid to the woman for a period of six weeks before confinement and six weeks after confinement.

With the introduction of this benefit it will be necessary to revise the existing Labour Ordinance affecting employment in the sugar industry. Employers should be entirely relieved of their financial obligations to provide special maternity benefits for any class of employees.

As regards the public service, we further recommend that the terms of service for Government employees (central and local) should be amended to make the granting of maternity leave subject to the same conditions. In particular, we have in mind the application of conditions 1, 2, 3 and 4 to the existing terms of service.

PROVISION FOR CHILDREN

We turn now to the main problem we have to discuss in this chapter—general provisions for children. The biggest problem of poverty in Mauritius is to be found among the large families in the lower income groups. Earnings from the economic system are not adjusted to the number of persons which those earnings have to support. Thus, earnings which may be adequate for a man and wife and one child become increasingly inadequate as the family grows. When, however, the older children are able to contribute to the family income the cycle is reversed and the family reaches a peak of prosperity which lasts until the children marry and have families of their own. It is for these reasons, among others, that in many countries in the world, money is taken in taxes or social security contributions from families with no children and with many earners and given to those with dependent children.

The problem of the poverty of large families in Mauritius cannot be met in future by means of public assistance because of the principle of the income or wage stop. This problem is discussed in our proposals for the reform of public assistance. If the Public Assistance Department provided money, subject to a means test, for all families with a large number of dependent children, there would be little incentive to earn; the more that was earned, the less would be received in payments from the Department. In terms of numbers, the largest cause of poverty in Mauritius today is excessive fertility, leading to families that are too large to be supported either by the existing wage levels or by public assistance allowances which must of necessity be related to those levels.

At present, as we showed in Chapter 4, the public assistance system encourages rather than discourages additions to already large families. It is the purpose of the many proposals we make under the general heading of social security to reverse this tendency. We have to recognise, however, especially for the children already born, that there are strong humanitarian and public health arguments for alleviating the hardships that undoubtedly exist among these larger families. There are also important social and economic considerations which cannot be ignored. The irrefutable facts of scientific knowledge, which have been accumulating over the past few decades, all confirm the long-term ill effects of malnutrition in early childhood. Poor physique, low standards of work, prolonged or intermittent sickness and general apathy can all have their origins in the malnourished child. It may well be that the low productivity of labour and the irregular work attendance complained of by employers in Mauritius today are partly attributable to inadequate nutrition in the past. According to a World Health Organisation Study Group: "In Mauritius also it has been shown that anaemia, because of its extent and severity, constitutes a major public health problem. Investigations indicate that 50% or more of certain groups of the population may be affected . . ."*.

Studies carried out in connection with this research on anaemia showed that, despite the eradication of malaria, the number of cases of anaemia treated at out-patient departments greatly increased between 1946 and 1955. In 1958 it was estimated that anaemia and allied nutritional disorders were responsible for something like 100,000 attendances a year at dispensaries and out-patient departments. Including the cost of drugs, treatment in hospitals and

* *Iron Deficiency Anaemia: Report of a Study Group*, W.H.O. Technical Report Series, No. 82, 1959, p. 3.

at dispensaries the annual cost was put at over Rs. 400,000.

The conclusion we draw from these studies by the Medical Services and by the W.H.O. Nutrition Survey Team in Mauritius is that higher standards of feeding for the present generation of children might well pay a dividend in better health and higher output in the future and in fewer demands on the health services.

Under existing arrangements, the provisions for the children of parents who are regularly at work consist of the supply of milk to school children and to a limited group of undernourished infants under the age of one year. The latter, after inspection by the post-natal services, can be granted milk if they show clear signs of under-nourishment. The service is, we understand, strictly limited by the supplies available and is not provided at all in the more remote parts of the island where possibly it is needed most. There were 24,600 live births in 1958, but the average number of children receiving milk during the year was only 1,994. Nothing at all is provided for children between the ages of one and five years when school begins. The school milk service then makes provision for all primary school children on the island, nearly all of whom take the milk provided for them.

In considering these questions of nutrition, we took note of the differences between the heights and weights of Mauritian children and children of corresponding ages in Britain and the United States.* The Mauritian child in infancy is shorter and lighter and falls increasingly behind up to the age of five. From this age, the relationship between the Mauritian child and children in the wealthier countries remains constant. Inadequate nutrition from birth to the age of five can probably never be made up by better nutrition later in life. "Perhaps the most important effects of malnutrition . . . may be cumulative, and manifest themselves through a long-term effect on constitution with resultant lack of resistance to infections and other stresses and liability to degenerative diseases."†

Family allowances

One obvious answer to this problem is the provision of family allowances. But a comprehensive system of family allowances would be extremely expensive. Thus, if an allowance were provided for every child under the age of 12 at the modest rate of Rs. 10 per month, the cost would be Rs. 30 million—four or five times the total cost of "outdoor relief" in the present public assistance budget.

---

* The evidence for these statements is drawn from the final report of the W.H.O. Survey Nutrition Team to be published shortly.
† Brock, J. F., "Nutrition and the Clinician", *Lancet*, 1959, *ii*, 859.

A more restricted family allowance programme could, of course, be considered. Allowances could be paid for each child from (say) the first to the sixth birthday. This proposal would cost Rs. 13 million—not so much as to rule it completely out on grounds of cost.

The objection which would immediately be made to any proposals of this kind is that they would provide—or appear to provide—an incentive or encouragement for increasing the size of families. At the very least, a comprehensive family allowance system is open to the criticism that it tacitly approves the procreation of large families.

At an early stage in our work, we thus found ourselves torn between the aim of not giving any encouragement or even tacit approval in our recommendations to the rearing of large families and the evident fact that such families are at present the biggest single cause of poverty, malnutrition and family hardship. The problem is to help children already born without encouraging further births. We have also to make recommendations in the next chapter which will "rationalise" the present public assistance system, reduce further demands for indiscriminate relief, and remove the present implied approval of the rearing of large families.

The needs of the large family are already recognised in public assistance scales and there are families on assistance who are receiving as much in aid as they would earn if they were at work. This has the undesirable consequence, which we have referred to earlier (see Chapter 4), that any additional earnings can be deducted from assistance, thus removing the incentive to work. This difficulty, and the need to limit public assistance by a "wage stop", can only be avoided if provision for the family is made both to those who are at work and to those who are not. In other words, there needs to be some general family benefit available to most of the population to make it possible to ignore or give only very limited recognition to dependent children when applications are made for public assistance.

This was the conclusion which Sir William (now Lord) Beveridge reached when he considered, in 1942, the problem of poverty among children in Britain. He pointed out that "the gap between income during earning and during interruption of earning should be as large as possible for every man. It cannot be kept large for men with large families, except either by making their benefit in unemployment and disability inadequate, or by giving allowances for children in times of earning and not-earning alike".*

We cannot follow Lord Beveridge in all his recommendations.

* Beveridge, Sir W., *Social Insurance and Allied Services*, Cmd. 6404, 1942, p. 154.

The population problem in Mauritius is far too menacing and every possible step must be taken by the Government and the people to avert disaster in the future. We thus set ourselves to devise a way of helping dependent children which gives no encouragement to parents to have more than three children. We have shown earlier that if married couples in Mauritius limited their families to three children, the long-term population problems of the island would eventually be overcome.

We also wished to support the growth of healthy family life and to link our proposals, constructively and positively, to a nation-wide campaign of family planning. We believe we have found the answer to these various objectives by recommending that any family with three dependent children under the age of 14 should be entitled to receive a "family benefit" of Rs. 15 per month. There should be no payment in cases where there are less than three dependent children and no increase in the family benefit if there are more than three.

We consider that this proposal satisfies the criteria which we have laid down. Parents will know that they will have no financial support whatever from the community for their first or second child. Thus, in normal cases, no family benefit will come until at least the third year of marriage. There will be no encouragement to parents to start a family. It may be said that as children reach the age of 14 there is then an incentive to have further children. This can only happen, however, when there have been three—and not more than three—surviving children born in the previous 14 years. The incentive only arises therefore among parents who have not been prolific before the age of 30 to 35. Nor, after this age, is there any encouragement for very large families. Indeed, looked at in terms of the child-bearing period as a whole, the proposed benefit encourages births to be spaced at four-yearly intervals at least. If such spacing were adopted, it would represent a major contribution to the future health and well-being of Mauritius. In our maternity benefit and marriage grant proposals we have already provided inducements for later marriage and for the longer spacing of births to women aged over 21. No family benefit should therefore be paid to any woman who is under the age of 21.

We estimate that this proposal will cost Rs. 7·5 million per year. It will, however, reduce substantially the cost of public assistance and other aids to large families and will thus be partly self-financing. We consider, taking account of other proposals in our Report, that this sum can be afforded and will pay dividends in the form of a healthier population composed of smaller families in years to come. At some time in the future it may be possible to introduce less restricted benefits for children but it can reasonably be argued that the vigorous family planning policy which we advocate in Chapter 12 should be thoroughly launched before any steps are taken in this direction.

This proposal for a family benefit, like our recommendations for survivors' benefits, is intended to improve the health and welfare of the child population today. It is also intended, as we shall explain in the next chapter, to make it possible to exclude children from the routine scales of the Public Assistance Department. We therefore want the benefit to be received by the great majority of families in the island with three or more children. We are particularly anxious to include families where ill-health or lack of employment opportunities have led to a bad contribution record in the social insurance scheme. We want also to include the families of the self-employed. It follows, therefore, that the family benefit should not form part of the insurance scheme but should be a non-contributory benefit.

Tax allowances for children

In view of our proposal for a family benefit, we are led to reconsider the place of child allowances in the income tax system. The 7,000 or so individuals in Mauritius with incomes above the generous exemption level pay less tax according to the number of their children. The allowance, which is deducted from the taxpayer's income before calculating tax liability, varies from Rs. 500 to Rs. 800 per child. It continues until the child reaches the age of 16, or longer if the child is still receiving full-time education. In addition to these benefits, there is an allowance of Rs. 1,000 for children studying overseas, and as from the year 1959-60 this was increased to Rs. 3,500 for children aged 16 and over. The cost of these special concessions for the children of income tax payers is by no means inconsiderable, particularly when account is taken of the number of children involved. It is estimated that the cost in the year 1957-58 was Rs. 1 million for children in Mauritius and Rs. 160,000 for children studying abroad (the latter figure is likely to rise very steeply to about Rs. 500,000 for 1959-60 because of the increased allowance).* This probably covers about 8,000 children in Mauritius and about 280 abroad. Thus, the average cost per child was Rs. 125 per year, or Rs. 10 per month, for children in Mauritius; and Rs. 714 per year or Rs. 60 per month for those studying abroad. These estimates do not include cases, of which there may be many, in which tax liability is extinguished altogether by the child allowances. For those paying tax in the

* See Appendix C on Income Tax Statistics.

highest band of income, the advantage of having a child can now be as large as Rs. 560 per year, or Rs. 3,010 if the child is receiving full-time education abroad. There is thus a very strong economic incentive for parents in this income group to have more children.

We are not alone in pointing out that child allowances in income tax systems are of the same character as family allowances and have very similar economic and social effects. These considerations have been recognised in many publications by international agencies and have been referred to in official literature in the United Kingdom. Some countries have found a system of child allowances in the income tax system incompatible with a policy of family allowances. It was to rationalise provisions for children that Sweden took the step of abolishing child allowances as an income tax concession.

As we are unable for the reasons given to recommend at the present time a comprehensive policy of family allowances, it logically follows that the child allowances in the income tax should be withdrawn. If it is held that family allowances cannot be introduced because they might be construed as an incentive to have larger families, exactly similar arguments can be applied to the child allowance in the income tax. It is clearly wrong for one income group to be given an incentive to have larger families when such an incentive is thought to be unjustified for other income groups.

At the same time, we have to recognise that these allowances are in force and that parents have already entered into commitments for the education of their children at the level of secondary and higher education. We propose therefore to allow time for adjustments to be made. Accordingly, we recommend that as primary education is free these special concessions should be abolished forthwith for all children under the age of 11. For children above this age we recommend that these concessions should continue for a further five years and should then be abolished. To this recommendation we attach two conditions (i) that family benefits should not be paid to any parents who, in the preceding year, were assessed to pay income tax, and (ii) that during these five years no further child allowances should be granted for children attaining the age of 11 whose parents have already received allowances for three or more children.

The pre-school child

We turn now to consider the question of services in kind for children. Because we are concerned to see the development of preventive health and welfare policies in Mauritius we wish to recommend extended provisions for children under the age of six.

We recognise that some provisions have been introduced for the school child, partly because it is much easier to administer a system of issuing milk to this age group than to the pre-school child. Nevertheless, we feel that if we were forced to make such a choice, it would be better to provide milk for the pre-school child than for the school child, since malnutrition in early childhood is more likely to produce permanent ill effects.

The policy of distributing free milk has been developed after much careful investigation. It has been found that the issue of milk is the cheapest way of ameliorating the major dietary deficiencies of childhood, though it would appear from Miss Dantier's findings in Mauritius and from studies in other countries that there may be a case for using whole rather than skimmed milk. The reasoning which has led to the provision of milk for the school child seems equally valid for the provision of milk for the pre-school child. We are not familiar with all the administrative complications involved in making such arrangements in Mauritius. It would, therefore, be presumptuous of us to attempt to make detailed recommendations laying down exactly how an issue of milk should be provided for this age group. All we can do here is to consider the alternatives and offer a few general observations.

It seems to us a sound principle that the issue of milk should be associated with the post-natal and infant welfare services. There are three reasons which substantiate this principle. First, the issue of milk acts as an inducement in Mauritius and also (for example) in Ceylon for mothers to sacrifice the time and possibly the earnings involved in a visit to the social welfare centres. We regard such visits as particularly important as it is at these centres that advice on family planning could eventually be available. Secondly, it makes it possible for the health and development of the children to be kept under observation and for education in diet and other health measures to be provided. Thirdly, it becomes possible to issue extra milk or other supplements in cases of special need.

There are, however, difficulties in basing the service exclusively on the social welfare centres. The centres or their equivalent do not reach the whole of the population. It would be wrong for there to be no service at all in the more remote areas. Secondly, while a mother may be expected to bring an infant to the centre, it is putting her to a considerable strain to expect her to bring all her children under six at the same time. One child that needs to be carried is a sufficient burden for any mother and it is not easy to bring, in addition, a toddler to a centre which is at any distance from the home.

For these reasons, it would be impracticable to expect all children under six to attend weekly or monthly for inspection.

Nevertheless, we think it right that children should be inspected, as a condition of receiving the milk, perhaps once a month for the first six months of life, once a quarter till the age of two, and once a year from the age of two to six.

This does not, however, mean that the milk should, in all cases, be drawn from the place where the inspection takes place. Every primary school in Mauritius has facilities for the issue of milk. These schools are within walking distance of virtually every home in the island. Where the post-natal services are not conveniently located, the primary school might be the place from which milk is issued. In other cases, the post-natal centres could be used.

We assume that as at present some member of the family, possibly a child, will draw the family issue of milk or milk powder. The administration of such a scheme would be greatly eased by a system of national registration so that cards could be issued for each child. Control would thus be exercised to ensure that the right issue is made to each family.

We do not consider that it is always necessary for powdered milk to be issued ready mixed. We recognise that there are dangers of the milk being badly mixed or used after the powder has deteriorated, or, indeed, mixed with water which is not properly sterilised. All these risks, however, already exist in the feeding of children and we feel that they are more adequately dealt with by health education than by taking away responsibility from the mother. As regards the possibility of milk powder being sold when it is received, we think that this difficulty could in large part be overcome by special packaging and by requiring containers to be returned to the place of issue.

On the question of how much milk or milk powder might be issued to those under the age of six, we are advised that 10 grammes a day would make a useful addition to the diet of the child. Provision of dried skimmed milk for all children under the age of six, except those attending school, would cost Rs. 350,000 a year. There is, of course, still no guarantee that the milk or milk powder which is intended for the child will be actually consumed by the child. Moreover, what is intended to be a supplement to the diet may lead to the withdrawal of food which the child might otherwise have received. If this does occur, it does not necessarily follow that the objectives of the whole scheme are being frustrated. In families where there are a large number of children, the diet is insufficient not only for the children but for the mother and father as well. If the effect of the better provision for the children is indirectly to secure better nutrition for the father or mother, this is not necessarily a loss.

It is important that the consequences of any scheme of this kind should be observed continuously and intensively. There are plans for establishing a Nutrition Unit in Mauritius. One of the tasks of such a Unit should be to observe the nutritional effects on the whole family of a scheme of this kind.

While we have recommended a basic issue of 10 grammes a day for each child below school age, there are good reasons to justify a larger issue in cases where there are signs of malnutrition, and for a specified list of diseases such as tuberculosis. Such issues should be prescribed, after inspection, by a medical officer.

The recommendations which we have made for the pre-school child should also apply to the pregnant mother during the last six months of pregnancy. She should also be entitled to an issue of milk. And, indeed, where her health requires it in the opinion of the medical officer, an additional issue should be made available.

The school child

There remains the question of extended services for the school child. We have described earlier in this chapter the steps which have been taken to investigate the possibility of providing school meals. These studies showed that a fairly substantial meal was needed to make a real supplement to the child's diet. Such a scheme was eventually rejected on the grounds of cost. We consider that this question should be seriously re-examined, on the lines suggested by Miss Dantier. We recognise that there are considerable difficulties in Mauritius which are related to the different eating habits of ethnic groups and the different customs with regard to cooking. Moreover, the provision of kitchen facilities is known to be expensive. One possibility which seemed to us to require investigation was the issue of a cold meal, not necessarily prepared at the school, with a balanced nutritional content. Such a meal need not necessarily be provided for all children free of charge. There are various means of trying to secure that free school meals go to those who need them most. One possibility would be to make the issue free where there are three or more dependent children in the family; there might be some test of means, though this would certainly involve administrative complications and should not be adopted until other methods have been exhaustively considered. We consider, however, that these and other alternatives need investigation as we think it highly desirable that a scheme should be started to provide some form of school meal as a free issue to those children whose parents cannot afford to pay, and subject to payment in the case of those who can.

There is one further matter to which we wish to draw attention in this section of the Report. We have mentioned earlier the fact that there is a dietary loss associated with the widespread hookworm and roundworm infestation. The size of this loss is not known but it may be quite considerable. In the long run the solution to this problem lies in the provision and use of proper sanitary facilities at home and in the community. It will, however, take some years before this is achieved. Meanwhile, we feel that other action might be taken to reduce the incidence of this infestation. One possible step would be to insist that all children come to school wearing adequate protective shoes. In cases where parents cannot afford to purchase them, free shoes might well be provided. This would not seem to be very expensive. Rubber-soled canvas shoes can be obtained wholesale for about Rs. 30 a dozen pairs, either imported or locally manufactured. This seems a good opportunity for encouraging the development of a local industry, provided that the local product is of adequate quality.

We are well aware of the fact that the compulsory wearing of shoes at school will not immediately eradicate hookworm in school children. Indeed, children are less likely to acquire hookworm at school than in the neighbourhood of their homes, and even if they have to wear shoes at school, they will not always wear them for the whole of the day. Nevertheless, we consider that the practice of compelling children to wear shoes at school would be a useful educative measure. In the long run we look to a new generation of Mauritians who are used to wearing shoes and who develop the practice for all purposes. Moreover, a measure of this kind, if the reasons were fully explained to the parents, might of itself prove a powerful educative influence on the parents as well as the children. It would not be the first time that school children had been used to educate their parents.

Children of Social Security Beneficiaries

We have outlined above our recommendations to meet the needs of all children in Mauritius. They amount to a limited benefit in cash for the family with three or more children and provisions in kind for all children from birth until leaving school. We do not propose that any allowances should be added to the insurance benefits for the sick and unemployed in cases where there are dependent children. In the case of survivors, however, we feel there is a need for additional children's allowances. The argument that such allowances will encourage further births is inapplicable in these circumstances and we are particularly anxious to help widowed mothers as their economic and social status is at present so pathetically low. We therefore recommend that where survivors' benefit is payable, an allowance of Rs. 5 per month should be paid for each dependent child in excess of three.

Orphans' Benefit

We are anxious to secure that orphans are looked after in a normal home rather than in an institution of the type that we have seen in Mauritius (see Chapter 11). As in the case of the children of widows, we would think it wrong that the welfare of orphaned children should depend on the contribution record of a deceased parent. Orphans' benefit should, therefore, be non-contributory.

We recommend that a person having the guardianship of a child, both of whose parents are dead, should be entitled to receive a guardian's allowance of Rs. 5 per month and in addition an allowance for the child or children at the following rates:—

Child under 5 years of age	Rs. 7 per month
Child aged 5 but under 10	Rs. 10 per month
Child aged 10 to age 14	Rs. 13 per month

Before this special benefit is paid, the placing of the child should be approved by a properly qualified officer (a Children's Officer) who should be empowered to visit periodically to see that the children are being well cared for. These responsibilities for supervision should also be extended to the care of children in public and voluntary institutions (see Chapter 11).

We associate this particular proposal with a further recommendation that the Government should consider the introduction of legislation in the light of modern practice relating to children in need of care and protection. The task of a qualified children's officer, soon after appointment, would be to assess the extent of the problem and to advise on legislation and methods of treatment.

SUMMARY AND CONCLUSION

Our recommendations may be summarised as follows:—

(*a*) A benefit of Rs. 20 per month to be paid to a widow without dependent children for three months after the death of her husband.

(*b*) An allowance of Rs. 30 per month to be paid to a widow and Rs. 20 per month to a widower having the care of dependent children. In addition, an allowance of Rs. 5 per month to be paid for a fourth or subsequent child.

(*c*) An investigation to be made into the means and circumstances of widows aged 50-59 with a view to the extension of benefits for widows in this age group without dependent children.

(*d*) A marriage benefit of Rs. 50 to be paid for a girl who has borne no children, is over the age of 21 on civil marriage, and satisfies other conditions as specified.

(*e*) A maternity benefit of Rs. 20 per month for six weeks before and six weeks after confinement, to be paid to a woman over the age of 21, who has given birth to no child for 24 months, who has no more than three living children, and who has attended an ante-natal clinic, been informed of family planning facilities, and lodged her insurance card with the insurance office. The existing Labour Ordinance should be revised to relieve employers in the sugar industry of their obligation to pay maternity benefits. Maternity leave arrangements for Government employees should be amended in line with the conditions stipulated in this section.

(*f*) A "Family Benefit" of Rs. 15 per month to be paid in all cases where there are three dependent children under the age of 14 in one family, subject to the condition that the mother is aged over 21.

(*g*) An allowance of free milk to all pre-school children.

(*h*) School meals (possibly cold) if these are found to be practicable, free to children of poor families.

(*i*) Compulsory wearing of shoes by children at school, with a free issue in cases of need.

(*j*) Child allowances in the income tax system should be abolished forthwith for all children under the age of 11. For children above that age they should continue to be granted for a further period of five years and should then be abolished. Meanwhile, no family benefits should be paid to parents who, in the preceding year, were assessed to pay income tax and no further child allowances should be granted to parents who have already received allowances for three or more children.

(*k*) Guardians of orphans to receive an allowance of Rs. 5 per month and allowances for the orphans varying from Rs. 7 to Rs. 13 according to age.

(*l*) A qualified children's officer should be appointed to supervise the welfare of orphans in the care of guardians or placed in public and voluntary institutions.

(*m*) The law relating to children in need of care and protection should be reviewed in the light of modern practice.

All these benefits should be non-contributory and subject to the conditions specified in respect to age, size of family, interval between births, assessment for income tax, overlapping benefits and other requirements.

THE COST OF NON-CONTRIBUTORY BENEFITS

The estimated cost of the benefits we have recommended in this chapter is set out in Appendix F. In total, the gross cost in a full year of cash benefits amounts to Rs. 11,750,000. For benefits in kind, which are much more hazardous to cost, the total might be in the region of Rs. 850,000 for free milk to pre-school children and some free issues of shoes for school children. The cost of a school meals service would depend on the type of meals given and on the charges made to parents.

When the tax allowances for children are completely abolished, there should be a saving of Rs. 1,500,000 yearly (see Appendix C). Meanwhile, a substantial saving will be effected by the restrictions we recommend.

It is far more difficult to assess the less tangible forms of savings. A considerable fall in the birth-rate could bring much relief in the costs of education, the provision of schools and the training of teachers. The same may be said of the provision of housing, public health, sanitation and amenities of all kinds. Improved standards of health, the reduction of such chronic and disabling conditions as anaemia, hookworm, tuberculosis and intestinal disorders could greatly reduce the present demands for medical care, hospitals and dispensaries, expensive and often completely ineffective drugs and so forth. Finally, the development of fuller, healthier and more purposeful patterns of family life could make a combination towards averting the threatened rise in juvenile delinquency, in the incidence of abortion, and in the consumption of gandia, rum and other harmful addictions.

CHAPTER 8

A National Assistance Board

The recommendations we have made in earlier chapters for family benefits, for social insurance and for improvements in the provisions for those injured at work will, we hope, reduce substantially the rôle of the Public Assistance Department in the relief of distress. But many needs will still have to be met by the Department—emergency payments, regular assistance to those who have not satisfied the contribution conditions for social insurance benefits, supplementary aid to those whose needs are not wholly met by social insurance, and relief for those who fall outside all these new provisions.

We explained in some detail in Chapter 4 the administrative procedures of the Department and the means by which the claims of applicants are assessed. A scale of need is applied to a family unit living in the same household and the resources of the household are calculated and used to determine the amount of assistance which is granted. The earnings of members of the household are disregarded up to a maximum which varies according to the number of persons and the composition of the household. All earnings in excess of this maximum are deducted from the assistance which would otherwise be available.

In this chapter we submit the present regulations of the Department to critical examination and suggest new regulations in the light of our earlier recommendations. Finally, we present proposals for the organisation and administration of a new Public Board to undertake the reduced and revised responsibilities of the present Department.

NORMAL EARNINGS AND ACTUAL EARNINGS

The concept of "normal" earnings lies at the root of the present public assistance system. An individual is assumed to have a certain earning potential, which may vary according to his or her occupation, state of health and family responsibilities. Assistance payments are based on this assumed potential rather than on the actual amount of earnings in a given month. Thus, the Darlow Report stated that "an able-bodied woman with one child should not as a rule be granted relief", as it was—and still is—assumed that her potential or "normal" earnings would suffice to feed herself and her child.

Again, if a doctor certifies that the applicant is fit for "light work", the amount that could "normally" be earned from light work is taken into account in assessing his resources. We stated in Chapter 4 that light work is seldom available, either for men or women, especially in the rural areas of Mauritius. This view was expressed to us by some of the doctors responsible for issuing the certificates. Earnings from light work are largely an administrative fiction. Indeed, opinion seems to vary considerably both among Government medical officers and public assistance officials as to what exactly is meant by "light work".

A system which bases the amount of assistance payable on a notional level of earnings which may bear no relation to actual employment opportunities is bound to operate unfairly. The alternative is to take the actual earnings of the individual for a given period into account.

There is, however, one important advantage in using "normal" rather than actual earnings. In many cases it does not remove the incentive for the individual and his family to earn as much as possible by their own efforts. In theory, any earnings above the assumed "normal" figure should be taken into account; but in practice, "normal" earnings are assumed to remain constant month after month, and unless the applicant goes to the trouble of informing the public assistance officer of his actual earnings each month, no adjustment will be made. Similarly, the widow with one child who decides not to work will not be encouraged to do so by additional assistance. If actual earnings were deducted from the assistance payable, the incentive to earn—and in particular to earn the little extra each week—might be reduced or removed.

This is an important consideration in Mauritius, where there are many opportunities to earn small sums by working for a few hours. In Britain, the National Assistance Board disregards only a small amount (15 shillings) of the weekly earnings of able-bodied applicants. Above this limit, all earnings lead to corresponding reductions in the assistance payable. This is appropriate because, in a highly developed industrial economy, there is a clearer distinction between employment and unemployment. The choice is often between a week's work or none. It is therefore of less importance in Britain to preserve the incentive to earn a few shillings by working for short periods.

The circumstances of Mauritius, however, are very different. Typically, work is on a daily basis for both men and women and there are extensive sources of casual income. Partial maintenance by work is much more practicable in Mauritius than in Britain. It is therefore important to preserve the incentive to earn even a small amount of additional income. The solution to the problem of doing this while at the same time taking actual earnings into account lies in the system of "disregards".

DISREGARDS

This term is used in Britain to describe the amounts of income disregarded in calculating the assistance payable. In Mauritius these are known as "concessions" and their operation is described in Chapter 4. We shall use the word "disregards" both because it indicates clearly what their purpose is, and because it seems desirable to distinguish the "disregards" which we shall propose from the "concessions" now given.

Under the present system, a fixed amount of earnings is allowed before any deduction is made from the assistance. This amount is calculated by reference to the composition of the household. Earnings in excess of the total concessions so calculated are deducted in full. If this method were applied to a system based on actual rather than normal earnings, the incentive to earn up to the amount of concessions given would be fully preserved; but there would be no incentive at all to earn small sums above this amount. To take an example: if the assistance payable, ignoring earnings, amounted to Rs. 80 per month, and the concessions to Rs. 40, any earnings between Rs. 40 and Rs. 120 per month would result in a corresponding reduction in the assistance. There would therefore be no incentive to earn anything in excess of Rs. 40 unless earnings of significantly more than Rs. 120 could be achieved. Moreover, the range of income where it is beneficial to earn varies under the present system according to the number of dependants. Thus, it is very advantageous for there to be earners in a household with a very large dependent family. When the family is small, there is only an incentive to earn a very small amount. Indirectly, therefore, there is also an incentive to have large families; this is one effect we wish to remove.

The logic of the present system is that the basic scale of assistance plus the concessions is intended to be equivalent to subsistence needs. Thus, at least in theory, if the household has earners it can reach subsistence level. But this logic breaks down if there are no earners. The family then has to live below subsistence level. We do not therefore feel that there is a strong case for retaining the present system as a means of providing subsistence.

The solution we propose is a system of proportional disregards. Instead of the present fixed concessions, one-quarter of the earnings of the applicant and his wife would be deducted from the assistance. We would have preferred to recommend that one-half of the applicant's earnings should be disregarded. This, however, would have meant that able-bodied men earning more than the minimum wage for a labourer could qualify for assistance. It is no part of the functions of public assistance to supplement the wages of able-bodied men in full-time employment. We should therefore have been driven to recommend that this generous scale of disregards should operate only up to a given level above which all earnings would be deducted in full. But this would leave unsolved the original problem of preserving incentives. We therefore came to the conclusion that the proportion of an able-bodied applicant's earnings to be disregarded must be limited to one-quarter, with certain exceptions.

In the case of sick applicants the question of preserving incentives to earn does not arise. On the contrary, if the applicant is genuinely sick, it is important that he should not be encouraged to take on work which might delay his recovery. In such cases, therefore, there should be no disregards, and of course no work test would be applied. In certain other cases, where the applicant's circumstances are such that he or she cannot be expected to manage unaided on minimum earnings, the proportion disregarded should be increased to one-half. This increase should be given to wives with sick husbands, and to women, whether widowed or separated, and widowers with the care of children under the age of 14.

Bus fares incurred in going to and from work should be deducted from earnings before calculating the proportion to be disregarded. Social insurance and pension scheme contributions should also be deducted. Insurance benefits and pensions (public and private) should not be regarded as earnings and should be wholly deducted from the assistance payable.

THE ASCERTAINMENT OF EARNINGS

To reform the procedure and to use actual earnings instead of a notional figure, we recommend that instead of assistance being paid to cover a period of a month without it being clear whether it is for the past month or the ensuing month, it should in future be based on a specific completed period—if possible, a week or a fortnight. A proportion of the actual earnings during that period would be deducted from the assistance payable.

We mentioned in Chapter 5 that one reason which led us to recommend a system of social insurance was that it would then be easier to establish whether an applicant was working or not and to find out actual as distinct from normal earnings. This advantage, however, would apply only to employment under a contract of service. The ascertainment of earnings from self-employment and casual occupations such as laundry work and hawking would continue to present difficult problems for the Public Assistance Department. These difficulties of course obtain in the public assistance systems of other countries as well as Mauritius.

At present, the Department ascertains the "normal" earnings of applicants and their families by the best means at its disposal. In addition to declarations by the applicant, enquiries are made of neighbours and employers and information may be provided by members of Public Assistance Advisory Committees. The Outdoor Relief Committee hoped that assistance officers would be able to rely on "public-spirited persons to give information about the means of applicants and recipients". In practice, however, we have gained the impression that the general public is not anxious to co-operate with the Department in these matters. We were told that it is not infrequent for information about undeclared earnings to reach the ears of public assistance officers in cases where neighbours have quarrelled with applicants. Understandably, reporting to the Public Assistance Department is not regarded as an act of public duty but rather as an act of spite.

No formal penalty is laid down in the existing legislation for the punishment of those who make false declarations of earnings. Public assistance can be withdrawn or refused to any person who has made a false statement or refused to give information regarding his means. This does not often occur, and relief is seldom refused on such grounds for more than one or two months. If relief has been forfeited in this way and the applicant is destitute, admission to an infirmary is offered. The present situation can be summarised without great exaggeration as a battle of wits between the general public and the Public Assistance Department. Social attitudes do not condemn attempts to deceive the public assistance officers and officers are, in their turn, tempted to use somewhat unscrupulous methods of obtaining information. We do not think that the total result encourages respect for Government, fairness to applicants or high ethical standards by either party. We recommend, therefore, that in future public assistance officers should only attempt to ascertain earnings from applicants themselves and from their employers. The applicant would be required to make and sign a declaration of his earnings and the earnings of his or her household (defined by regulations). Severe penalties for false declarations should be written into the Ordinance. These and other changes we recommend may go some way towards building up public confidence in the system.

THE WORK TEST

In the past it has seemed impossible to grant assistance to unemployed men and women because it has not been possible to test their willingness to work. The introduction of a social insurance scheme with an effective Employment Service will make it possible to apply a test of willingness to work not only to those eligible for unemployment benefit but also to able-bodied public assistance applicants who, although claiming to be unemployed, are ineligible for such benefit. Since no such test would be applied to sick applicants, Government medical officers would have to decide whether an applicant's condition required him or her not to work. We have stated above that the whole of a sick person's earnings would be deducted from the assistance payable to him. It follows that the category "fit for light work" should be abolished. Indeed, we suspect that this category is frequently used by the over-pressed medical officer in cases when he is not really sure whether there is or is not a case for certifying that the applicant is sick.

No clear-cut principles can be applied to the other categories of persons applying for public assistance. The extent to which family responsibilities make it impossible for some people to work differs from one community to another. The separated or deserted wife, the unmarried mother and the widow may be regarded as unable to work if they have very young infants to care for. But many married women go to work in Mauritius despite their responsibility for young children and criteria developed for other women with children must be largely in line with the generally accepted habits and customs of the community. When, however, available work is limited, as is the case in the inter-crop season and may be increasingly the case in years to come, we suggest (as already outlined in Chapter 5) that available work should be offered first to those with more limited family duties and those who are younger. We therefore recommend the following order of priority in applying the work test for assistance cases:—

(a) able-bodied men aged 14-55 with and without dependent children (self-employed as well as those normally under a contract of service) should be singled out first: that is to say, all available work in the district should first be offered to this group;

(b) able-bodied women aged 14-55 with no dependent children;

(c) wives aged under 55 of able-bodied men with dependent children;

(d) all men and women over the age of 55 excluding the following groups;

(e) wives of sick and disabled husbands with dependent children;

(f) widows with dependent children;

(g) the position of deserted wives with dependent children and unmarried mothers will have to be dealt with by public assistance officers under their discretionary powers;

(h) no work test should be applied to sick and severely disabled persons, and to men and women over the age of 65.

Those who are involuntarily unemployed (including the partially disabled) should receive assistance based on the number of days that the Employment Service has been unable to find work for them.

LIABLE RELATIVES

Under the existing system, the resources and earnings of husband and wife are aggregated for the purpose of assessing their rights to public assistance. Unmarried children living in the same household as their parents are expected to contribute part of their earnings to their parents' maintenance, and a deduction of up to Rs. 10 or Rs. 15 can be made from the assistance payable to take account of this contribution. The method of treating other adults is laid down by the Darlow Report as follows: "adults other than mother, father or children living in the same household should, however, be treated as recipients living separately in order to keep them within a related group. Otherwise these adults, if penalised by a lower scale rate, would leave the group".

We accept the argument for the exclusion of relatives other than children. In the case of unmarried children's earnings we recommend that a more precise formula be substituted for the present somewhat arbitrary arrangement. The first Rs. 30 a month of each child's earnings and one-half of the remainder should be disregarded. The rest should be deducted from the assistance. We consider that this arrangement should be sufficiently generous to prevent earning children from leaving the household in order to increase the assistance payable to their parents.

Married children should not normally be treated as living in the same household as their parents. Nor should their earnings be taken into account in assessing the assistance payable to the parents. We would, however, make an exception in the case of widowed, divorced or separated children living with their parents. These children should be treated as unmarried.

We consider that the provision of the Public Assistance Ordinance which makes various relatives of the applicant liable to assist him, whether or not living in the same household, should be repealed, since it is very seldom enforced and could be a source of hardship to the applicant. Any contributions made voluntarily by such relatives or from other sources should be ignored if they do not exceed Rs. 10 a month for each member of the household. One-half of any contributions in excess of this sum should be deducted.

SCALES OF PUBLIC ASSISTANCE

Having made our recommendations on the questions of the ascertainment and treatment of earnings, we come next to consider the level of public assistance scales. We have mentioned earlier that the scales laid down by the Darlow Committee were fixed by reference to a calculation of minimum needs, substantially reduced to allow for undisclosed resources. We are unable to endorse the method of calculating the cost of maintenance used by that Committee, not only because the enquiry covered too few households but also because it was unrealistic to use as the basis for new assistance scales the actual expenditure of persons attempting to live on earlier assistance scales. Information is now available from which calculations of subsistence could be made which would not be open to these objections. We do not think, however, that this is the most useful starting point, though we would urge the need for data to be collected on standards of living as part of Government planning in general.

The problem of deductions for earnings and other matters which we have discussed are so intimately related to current wage levels that we are forced to the conclusion that new scales should be fixed in relation to these levels. We see no alternative to this conclusion despite the fact that, over the year as a whole, some wages paid are inadequate for the maintenance of a small family and few manual workers earn enough to support the large families which are typical of Mauritius. The value of the social insurance benefits which we recommend in this Report are also relevant to the problem of determining new scales of public assistance. While we hope that these benefits will lead to a considerable reduction in applications for public assistance we recognise that they will not by any means meet all cases of need. There will be many families with inadequate contribution records who will be ineligible for insurance benefits and many others with exceptional circumstances which will need consideration case by case. But, in general, we hope that the automatic granting of insurance benefits and the absence of enquiries about means will make many families prefer to manage on their benefit even though they might gain a few more rupees by applying to the Public Assistance Department for a supplementary grant.

We have gained the impression that the present scales of public assistance are generally regarded as inadequate. This was the view expressed to us by some public assistance officers and by many sections of public opinion. An applicant who cannot earn and receives no assistance from relatives has to live considerably below subsistence level, unless he is rescued by charity or extensive loan facilities. But although the basic scales are low, some recipients of public assistance are no worse off than many other people in Mauritius. This is particularly true of recipients with large families.

In many ways, this is the crux of the problem: how to provide some measure of subsistence in and through public assistance and social insurance without endangering incentives to work for wages which may be inadequate and, furthermore, how to do so without giving direct encouragement (as the present system does) to the procreation of large families. We are thus led to consider two further and related questions; the payment for rents and provision for children under public assistance.

At present, half the actual rent is allowed (up to a maximum of Rs. 12) as an addition to the basic assistance scale. In cases of prolonged illness the allowance can be increased to 75% of the rent. Rents vary widely over the island. A considerable proportion of the population are owner-occupiers, but the majority pay rent. We were told that in the rural areas a reasonable rent for a labourer with a wife and three children to pay would be between Rs. 8 and Rs. 15 a month. In the main built-up areas, particularly in Curepipe and Port Louis, a rent of Rs. 20 (and sometimes much more) may be the minimum cost of housing a family at a far from adequate standard. Thus, the system of providing half the actual rent leaves serious inequalities between different parts of the island. Applicants in rural areas find it easier to subsist on public assistance than applicants in the expensive urban areas. The only equitable solution to this problem is to pay the actual rent up to a maximum fixed for different areas.

The public assistance officer should have discretion to refuse payment if he considers the rent wholly unreasonable and to pay more than the new maxima in exceptional cases.

The most difficult problem which needs to be settled before we can make recommendations about the level of assistance scales concerns children's allowances. It constitutes the basic dilemma of public assistance in Mauritius today. If the scales are to include allowances for children, then the amount of aid for adults must be kept very low to prevent it being too frequently the case that public assistance could, but for the "wage stop", provide a better standard of living than normal wages. If, therefore, the scales for adults are to be improved, there can be no separate allowances for children.

The family benefit which we have proposed as a comprehensive measure will, we believe, go a long way in helping many families receiving public assistance. Indeed, this was one of the principal reasons which led us to recommend it. We recognise, however, that the automatic granting of a family benefit of Rs. 15 a month in all cases of three or more dependent children under the age of 14 will not meet the exceptional needs of very large families. These must be left to the discretionary powers of the Public Assistance Commissioner himself with the intention that they should be used only in exceptional circumstances. No formal system of public assistance and social insurance can solve—or should be expected to solve—all the problems of poverty caused by low wages, underemployment and large families.

With the introduction of a family benefit on these lines we therefore recommend the abolition of the present system of children's allowances under public assistance.

To this recommendation we make one exception; that is the case of one parent still responsible for the upbringing of a large family. The argument about encouraging further births is hardly applicable when the marriage is already broken. Thus, we recommend that widows and widowers who have not formed a new union should have children's allowances added to their scale for the fourth, fifth, sixth and seventh children (and for the first and second children if there are less than three) at the rate of Rs. 5 per child per month. These additions should also be made to the scales of assistance for deserted, separated or divorced wives and unmarried mothers at the discretion of the public assistance officer.

As we have said, it is in the present circumstances of the Mauritian economy impossible to reconcile completely a policy of meeting need with the two objectives of limiting parenthood and encouraging the incentive to work. Our recommendations therefore represent a compromise between conflicting principles and aims. But if all our earlier recommendations are accepted, we find it possible to recommend a modest increase in the scales of public assistance for adults. Tentatively, we suggest that the scale for the first adult (the husband, the single person or the widowed mother) might be Rs. 20 a month with Rs. 17 each for other adults and Rs. 13 for any unmarried children of working age. Widowed, divorced or separated children should be scaled as adults and grandchildren as children. By the strict limits we have imposed in our provisions for dependent children and by our area maxima for rents, we have made it unnecessary to specify any principle of a "wage stop". In suggesting these increased scales we have taken account of the current wage levels for the lowest paid workers. We suggest that there should be an additional allowance of Rs. 15 per month in all cases of tuberculosis irrespective of age.

So far we have said nothing about the discretionary allowances. Our remarks have been solely confined to the basic needs of the great majority of applicants. We recognise, however, that discretionary allowances to meet exceptional needs are essential to the effective working of any system of public assistance. We suggest, however, that the addition of Rs. 5 for sickness and the deduction for rural amenities should be abolished.

THE ADMINISTRATION OF PUBLIC ASSISTANCE

The remaining comments we wish to make about public assistance concern organisation and administration. We have mentioned earlier the administrative procedure for granting benefit. Each case is dealt with twice by the local officer on his own account, and once more when he brings it before the Public Assistance Committee, twice by the district officer and once by the adjudicating officer in Port Louis. The applicant is interviewed on three or four separate occasions. This procedure seems to us cumbrous, lengthy and expensive. It is also unnecessarily troublesome for the applicant and unlikely to build up the self-confidence and sense of responsibility of the local officers.

We gather that the present system has developed as a result of strong pressures of opinion by the general public and from members of the Legislative Council on the Public Assistance Department. The administrative system has become highly centralised, partly to standardise procedures all over the island, and partly as an attempt to prevent corruption by extensive cross-checking by officials of other officials' work. It seems to us, however, doubtful if this system is very effective either at checking on junior officials or at providing the best possible service to the applicant. Adjudicators can only form their decisions on the basis of the facts presented to them. If relevant facts are omitted or if the information is incorrect, the adjudicator can seldom do more than agree with decisions made by more junior officers.

The value of the Public Assistance Advisory Committee varies between different areas. With so many cases before it, the Committee obviously cannot devote much time to each. The only value of every case coming before the Committee lies in the possibility that some member will know more about the earnings of the applicant than he or she has in fact disclosed. If in the future it becomes feasible to verify actual earnings over a much wider field of applications, the arguments for placing every case before the Committee will become much less strong.

The key to the whole administrative system is inevitably the quality of the local officer. It is the officer's responsibility to collect all the relevant facts. These officers must be carefully selected and systematically trained. We were, therefore, very disturbed to learn that there has been no organised training provided in recent years, owing to shortage of staff available to carry out the work as planned. We feel that the whole future of the Public Assistance Department depends on proper training, adequate staffing and good selection. We do not suggest elaborate theoretical courses carried out in Port Louis. What we consider most important of all is for there to be a training officer who should be responsible both for the induction of new entrants and for refresher courses for existing staff. Training should involve instruction in Port Louis and supervised practice all over the island. Officers in training should be attached to experienced and skilled district officers and field officers for short periods and required to make detailed reports on their experiences which they can discuss individually and in groups with the training officer. It might prove of value to bring over to Mauritius on a short assignment an experienced officer from the National Assistance Board in London so that the new regulations of the Department can be introduced after new training, and with a new sense of purpose in the discharge of important public duties.

If local officers were more carefully selected and better trained, it would be possible to give them greater responsibility. This would go far to raise the confidence of the Department. Thus, we feel that if the district officer is satisfied, and if the applicant does not wish to appeal, it should be possible to settle a case at the district level without any reference to the Public Assistance Advisory Committee or Port Louis.

The first step should be for the district officer to notify the applicant of his decision. It would still, however, be possible for the district officer or the applicant to have the case raised before the Public Assistance Advisory Committee. If the applicant is dissatisfied, this would be his first court of appeal. If the officer wanted special help or advice from the Committee, then again he could raise the case with the Committee before making his decision. If either the district officer or the applicant is dissatisfied with the decision of the Committee, there should be a further appeal to an adjudicating officer in Port Louis. The applicant should have the right to attend all appeal hearings.

This does not mean that there should be no supervision of

district officers by the Commissioner or his adjudicating officers. We would prefer the headquarters' staff, in addition to dealing with cases of appeal, to go out into the field unannounced, visit district officers and discuss recent decisions with the officer concerned. We feel that this close contact between the adjudicating officer and the district officer in the latter's own office would have a beneficial effect on all concerned. It would make it possible to standardise practice throughout the island and it would assist the headquarters' staff to keep in touch with problems which are arising in the field.

What is needed most of all is to build up the confidence of the officers of the Department. It seems to us that this can only be achieved if they are trusted and given responsibility. The same is true of both the district officer and the officers working under him.

We hope that by the new procedure it will be possible to deal with claims more swiftly than in the past. It would also expedite payments if the system of the monthly pay day were abandoned. There are two further reasons for this recommendation. First, we regard it as humiliating for the applicant to have to queue in the open for long periods while he or she is waiting to receive benefits. Secondly, we suspect that in many cases payment could be made as effectively and at lower real administrative cost through the Post Office. We have not had the time to investigate closely this last aspect. We have been told, however, that the flow of work in Post Offices is uneven. There are many periods of the day when the staff is under-employed. This period of staff-time could be utilised in the cashing of public assistance vouchers. Payments of public assistance are generally made through the Post Office in Britain and we see no reason why this system should not operate in Mauritius—at least in urban areas. We understand that a start is being made by arranging for old age pensions to be paid through the Post Office.

If payments could generally be made in this way, it might be possible to arrange for applicants to be paid weekly or fortnightly rather than monthly as at present. The working family of Mauritius normally budgets on a weekly basis. This practice should be reflected, wherever possible, in the operation of public assistance.

THE CASE FOR A NATIONAL ASSISTANCE BOARD

Up to this point, we have been concerned with the conditions upon which assistance should be granted and the organisation of the Department at the lower and local levels. We now turn to the question of the future administration of assistance at the centre.

We have said earlier that we want to create confidence in the public mind and among representatives of the people in the administration of assistance, and we also want to raise the confidence of public assistance officers in themselves as trusted public servants. The key to establishing this confidence is the provision of a service of such a standard that criticism is clearly unwarranted. Our many recommendations are intended to help to secure this. But it cannot be achieved unless the Department is given some respite from the pressure which is exerted upon it by members of the Legislative Council at all levels of administration. No officer can be expected to perform his job impartially if he has to work under the continuous scrutiny of the local M.L.C. No Commissioner can run a department if the volume of complaints channelled either through the legislature or through the personal intervention of leading citizens is so great that he is left with no time to give to wider questions of policy.

We are not saying that injustice or inefficiency should be tolerated or that relevant facts should not be brought to light which the applicant failed to disclose in the first place. What we want to prevent, to put it bluntly, is political pressure being exercised to secure for a constituent more than he or she is strictly entitled to under the regulations. We are not suggesting that much of the pressure applied to the Department has been of this character. M.L.C.'s have a legitimate right, indeed a duty, to see that their constituents receive what they are entitled to and to represent them when they themselves believe that they have been unfairly treated. What is wrong is for an M.L.C. to support a constituent in asking for more than he himself knows the constituent is entitled to under the regulations. The proper course, in such circumstances, is to raise in the Legislative Council the whole question of the regulations and suggest amendments which will apply to all applicants.

We appreciate that one purpose of the pressure put upon the Department has been to secure an enquiry such as we have undertaken. We hope that now the enquiry is completed, M.L.C.'s will allow the Department time to show the advantages of applying the new regulations, and time to allow new administrative procedures to take shape.

We think it would help if the day-to-day administrative work of the Department were largely removed from the political arena in so far as it is possible to do so. We recommend, therefore, that a National Assistance Board should be established, and that, as in Britain, it should not be possible to put to the relevant Minister detailed questions dealing with individual applicants. Such questions should be referred directly to the Board itself and its regular tribunal for appeals. The Minister of Labour and Social Security would remain answerable to the Legislative Council on questions concerning the *general policy* of the Board and its administrative development.

The Board would be appointed by the Governor-in-Council and would consist of three persons, one of whom should be a woman. The success of the Board will, however, largely depend on the status of the chairman. We hope that this post would be accepted by a distinguished lawyer who is highly respected by all sections of the population.

Apart from the proposals made here for administrative reforms, we now summarise our recommendations concerning the system itself:—

1. The assessment of all earnings by applicants and relatives should be based on actual earnings during the preceding two weeks. Re-assessments, where necessary, should be made fortnightly.

2. Payments should, if at all possible, be made weekly (or at least fortnightly). We hope that arrangements can be made, especially for long-term cases (widows with dependent children, the disabled, chronically sick, and elderly people), for assistance to be paid through the agency of the Post Offices.

3. We consider that so far as individual applicants for assistance are concerned, the severity of the work test should be applied in the following order:—

(*a*) able-bodied men aged 14-55 with and without dependent children (self-employed as well as those normally under a contract of service) should be singled out first; that is to say, all available work in the district should first be offered to this group;

(*b*) able-bodied women aged 14-55 with no dependent children;

(*c*) wives aged under 55 of able-bodied men with dependent children;

(*d*) all men and women over the age of 55 excluding the following groups;

(*e*) wives of sick and disabled husbands with dependent children;

(*f*) widows with dependent children;

(*g*) the position of deserted wives with dependent children and unmarried mothers will have to be dealt with by public assistance officers under their discretionary powers;

(*h*) no work test should be applied to sick and severely disabled persons, and to men and women over the age of 65.

4. The rules concerning liable relatives should be amended to

embrace only liability towards husbands, wives, dependent children up to the age of 14 (but including unmarried and handicapped children above that age) and parents of unmarried children.

5. Applicants for assistance, other than married couples where the husband is sick and single applicants with the care of children under the age of 14, should be entitled to retain one-quarter of their earnings which should be disregarded when public assistance is granted. Married couples where the husband is sick and single applicants with the care of children under the age of 14 should be entitled to retain one-half of their earnings. Persons with certificates of sickness should be forbidden to work. Unmarried earning children should retain the first Rs. 30 of earnings a month and one-half of the remainder.

6. Pensions and social insurance benefits should be deducted from the assistance payable.

7. One-half of any contributions from relatives and other sources in excess of Rs. 10 a month should be deducted from the assistance payable.

8. Penalties should be imposed on employees, employers and the self-employed for failure to report earnings correctly. The attempt to get neighbours to voluntarily "inform" on earnings should be abandoned.

9. The system of rent allowances should be revised so as to pay the actual rent up to maxima fixed for different urban and rural areas.

10. Medical certification and public assistance practices should no longer employ the category of "light work".

11. In the calculation of need, no allowance should be made for dependent children where the household includes both parents. In other cases, a benefit of Rs. 5 per month should be paid for the fourth, fifth, sixth and seventh children, and for the first and second where there are less than three children.

12. The scales of public assistance should be increased as follows:

	Rs. a month
First adult	20
Other adults	17
Unmarried children of working age	13

13. The "wage stop" should be abolished.

14. No public assistance grants of whatever nature should be made in cases where the net grant has a value of less than Rs. 2 a month.

CHAPTER 9

The Fundamental Problems of Medical Care

There are three separate systems of providing "free" medical services in Mauritius. The first and largest, the Government Medical Service, has evolved from the provision of medical care to paupers under the Poor Law. The second consists of the medical services which are provided by sugar estates for their employees as required by the Labour Ordinance. The third and most recent consists of the maternity and child welfare services provided partly by the Government and partly by a voluntary body—the Maternity and Child Welfare Society. In this section, we sketch the history of each of these three systems of medical care.

THE HISTORICAL BACKGROUND

The Government Medical Service

In the nineteenth century, both dispensaries and hospitals were provided by the Poor Law Medical Service. In 1871, there were about 400 patients in the Civil Hospital and the six Poor Law Hospitals.*

By 1901 there were about a thousand patients in the general hospitals, about 400 in a Lunatic Asylum and 50 in a Leper Asylum. The general hospital beds were concentrated at the Civil Hospital in Port Louis and the Barkly Hospital in Plaines Wilhems. The other five Poor Law Hospitals had only 362 patients between them.† The hospitals beds were distributed in this way although as early as 1859 a committee of enquiry had recommended that there should be large district hospitals for serious cases, paid for by an additional tax.‡

According to evidence by the Acting Head of the Medical and Health Department to the 1909 Royal Commission, none of the hospital buildings in Mauritius had been originally constructed for the purpose.§ Some of them were considerably overcrowded. The Civil Hospital had 220 beds but an average of 240-250 patients.‖

---
* *Census of Mauritius and its Dependencies*, 1871, Part I, p. 23.
† *Census of Mauritius and its Dependencies*. 1901, p. 165.
‡ *Report of the Royal Commission on the Treatment of Immigrants in Mauritius*, Cmd. 1115, 1875, p. 356.
§ *Mauritius Royal Commission*, 1909, Minutes of Evidence, Cmd. 5186, 1910, p. 348.
‖ *Ibid.*, p. 347.

At Pamplemousses the hospital had 30 beds with usually 35-40 patients.* It was difficult to get suitable nurses. By 1909, the Government had been induced to grant a number of special scholarships for girls to take up nursing.† Only about 4% or 5% of the hospital patients paid for their maintenance.‡ The charges levied were Rs. 2 a day for first-class patients, Rs. 1 for second-class patients and 50c. for labourers and servants under contract and engagement.§

When the hospitals were inspected in 1921 by Dr. Balfour, the Director-in-Chief of the Wellcome Bureau of Scientific Research, he had much to say about their deficiencies. He complained of the absence of ambulances, laundries, incinerators, disinfecting apparatus, poison cupboards, lavatories, and temperature charts. He found that the facilities for isolation were inadequate and that the medical staff was insufficient and that some of them did not conduct their treatment on scientific lines. He summarised the position as follows: "In a new country one expects to find rough and ready conditions and many deficiencies but, in an old colony like Mauritius, it is distressing to find so much that is faulty and out-of-date". ||

In 1931, the Report of the Commission on the Financial Situation of Mauritius drew attention to the inadequate nursing staff in the hospitals. "There can be no doubt that the nursing staff both in the larger hospitals and in the country hospitals is far smaller than is desirable in the interests of the patients, even taking into consideration the fact that owing to social conditions in Mauritius some of what are the normal duties of nurses are placed upon the servants. . . . The total number at present employed is only 50 for all other institutions than the Mental Hospital."¶

By the Second World War, there were still only eight hospitals with about 1,100 beds.** The problem of over-crowding remained. "With the exception of certain district hospitals . . . over-crowding in wards is general . . . two children not infrequently occupy one bed"; or two beds were put together to hold three patients.††

Dispensaries had been opened in many parts of the island as outposts of the hospital service. They served as centres for a rudimentary general practitioner service. Some of them had beds where patients could be cared for until they could be removed to the

---

* *Mauritius Royal Commission*, 1909, Minutes of Evidence, Cmd. 5186, 1910, p. 345.
† *Ibid.*, p. 473.
‡ *Ibid.*, p. 347.
§ *Ibid.*, p. 399.
|| Balfour, A., *Report on Medical Matters in Mauritius*, 1921, p. 6.
¶ *Report of Commission on the Financial Situation of Mauritius*, Cmd. 4034, 1932, pp. 53-4.
** Rankine, A., *Report on Health Conditions in Mauritius*, 1944, p. 11.
†† *Ibid.*, p.12.

nearest hospital.* In Port Louis, the medical officer went out to visit paupers in their own homes.† The medical service was also responsible for the administration of poor relief.‡ This last function was wasteful of medical man-power. The Royal Commission of 1909 remarked that "the services of well-paid medical men are largely occupied with the performance of clerical and other duties which could be carried out as well by officers without professional qualifications, while the professional officers themselves are so tied down by laws and regulations that their real usefulness is largely impaired".§ Thus the Poor Law medical officers at the dispensaries provided not only medical care, but food. The dispensary was "a kind of soup-kitchen".

In his survey of the medical services in 1921, Dr. Balfour had much to say about the dispensaries. He found "dirty ointment pots, instruments wrongly stored, untidy cupboards and slip-shod entries in the books".‖ He also found what he called "abuse". "Many persons frequent the dispensaries who are quite able to afford the services of a medical practitioner. I understand, also, that the Dispensers are accustomed to prescribe, a custom which cannot be too strongly condemned, although, under existing conditions, it is perhaps to some extent unavoidable. . . . Dispensary practice in Mauritius is inefficient chiefly because the cases applying for medical relief cannot be followed up at their own homes. . . . It is, in my opinion, essential, in a place like Mauritius, that dispensary cases should be followed up and treated properly in their own homes."¶

In 1931, the Report of the Commission on the Financial Situation approved the dispensary system. "The qualifications of a country Dispenser are low and it cannot be expected that his medical work should be very effective, but we consider that most of these dispensaries have a real use which justifies their approximate annual cost of Rs. 30,000. In the first place they serve as consulting rooms for the Government Medical Officers in charge of the country hospitals, who visit them at fixed times during the week; this is an excellent device for giving direct medical relief to the poorer classes. The Dispenser is at least able to ascertain the more serious cases of illness and to bring these cases to the notice of the doctor. Secondly, the Dispenser acts as a local chemist, who is able to provide simple remedies and to make up simple prescriptions on the doctor's orders; it must be remembered

---

* *Mauritius Royal Commission*, 1909, Minutes of Evidence, Cmd. 5186, 1910, p. 345.
† *Ibid.*, p. 344.
‡ See Chapter 4.
§ *Report of Mauritius Royal Commission*, 1909, Cmd. 5185, 1910, p. 40.
‖ Balfour, A., *op. cit.*, p. 12.
¶ *Ibid.*, p. 11.

that in the country districts there are no chemists' shops, and though distances are small there are gaps sufficiently large to justify the provision of a Government chemist for the area."*

By the Second World War, there were 39 dispensaries scattered over the island. The dispensaries and the eight Government hospitals constituted the personal health services provided by the Government. Not until after the Second World War were school health services developed or any specific provision made by the Government for maternity and child welfare.

The Estate Medical Services

Under Ordinance No. 6 of 1845, every sugar estate with 40 or more labourers was required to have a hospital. This Ordinance was largely ignored by the planters, and in 1865 a new Ordinance was enacted, reducing the number of labourers for whom a hospital must be provided to 30.† The Royal Commission of 1875 found little improvement, such observance as there was being to the letter rather than the spirit of the law. It was found that the "hospitals" were being used for a guano store, a room for new-mown oats, a tool-house, a "manufactory of vacoa bags", a stable for mules or a dog-kennel.‡ They lacked sheets, blankets, beds, chamber utensils, bathrooms, and latrines. Where there were patients, they were not properly fed.§ The people employed as hospital attendants were "unable to read or write". They were "labourers without any qualifications". ‖

The planters said that the labourers refused to occupy the hospitals when they were sick. They preferred to be treated in their own huts and refused to take the medicines prescribed by the doctors. Some planters concluded that there was "no necessity to keep an hospital on a proper footing for the labourers, when they cannot force them to go there".¶ Accordingly, the 1865 Ordinance authorised employers to compel sick labourers to enter the hospitals.** Some employers, however, forced labourers who were not sick to be illegally detained in hospital. This led to a circular being issued stating that "it had been brought to the notice of the Governor that some planters had used their hospitals as prisons".††

Doctors did not visit the hospitals as often as the law required;

---

* *Report of Commission on the Financial Situation of Mauritius*, Cmd. 4034, 1932, p. 58.
† *Report of Royal Commission on the Treatment of Immigrants in Mauritius*, Cmd. 1115, 1875, p. 361.
‡ *Ibid.*, pp. 369-370.
§ *Ibid.*, p. 364.
‖ *Ibid.*, p. 368.
¶ *Ibid.*, p. 355.
** *Ibid.*, p. 361.
†† *Ibid.*, p. 356.

in some cases a period of months passed without a single visit.*
Planters did not pay the doctors the remuneration required by law,†
and sacked them if they made complaints about the standard of the
facilities provided.‡

After the revelations of the Royal Commission of 1875, the estate
hospitals were gradually improved. Dr. Balfour, who visited them in
1921, summed up the position as follows: "Some were good, some
bad, some indifferent. One thing they all possessed in common, a
great lack of comfort".§ Dr. Balfour thought that before long the
sugar estate hospitals would cease to exist, "in which case Government will be faced with the necessity of erecting several large
hospitals in the Districts". ‖

By the outbreak of the Second World War, employers with 20 or
more labourers living on the estate were required to maintain a
hospital. In 1938 there were 40 hospitals under the care of 12 doctors.
According to the Annual Report of the Labour Department for 1938,
"they were well maintained and equipped, but it is felt that if a
system of group hospitals to serve three or four estates could be
arranged, it would lead to greater efficiency and economy".¶ By 1945
the Labour Department was able to report that "several neighbouring
estates have agreed to combine to set up a group hospital and to
engage two doctors, one of whom is to treat the sick and the other is
to watch over the health of the camp-dwellers".** In 1939, the 13 estate
doctors were paid the total sum of Rs. 74,275. The total expenditure
by estates on the provision of medical facilities was then about
Rs. 380,000.††

An independent inspection of the estate hospitals was undertaken
by Dr. Rankine in 1944. "The hospitals vary greatly both in equipment and in the advantage taken of them, some being well equipped
and furnished whilst others provide the bare necessities and show
little evidence of care or attention. The latter are seldom used by the
labourers, but the former are well patronized and I have been told by
more than one manager that the withdrawal of the hospital facilities
provided by the estate would be immediately followed by a loss of
labour", because the labourer regarded hospital treatment as a
perquisite and his relatives could easily visit him in the hospital.‡‡

---

* *Report of Royal Commission on the Treatment of Immigrants in Mauritius*, Cmd. 1115, 1875, p. 374.
† *Ibid.*, p. 375. ‡ *Ibid.*, p. 392.
§ Balfour, A., *Report on Sanitary Matters in the Districts of Grand Port and Savanne*, 1921, p. 6.
‖ Balfour, A., *Report on Medical Matters in Mauritius*, 1921, p. 8.
¶ *Annual Report of the Labour Department*, 1938, p. 15.
** *Annual Report of the Labour Department*, 1945, p. 3.
†† *Majority Report of the Social Insurance Committee*, 1941 (unpublished).
‡‡ Rankine, A., *op. cit.*, p. 43.

Maternity and Child Welfare

While the Government Medical Service and the estate medical services owe their origin mainly to legislation, the development of the child welfare and maternity services was due to private initiative. In 1913, the Governor called attention to the heavy infant mortality in Mauritius, and in 1916, Dr. E. L. de Chazal gave Rs. 100,000 to the Government as a fund to be used for the training of midwives and nurses, the establishment of a maternity ward and a ward for the treatment of infantile complaints. Part of the fund was used to open a crêche in Port Louis but this was closed down a few years later because of high mortality. Midwives were trained at the Civil Hospital and employed on sugar estates with their salaries paid jointly by the fund and by the estate. A number of the estates withdrew their contribution to midwives after the passing of the Labour Ordinance in 1922 and the fund withdrew its contribution in 1927. Trained midwives disappeared from the estate areas.*

Meanwhile, in 1925, the Maternity and Child Welfare Society had been formed by Lady Read, the Governor's wife. In 1926, the first Maternity and Child Welfare Centre was opened at Rose Hill, with an honorary physician, a resident health visitor and a certified midwife. From 1927 onwards, the de Chazal Fund stopped paying for the training of midwives and devoted its whole income to the Maternity and Child Welfare Society. By 1935 the Society had seven centres with four honorary physicians, a superintendent midwife and 17 midwives.†

In 1927, the Oeuvre Pasteur opened a "goutte de lait" in Port Louis to distribute milk to infants and to provide ante- and postnatal services. By 1935 both the Maternity and Child Welfare Society and the Goutte de Lait were receiving Government subsidies.‡ In the year 1942-43, 69% of the Society's income came from the Government.§

In 1938 the Maternity and Child Welfare Society supervised 2,177 confinements and there were more than 9,000 attendances of children at the clinics. The Society employed 20 midwives.|| By the middle of the Second World War, the Society had eight centres and one branch centre. The staff consisted of a superintendent, seven senior midwives and 40 other midwives. The Society charged up to Rs. 10 for a confinement.¶

---

* *Annual Report of the Medical and Health Department*, 1935, pp. 22-25.
† *Ibid.*, pp. 26-27.
‡ *Ibid.*, p. 28.
§ Rankine, A., *op. cit.*, p. 29.
|| *Majority Report of the Social Insurance Committee*, 1941 (unpublished).
¶ Rankine, A., *op. cit.*, p. 29.

Post-war developments

So far we have described the development of the three streams of the health services in Mauritius up to the end of the Second World War. The history from 1945 to the present day is one of further extension and development—particularly in the Government service.

Perhaps the most important improvement other than the eradication of malaria has been in the quality and quantity of the nursing staff. We have quoted earlier the comment of the 1931 Commission, pointing out the inadequacy of the nursing services at that time. In 1938 there were only 139 "qualified" nursing officers in the whole Government service. By 1946 the number was still only 156. The qualification was acquired in two years and included midwifery. No lectures were given to nurses in training and nursing was not included as an examination subject.

By 1949 the course had been lengthened to three years, with a further year for midwifery. The syllabus was revised to include nursing and lectures were introduced for both trained staff and nurses in training. At the end of 1950 there were nearly 100 students and by 1956 the number of qualified nurses in the service had increased to nearly 400. In that year, a residential school of nursing was opened and the "block system" of training was introduced under the first whole-time nursing tutor to be employed in Mauritius. There are now two tutors and nearly 500 qualified nurses for over 2,000 hospital beds (including those in the mental hospital). From 1959 a special combined course in mental and physical nursing has been introduced.

The large increase in the population and the even larger proportionate growth in the number of nursing staff has not been accompanied by a corresponding increase in the number of hospital beds. It was felt in 1952 that this would be "beyond the financial resources of the Colony".* It was planned instead to develop the ambulatory and domiciliary services. In 1955, the heavy demand on the hospital services led to chronic sick cases being moved to infirmaries "which can adequately look after this class of case".† To relieve the congestion in the mental hospital, "harmless patients not in need of constant medical care and supervision [were] transferred to suitable infirmaries".‡ The most important additions to the hospital service since 1945 have been the orthopaedic centre which was opened in 1956 with 195 beds and the pathological laboratory which opened in 1958.

* *Annual Report of the Medical and Health Department*, 1952, p. 28.
† *Annual Report of the Medical and Health Department*, 1955, p. 17.
‡ *Ibid.*, p. 21.

The dispensary services have been extended and there are now 48 static dispensaries. The first mobile dispensary started in 1947 and there are now four.

Other important developments since the war have been in services for children and mothers. The provision of maternity and child welfare services by the Maternity and Child Welfare Society in the towns has been supplemented by a Government service in the rural areas, mainly in buildings provided by the Sugar Industry Labour Welfare Fund. These services are provided by the Government in 15 social welfare centres with two midwives attached to each centre.

A school dental service was started in 1946 with one dentist. There are now five dentists employed providing a service mainly to preschool and school children and expectant and nursing mothers. In 1952 a school medical service was started. There are now three doctors employed on this work.

This brief historical sketch, which provides some of the background to the detailed account of the present position of the health services given in Chapter 2, shows that considerable extensions and innovations have taken place in the Government services in the last ten years or so. It seems to us that these developments have, in general, been on the right lines with the emphasis falling on preventive work. The progress so far made in building a comprehensive health service would have been more impressive but for the growth in population of 50% since 1945 and the continuing shortage of doctors in the island.

FUTURE PLANS

The Government is fully aware of the fact that a rapidly growing population and other factors make necessary further extensions to the existing services. Among the projects which have been envisaged are a number of additions to the general hospital services, including a new tuberculosis hospital, a unit for the treatment of cancerous conditions and an ophthalmic unit. The plan also provides for the construction or reconstruction of 17 dispensaries, thus extending the areas in which a permanent service is available to the public. "This network of local treatment will be geared to a system of District Hospitals of an improved standard. The Hospitals at Moka, Flacq, and Mahébourg will be extended, a new Central Hospital will be constructed to serve the North and to replace the services now provided by the inadequate small hospitals at Poudre d'Or and Montagne Longue; Rodrigues will be supplied with a new hospital; and significant modernisation and extension work will be—in some cases is being—carried out at the Civil and Victoria Hospitals, attention being particularly paid to Out-patients Departments."*

In addition to the Government's capital programme, the Sugar Industry Labour Welfare Fund plans to build 16 more social welfare centres in the next five years. This will make it possible to extend the maternity and child welfare services in the rural areas. There are also plans for the expansion of the school health services; for further developments in the control of tuberculosis, malaria, hookworm and bilharzia; and for a major campaign for the improvement of environmental sanitation and for public education in such matters.

THE REPORTS OF RECENT ENQUIRIES

The Majority Report of the Committee on Social Insurance of 1941† decided that a much improved medical service for the labouring classes was required. Medical supervision under the system of dispensaries was inadequate and the estate and industrial medical facilities were "costly to employers without giving an effective public service in their neighbourhood". It would be expensive to improve the Government service. Accordingly, the Committee recommended that "the most practical and equitable way of making improved provision is by a compulsory contributory Health Insurance Scheme". The Labour Ordinance requiring employers to provide medical services should be repealed. All estate hospitals would ultimately be closed and additional provision would be made in Government hospitals and dispensaries.

Under the proposed Health Insurance Scheme, insured persons would be entitled to hospital benefit, medical benefit and dental benefit. The benefits were, *if possible*, to be extended to an insured person's wife and children. The contribution required for these benefits and for cash sickness, disablement and maternity benefits was calculated at 2c. per day.

The members of the Committee were not agreed as to the desirability of adopting the panel system of organising general practitioner services. They recommended that if it were adopted no doctor should have a list of more than 2,000 patients and noted that the medical profession had asked for Rs. 6 per annum as a capitation fee. If 280,000 persons were to be entitled to medical benefit (including dependants), 140 medical officers would be required. "It is quite clear that for many years to come it will not be possible to provide

---

* *A Plan for Mauritius*, Sessional Paper No. 4 of 1958, pp. 38-39.
† The Social Insurance Committee was appointed in January, 1940, with the Director of Labour, Mr. (now Lord) Twining, as Chairman. Its Report was not published and we were unable to trace a copy of it in Mauritius. A copy was eventually made available to us by the Colonial Office, together with the dissenting memoir by Dr. Millien.

this number for the reasons that there are insufficient doctors available, the inability of the scheme to meet the costs and the lack of any reliable information as to how many dependants will be entitled to the medical benefit." They therefore considered it impracticable to introduce the panel system in the early stages of the scheme. They recommended that "additional medical officers should be engaged on the same terms pertaining to the present posts of Government Medical Officers". Drugs were to be limited to those contained in a special pharmacopoeia drawn up for the scheme. The drugs would be distributed by pharmacies and branch pharmacies established for the purpose.

Messrs. Marc de Chazal and Raymond Hein had reservations to the Report. They considered that in view of the cost the panel system was outside the range of possibility. They did not agree that estate hospitals should be closed down, and they feared that the whole burden of the cost might eventually fall on employers.

In a "dissenting memoir" Dr. Millien objected to the whole conduct of the Committee. The enquiries had not been sufficiently thorough. He feared that the proposals made would lead to the function of providing medical care being handed over to dispensers— to "half-trained men".

Dr. Millien was highly critical of the estate medical services. Although doctors were expected to live within a certain distance of their estate, the Director of the Medical Department was able to make exceptions. Every doctor had become an exception. They lived in areas which were most profitable for private practice with the result that serious cases inevitably fell upon the Government Medical Service in rural areas. Employers avoided their legal obligation of providing medical care for their servants by sending them as paupers to consult and get free treatment at the Government dispensaries and hospitals.

Dr. Millien based his own proposals on the assumption that patients would ask for two consultations per year from their doctor. If 314,957 persons were entitled to insurance benefit, there would be about 630,000 consultations. He felt that this work could be easily done by 45 private practitioners. He thought that there ought to be 125 centres in the island where patients could receive general practitioner services. He wanted each dispensary to be visited by two doctors daily, one in the morning and one in the evening. Each doctor was to have his own register of insured persons and was to be responsible for doing home visits. Dr. Millien suggested a yearly capitation payment of Rs. 2 per head to the insurance doctor and thought that it was desirable to make the patients pay 10c. for a consultation and 25c. for a home visit.

When forwarding the Report to the Secretary of State in March 1941 the Governor stated that he regarded the scheme of health insurance as "too ambitious, premature and expensive. The people most in need of such facilities are at present too ignorant to avail themselves of many of the proposed benefits. Much more primary education is necessary before such a scheme will be really understood by a lot of the local people." He therefore proposed that there should be an expansion of Government medical and sanitary facilities before any such scheme was introduced.

In September 1950 the then Governor set up another Committee to investigate health insurance. Its terms of reference were "to advise the Government as to the action required to set up a Health Insurance Scheme in Mauritius and to furnish an estimate of the cost". The Committee consisted of the Public Assistance Commissioner as Chairman, three other officials, four doctors, including Dr. Millien, and three other persons including Mrs. L. M. D. de Chazal.

The Committee recommended that compulsory insurance should apply to employed persons between the ages of 14 and 65 (excluding non-manual workers in receipt of a basic wage in excess of Rs. 2,000 per annum). On this basis the number of insured persons was put at 90,000 and the Committee thought that the average patient was likely to come for treatment "at least four times a year"—making a total of 360,000 attendances per year.* Panel doctors were to have a maximum of 4,000 patients on their lists and were to be allowed to engage in private practice.† The Committee hoped to induce doctors to reside in rural areas by financial incentives. Patients were to be allowed to go to private pharmacists for free medicines and it was recommended that a pharmacopoeia should be devised by a Committee on which both doctors and pharmacists would be represented. Doctors were to be instructed to use the formulary whenever a patient's condition allowed it.‡ The insurance scheme would replace the estate medical services. Estate doctors would be compensated for their loss of office.§

The Committee calculated the remuneration of insurance doctors in the following way. The average remuneration of a Government medical officer was then Rs. 11,000. To this they added 46% for overseas leave, pension rights, etc., plus cost of living allowance. They also added Rs. 2,400 for the cost of a dresser, Rs. 3,000 for a car and Rs. 2,000 for a surgery—and arrived at a total of nearly

---

* *Report of the Committee on Health Insurance*, Sessional Paper No. 4 of 1953, p. 2.
† *Ibid.*, p. 3.
‡ *Ibid.*, p. 4.
§ *Ibid.*, p. 7.

Rs. 28,000 (precisely how they reached this total is not entirely clear). From this calculation the Committee recommended a capitation payment to doctors of Rs. 8 per patient, excluding mileage allowances and special payments to doctors working in rural areas.*

The scheme was to be financed by contributions, paid by weekly stamps, of 21c. per day (based on a five-day week) shared equally by the employed person, the employer, and the Government. Lower rates were proposed for women and juveniles. The first employer in the week would be responsible for the employer's share of the contribution. The Committee assumed that the contribution would be collected for each week in which the insured person was employed, if only for a day.†

Mrs. de Chazal wrote a minority report.‡ While she was not against National Health Insurance, she felt it was not the time to start it in Mauritius. She emphasised the lack of panel doctors. In general, she felt that the money would be better spent on providing more dispensaries, extending the system of travelling dispensaries, increasing the number of doctors in the existing hospitals, building further hospitals, and training more dressers and nurses.

Dr. Millien also contributed a minority report.§ He considered that the preliminary studies were not sufficiently thorough. The medical profession had been too strongly represented on the Committee and the consequences were apparent in the conclusions reached. He thought that there was no reason why estate doctors should receive compensation for the loss of their jobs.

If patients did come to see their doctors four times a year, which he thought was an under-estimate, the burden on the doctor "cannot be conducive to efficient service, the more so that the panel doctor is to be allowed private practice". Dr. Millien took the view "that at the rate offered, nearly every doctor will accept to register a certain number of insured, and that even medical men nearing retiring age in Government Service will gladly add revenue earned in the Scheme to their pension". If panel doctors were allowed Rs. 32,000 plus private practice, "there is no doubt that the Health Department will not be able to recruit medical men for its services". Doctors would gain more from the scheme than the insured.

The 1958 Committee of Ministers also dealt with the question of health insurance. This Committee felt that the present medical arrangements were faulty in two respects. First, there was no provision for the visiting of patients in their homes. Secondly, "the fact

---

* *Report of the Committee on Health Insurance*, Sessional Paper No. 4, of 1953, p. 3-4.
† *Ibid.*, pp. 5-7.
‡ *Ibid.*, p. 8.
§ *Ibid.*, pp. 11-13.

that the Government Doctors are located in hospitals at specific points in the Island means that the pressure on their services for the treatment of minor complaints leads to serious congestion at the Out Patients Departments—which moreover do not exist in proper form at every hospital, so that confusion exists in the handling of out patients and the normal work of the hospital is disrupted in consequence. As a result, very many members of the public, including many who cannot afford it, go to private doctors instead of using the free public facilities, and many go to pharmacies and other sources of no doubt well-intentioned but nevertheless unqualified advice".

The Committee recommended the introduction of the panel doctor system for the working population. Panel doctors were to dispense simple medicines, and private pharmacies were to dispense medicines against National Insurance prescriptions in heavily populated areas. Prescriptions were to be related to a national pharmacopoeia. Special or specially expensive drugs, medicines, etc., were only to be available at public hospitals. "This safeguard is necessary because, as noted above, the population of Mauritius is very 'medicine-conscious' and tends to spend an unduly and unnecessarily large part of its income on 'fashionable' remedies and patent medicines which are no more efficacious, even when they are indicated, than simpler and less costly preparations."

OUR OWN VIEWS

Before we set out our criticisms of the present health services of Mauritius and outline our proposals for improvements and developments, we wish to record our view that the achievements of the Government Medical Service, particularly since the Second World War, have been impressive. To a substantial extent, Mauritius already has a free health service. The standard of this service is in various respects in advance of that of many countries at a similar stage of economic and social development. But for the rapid growth in population in the past few years the achievements and repute of the Service would have stood much higher. It is a tribute to the work of doctors, nurses and other staff that, despite the increasing pressure of demand, much progress has been achieved.

We have, however, received evidence from villagers and townspeople, from trade unions and other organisations expressing serious dissatisfaction with the curative services provided by the Government. There is dissatisfaction with the in-patient services: there are not enough staffed beds and care in hospitals is not always believed to be of a high standard. But the major complaint concerns the ambulatory medical services provided at dispensaries and out-patient departments: patients are kept waiting for long periods and the time given for consultations is thought inadequate for careful examination and treatment. Frequently we were told that doctors did not listen to what the patient had to tell them and that patients were "palmed off" with "inferior" drugs. There were also complaints in a number of areas about lack of courtesy of Government medical officers, dressers and nurses. It is this dissatisfaction with the dispensary and out-patients services which has led to the demand for health insurance.

We are in no doubt, from the evidence and testimony we collected and from our own investigations, that patients have to wait a long time to see a doctor and that the time given to each patient is extremely short. This does not necessarily mean that the standard of care provided is in all cases grossly inadequate. We ourselves observed a doctor carrying out what seemed to us as laymen thorough investigations, keeping detailed notes, and making careful diagnoses in a relatively short time. No doubt the quality of the service, as indeed of any medical service in any country, varies greatly from one area to another in the island, and, indeed, from one doctor to another.

The shortcomings of the Government Medical Service seem to us to be due to a number of different causes and they cannot be remedied solely by changes in organisation or in methods of payment. The more fundamental problems of the quantity and quality of doctors, nurses and other skilled personnel need first to be tackled. If these problems are not dealt with, changes in organisation such as have been envisaged may at best provide only a temporary alleviation of the position; there is, on the other hand, a real danger that they will make the situation worse rather than better.

There is at present a serious shortage of doctors and nurses. Any plan for the re-organisation of the health services must take account of this fact. Careful thought must be given to the priority of different needs in the population and any plan for re-organisation must be designed to maintain these priorities. We leave over to the next chapter these questions of priorities and we make there our proposals for changes in the structure of the health services. The remainder of this chapter is devoted to what we consider to be an essential pre-requisite of any developments; namely, improvements in the recruitment, training and standards of practice of medical personnel.

We would be failing in our duty if we did not speak frankly about the unethical behaviour of certain professional people in Mauritius. We have received evidence from doctors inside and outside the Government Medical Service and from a large number of other persons in responsible positions complaining of lapses in conduct in all grades of personnel from doctors to hospital orderlies.

There are many Mauritians who cannot afford to pay for the services of a doctor. There are others who can afford a doctor's fee but are not content to rely upon the services of one medical adviser. In general, neither the potentialities nor the limitations of modern medicine are properly understood. A Mauritian faced with an illness will often seek advice from a number of different doctors, pharmacists, nurses, herbalists and self-appointed lay experts. He will purchase both modern drugs and traditional herbs, make vows to different deities and visit shrines of more than one denomination. It is an eclectic pattern of behaviour which offers singular opportunities for the sick to be exploited for monetary gain. Those who exploit suffering, be it in good faith or bad faith, include doctors, nurses, dressers and pharmacists.

We have heard of doctors who are said to recommend treatments which they must know are ineffective. We learnt of doctors who prescribe expensive pharmaceuticals for poor patients although cheaper remedies of equivalent value are available. We were told of doctors who are said to prescribe brands which can only be obtained at a pharmacy in which the doctor concerned has a direct or indirect financial interest. We were informed about a Government medical officer who is alleged to take payment for commanding the admission of a patient to an already overcrowded hospital. We learnt of a doctor who claims on his writing paper to be a specialist in a number of fields for which he has in fact no specialist training. We received much evidence of the waste and misuse of antibiotics and other modern drugs purely as a result of financial relationships between doctors, chemists and other interests.

None of these allegations have we investigated closely. Nor would it have been proper for us to have done so. We are led to believe, however, from the large number and variety of different and responsible persons who brought these facts to our notice that they are not just part of the extensive mythology of Mauritian gossip. We are impressed by the number of doctors in private practice and in Government service who went out of their way to draw our attention to these matters, and we have no doubt that the majority of doctors in Mauritius condemn these practices as whole-heartedly as we do and are every bit as anxious to stamp out all conduct which brings the profession into disrepute. It is therefore a matter of urgency that legislation should be introduced to establish a General Medical Council. This would give the profession the opportunity it needs and asks for to put its own house in order.

In view of these lapses in professional conduct among some

doctors, it is not surprising that low ethical standards are also to be found among dressers, nurses and pharmacists. We are in no doubt that there are many dressers and nurses who take illicit charges from patients. Some engage openly in private "medical" practice after their hours of duty. It is even alleged that there are members of the nursing staff who have such a low code of honour and such a high desire for financial gain that they are prepared to steal injections from their own hospital patients for sale in their "private practice", thus risking the lives of both patients for whom they have taken more responsibility than their training warrants. In view of the behaviour of some members of the nursing staff, it is not surprising that there are attendants who demand payment from the patient or his relatives for performing the services which they are paid by the hospital to provide.

As in the case of the doctors, the solution lies in the discipline of the profession by the profession. We recommend that a General Nursing Council should be set up to maintain a register and to strike off those whose conduct does not befit the profession. We are confident that such a body would insist on the highest professional standards. A man or woman who refuses to handle a bed-pan without exacting a fee is not fit to bear the title of "dresser" or "nurse".

Owing to the shortage of doctors in Mauritius, it is inevitable that the sick should ask not only nurses and dressers but also pharmacists (or indeed any person selling pharmaceuticals or medicinal herbs) to diagnose and prescribe. In such circumstances, it is not altogether surprising that dangerous drugs should be sold without a doctor's prescription. In Mauritius, however, the unauthorised sale of drugs extends far beyond what could be justified by sudden emergencies. Nearly any preparation can be obtained without a prescription—sedatives, stimulants and antibiotics. Some are even hawked from door to door. Others are recommended by qualified pharmacists who should know the limitations of their professional competence. Such drugs as isoniazid and streptomycin are handed out indiscriminately. Other drugs which are sold include some of such low quality as to be valueless, if not dangerous, if used for the purposes for which they are recommended.

The consequences of the indiscriminate sale of patent remedies to the health of the population of Mauritius are undoubtedly menacing. The patient who uses a preparation without medical advice undergoes the risk of doing himself more harm than good. It may be that the drug was unsuitable in the first place; it may be that certain precautions should have been taken of which he was not aware while using the drug; it may be that dangerous side-effects are involved of which the purchaser is totally ignorant. And last, but not least, the use of antibiotics when they are not needed encourages the growth of resistant strains and thus increases the risk that the patient will not respond to the drug later on when it is really needed. The ultimate cost of such consequences to the economy of Mauritius cannot, of course, be measured.

With these standards prevailing, the pharmacist who is asked to prescribe at the counter is inevitably tempted to try and dispose not of the customer's disease but of his own expensive and unwisely purchased stock. It is alleged that there are pharmacies in Mauritius where this temptation is not strongly resisted. It was also alleged in evidence to us that some pharmacists are prepared to substitute a preparation for that prescribed by the doctor, to change the dosage, and even to persuade the patient who cannot afford to pay for the whole dose that it is efficacious to purchase half the dose now and postpone to a later occasion the purchase of the other half. The cost of some preparations in Mauritius is extremely high. Some retail margins are at the fantastic figure of 3-400%. One chemist may have exclusive sales of one preparation and not hesitate to make exorbitant profits out of this monopoly power. In such circumstances, a co-operative doctor is worth more to the chemist than the cost of giving him free surgery facilities. We came across more than one instance of doctors approached by representatives of chemists with offers to enter into such relationships on returning to Mauritius after qualification.

The remedies to the malpractices of the pharmaceutical trade must surely be found by the better enforcement of existing legislation and by the introduction of new legislation to control more closely the importation and distribution of drugs and to fix appropriate maximum prices. In addition, the profession must be given powers to regulate itself as we have proposed for other professions. We are not in a position to make detailed recommendations about all these matters but the allegations which have been made to us are of such gravity as to require detailed investigation. Accordingly, we recommend that an expert committee should be set up to carry out such investigations and make recommendations for controlling the import, sale and profit margins of pharmaceutical products in Mauritius.

The problem of ethical standards among nurses, pharmacists and dressers in Mauritius is partly due to the shortage of doctors. It is also partly due to the standards which the doctors themselves set. These two problems of ethical standards and medical recruitment are therefore closely related. If there were more doctors, and particularly more doctors working in the Government Medical Service, patients would have no need to seek advice from persons who are not qualified to give it. We reach the conclusion that an increase in the number of doctors in Mauritius is an essential prerequisite to improvements in the health services.

THE SHORTAGE OF DOCTORS

There is at present only about one doctor to 4,500 people in Mauritius. This may be compared to one doctor per 1,000 in the United Kingdom and to one doctor per 600 in Czechoslovakia and one doctor per 500 in Israel. The shortage is a problem of long standing. In 1851 there were 60 doctors and dentists for a population of 183,506. In 1861 there were 52 doctors and dentists for a population of 313,462. In 1871, the number of surgeons and physicians was 62 and the number of dentists was seven for a population of 317,069.*
In 1909 there were 68 registered medical practitioners of whom 37 were employed by the Government.† In 1954, there were 99 doctors on the island and by the end of 1959 there were about 140 for a population of 640,000. Thus, while the position has improved in the last five years, the ratio of doctors to population is still not much larger than it was 100 years ago. The shortage of doctors has been recognised for many years as a major problem. It was suggested far back in the nineteenth century, and this suggestion was repeated by Dr. Balfour in 1921, that doctors should be specially recruited from India to serve in Mauritius.

The problem of the recruitment of doctors takes on a new and more urgent aspect in view of the large population increase which is now inevitable. To aim at a target of one doctor for 3,000 patients in 1980, assuming that the population grows to around 1,250,000 by then, would mean increasing by more than 25% the annual net addition to the number of doctors practising in some capacity in the island.

One possible way of attempting to increase the number of doctors would be by recruitment of doctors from abroad. An attempt could be made to attract doctors from Britain, France or those countries at present liberally supplied. It would seem, however, unlikely to have much prospect of success. Doctors unfamiliar with the island would probably not be willing to abandon their work in their country of origin and settle in a relatively poor country. Mauritius does not, and cannot, offer the same opportunities for the development of specialised medical knowledge as larger centres. Nor can Mauritius afford to offer salaries which compete with other possible places for emigration such as Canada. There is, moreover, a danger that a

* *Census of Mauritius and its Dependencies*, 1851, 1861 and 1871.
† *Mauritius Royal Commission*, 1909, Minutes of Evidence, Cmd. 5186, 1910, p. 475.

policy of recruiting "foreign" doctors would not in practice be acceptable to public opinion.

Thus, we do not expect that an attempt to recruit doctors from abroad can make more than a small contribution to the problem. Nevertheless, we consider that the effort should be made. Careful thought must, however, be given to the most suitable rôle which such doctors can play in Mauritius. There is the language difficulty which means that doctors without fluent French are unlikely to be of much use in the general practitioner services—at least for a year or so. This, however, is not important in specialities such as pathology and radiology, where contact with the patient is not so close. On the whole, it seems that "foreign" doctors with specialist qualifications could be more readily fitted into the hospitals than general practitioners could be fitted into the dispensary system.

There are in British hospitals many young doctors with excellent qualifications who have been unable to obtain consultant appointments simply because of the lack of vacancies. Some of these doctors might be willing to take specialist appointments in Mauritius. It would be absurd, however, to expect to find doctors of this type by advertisement alone. What is needed is a visit to Britain of a senior medical representative of the Mauritian service with powers to constitute appropriate appointment committees and to offer temporary or more permanent positions.

Although we are not qualified to offer expert opinion on these matters, we believe that opportunities to engage in research should be made available in the hospitals and the Government Medical Service. In many ways, Mauritius is ideally situated and ethnically constituted to provide an interesting "laboratory" for the study of the pattern and aetiology of certain diseases and mental disorders. We would hope that some way might be found of offering appointments which would combine clinical work with the pursuit of such research. An infusion of research and graduate studies would help to raise the quality of medical care.

There are many ways in which Mauritius might gain the services of foreign doctors. It might be possible to arrange for a teaching hospital in Australia or Britain to enter into some system of exchange of personnel. This could be of mutual benefit. Young doctors from the wealthier countries would have the opportunity of treating conditions which are rare in their own countries while the doctors from Mauritius would benefit from working with better facilities than are available in Mauritius. Alternatively, one of the Regional Hospital Boards in Britain might assign doctors for work in Mauritius to gain special experience for limited periods. Thirdly, the Medical Research Council might be willing to set up a demonstration area in Mauritius on the lines of the service now provided in one area of Jamaica. The study of the epidemiology of different ethnic groups by highly skilled personnel would not only contribute to knowledge about the health of the people of Mauritius but set an example of what could be achieved by a high standard of medical care. All these possibilities deserve investigation.

Whatever comes of these possibilities, the *major* source of permanent recruits to the Government service is likely to be restricted to persons born in the island. Thus, the intake of doctors will depend on the number of Mauritians being trained, on the number of doctors who are prepared to return to Mauritius after training, and on their willingness to remain and practise in the island.

The Government of Mauritius at present provides a general scholarship system for higher education, and medicine is certainly a popular subject of study. Out of the 36 English scholarships awarded between 1953 and 1958, 21 were for medicine. The Indian Government also awards scholarships. Out of the 35 awards between 1951 and 1959, 14 were for medicine. There are many others studying medicine abroad by private arrangement. In total, there were known to be 200 Mauritian medical students at the end of 1959, 61 in the United Kingdom, 50 in Eire, 59 in France, 29 in India, and one in the United States. Mauritius has more medical students than doctors.

Under the income tax, generous concessions are at present given to parents whose children are being educated abroad. At a level of income of Rs. 60,000 per annum, a course is subsidised by the Government to the extent of Rs. 2,450 per year (£184). Thus, a not inconsiderable proportion of the cost of privately financed medical education falls indirectly upon the Government. There are, therefore, two systems of encouraging higher education. The first, which is wholly Government financed, is available to those selected on grounds of merit. The second system, which is indirectly Government aided, is available to those whose parents pay income tax. Indeed, both can be received for the same student. And in neither case is there any undertaking required of the student that he will return to Mauritius when his course is completed. We understand, however, that students on Government scholarships may be asked to refund travel expenses in certain circumstances. (There is, of course, no similar provision for the repayment of tax concessions.)

Some witnesses have suggested to us that as there are known to be over 200 Mauritians studying medicine, the present shortage of doctors will soon be remedied. It is certainly true that if all these young people returned to Mauritius after qualifying, there would not only be a very large increase in the absolute number of doctors in the island, but an increase in the ratio of doctors to the population.

But we ourselves doubt whether all these students will return to settle in the island. We have been told that the proportion of recent medical students who do not return after medical training is extremely large. It has been suggested that there may be at present not only more Mauritian medical students training abroad than doctors in Mauritius, but also more Mauritian doctors working overseas than in the island itself.

We have tried to find out exactly what proportion of medical students have failed to return to Mauritius in recent years, but no records are kept. And even if such information were available it would be dangerous to make predictions on the basis of past experience and even more dangerous to undertake a reorganisation of the medical services which could only be implemented if there was a great increase in medical staff. We note that the vast majority of the present medical students are privately financed and we think it wise to take a pessimistic view about the proportion of them who will return to Mauritius. In short, we fear that the Government's policy for promoting higher education may be encouraging the permanent emigration of some of the most able and talented young people in the island. These are precisely the people that Mauritius most badly needs.

It is for this reason among others that we wish to make proposals for changing the system of Government aid to higher education. It seems to us that the policy of granting tax concessions on expenditure incurred in educating children abroad is undesirable. First, it contradicts the population policies we advocate by easing the financial burdens of parenthood for a selected group in the island. Secondly, we suggest that the state's financial assistance to education, be it direct or indirect, should be restricted to candidates selected strictly according to merit. For these reasons we recommend that this tax allowance should be withdrawn and that the resulting addition to the revenue should be used to increase the number of state scholarships. To make the maximum use of this money, there should be an examination of parental capital and income to determine the amount granted to each individual scholar.

It also seems important to ensure that, so far as possible, the people of Mauritius receive some return for their considerable expenditure on the education of medical students. We do not want to imply that the actions of students who do not return home after completing their education are unreasonable. We appreciate that the opportunities, professional and otherwise, of a career outside Mauritius are in some ways more attractive than in the island. Doctors who show special abilities during their training may be offered prospects in Britain and elsewhere which are considerably greater than they could expect if they returned home. It seems to us, however, only right that in such cases the Government which has given them such good opportunities for personal advancement should receive some financial recompense.

A number of conclusions emerge from this discussion of the problem of medical recruitment. First, we suggest that more scholarships should be made available for selected candidates to study medicine. Secondly, we suggest that some of these scholarships should be reserved for women candidates. The British medical schools have for a number of years reserved a proportion of places for women students. Today, and increasingly in the future, women have a special contribution to make to the medical services of Mauritius—especially in the important fields of maternity, child welfare and family planning. Moreover, we would expect the wastage in non-return to be less among women than men. Thirdly, we question whether Britain, Eire or France are necessarily the best places for the bulk of Government financed medical students to pursue their education. We suggest that some scholarships for medical study should be given nearer at hand (possibly in Australia) where opportunities for taking up practice are not so readily available. Fourthly, we recommend that where medical students are being wholly financed by the Government they should make some undertaking to return to practise in Mauritius for a limited period or repay the cost of their medical education over a number of years. This recommendation is in line with that made by the *Ministerial Committee on Recruitment and Training* (1959).*

The Government in its turn should do everything possible to make it easier for doctors to return to Mauritius immediately after they have completed their studies. The Director of the Mauritius Students' Unit in London should keep regularly in touch with all medical students and ensure that contracts (conditional on satisfactory examination results) are offered to them and passages are arranged for them *before* their final examinations. We understand that the present complicated formalities involve considerable delay and some losses. We also suggest that Mauritian doctors practising abroad should be kept constantly informed of the prospects in their own country. Short-term assignments with travel fees paid might be offered to doctors practising abroad in the hope that having returned to Mauritius they may decide to settle permanently in the island.

We recognise that none of these measures, however energetically pursued, can secure a great increase in the number of doctors within the next few years. There are at present 200 Mauritians training to be doctors. If they all returned to Mauritius, and if allowance is

* Sessional Paper No. 5 of 1959.

made for retirements and deaths, the number of doctors in the island would more than double in seven years' time. The preventive and curative services could be extended as more doctors became available, though not sufficiently to meet all needs. Taking account of population growth, this increase would allow a reduction in the patient-doctor ratio to 2,600 by 1967. But if only 25% of them returned to Mauritius, there would be no increase in the patient-doctor ratio.

We conclude therefore that the fundamental prerequisites to any improvements in the health services are the introduction of legislation to enable the professions to raise their ethical standards; greatly increased control over the import, distribution and sale of pharmaceutical products; and a variety of measures designed to increase the number of doctors in Mauritius. These matters require immediate attention if the standard of medical care is not to deteriorate in the coming years.

CHAPTER 10

A National Health Service

We drew attention in the last chapter to criticisms of the curative health services provided by the Government. Given the present serious shortage of doctors and other health workers, dissatisfaction is to a large extent inevitable. There are too few doctors to provide the whole population with even a moderate standard of service. There are, in consequence, long queues at the Government dispensaries and outpatient departments and consultations are necessarily very short. And as we have pointed out in earlier chapters, the position is made much worse by the heavy demands for public assistance sickness certificates.

In this situation there are many patients, even among the poorer families, who express their dissatisfaction with the Government Medical Service by going to private doctors and chemists on a considerable scale. They also seek out unqualified advisers and indulge extensively in self-medication, often with dangerous drugs. Private expenditure on pharmaceuticals in Mauritius is by almost any standard extraordinarily high. Less than a quarter of the pharmaceutical products imported are purchased by the Government. Private expenditure on drugs now amounts to nearly 2% of consumer expenditure. The corresponding figure in Britain is about $\frac{1}{2}$%. If all the costs of purchasing private medical care could be brought into account, it would probably emerge that private expenditure on medical care was as large as the expenditure of the Government Medical Service.

THE NEED FOR PRIORITIES

To assist us in assessing the priorities for the future development of the health services, we wanted to have exact information showing the proportion of time which doctors working in the Government Service were devoting to different activities. Accordingly we asked the Director of Medical Services to send out a questionnaire to most of the doctors and a high proportion of them kindly supplied answers. As this enquiry was confidential, the information cannot be published, but it enabled us to gain a clearer knowledge of the present organisation and working of the Government Service. We wish to thank the doctors who cooperated with us in this way.

Although the case for extending and improving the curative services provided by the Government is obviously very strong, we do not think that this is the most urgent immediate need. We would like to see the highest priority given to the preventive health and welfare services—especially where the health of mothers and children is concerned. We are therefore glad to learn that plans have reached an advanced stage for the reorganisation and extension of these services. We particularly welcome the plans (referred to in the last chapter) for the pre-natal and midwifery services, the expansion of the school health services, further developments in the control of tuberculosis, malaria, hookworm and bilharzia, and the launching of a campaign for the improvement of environmental sanitation and for health education. In our view, these developments should receive the highest priority in the allocation of financial resources.

Later in this chapter we discuss the question of the dental services. At this point, we wish to select two problems of preventive medicine for special mention. The first is hookworm infestation. This is extremely common in the rural parts of the island. It seems to us that the most serious aspect of this problem is the nutritional loss which it causes. The diet of the people of Mauritius is not so generous that it can be shared with these worms. We are, therefore, glad to hear that plans are being made to attack this problem. From expert advice we received both in Mauritius and in the United Kingdom, we understand that a policy of disinfestation alone is of limited value. The solution lies in the provision of latrines all over the island and their use by the whole population. The demand for these facilities and their provision must depend in large part on action by local communities. To support this development, a large scale campaign in public education should be inaugurated. Everything possible should be done to encourage people to wear shoes. We have proposed earlier that a start should be made with school children.

The second preventive service to which we attach great importance is that for mothers and children. In 1958 there were 26,303 births in Mauritius. Of this total, it is not known where 7,686 took place owing to a failure to comply with the Notification of Births Ordinance. Of the remaining 18,617, only 3,146 took place in Government hospitals and 10,022 occurred at home with a qualified midwife or doctor in attendance. Thus, there were 5,449 births which took place at home without the attendance of a qualified midwife or doctor. It is important that a qualified midwife or doctor should be present at all births.

Only about half all expectant mothers in 1958 received any antenatal care. Though there is a service for infant welfare, very few mothers received any post-natal care. Everything possible should be done to develop a post-natal service and to encourage its use. It is essential that such a service, at clinics, maternity centres and hospitals, should include advice and assistance with family planning.

A FAMILY PLANNING SERVICE

The provision of a family planning service is the most important single measure we have to propose in this report. It goes without saying that it should be within reach of every mother and father in the island. All should have the right voluntarily to use the service.

We recommend that a start should be made immediately with a family planning service in such premises and with such staff as are at present available. At the same time, we suggest that a consortium of charitable foundations should be approached by the Government for a large-scale programme of aid for health and family planning developments covering a period of at least ten years. The total sum we have in mind would be of the order of Rs. 200 million. Mauritius could serve as a demonstration area to show that an alliance of social, economic and family planning can resolve the problems of population growth. Such a programme would need to be closely associated with the maternity and child welfare services.

The Family Welfare Association has done important pioneering work in this field since its foundation as the Family Planning Association in October 1957. The scale of the problem and the urgent need for immediate action now demands a comprehensive service provided by Government as an integral part of the health and welfare programme. Had such a service been started in the early 1950's the future of Mauritius might look less sombre than it does today. In the development of a nation-wide educational campaign the Family Welfare Association will clearly have an important part to play.

Medical and sociological studies in many countries with different religious faiths and faced with similar problems of over-population have shown the need for married couples to be offered a free choice of various methods of family limitation. The available literature on the results of experimental services and programmes of education in family planning in India, Pakistan, Japan, Puerto Rico, Jamaica and other countries is now very extensive. We do not propose to attempt a summary here. Nor shall we reproduce the evidence which shows the extent to which peoples of all religions in all countries of the world are limiting their families by the use of different methods of control and self-discipline. There are now a variety of methods available—condom, diaphragm and jelly, foam tablets, jelly-and-syringe, the safe period, sponge-and-water solution, suppositories and withdrawal.

The measures which will be necessary to inform the public, to provide the facilities, and to offer a free choice of different methods of family limitation are matters which must be determined in Mauritius and by Mauritians. All that we can stress is the need for education and the need for the provision of facilities. It may be that an extensive service of home visitors will be required. It may be that many measures will have to be taken to prevent the harm now being done by the practice of illegally induced abortions and by the use of toxic abortifacients by Catholics and non-Catholics alike. Social, biological and medical research will certainly be required on attitudes to family planning, on the efficacy of different contraceptive practices, and on the scientific aspects of human fertility among different ethnic groups. Hence, we express the hope that studies of this kind will form part of a programme of aid from foundations in the United Kingdom and the United States.

We are very conscious of the fact that in urging the need for a policy of family limitation we are challenging the attitudes and beliefs of a considerable section of the population. Nevertheless, we do so on the grounds that every man and woman should have the dignity of freedom to make decisions for themselves in obedience to conscience; a doctrine of society in which men and nations are bound to care for one another, and to help one another to ease the present suffering, and avert the threatened cataclysm, of over-population.

While this knowledge and these services should be available to everyone in the island it would be illiberal to compel anyone to take advantage of them. We could not subscribe to any policy which entailed compulsion. Similarly, we would think it wrong if medical officers and others with religious scruples were not permitted to abstain from taking part in the provision of family planning facilities. The right of any individual on religious or any other ground to refuse to use these services or any particular method of family limitation must be safeguarded. The right of those who wish to know and who wish to use the services must equally be upheld. The tolerances and courtesies of a liberal society must be practised by all. The illiberalities of some must not thrive on the courtesies of others.

The development of preventive health and welfare services for mothers and children and a nation-wide provision of family planning facilities are essential elements in a single social policy of supporting the growth of healthy three-child families among all classes in the community. As we said in Chapter 3, the appeal is to a more healthy and secure family life.

THE HOSPITAL AND CURATIVE SERVICES

We turn now to consider needed developments in these services. The first point we would make is that an effective chain of district hospitals is as essential today as when it was recommended by a Committee of Enquiry in 1859. Nor is the need only for more hospital beds. Proper isolation facilities and separate labour rooms should also be made available. There is room for improvement in the diagnostic services so that doctors are provided with more accessible X-ray and pathological facilties. The more complex pathological work should continue to be concentrated at the Victoria Hospital, but we would like to see some facilities gradually made available in other parts of the island. We make no recommendations on the subject of hospital administration as we understand that an adviser in this field is to visit Mauritius in the near future.

We are not in a position to make specific recommendations about the number of beds which should be provided or where they should be located. This is a matter of detailed local planning. We hope, however, that the provision of a limited domiciliary service (which we refer to later) will reduce somewhat the need for additional hospital beds. We do not, however, expect that the rapid expansion of the population over the next 20 years can be absorbed without a considerable increase in hospital facilities. Without more provision, we see a real danger that chronically sick patients, both mental and physical, may increasingly be "dumped" in infirmaries where they will not receive proper supervision from the medical department. In the next chapter we show the extent of this problem today. To shift patients into unsuitable "welfare" institutions can all too easily result in neglecting the need for rehabilitation and in creating a costly and long-continuing burden for the Public Assistance Department. The needs of the individual are not changed by the transfer of responsibility from one authority to another less qualified to meet them.

Apart from the additional demands that will be created by the rapid growth in population, there is already an obvious and well-recognised need for a special hospital and training centre for mental defectives. The number of cases needing care of this kind is unknown but it is clearly undesirable that mental defectives should be scattered around the different types of institutions. At present, they are to be found in the mental hospitals, the general hospitals and in the institutions subsidised by the Public Assistance Department. If all these patients were brought together, better care and training could be provided. Such a combined institution and training centre needs to be placed somewhere in the built-up area of the island to facilitate visiting and to enable patients living at home to attend for training. Senior staff should be sent abroad at an early date to gain experience of this type of work.

We would also like to see some improvements in the mental health services. We welcome the fact that so many patients are now treated on an outpatient basis and indeed in this respect the mental health services of Mauritius are in advance of those of many comparable countries. This type of service could, however, be made more effective if a psychiatric social worker were employed. We therefore recommend that a suitable candidate or candidates should be sent at an early date for training in the United Kingdom.

These developments in the hospitals, both general and mental, must be accompanied by an improvement in the ambulance services. At present, they are quite inadequate.

THE ESTATE MEDICAL SERVICES

In addition to the accommodation available in the Government hospitals, there are the hospitals provided by the sugar industry on the estates. It has been suggested to us that one possible solution to the shortage of hospital beds is for better use to be made of these hospitals. Partly for this reason and partly because conflicting statements had been made to us about the present rôle played by the estate medical services, we asked the Labour Commissioner to obtain for us certain information which was not previously available. We wish to thank the Commissioner and his staff for the information they have collected for us.

There are 575 hospital beds available in the estate hospitals—308 for men, 221 for women, 12 for children and 34 for maternity cases. When the hospitals were visited by the labour inspectors only about a quarter of the beds were occupied. The majority of the patients were monthly paid and regular employees of the estates and their relatives. The inpatient services were hardly used at all by daily paid workers. There had, however, been about 200,000 visits from ambulant patients for first aid and other needs during the preceding year.

In the week preceding the visits of the inspectors, doctors spent a total of about 200 hours in the hospitals and dispensaries. There were 50 whole-time and four part-time nursing staff. The whole-time staff comprised 35 dressers, 10 midwives and five nurses; six of them were over 60 and 11 were between the ages of 55 and 59.

The staff of the estate medical service is relatively small. In terms of whole-time equivalents it amounts to about one-twentieth of the staff of the Government Medical Service. There are, however, between 300 and 400 vacant beds. This may be compared to the total of about 1,400 beds in the Government hospitals for the physically sick, which are very fully occupied. In practice, the estate hospitals provide little more than a place for treating the minor illnesses of monthly paid workers and looking after more serious cases for short periods until they can be moved to the Government hospitals. The staffing and equipment of the estate hospitals is, in general, inadequate for the care of the seriously ill and injured. The best of the buildings are, however, greatly superior to the worst of the Government hospitals.

The future of the estate hospitals was an issue on which many witnesses had strong views. It is clear that the service does not enjoy the confidence of the majority of the estate workers; this is shown by the scant use which is made of it. They view the service with suspicion; and believe that it is organised to serve not their own interests but those of the employers. It was therefore suggested to us that the service should be taken over by the Government. Some employers, on the other hand, pointed out that they were doing more for the health of the workers than was strictly required by the Ordinance. We gained the impression that at least some of the estates like to regard the provision of these services as an act of enlightened philanthropy. They are not, however, altogether consistent in holding this view as the cost of these medical services is quoted at arbitration tribunals as forming part of the remuneration of estate workers. If the services are financed indirectly by employees in wages forgone, it seems only right that what is being paid for by workers should be run in a way which gives satisfaction.

Those who urged us to recommend that the estate hospitals should be taken over by the Government supported their arguments with the suggestion that the under-utilised facilities on the estates would relieve the Government Service. We give little weight to this consideration. The estate hospitals are too small to be of much value to the Government Service, nor are they sited where hospital beds are most needed. The time may come when the Government could profitably use some of the estate hospital buildings as maternity or other specialised units for a rapidly growing population. But such hypothetical advantages cannot be used to justify taking over immediately all the estate hospitals.

Alternative uses for the existing staff and buildings seem to us a minor issue at the present time. The question which is important is to settle the rôle the estate medical service should play in the future in relation to the general provision of medical care. Before the Government Service was so well developed and before transport and communications in Mauritius became efficient, there undoubtedly was a need for employers to provide some system of medical care for their employees at their place of work. This need no longer exists in its nineteenth-century form. As employers have increasingly recognised, the best place for care to be provided for the seriously ill and injured worker is in the larger and better equipped Government hospitals. It seems to us that the appropriate rôle today for the estate service is to provide first-aid and to care temporarily for a few patients who are not acutely ill. The service is doing little more than this at the present time.

There are, of course, advantages in having a medical service provided by employers—for example the advantages of decentralisation and of increasing the opportunities for nursing staff outside the Government Service. But such advantages have to be weighed against the fact that the service is unpopular and that it is little used by the mass of the workers. If sugar employers were faced with powerful and recognised trade union representatives at the local level, the detailed arrangements for medical care might be left for local negotiation and there might be some reason to hope that the attitudes of employees would in time be changed. At the present time, however, the trade unions have little local representation.

We considered the possibility of placing the control of the estate medical services in the hands of a joint board of employers and employees or of the Committee of the Sugar Industry Labour Welfare Fund. But we did not think that a special agency with such limited functions would work effectively and the Welfare Fund did not seem an appropriate body to carry this responsibility. After reviewing all the possibilities, we ultimately decided that the best solution for the estate medical services was to recommend that they should be taken over by the Government Medical Service. The relevant sections of the Labour Ordinance should thus be repealed.

The main and deciding factor which forced us to this conclusion was the shortage of doctors. The seriousness of this shortage requires that the public health services should be planned as a whole. We shall be making proposals later in this chapter for a reorganisation of the "general practitioner" services. To provide a properly coordinated service, the needs of sugar estate employees should be regarded as an intrinsic part and not as a separate part of the general practitioner services.

The effects of this recommendation should not be misunderstood. We are not suggesting that the Government should "upgrade" all the estate hospitals, appoint new staff or attempt to provide the best services that money can buy. The standard of service for sugar employees should be in line with that provided for the rest of the community. These workers should participate in the same services as the population as a whole. The branches of the service located on the estates should be little more than first-aid stations.

Claims for compensation may be presented when the Government takes over the estate services. Though there may be special circumstances in particular cases, we see no reason why the general principle of compensation should be allowed. The estates will have relinquished buildings from which they can hardly claim they were obtaining any profit. Indeed, as the running costs will be transferred from the estates to the Exchequer, it would be more appropriate for the estates to pay the Government for relieving them of a substantial financial liability. In the case of the staff at present working in the estate medical service, appointments should generally be offered in the Government Service on appropriate terms.

A NATIONAL FAMILY DOCTOR SERVICE

From the recommendations we have so far made it will be clear that we give higher priority to developments in the preventive and hospital services than to the dispensary and general practitioner services. But many of our recommendations have been specifically directed at relieving some of the heavy burdens now being carried by the latter services. In all sectors, however, the rate of development must depend on the availability of resources and, in particular, on the supply of newly-qualified doctors. If more doctors were available in Mauritius, it would be possible to make dramatic improvements in every field within a short period. At present, this seems unlikely to happen.

It is against this background of a grave shortage of doctors that we come to consider the proposals which have been made for a panel service in Mauritius. We have examined carefully the reports of earlier committees which have investigated this proposal. All of them have been aware of the shortage of doctors. It was for this reason that all the three Committees (1941, 1951 and 1958) recommended that in the first instance any panel service should be confined to insured persons. There were not enough doctors to provide a service for the whole population.

We ourselves do not favour a panel service *restricted to insured persons*. Such a system operated in the United Kingdom from 1913 to 1948 and the lessons of history do not lead us to recommend the adoption of the system in Mauritius. It seems to us wrong in principle that priority should now be given to providing medical care for the working population, consisting, as it does, mainly of men. The effect of such an arrangement in Mauritius would almost certainly be to *lower* the standard of care provided for children, dependent wives, old people and, in general, the poorer sections of the population. It would also be against the long-run economic and social interests of Mauritius. It would make it more difficult to provide a family planning service and to develop adequate ante-natal and post-natal services for mothers. We also think it important that the next generation of Mauritians should be better cared for in childhood and achieve greater earning capacity in adult life. This can only be secured if better nutritional and health services are provided for mothers and children. If a panel service can only be provided for the insured population, we would think it better that no such service should be provided at all.

A further argument against a panel service for insured workers is that it would have to exclude the "self-employed". We mentioned in Chapter 5 the administrative difficulties of defining the self-employed and extracting contributions from them. In time these difficulties may be overcome but we recommended that our social insurance scheme should be confined in the first instance to employed persons. This means that if the right to medical benefit were to depend on separate contributions, the self-employed would have to be excluded. This would be unfortunate. Among the self-employed are many people who are as poor and as much in need of better medical care as many employees. If an insurance service were developed for employed persons, there would thus have to be a separate "poor law" or "assistance" service for the self-employed. This would create numerous administrative complications and endless anomalies.

For all these reasons we believe that any reorganisation of the "family doctor" services should lead to a scheme which would include anyone who wished to make use of them. There must, therefore, be no separate contribution for medical care. The service would still be a health insurance or social security service in the sense that it would be paid for from taxation, both direct and indirect, to which virtually everyone has to contribute.

In proposing a new family doctor service for Mauritius, we have had to take account of a number of specially difficult problems; the shortage of doctors, the ethics of the medical and pharmaceutical professions, the present exorbitant demand for drugs, and the concentration of the population and particularly the wealthier section of the population between Port Louis and Curepipe. We have also had to take account of the lessons which have been learnt from introducing different types of service in Britain, France, Sweden, Czechoslovakia and other countries. And, finally, we have had to think out clearly what objectives any new service should aim to secure. After studying the reports of the three earlier committees, the evidence we have received, and from our discussions in Mauritius, we have come to the conclusion that the objectives to be sought from any reorganisation should be:—

(i) to increase the amount of medical work performed in the whole island by making greater use of those private doctors who are at present (or who may be in the future) under-employed;

(ii) to encourage more people to take up medical practice and to attract more qualified doctors to return to Mauritius;

(iii) to secure a more even distribution of doctors over the island. At present, it should be noted, a private doctor cannot make a living outside the main urban centres. If he were able to obtain payment for services to poorer patients in more remote rural areas, there would be an incentive to develop practice in such areas;

(iv) to lead to more consultations taking place in the more homely surroundings of the doctor's own home or surgery rather than in the dispensary or outpatient department;

(v) to develop a home visiting service for the poorer patient;

(vi) to offer patients a free choice of doctors;

(vii) to encourage continuity of care;

(viii) to provide better medical care for mothers and children.

It should be appreciated that certain of these objectives are in conflict with one another. Some features which could be introduced into a new scheme to make it attractive to private doctors would have the effect of discouraging residence in the more remote areas. There is also an obvious conflict between the need for continuity of care and for free choice of doctor. Our proposals are presented after a careful assessment of the importance of the different objectives in the special circumstances of Mauritius which we have discussed in this and the preceding chapter.

We recommend that a new family doctor service should be started giving free treatment to anyone who has registered with a doctor participating in the new service. The scheme would be based on geographical areas. The island would be divided into a number of areas with three or four doctors offering general practitioner services at stated times and places in each of those areas. Patients could only register with one of the doctors serving their area. There would have to be a maximum number of patients which any doctor could take on his list. This would mean that patients who were late in applying for registration might not be able to be accommodated with their first choice of doctor. A patient wishing to change his doctor would have to give three months' notice; six months' notice was required at the start of the British health insurance scheme in 1913.

The number of areas would be determined by the number of doctors available and willing to take part in the scheme. Some doctors would be assigned to this work from the Government Medical Service, and we hope that a number of private doctors would also be willing to accept contracts under the scheme. In return for a monthly fee, the community doctor would contract to attend certain named surgeries and branch surgeries at stated hours. The existing Government dispensaries would form the nucleus of this network of surgeries. Doctors in more remote areas would be provided with a service tenancy. The level of monthly contractual payments would vary according to whether accommodation was provided and according to the popularity of the area. It would not, however, vary *pari passu* with the number of patients registered with the doctor.

As more doctors became available, the number of doctors working in each area could be increased or the size of areas reduced. Each patient would be given a card saying where and when his doctor was available. It might also be possible to operate a regional night emergency service. The patient would be given the regional telephone number and the doctor on duty would make a domiciliary visit if requested.

Such in outline is our plan. We hope it will prove popular with both patients and doctors. We attribute the reluctance of doctors to join the present Government Medical Service to a number of factors. One is the heavy burden of public assistance certification which we hope to reduce by other proposals in our Report. Another is the large number of patients to be seen, which makes a high and professionally satisfying standard of medical care hard to provide. A third is the lack of continuity of care as so many patients "shop around" between different dispensaries and outpatient departments.

Owing to the shortage of doctors it will be impossible to reduce the load on each doctor to what we would consider desirable. But if more private doctors agree to join the new service, the burden of work on each doctor will be correspondingly reduced. Also we hope that doctors will be attracted by the prospect of having their own patients who have chosen to come to them and whom they have agreed to treat. It is clearly undesirable to allow patients to "shop around" among different Government doctors looking for a "dramatic cure", a prescription for a new drug, or someone who will sign a certificate of sickness. Continuity of care must be encouraged. Moreover, hospitals should not be burdened with general practitioner work in their outpatient departments. Their proper function is to provide more specialised services and diagnostic facilities. On the other hand, it is equally undesirable for a patient to be attached permanently to a doctor in whom he has no confidence or for a doctor to have a patient whom he regards as uncooperative. Mutual confidence between patient and doctor is essential to an effective relationship. This is what we hope will develop in the new service. It would, however, clearly be impractical to allow patients to choose any doctor in the island. If doctors accepted patients from all over the island, they would spend more time travelling than being doctors.

Experience in other countries has shown that it is very difficult to induce doctors to live outside the main urban centres where there are substantial opportunities for private practice even though many doctors living in such centres are not themselves benefitting greatly from them. The introduction of a standard "capitation" payment to the doctor for each patient on his "list" certainly failed to solve this problem in Britain between 1913 and 1948. Under the National Health Service, a special system of indirect control had to be introduced which is only very gradually evening out the distribution of doctors in different parts of Britain.

We hope to solve this problem in Mauritius by the incentive method which is used in Sweden. We believe that doctors will be attracted to live in less popular areas by the offer of a free house and some monetary differential. Moreover, it would be clearly understood that doctors taking such assignments were not necessarily taking on an appointment for life. One of the features of the British National Health Service, and indeed of the system of medical care evolved earlier, which general practitioners find unwelcome is their continued isolation from the hospitals where new treatments are being developed. It seems to us desirable that doctors who have served for several years as general practitioners in more remote areas should be offered hospital appointments either permanently or as a prelude to general practitioner work in another area.

Where residences are provided it should be possible for some consultations to take place in the more homely surroundings of a surgery attached to the residence. Also, the existing dispensaries could be converted into branch surgeries. They should be made more private, more pleasant to work in and the waiting facilities should be improved. We think that this could be done without a heavy expenditure of money. We would also like to see an increasing number of consultations taking place in the patient's own home. There is no need to stress the important part that can be played in any health service by an efficient home visiting service, not only in the practice of good medicine but also in preventing unnecessary admissions to hospital.

The main difficulty with our plan, as indeed of any system which could be devised for bringing better family doctor services to the population of Mauritius, is the heavy burden of work which will fall upon the doctors at the surgeries and branch surgeries. Until there are more doctors, no dramatic improvement can take place in the amount of time which, on average, each doctor can give to patients. Everything possible must, therefore, be done to save the doctor's time and to make sure that he only sees cases which require his personal attention. If a doctor feels that he can delegate responsibilities, the staff must be available to take them. And the more skilled the doctor's assistants, the more he will feel able to delegate.

This raises the question of the training of the nursing staff who at present work at the dispensaries. Already they diagnose or "spot" simple complaints and undertake other semi-medical duties. In Ceylon, there is a category of "apothecary" who is specially trained to do work of this kind. It would seem possible to develop in Mauritius, possibly with the help of the World Health Organisation, a special form of training (lasting perhaps from one to two years) for selected people, both men and women, who will then be able to take greater responsibility and be more effective assistants then the present "dressers". We envisage that this training would be taken after the basic nursing qualification. These assistants might then be more safely trusted by the doctor to screen the patients coming to the dispensaries, treat the simpler cases, and discharge other duties under the direction of the doctor.

One reason for recommending a greater use of auxiliaries than is customary in wealthier countries is the cost which would be immediately involved in providing a medical service in Mauritius on the same scale as that obtaining in such countries. Inevitably, salary scales for doctors cannot be far out of line with those in the United Kingdom and other high income countries. Already, doctors' incomes amount to nearly $\frac{1}{2}\%$ of the Mauritian national income. The proportion of the national income which is spent on National Health Service doctors in the United Kingdom is about $\frac{2}{3}\%$. If it were possible to provide immediately the same number of doctors per head of the population as there are in the United Kingdom, nearly 2% of the national income of Mauritius (or one-twelfth of the present total Government revenue) would be spent on Government and private doctors alone. Rapid population growth in the next few years might push the proportion even higher.

One duty which would fall upon the doctor's assistants would be the control and issue of the drugs prescribed by the doctor. We envisage that this duty would be very much in mind when the special "post-graduate" training courses are designed. We do not recommend that the prescriptions of Government doctors should be made up by private pharmacists. Such a system would not be economical and would open the door to many expensive abuses which could not possibly be afforded. We recommend therefore that a wider range of preparations should be made available locally than is at present the case in the Government Service.

Given goodwill on all sides, we believe that this system of organising the general practitioner services will gain the cooperation of the medical profession in Mauritius. We are convinced that it would provide a better service to the patients. It also has many intrinsic advantages for the doctors. They will have more contact with the hospitals, more opportunities than in private practice for regular leave abroad and periods of advanced study, more freedom to prescribe on medical grounds alone, greater possibilities of developing a preventive approach to medical care, and guaranteed pensions on retirement.

We consider, therefore, that the form of panel practice which we have outlined above represents a substantial improvement for both doctors and patients on the type of practice recommended by our predecessors. Under a capitation system of payment, it would be impossible to give doctors the same variety of experience and the same leave and study opportunities. It would also be extremely difficult to agree upon a level of capitation payment which seemed fair to the doctor in view of what is paid for similar services in the United Kingdom and yet was not so high as eventually to destroy the vital preventive, hospital and specialist services.

If, for example, the British system of organising general practice were introduced in Mauritius in the present circumstances, the cost of the pharmaceutical service might well reach fantastic heights. Even if Mauritian doctors prescribed as British doctors do, the cost would amount to about Rs. 12 million—nearly the total cost of the present medical service. Because of the social, economic and ethical reasons we have mentioned earlier the cost of prescribing might well be much higher. In the present state of the economy and the prospect of rapid population growth, we do not think that Mauritius can risk a bill of this magnitude. Such studies as have been made suggest that Britain has by no means the highest bill for pharmaceuticals. The cost in France has been reckoned to be greater than in Britain and the traditions of French medicine among some of the doctors in Mauritius could lead to even higher costs than if British standards were followed in Mauritius.

THE DENTAL SERVICES

Our recommendations to this point have been confined to the medical services. We now wish to make some comment about the existing dental services and the availability of dentists. The situation here is very different from that in the medical services. There is no shortage of applicants for service with the Government. Yet at present there are only five dentists employed and about 20 dentists in the island engaged partly or wholly in private practice. We understand that when a new post was recently advertised for a Government dental officer there were 12 applications. This and other evidence we have received indicates that the only restriction on the development of the dental service is the willingness of the Government to pay for it. In our view, the public dental services should be developed and enlarged and for the following reasons. First, it seems to us wrong in principle that medical officers and even dressers should be attempting extractions without any training at all. Secondly, there would be some relief to the over-strained medical service if this work were undertaken by qualified dentists. Thirdly, it is a misuse of resources for many extractions to take place in hospitals. Fourthly, the preventive services are sadly inadequate.

We therefore recommend the extension of the Government Dental Service on the following lines. First, we would like to see the development of a free, priority dental service for *all* children and expectant mothers. One of the purposes of this service in the schools and through the maternity and child welfare services would be to encourage habits of oral hygiene as a preventive and educative measure. In addition, there is a need for the provision of more mobile dental units. We see no reason why moderate charges should not be levied. The charges should be waived in cases where the patient is an old age pensioner or receiving public assistance or insurance benefits.

We recommend also that use should be made in the priority services of dental assistants of the New Zealand type. A school has recently been opened in Ceylon for training such assistants and there might be a case for a similar school or course in Mauritius. Experience gained in New Zealand and elsewhere has shown that the dental assistant is able to provide certain limited treatments for school children under the direction of a qualified dentist.

A NATIONAL HEALTH SERVICE

After this review of the medical and dental services, preventive and curative, in Mauritius, it remains for us to consider whether free services should continue to be provided only for the indigent and certain categories of Government employees or whether minimum services should be provided free for the whole population subject to the charges we have named. At present, free services are available to:—

(1) Government officers and artisans if injured in discharge of their duties.

(2) Government officers, servants and employees and their dependants if treated as outpatients. Inpatients are charged according to their salaries.

(3) Labourers in Government service.

(4) Police and prison officers of and below the rank of inspector and chief warden and their wives and children under 14.

(5) Paupers.

The remainder of the population are, in theory, paying patients. There are standard charges for dressings, X-rays, laboratory investigations and other services. The charges are in general far below the cost of providing the service. Inpatients are divided into three classes at the discretion of medical officers and pay Rs. 5·00, 2·50 or 1·00 per day according to the class into which they are placed. All these charges are substantially below cost.

Not only is the classification of paying inpatients arbitrary but no proper tests are applied to ascertain whether a particular patient should pay nothing or the subsidised charge. As a result, the amount collected from all charges is below Rs. 100,000, considerably less than 1% of the cost of the whole medical service.

Experience in other countries has shown that it is extremely difficult to operate any effective system of charging according to means unless services are refused to persons who do not make payments in advance or produce concrete evidence that they are entitled to free services. Such a practice if ruthlessly enforced would be in conflict with the whole spirit and purpose of our recommendations. Medical need must be met first and enquiries made afterwards. Moreover, such enquiries can involve a very heavy administrative cost and much misuse of the doctor's time. Serious illness interrupts earning capacity and unless wages and salaries are continued during periods of incapacity even those with relatively high incomes may be unable today to pay their medical bills.

It is clear from the evidence we have received that the present system of charges is not operating in the way it was intended to work. Many patients who should pay charges are receiving free treatment. For the reasons given above it would be extremely difficult and costly to operate any system of administration which would succeed in extracting charges from all those who should be paying them. Moreover, the medical service is financed out of taxes and we have suggested that it should continue to be paid for in this way.

Thus, we recommend that the Government Medical Service should be available to anyone who wishes to make use of it without any examination of their means. Those parts of it which are available without payment should be available to the whole population. But the service must be regarded as an integrated single system. Admission to a free bed should only be allowed on the recommendation of a doctor working in the service. Hospitals must not be allowed to admit patients to free beds on the recommendations of private doctors. There will inevitably be more demands for hospital beds than can be met immediately, and the assessment of priorities must be in the hands of those doctors who are responsible for the service and for the allocation of resources in the face of conflicting needs.

We are aware that the provision of free hospital places will make it cheaper for some patients to be admitted to hospital than to be looked after at home. This is a particularly relevant consideration when employees receive full pay during illness. We consider that this problem is much better and more easily dealt with by reductions in sick pay and sickness benefit while the patient is in hospital than by imposing charges for hospital care.

All this represents a major change in principle. No longer will the free service cater only for paupers and certain other classes of patients. It will be a national service available to the whole population. This significant development in policy should be marked by changing the name of the service to the National Health Service of Mauritius. We hope that as our recommendations are adopted the free service will acquire a higher reputation among patients and doctors alike and that it will be used increasingly by the better-off sections of the community, who expect good standards of care and will not passively accept inconvenience or discourtesy. The use of the service by the more fortunate members of the community could bring greater public awareness of its achievements and shortcomings.

Our proposals do not mean that private patients and private doctors should be unable to make use of the facilities in the Government hospitals. In principle, we feel that the services should be available privately, but that the *full* cost should be charged to the private user. This means that the full cost should be charged for X-rays, pathological examinations and other services provided for private patients through the agency of private doctors. We also consider that Government specialists should continue to be entitled to give private consultations at the request of private doctors, providing they take place outside their normal hours of duty. Standard charges should be made for these services which should be subject to regulations laid down by the Minister.

We appreciate that it will be some years before the standard of care provided free in the general wards of the public hospitals will satisfy the wealthier sections of the population. Moreover, this group will expect and be able to pay for higher standards of amenity while in hospital than the country can afford to provide for all patients for many years to come. In these circumstances, we suggest that private wards should be provided as part of the public hospitals and that charges should be made to cover the cost of *all* the services including the depreciation charges on the buildings. The private sector of hospital care would thus develop as an integral part of the hospital services. This is in the best interests of the Government Service as nursing and other staff will more readily appreciate what is involved in a high standard of service. Private patients will also have the full advantages of being cared for in a large hospital with its complement of specialist and diagnostic services.

We recognise that our proposals will bring the private wards into competition with the five existing nursing homes and with the new clinic which opens this year. This seems to us to be a desirable development. It would certainly be wrong to deprive private patients of the services of Government specialists should they need them. Specialists can also be expected to do their best work in surroundings with which they are familiar and with modern equipment and services at their command. We therefore believe that private facilities will be better deployed in the long run as an integral part of a large public hospital where a full range of diagnostic aids and other costly services can be provided economically. In terms of good medical and surgical care, there is no future for small private clinics.

SUMMARY OF RECOMMENDATIONS

Our main recommendations in this and the preceding chapter are aimed at transforming the Government Medical Service into a comprehensive National Health Service, including a general practitioner service providing each patient on an area basis with his own personal medical adviser. The National Health Service of Mauritius should not be a second-rate service. It must offer the highest standards of medical care that Mauritius can afford.

The greatest single obstacle to the attainment of this aim is the acute shortage of doctors. Our proposals for the alleviation of this shortage may be summarised as follows:—

(*a*) as a short-term measure, efforts should be made to recruit doctors from abroad, especially for the hospital service;

(*b*) arrangements for the recruitment of Mauritian doctors should be streamlined so as to eliminate the delays and wastage which occur at present;

(*c*) more scholarships should be given to medical students, subject to a test of parents' financial resources and an undertaking to return to Mauritius after training or to repay the value of the scholarship over a number of years;

(*d*) a number of scholarships should be awarded for study in countries such as Australia, where opportunities to remain after qualification would not be so readily available as in Britain and France;

(*e*) a certain number of scholarships should be reserved each year for women students.

In accordance with the policy of giving Government aid to students on grounds of merit only, we recommend the abolition of the special income tax allowance for children educated abroad. The extra revenue collected should pay for the additional scholarships.

The second major obstacle to the improvement of the health services of Mauritius is the problem of professional ethics. We recommend that a General Medical Council should be established and also appropriate professional bodies with responsibilities for the nursing and pharmacist professions. In addition, an expert committee should be set up to enquire into the import, distribution and control of pharmaceutical preparations.

Priority should be given to the preventive services. We particularly stress the need for developments in the maternity and child welfare services. A start should be made immediately to provide a family planning service throughout the island. We hope that a consortium of charitable foundations might make a grant to improve and develop such a service. We would also recommend a campaign of health education aimed particularly at the elimination of hookworm.

We propose a number of improvements in the hospital service. Efforts should be made to reduce the shortage of hospital beds, partly by the development of district hospitals. A hospital and training centre for mental defectives is an urgent need. We recommend the appointment of a psychiatric social worker for the mental services as soon as training can be arranged.

The sugar estate medical services have a useful function to perform in tending minor injuries and ailments. We recommend that they should be taken over by the Government. Except in special cases there seems no case for compensation to be paid either to the existing staff for loss of office or to the sugar estates for the premises acquired by the Government Service.

The island should be divided into areas and three or four family doctors should be established in each area. The duties of the doctor would be to provide general practitioner services at stated hours in surgeries and branch surgeries. He would be encouraged to do home visits. Such doctors would eventually be assisted by specially trained nursing staff. Pharmaceutical services would be provided by the Government and it is recommended that a larger range of preparations should be kept in stock in each area than is at present provided at the dispensaries.

We recommend that the priority dental services for mothers and children should be expanded and improved. Dental assistants should be trained to work in this service under the direction of qualified dentists. The mobile dental service should be further developed.

Hospital facilities should be free where recommended by doctors working in the service. Private patients should be charged the full cost of any services provided for them and pay beds should be provided at the Government hospitals.

The adoption of all our recommendations will call for far-reaching developments in the organisation and provision of medical services. We think that these should be marked by changing the name of the service to the National Health Service of Mauritius.

CHAPTER 11

Institutional Care

In Chapters 4 and 8 we set out the history of "outdoor relief" and made recommendations for improvements in the assessment and administration of financial assistance granted to people in their own homes. This chapter is concerned with the other principal responsibility of the Public Assistance Department—"indoor relief".

THE HISTORICAL BACKGROUND

The system of institutional care is largely a legacy from the old Poor Law. There is a wealth of historical material in the reports of numerous official enquiries, but in this summary we shall only deal with the history of the institutions since 1900. The Poor Law Ordinance of 1902 laid on the Commissioner the duty of establishing and directing the management of "almshouses, workhouses, infirmaries and other asylums for the poor". It also provided a "workhouse test" for the payment of outdoor relief (see Chapter 8). The duties of the Poor Law Department regarding the care of children were laid down in sections 10 and 11 of the Ordinance:—

"10. The Commissioner shall provide for the protection and care, and for the instruction and employment of destitute orphans, and of children whose parents are paupers.

"11. If any parent abandon, or otherwise neglect to take care of any of his children, and such child be under fifteen years of age, and be found destitute and in want of relief, the Poor Law Officer shall provide for the protection and relief of such child, and the expense so incurred shall be recoverable from such parent.

"Any parent guilty of such abandonment or neglect of any of his children shall, on complaint of the Poor Law Officer, or of any person authorized by him, be liable to imprisonment not exceeding one month and a fine not exceeding fifty rupees for the first offence, and not exceeding one hundred rupees for each subsequent offence".

The institutions to which paupers were sent at this time included the Barkly Asylum and a number of Catholic infirmaries, orphanages and convents. The Barkly Asylum, situated at Beau Bassin, was the only non-medical institution managed by the Poor Law Department. It was apparently intended to provide accommodation for destitute old people and children, with a small infirmary attached. However, the infirmary had grown into a public hospital,* which contained 373 patients at the time of the 1901 census. The asylum itself, according to the same source, had a population of only 48.† The building had originally been a sugar factory, and was condemned in the strongest terms by Dr. Balfour in 1921.‡

When accommodation was not available at the Barkly Asylum, the paupers were sent to one of the Catholic institutions, of which ten are listed in the 1901 census report—five orphanages and five infirmaries.§ Although a "workhouse test" was provided for in the Poor Law Ordinance, there were no workhouses in the sense in which the term was used in Britain. ‖ Nor were there any almshouses or other institutions, religious or otherwise, specifically for the care of the old.¶

In 1909, the Poor Law Department paid Rs. 10 a month for each pauper committed to the care of the nuns.** This *per capita* grant has survived to the present day. It has been raised many times and reduced at least once (in 1931 after a fall in the cost of living).††

In the various Royal Commissions and Committees of Enquiry which have studied these problems since 1900 the subject of indoor relief received much less attention than that of outdoor relief. The 1909 Royal Commission, as a corollary to its proposal to abolish the Poor Law Department, suggested that the Medical and Health Department should take over the administration of indoor relief.‡‡ However, as the Poor Law Department was not abolished but amalgamated with the office of the Protector of Immigrants, this suggestion lapsed.

In 1929, the Poor Relief Enquiry Commission§§ visited five institutions in one day, and reported that conditions in three of them were "good", one was "not so good", and the last, Calebasses, was "fairly good" but nevertheless in urgent need of improvements, especially for the "tuberculosis infirms". They noted a lack of

---

* *Mauritius Royal Commission*, 1909, Minutes of Evidence, Cmd. 5186, 1910, p. 347.
† *Census of Mauritius and its Dependencies*, 1901, p. 165.
‡ Balfour, A., *Report on Medical Matters in Mauritius*, 1921, p. 3. The asylum was closed in 1926, being replaced for medical purposes by the Victoria Hospital, while Calebasses Infirmary became the only Government-owned Poor Law Institution.
§ *Census of Mauritius and its Dependencies*, 1901, p. 165.
‖ *Mauritius Royal Commission*, 1909, Minutes of Evidence, Cmd. 5186, 1910, p. 127.
¶ *Ibid.*, p. 130.
** *Ibid.*, p. 128.
†† *Annual Report of the Poor Law Commissioner*, 1932, p. 7.
‡‡ *Report of Mauritius Royal Commission*, 1909, Cmd. 5185, 1910, p. 43.
§§ See footnote ‡, p. 70.

discipline at Calebasses and a refusal of the inmates to perform any work. They proposed that all "infirms" should be concentrated in one institution, with separate quarters for tuberculosis cases and the chronic sick. Since this proposal was made "subject to the finances of the Colony being available to meet expenditure", it is fair to assume that the Commission did not anticipate any financial saving from the transfer of the infirmary inmates to a single Government institution. No similar proposal was made regarding the orphanages.

Mr. G. Atchia, dissenting from the findings of the majority of the Commission, urged that the "workhouse test" should be abandoned. It was, he complained, very much more expensive to insist on paupers entering an institution when a small cash payment could have kept them out. He also criticised the failure of the authorities to supply orphans as domestic servants to all who applied for them, and the fact that some of the orphans supplied were "notoriously bad characters".

The Commissioners' proposal for a single Government infirmary was not implemented. Dissatisfaction continued to be expressed with a situation in which non-Christians were obliged (and could be required as a condition of relief) to enter Christian institutions. Most of the institutions were managed by the Catholic nuns (including the Government-owned Calebasses Infirmary), the only non-Catholic institutions being two Church of England orphanages and a Presbyterian infirmary. The first step away from this Christian "monopoly" was the opening of the Muslim Orphanage in 1937. By the end of the year, 62 children had been admitted, and the number of children in all the orphanages had risen to 163 from 97 at the beginning of the year.* It seems that the new orphanage satisfied a real need and that Muslim children had not been entering the orphanages previously.

In December 1941 one ward of 50 beds at Calebasses was taken over for direct administration by the Government on non-denominational lines. It was hoped that this ward would become a model for the other institutions and at first it seems to have been a success. Nevertheless, in October 1946, this promising experiment was terminated on the recommendation of the Central Poor Law Advisory Board. The only explanation given in the Annual Report of the Poor Law Department was that "the senior officers of the Department could not give adequate attention to the running of the institution".†

By that time, however, the denominational basis of the institutions

---

* *Annual Report of the Poor Law Department*, 1937, p. 7.
† *Annual Report of the Poor Law Department*, 1946, p. 4.

had been broadened by the opening of a Muslim infirmary and a Hindu infirmary and orphanage. While the Muslim institutions admitted only Muslims and the Hindu institutions only admitted Hindus, the Christian institutions, with more beds at their disposal, continued to welcome inmates of all denominations.* By the end of 1946 there were 538 adults and 179 children in the institutions.†

After the war, a more critical attitude to the running of the institutions began to emerge, perhaps partly as a result of the Calebasses experiment. The need for cheerful surroundings, good food, contacts with the world outside the institution, useful occupations and in general a more constructively human approach was increasingly recognised.

In 1946, a Lady Visiting Officer was appointed. Her duties were roughly those of welfare officer to the institutions and included visits to the foster-homes of children boarded out from the orphanages. Boarding-out was done on a very small scale, care being taken to find homes whose religious and cultural background did not conflict with that of the child. Unfortunately, neither the employment of a Lady Visiting Officer nor the boarding-out of children seems to have continued for long. The practice of placing orphans in domestic service was also discontinued—at least in theory. Another scheme started about the same time was the provision of a "god-mother" for each of the 180 children in the orphanages. By the end of 1947, every child had such a "god-mother" to act as a friendly contact outside the institution. This scheme also, however, seems to have been largely abandoned when the initial enthusiasm waned,‡ though a few "god-mothers" have continued to visit the children.

Much of the domestic work of the institutions, including cooking, gardening and cleaning, had always been done by the inmates, but in most cases no payment had been made for the work. In 1947, a scheme was devised for growing fruit and vegetables and for developing other occupations by which the inmates of the infirmaries could earn a small but welcome amount of pocket-money instead of begging in the streets. This scheme was envisaged as part of a general process of rehabilitation. At the same time, therefore, an attempt was made to classify the inmates so that those who could be rehabilitated might be segregated in one of two infirmaries, tuberculous cases in a third, and "discharged lunatics" and epileptics in a fourth.§ Although the process of classification does not seem

* *Annual Report of the Poor Law Department*, 1946, p. 4.
† *Ibid.*, p. 19.
‡ See Annual Reports of *Poor Law Department*, 1946, and *Public Assistance Department*, 1947.
§ *Annual Report of Public Assistance Department*, 1947, p. 6.

to have been taken as far as was intended, some degree of segregation was in fact achieved.

An enquiry into the diet of the institutions was carried out by the Nutrition Officer, Miss J. C. Chettle, in 1947. Her findings, based on measurements of all food issued in four institutions during a given week, were alarming. "At this level of intake", she reported, "the adults of the infirmaries cannot be expected to be in a reasonable state of health, mentally or physically, and they must be incapable of doing any regular work".* In the case of the children, the situation was even more serious: "With the diet they are at present getting, they cannot be satisfying their energy needs, let alone their requirements for growth".† Owing to deficiencies of equipment the food was usually cold by the time it was served, and before being served it was often covered with flies.

Miss Chettle worked out minimum diet scales for adults and children, the cost of which she estimated at 60c. a day in each case. These diets, however, would only be adequate if the inmates were doing no work; they were to be regarded as "a preliminary improvement only".‡ Although there was some doubt as to how much of the *per capita* grant then being paid (60c. a day for adults, 40c. for children and 70c. for "imbeciles") was intended to be spent on food, it was clear, Miss Chettle stated, that it could not cover the cost of an adequate diet as well as fuel, clothing, medicine and other essentials.§ As a result of this report the grants were increased by 10c. a day per head, and a committee was appointed by the Public Assistance Commissioner to consider what further steps should be taken. This committee recommended that the grant for children should be raised to 85c. a day for food alone, and that an increase of 20% should be given for adults.

It is barely credible that anything should have been allowed to delay the implementation of Miss Chettle's minimum diet which she herself considered inadequate. And yet in the Poor Law Department's Annual Report for 1948, it was said that "owing to a reduction in the vote it was unfortunately not possible to enforce the diet laid down by the Nutrition Officer last year".‖ The 1949 report states that although "steps have been taken to secure the implementation of the diet worked out by the Nutrition Officer . . . there have been difficulties such as seasonal shortage . . ."¶ Not until 1950 was the *per capita* grant increased to Rs. 25 per month,

* Chettle, J. C., *Report on the Feeding in Infirmaries and Orphanages*, 1949, p. 4.
† *Ibid.*, p. 4.
‡ *Ibid.*, p. 6.
§ *Ibid.*, p. 7.
‖ *Annual Report of the Public Assistance Department*, 1948, p. 5.
¶ *Annual Report of the Public Assistance Department*, 1949, p. 7.

for both adults and children—roughly the level recommended two and a half years previously. Since then, rises in the cost of living have led to three further increases, bringing the grant to its present level of Rs. 1·20 a day per head. In 1954 the Commissioner reported that "the nutritive value of the ordinary diet has . . . considerably improved",* though it is not clear on what evidence this statement was based.

In 1950, an additional grant of Rs. 100 a month was given to each institution "towards the expenses of the building";† clothing, bedding, and other articles were also issued by the Public Assistance Department on an approved scale for each inmate.

Special provision has been made since 1946 for the institutional care of the blind. A school for the blind was opened in a private residence, and subsequently transferred to a temporary building in the grounds of the Poor Law Office in Port Louis. Blind people, mostly from the infirmaries, came each day, the cost being borne largely by private subscriptions. Basket-making was taught, and a few individuals who were not blind but suffered from other disabilities gave assistance.‡ The school was managed by the Welfare of the Blind and Prevention of Blindness Society. In 1958, the Loïs Lagesse Residential and Training Centre was opened, providing not only occupational facilities for about 40 people, but also residential accommodation for about 20 men. A small number of blind women who at first attended the Centre ceased to do so, as it was felt to be inadvisable for blind men and women to work together.

THE INFIRMARIES AND ORPHANAGES TODAY

From our own observations and inquiries we have formed the opinion that some of the existing institutions in Mauritius still do not provide an adequate standard of care. The reasons for this are partly financial, but an important factor is undoubtedly the lack of properly qualified staff.

Too many of the 16 institutions still bear the stigma of the Poor Law. There is a serious failure to understand the emotional needs of children, the aged and the infirm. What is provided is not the humane atmosphere of "home", but the bare, dehumanised minimum of "indoor relief". It must be emphasised that this general and depressing impression conceals many individual examples of devotion and humanity, though even these tend to be stultified

---

* *Annual Report of the Public Assistance Department*, 1954, p. 7.
† *Annual Report of the Public Assistance Department*, 1950, p. 6.
‡ *Annual Report of the Public Assistance Department*, 1947, pp. 9-10.

by financial stringency. It is only fair to add that some of the shortcomings of institutional care in Mauritius are broadly typical of what is to be found in some European countries. Indeed, a similar picture was painted by investigators of the English Poor Law only a decade or so ago.

The institutions are classified as "orphanages" and "infirmaries". With the exception of Calebasses Infirmary, all of them still belong to bodies representing the various religious communities: Roman Catholic, Church of England, Presbyterian, Hindu and Muslim. Even Calebasses, though owned by the Government and in theory non-denominational, is run by the Catholic Sisters of Mercy and has a newly-built Catholic chapel. There is as yet no Hindu infirmary for men.

The institutions have three sources of income: the allowance of Rs. 1·20 per day from the Public Assistance Department for each eligible inmate; contributions from the inmates themselves, their relatives or other interested persons; and money raised by the institution in the form of donations, profits from "fancy fairs" and other activities.

As we have seen, the subsidy of Rs. 1·20 per head paid by the Department is derived from the old Poor Law. Although the "workhouse test" is no longer applied, the Department remains responsible for the destitute inmates of the infirmaries and orphanages. Nearly 700 of the 800 inmates of the infirmaries are maintained by the Department, but well over half of the 400 children in the orphanages derive their maintenance from other sources. The Poor Law Regulations of 1946 authorise the Commissioner to make grants to any charitable institution "for the upkeep of paupers", such grants to be "fixed from time to time . . . in accordance with the cost of living and . . . proportionate to the number of its inmates".

In December 1959 and January 1960, the Public Assistance Department, with the generous assistance of a number of voluntary workers, carried out at our request a survey of the population of the institutions. By analysing the results of this survey, we were able to obtain a more detailed picture than was previously available of the circumstances of these 1,200 men, women and children. Owing to the speed with which the survey was carried out, the statistical results are not sufficiently reliable for full publication. However, the broad results are informative and raise a number of questions on which further enquiry seems desirable.

The survey covered 11 infirmaries and 11 children's homes—a somewhat more accurate description than "orphanage" since most of the children have at least one parent living but for one reason or another are deprived of family life. Six of the institutions comprise both an infirmary and a children's home. Most of them are fairly large, in population if not in size. Only one has less than 30 inmates, while the largest, Calebasses Infirmary, has nearly 200.

In general, residence in an institution seems to result as much from the lack of a normal home as from any other cause. Although most of the children have one parent living, few have both parents living together. In the infirmaries there are very few married people. Most are single or widowed. By contrast with the children's homes, few even of the younger inmates have parents living. Such evidence as was collected regarding inmates' children suggests that few of those who are or have been married are the parents of large families. In short, a large proportion of these people cannot obtain the support which the Mauritian family traditionally gives to its less fortunate members because they do not have the extensive network of family connections on which such support depends. Thus, any infirmity which prevents them from being self-sufficient drives them inexorably into an institution. Once there, with no home to return to, they are likely to remain for many years—perhaps for the rest of their lives. Of 319 infirmary inmates aged under 55, as many as 48 had been in the same institution for more than 10 years.

The basic problem is a social one—that of enabling those who lack the support of a family to weather the crises of everyday life without being compelled to find shelter in an institution, whether it be a hospital, an infirmary or an orphanage; and of ensuring that those who are admitted to such institutions as a result of short-term difficulties do not become long-term residents. Part of the answer, especially in the case of children, lies in a policy of "boarding-out", which we shall discuss more fully when we come to consider the future of the institutions.

Some attempt is at present made to classify inmates by age, sex, religion, social class and type of disability. Because these various classifications do not coincide, the population of some of the institutions is extremely mixed. The infirmaries are in many ways reminiscent of the "general mixed institutions" which flourished in England in the nineteenth century and were roundly condemned in the Minority Report of the 1909 Royal Commission on the Poor Laws. The same institution may house the aged, the paralysed, the mentally deficient, young asthmatics, unmarried mothers and cripples, together with convalescents from the hospitals, cases of tuberculosis and even juvenile offenders. The situation in the children's homes is in some ways even more disturbing. In one boys' home, for example, youngsters of eight and nine share a dormitory with handicapped men in their twenties.

If the need for classification is not sufficiently appreciated, such attempts as are made to segregate the inmates by age groups or types of infirmity are largely frustrated by chronic overcrowding and by the size of wards or dormitories. The boys' home referred to above, built very recently, has only one dormitory containing 60 beds. In another home we saw a girls' dormitory with about 20 beds so close together that there was barely room to move between them. On the wall was a prominently displayed notice bearing the single word "SILENCE".

Classification by religion is strictly adhered to in children's homes. There are nevertheless a few exceptions—mainly children in Catholic homes whose fathers are stated to be (or to have been) Hindu or Protestant. In the infirmaries the inmates are classified by religion as far as possible, but as most of the infirmaries are owned or managed by the nuns, and there is no Hindu men's infirmary, inevitably a number of non-Catholics are to be found in Catholic institutions. In addition, 37 Indo-Mauritians in Catholic infirmaries were stated to be Catholics—a surprisingly high number which may, however, be due to inaccurate reporting.

Classification by sex is also applied rigidly, sometimes resulting in total segregation even where the two sexes are housed in the same institution. Given the limited number of institutions and the nature of the buildings, it is clear that if the inmates are to be classified at all strictly in terms of religion and sex, it must be physically impossible to provide separate accommodation for those who have particular needs for treatment or rehabilitation, or for different age groups. There simply are not enough different buildings. Thus, while the majority of mentally deficient inmates are to be found at the Calebasses and Père Laval infirmaries for men and women respectively, the rest are scattered among all the other infirmaries. In general, there is more opportunity of classifying the inmates of the Catholic institutions than of the non-Catholic institutions. There is, for example, only one Muslim children's home, which is therefore compelled to accommodate Muslim children of all ages from birth to the late teens, though the strictest segregation of the sexes is practised. Similarly, there is nothing in the nature of an old people's home, since old people, whether in possession of their faculties or not, have to be accommodated in the same premises as infirm people of all ages.

Most of the institutions' population are housed in buildings which, in terms of construction and materials, must compare favourably with the homes from which many of the inmates come. Although solidly built, however, they are mostly cheerless and uninviting, sparsely furnished and, above all, lacking in privacy.

In one of the orphanages, for example, there was nowhere for the boys to keep any private possessions; we were told that they had none, and that if they were given toys they would only break them. In another orphanage the children are bathed *en masse* in large concrete tubs.

Unpleasant and psychologically harmful though this lack of comfort and privacy must be for the children, it is perhaps even worse for the old people in the infirmaries, especially for the sick. They usually have bedside cupboards, but these are pitifully small. Apart from their beds, they often have nowhere to sit except an open verandah or, in fine weather, a garden. At Calebasses (which is considered a show-piece) there is not even an adequate dining-room, and meals have to be eaten in the wards, on the verandah or in the garden.

The scheme by which the inmates are paid a small wage for giving some help with the domestic work, the gardening or the rearing of animals is still in operation, though no standard wage scales have been laid down. At Calebasses, they receive 35c. a day for four hours' work, and higher rates for the more responsible jobs.

The staff of the institutions are, with few exceptions, untrained, but some of them bring to their work a devotion and sympathy which reflects many years of experience in this field. In the case of the nuns who run most of the institutions (more than half of which are Catholic) we know little about the training they receive, but what is impressive is the selflessness with which they devote themselves to their allotted tasks. Nevertheless, in visiting the institutions we frequently observed a need for training in modern methods of institutional care. In one non-Catholic infirmary, the staff employed seemed totally unsuitable, and we felt that what was needed in this instance was not training but replacement.

In some of the infirmaries the latrines and washing facilities leave much to be desired. In most cases water closets have been installed, but pit latrines are still to be found. In at least one infirmary buckets are the only provision: they are not emptied every day. Equally important is the location of latrines. They are often situated some distance from the main building, and it must be difficult, if not impossible, for many of the inmates to use them, especially at night. The bathrooms, which usually contain only a douche, are also often inconveniently situated.

We heard a number of complaints regarding the food served in the institutions. From what we saw, we could not judge the nutritional adequacy of the diet, but in other respects many of the criticisms made by Miss Chettle in 1947 still apply. The meals are lacking in variety and have most of the defects usually associated with institutional cooking. This is partly a financial question and partly the result of rather primitive cooking facilities, often some distance from the point where the food is served. Lack of money affects not only the kinds of food that can be purchased but also the kitchen staff that can be employed. At Calebasses, for instance, one of the inmates acts as cook, for which he is paid a pocket-money wage (we would add that we have no reason to suppose that in this particular case the effect on the meals is bad).

We were able to visit 14 institutions in all, but as none of these visits lasted much more than an hour, and some of them considerably less, our impressions of the general atmosphere were inevitably subjective and superficial. However, from what we saw, from the answers to the questions we asked, and from other inquiries we made, we considered that financial stringency, overcrowding and lack of trained staff were preventing the development of a homely and socially constructive environment. Among the factors which we felt to be symptomatic of an unimaginative approach were the following:—

(1) The wearing of uniforms occurs both in the infirmaries and in the orphanages. We recognise that this may be a result of the need to provide clothing as cheaply as possible. In some cases, the clothes, although identical, may not be thought of as a uniform. Nonetheless, the wearing of identical clothing, whether by adults or children, seems to us to be most undesirable. We were told that the blue and white uniform worn by mental defectives is intended to prevent them from straying away from the institution. This did not seem to us to justify the practice.

(2) We have mentioned the lack of space for private possessions. It is most important that children should have the experience of owning and caring for their own possessions, however small, however ragged. A child with nothing (not even the clothes he wears) which he can call his own is unlikely to develop much respect for the property of others. We were told by one senior official that a high proportion of criminal offenders had been brought up in the orphanages.

The propensity of old people to treasure small personal possessions is well known, and to deny them the right to surround themselves with these possessions, even at the cost of a certain untidiness, can only be condemned.

(3) We found that social contacts between the sexes were generally discouraged. At one infirmary, the men and women, although housed some 20 yards apart, were not allowed to visit each other, the only exceptions to this rule being a married couple who are allowed to meet once a week. In the orphanages,

segregation of the sexes can only encourage homosexual tendencies and the feelings of guilt which almost inevitably accompany them.

To the administrator, these may seem unimportant details. To the individuals concerned, they are not. The fact that they are apparently accepted without question by the staff of the institutions seems to us to indicate the very great need for staff training and some method of selection.

PROPOSALS FOR THE FUTURE

Many of the proposals we have made in earlier chapters are aimed at helping to sustain the individual during periods of incapacity and interruption or diminution of earnings without placing an intolerable burden on the family. One of the objects of these recommendations is, therefore, to make it possible in appropriate cases for the family to accept responsibility for its handicapped and weaker members. We consider that more should be done to safeguard the right of the individual, whatever his circumstances, to determine his own way of life, to receive at least a basic minimum income in times of adversity, and to spend it as he thinks fit.

It follows from the acceptance of these aims that when an individual is obliged to leave his own home and live permanently in an institution, the social services have to some extent failed. That is the conclusion we draw. Institutions must be regarded as a necessary last resort, and they should only be used when the situation can no longer be remedied by other services. The guiding rule should be to keep people out of institutions. If they must enter them, temporarily, the aim should be to return them to normal life as soon as possible. Those with severe handicaps, mental or physical, who may have to stay for long periods, should have the treatment which modern institutional care now requires.

Admission to an institution normally occurs because the social or medical needs of the individual cannot be met in his own home. At least two measures are essential if the population in institutions is to be kept to a minimum. Where someone has been admitted to an institution because his own family cannot or will not look after him, the first step must be to try and find another family prepared to accept the responsibility. Efforts are most likely to be successful in the case of children and arrangements may be made either for adoption or "boarding-out". Secondly, when residence in an institution is partly due to some physical or mental disability, an intensive effort must be made to rehabilitate and re-train the individual so that he can return to live in the community with support from the social services.

There are two consequences to the adoption of these principles in Mauritius. The first is the development of an organisation to arrange boarding-out and adoption. Some attempt at boarding-out was made in the post-war years, but it does not seem to have been actively sustained. There must be many widows and some childless couples in Mauritius who would welcome the opportunity to care for a child, especially if adequate financial assistance were provided. We have recommended in Chapter 7 scales of Orphans' Benefit, which should be paid to foster parents. These should be supplemented if necessary. The present cost to the Public Assistance Department of keeping a child in an orphanage is very much higher—Rs. 36·50 a month for the *per capita* grant alone. "Boarding-out" would lead to a substantial saving of public funds. But this is not the reason which has led us to recommend it.

A child needs the atmosphere of a normal home: it needs the security of knowing that there is at least one person with whom it can share a continuous affectionate relationship. A child must love and be loved. This can happen in an institution provided the children are cared for in small groups and the staff is dedicated and permanent. In general, the orphanages of Mauritius do not lend themselves to the formation of small groups: the buildings are not planned for this purpose and the staff is inadequate. For a variety of reasons the large group almost always leads to more formal control, stricter discipline and a rigidity of outlook among the staff. This explains many of the restrictions which we observed in the orphanages. A child brought up in these conditions has far less opportunity to develop, experiment and explore than a child brought up in a normal home.

"Boarding-out", however, has dangers of its own. A child may be exploited or ill-treated by foster parents for reasons of financial gain or as a cheap domestic servant. Harm may be done to the child if it has been taken simply to solve the psychological problems of the foster parents. Where there are other children in the family, there must be no differences in treatment between the children. We have no doubt that foster parents can be found in Mauritius who would live up to these precepts. But some people may offer themselves as foster parents who are unsuitable. It is therefore essential in the interests of the child that the selection of foster homes and the supervision of "boarding-out" should be in the hands of a professionally trained officer.

The duties of such an officer, a "children's officer", would be to find prospective foster parents and satisfy herself that they are really suitable. It would be her task to see that a proper relationship is established between child and "foster parent" before any arrangement for "boarding-out" is made. She would also have to visit the home regularly to make sure that the child was adequately cared for and that everything was being done for its education and welfare. This task requires a woman of integrity, maturity and good education who has been professionally trained. We therefore recommend that the Government should pay for the training of a children's officer in the United Kingdom.

Another duty which would fall upon the children's officer would be to arrange adoptions. The legal procedures are necessarily complex and no doubt many couples are deterred from adoption by the difficulties involved. It should be the duty of the children's officer to explain these procedures and even represent the couple in Court when she is satisfied that the persons concerned are suitable to have the responsibility of an adopted child.

The second consequence of the principles we have stated above is that all persons with physical or mental disabilities who require skilled nursing, training or supervision should be the responsibility of the Medical Department. We have mentioned in Chapter 9 the tendency of the Medical Department in recent years to shift the responsibility for people with "chronic" mental or physical handicaps on to the infirmaries. The reasons for this can be understood. Medical superintendents are very conscious of the urgent needs of people waiting to enter hospital and are naturally anxious not to have their beds "blocked" by those staying for long periods of time. But if these ill or handicapped people are shifted outside the responsibilities of the Medical Department to places where they will get much less medical supervision and nursing care, they are likely to become permanently unable to live outside an institution.

We are not necessarily suggesting that all these people should be retained in the hospitals, but we do recommend that any institutions to which those with severe mental or physical disabilities are sent should be under the control of the Medical Department. We are convinced that more could be done in the field of medical and social rehabilitation. We were therefore glad to learn that plans for a rehabilitation centre with proper facilities for treatment have been drawn up and that part of the funds required to put them into effect are already available. We understand that an application has been made to a charitable foundation for the balance of the sum required and we earnestly hope that this application will be successful.

Similar reasoning lies behind the proposal which we made in the last chapter for the establishment under the control of the Medical Department of a special institution to care for mental defectives.

This should provide training for residents and an occupation centre for non-residents. The construction of such an institution in an urban area would relieve the infirmaries and orphanages of a large number of handicapped individuals.

All these proposals for boarding-out, adoption, a rehabilitation centre and a special institution for mental defectives would, by reducing the load on the grant-aided institutions, pave the way for many of the improvements we would like to see—in particular for better classification, for a reduction in overcrowding and for the abandonment of unsuitable premises.

At present the main classification of the residents of institutions is not by social or medical need but by religion. While all denominations attend the Government schools, are admitted to the Government hospitals, stay at Government supported hotels, and are detained in the Government borstal and prisons, the different denominations tend to be segregated in the infirmaries and orphanages. The preservation of religious classifications in a multiracial society like Mauritius makes the creation of any other system of classification much more difficult. As a minimum there should be separate institutions for the aged, for the physically handicapped, for the convalescent, and for homeless children. Each of these groups is large enough to justify a separate institution in Mauritius. A satisfactory classification of residents on these lines could be achieved in the Catholic institutions, but for the other religious denominations it could only be done by opening a considerable number of very small, and therefore very expensive, specialised institutions.

For this reason and on general grounds we would like to see the denominational classifications abandoned, but it would be unreasonable to expect the other denominations to agree to their members being compelled to enter Catholic institutions. Indeed, we do not believe that the Catholic authorities themselves would wish to have a monopoly of institutional care in Mauritius. The obvious solution to this dilemma is for the Government to open a number of non-denominational institutions. This would not involve an extensive building programme. Calebasses Infirmary is already the property of the Government, and for some years part of it was taken over as a Government institution (Calebasses is in theory "non-denominational", but it is run at present as a Catholic institution). It is possible that arrangements could be made for some of the other institutions to be acquired by the Government, it being understood that facilities for denominational worship would be provided.

In the case of the orphanages, what is needed is not only classification but the placing of children together to form something a little more like large family groups, with not more than about 15 to 20 children in each. It must be said at once, however, that this cannot be done without a great increase in staff (or a corresponding reduction in the number of children living in institutions), and that most of the existing buildings are quite unsuitable for this kind of grouping. We therefore recommend that family groups should be organised where this is possible and that the appropriate buildings should be obtained and staff engaged as soon as resources permit.

In addition to the advantages of classifying children and adults according to age and type of disability, there are other reasons for advocating the development of Government institutions. A large proportion of the cost of the existing institutions is borne by the whole community through the agency of the Public Assistance Department, and it seems reasonable that the Government should have control over at least a part of this expenditure. The Government institutions could set a high standard of institutional care, and provide a criterion for judging the standards of the other institutions. This we regard as an important matter. The Public Assistance Department already has the responsibility for ensuring that any institution to which grants are made from public funds satisfies certain conditions, laid down in the Poor Law Regulations of 1946:—

"(a) The buildings and site of the institution and its accommodation have previously been approved by the Commissioner on the report of the Director of the Health Department;

(b) such books and accounts as the Commissioner may direct are kept by the Manager of the institution;

(c) diet sheets approved by the Commissioner are drawn up and are adhered to as exactly as possible;

(d) religious instruction in the faith professed by the Institution Authorities is given to such inmates as desire it, and

(e) in case inmates of different faiths are admitted by the institution, any inmate is authorised to practise his own faith in so far as such practice does not interfere with the peace and comfort of other inmates."

Although an officer of the Public Assistance Department is responsible for the welfare of inmates of the institutions, there is at present nothing approaching the rigorous system of inspection that would be required to ensure that these conditions are complied with. What is needed, therefore, is the setting of standards by Government institutions, the establishment of a proper system of inspection of all institutions, and the training of staff to do this work.

We cannot offer any estimate of the probable cost of running Government institutions. The cost of the Calebasses experiment would have been a useful guide, but we were unable to obtain information on this point, apart from expenditure on food. However, it should be possible to ascertain the cost of running the existing institutions, and from this a fairly close estimate could be made, taking into account the additional cost of staff, training needs and any necessary improvements in conditions and amenities.

There are many improvements which we would like to see in the general equipment and management of the institutions. There is a strong case for dividing the large dormitories and wards now found in some institutions into smaller units. A *maximum* of 10 beds to award would not be an unreasonable target. This would automatically reduce the number of beds that could be fitted into the existing buildings, even if no improvement were made in the spacing of beds; and as we have indicated, there is urgent need for such improvement in some institutions. It is also essential that sufficient living space should be provided in addition to sleeping accommodation. For the older residents there should at least be a room where they can sit in comfort during the day; at present, there is often only an open verandah. For children, adequate play space is a prime necessity, as well as a supply of toys and play equipment.

The provision of adequate and suitable toilets and bathrooms can and should be given immediate attention. The lack of indoor, or easily accessible, toilets is particularly distressing, and should not be difficult to remedy.

The question of adequate and nourishing food needs careful investigation. The first essential is that the grant made by the Public Assistance Department should be sufficient to pay for a good diet. We reproduce as Appendix E a diet sheet submitted to us by the Mother Provincial responsible for a number of the Catholic institutions, which shows the daily cost of feeding a child as Rs. 1·68, excluding the cost of fuel and extra diets in case of illness. We had no opportunity of checking the prices of the various items; nor could we judge the adequacy of this diet. Assuming that the cost of an adequate diet is about Rs. 1·70 a day, there would appear to be a strong case for higher grants than at present. It should, however, be borne in mind that with good marketing many foods could be purchased at less than retail prices, and that some of the institutions have their own gardens and livestock.

However large the grants may be, they cannot guarantee that the diet will be not only adequate in quantity but appetising, varied and well cooked. This is not a mere detail. For those, especially the old, whose days are spent in the unvaried routine of an institution, with little or no occupation, meals acquire a special importance. We strongly recommend, therefore, that in any plans for building or modernising institutions, priority should be given to the provision of adequate cooking facilities and attractive dining-rooms, and that the distance between them should be as short as possible. We also feel that more attention could be given to the appointment and training of kitchen staff. Cooking is a skilled job at any time, but especially is this true in the setting of an institution.

We heard it suggested that in some of the institutions the public assistance grant was being spent partly on residents who were ineligible for it. We do not know whether this is true, but the fact that such accusations are made emphasises the need for proper control over the spending of the grants. Such control could most easily be exercised by annual returns of income and expenditure submitted to the Public Assistance Commissioner by each aided institution, and by a system of audit and unannounced inspections.

Whatever the rôle of the Government in the provision of institutions, it is inevitable that most of the cost will be defrayed from public funds. It is therefore necessary to consider whether the present system of a *per capita* grant is the best system of calculating the aid available to each institution. The present system has the merit of simplicity. But it takes no account of the varied needs of the different institutions which arise from the state of the buildings, the availability of cultivable land and the age, health and religion of the residents. A *per capita* grant creates an incentive to run a mixed institution so that those who consume least and contribute most can subsidise those less favourably placed.

We therefore recommend that the grant should in future be based on the total net annual running costs of each institution, or the proportion of such costs which are applicable to those inmates for whose maintenance the Public Assistance Department is responsible. We recognise, however, that this system cannot be introduced until the Department is satisfied that proper account books are kept by each institution on a standardised basis. The annual expenditure would have to be checked by a qualified auditor, and any unreasonable items disallowed. As at present, the institutions would be free to increase their income by "fancy fairs" and private donations to cover the cost of any "extras".

Assumptions about institutional care and the training of staff derived from experience in other countries may not be appropriate in Mauritius, and we do not, therefore, suggest that staff training methods used in the United Kingdom are necessarily applicable.

On the contrary, short courses of training devised in the light of Mauritian conditions and needs, and carried out on the spot, are likely to be much more successful. These could be instituted at no great expense and we recommend that the Government should arrange for such facilities to be made available.

Much can be done by voluntary effort to make institutional life less drab. A notable example has been set by the "Amis du Moulin à Poudre", who not only pay regular visits to the patients at the Leper Hospital, but have provided them with many extra comforts and amenities, including a recreation hall. It should not be impossible to form a similar group of voluntary workers for each infirmary and orphanage. Valuable work is done by the Red Cross in visiting and distributing gifts. What is needed, in addition, is a group of people who will take a personal interest in each institution, paying frequent visits, supplying the small extra comforts that can make a lot of difference, and watching out for individual needs which may be overlooked by an overworked staff.

Lastly we come to consider the future of institutional provision for the blind in Mauritius. Unlike the other institutions we have mentioned, the Loïs Lagesse Residential and Training Centre is not financed by a *per capita* grant from the Public Assistance Department, but by a lump sum annual grant made by the Government to the Welfare of the Blind and Prevention of Blindness Society. Of the Society's total income of just over Rs. 40,000 for the year 1958-59, Rs. 15,000 came from the Government grant, Rs. 11,600 from subscriptions, donations and the proceeds of a public collection, and the remaining Rs. 13,500 from profits on sales of baskets made at the Centre. Not only, therefore, has the Society a modern, purpose-built residential centre, but also an annual income which must certainly be the envy of the managers of the infirmaries and orphanages, and which in fact leaves a substantial surplus after meeting current expenditure. The Society is thus able to pay the local trade rate of wages for basket-making and, in addition, a monthly allowance to all blind persons, whether living at the Centre or not, of Rs. 9 for men and Rs. 5 for women. Further assistance, varying from Rs. 10 to Rs. 20 a month, is given in a few needy cases. Those who live at the Centre do not receive the Government pension of Rs. 22 a month which is otherwise payable to blind people from age 40.

The Government has recently had the benefit of expert advice on the welfare of the blind from Mr. E. W. Christiansen, Director of the New Zealand Foundation for the Blind. His main recommendations were as follows:—

(1) Appointment of a qualified handicraft teacher as manager of the Centre.

(2) Provision of adequate teaching facilities for children at the Centre, including the building of at least two classrooms and the seconding of teachers from the Education Department.

(3) Construction of a suitable workshop.

(4) Measures to expand the production of baskets and to develop other lines of production such as brushes, coir mats and furniture.

(5) Compilation of a complete register of blind people.

We would emphasise the part that Government and the sugar estates can play in providing a regular market for goods produced by the blind, thus avoiding the seasonal variations in activity which are a regrettable feature of the present arrangements.

The only other recommendation we would add is that similar provision to that now made for blind men and children should also be made for blind women. The decision to exclude women from the Lagesse Centre seems to us an unfortunate one, though we appreciate the grounds on which it was made. It is of course true that marriages between blind persons can lead to difficulties, especially in child-rearing. A possible solution for such difficulties would be the provision of special quarters for married couples at the Centre. If this is not considered feasible, we would suggest that the Government should include a training centre for blind women in its plans for the provision of specialised institutions for the handicapped.

Our main proposals for the future of the institutions may be summarised as follows:—

(1) Everything possible should be done to avoid the necessity for individuals to enter institutions, or if they must do so, to return them to their homes as soon as practicable. Particular attention should be given to the training and rehabilitation of the physically and mentally handicapped.

(2) A children's officer should be sent for training in the United Kingdom. It would be the duty of such an officer to find suitable foster parents and arrange and supervise "boarding-out". She should also help to arrange adoptions in suitable cases.

(3) Separate institutions should be provided for the aged, the mentally deficient and the physically handicapped. Other specialised institutions (including a home for unmarried or deserted mothers and their children) should be provided as and when a sufficient need for them is found to exist.

(4) There should be a number of Government-managed institutions, which should set a high standard of care.

(5) Small children's homes, for not more than 15 to 20 children, should be opened as staffing and other factors permit.

(6) Adequate and conveniently situated toilets and bathrooms should be provided as a matter of urgency wherever they do not exist.

(7) Attention should be paid to improving the food in the institutions, by the provision of better kitchens and dining-rooms and trained kitchen staff, as well as the enforcement of minimum diet scales.

(8) If married quarters cannot be provided at the Lagesse Centre, a similar institution should be opened for blind women.

(9) Arrangements should be made for the training of staff in Mauritius.

(10) The grants paid by the Public Assistance Department to the institutions should in future be based on the actual running costs of each institution.

(11) An effective system of inspection and audit should be introduced, and minimum standards rigorously enforced. Annual financial returns should be submitted to the Public Assistance Department by each institution.

(12) The formation of groups of voluntary workers to visit the institutions and provide additional amenities should be encouraged.

CHAPTER 12

Social Policies and Population Growth

The gravity of the economic problems confronting the people of Mauritius is explained at length in the Meade Report. We have attempted to summarise some of the salient facts as they relate to the development of the social services in Chapter 1 of this Report. The national income per head is now declining; unemployment is growing; the increasing casualisation of the sugar industry, which commands the economy, is accentuating a host of social and educational problems; the cost of public assistance has risen tenfold in ten years; the demand for sickness certificates, as a concealed form of unemployment relief, and the growing consumption of proprietary drugs, indiscriminately promoted by the unethical activities of a section of the medical and pharmaceutical professions, are throwing intolerable burdens on the Government Medical Service; and the educational system, which at the primary school level has had to absorb 40,000 more children in the last five years and faces the prospect of an even larger increase in the next five years, is in serious danger of collapsing under the strain of shift-work teaching, obsessional cramming for academic prizes, and the problem of teaching three languages to little children who are often ill-fed and ill-housed. The onslaught of two cyclones in 1960 magnified all these national issues, and presented new bills for reconstruction, the building of new and sturdier houses, and the relief of distress. Confronted as the Government is with all these heavy and competing claims, our proposals for further expenditure on social welfare require justification.

Nothing would be more misleading than to interpret our proposals as well-intentioned measures designed to bring about some kind of benevolent "welfare state" in Mauritius. On the contrary, many of the recommendations we have made, for instance, to reform public assistance, are painfully stern. If they are accepted and implemented by the Government it will not be the privileged classes of Mauritius who will experience the austerities of "work tests", "waiting days", and public assistance and insurance benefits on a scale below any reasonable standard of subsistence for large families. There is little margin in the present situation for generosity; only justice and sheer economic necessity forces an immediate expansion of social welfare expenditure. What we propose, however, is not social welfare for its own sake, a political bribe for the masses, or a bonus for the workshy. Our recommendations are designed actively to assist and not retard the processes of economic growth; to spend less rather than more on public assistance; to prevent rather than treat ill-health; to use more efficiently and more fully the scarce and precious social resources and skills of the community and, ultimately, to bring about, by calling on the self-discipline of all parents, a more purposeful and dignified family life.

For Mauritius to set its governance in this direction it is necessary to accept realistically the facts of population. These are the facts which dominate the present economic situation and which we, risking the charge of censoriousness, have not been able to avoid. We have thus attempted in many of our recommendations and through a combination of social incentives and disincentives to propose measures for slowing down the rate of population growth. As a condition of survival family control must come; but it cannot be imposed. It has to be assisted and given the freedom to develop. For this to happen money must first be spent on providing the necessary information and facilities; on staffing and expanding the health and welfare services through which these facilities may be utilised; and on other essential measures described in this Report. The need for population control is one justification for further public expenditure on social welfare. Before, however, we develop this theme of the connections between economic growth, social justice and family planning we must first gather together our estimates of the cost of our proposals.

THE COST OF EXPANDING SOCIAL WELFARE

In this particular field it is necessary to distinguish between two different types of cost—*real* costs and *transfer* costs. Real costs involve the purchase by the Government of goods and services for social or other purposes. Thus if more resources are used to provide hospitals, schools, doctors and teachers, fewer resources are available to be used for other purposes—for industrial investment or for private persons to purchase their day to day needs. Transfer costs simply involve transfers of spending power from one person to another. Thus, apart from the *real* cost of administration, the population as a whole has as much money to spend as before.

We have made recommendations in this report for both real and transfer expenditures. Among the real expenditures are our proposals for improvements in the hospitals and other institutions and in the preventive services. Our proposals for social insurance and for non-contributory benefits will make it necessary for more persons to be employed by Government in administration, though part of the staff may be found from the Public Assistance Department whose responsibilities will be reduced. Most of our proposals for more *real* expenditure will take time to be implemented as neither the trained staff nor the buildings are at present available. Moreover, we hope that external aid will be made available to help finance the development of the health and family planning services.

It should not be thought that our proposals for improvements in the health services involve wholly new burdens for the people of Mauritius. Expenditure by the Government on health services in 1957/8 was about Rs. 15·8 million. We have reason to believe from figures which have been made available to us that private expenditure on medical care including doctors, chemists, drugs, herbs, travelling costs and a variety of illicit payments ranging from tips to dressers to fees to abortionists may well be as large as the expenditure incurred by the Government. Thus, if the Government services are improved, less may be spent on purveyors of unqualified advice, on the services of untrained persons and on expensive pharmaceuticals which are ineptly chosen and potentially dangerous both to the individual and to the community.

The improvements in the health services which we have recommended may be expected to increase in the short run and even more in the long run the working capacity and thus the economic potential of the people. Both the incidence and the duration of periods of incapacity for work can be reduced. If there were better preventive services, there would be less illness. If there were better curative services, there would be a swifter return to work. If there were better rehabilitation services, there would be less economic waste and less drain on the medical and public assistance budgets. If the maternity and child welfare services were improved, the women of Mauritius could bear healthier children with fewer debilitating pregnancies and employers would benefit from a new generation of workers with a greater output and more regular attendance at work. And an effective family planning service cannot be provided on a nation-wide scale without the support of improved health and welfare services.

Our proposals for the reorganisation and development of the health services have been given in general outline. The next stage requires the working out of detailed plans. Until this is done it is impossible to give any estimate of the new real expenditure involved. We have seen it as our task to set out the main principles and to identify the major needs and priorities so that policy can be settled and the work of planning started as soon as possible. Much depends upon the rate at which additional doctors and other staff are recruited and the willingness of private doctors to accept contracts in the new general practitioner service. These factors will, in turn, depend to some extent on the exact terms of service which are settled after discussion with the profession.

We have suggested that the existing charges levied on persons who are not entitled to free service should be abolished. This would raise the annual cost of the health service immediately by less than Rs. 100,000. We have also recommended that private pay beds should be provided in the Government hospitals offering a higher standard of amenity and that charges should be made by dentists for certain specified services. Part of these charges will add to the revenue of the Government. It would be absurd to attempt an estimate at this stage of what this might amount to.

The bulk of our proposals, however, involve increases in the transfer services—unemployment benefit, sickness benefit, survivors' benefit, family benefit and a number of other benefits. Again these will not impose wholly new burdens on the community. In many cases needs are already being met—not only by the Public Assistance Department but by gifts from the family and loans, often on extortionate terms, from money-lenders, shopkeepers, job contractors and others. To a considerable extent we are redistributing existing burdens so that they are borne more fairly and at less cost by the whole population. We are proposing the replacement of the costly, inefficient and demoralising loan-raising machinery which exists all over the island with a cheaper and more rational system of compulsory saving to meet the needs of sickness, unemployment and other contingencies. Only in so far as we are meeting needs which have previously been unmet are we laying new charges and new responsibilities on the community. This should be remembered when the financial aspects of our proposals are debated. Many of those who will be asked to pay more in the form of taxes and contributions will be relieved of part of the disproportionate charges which they are already paying in other ways.

The additional expenditures we propose, relatively modest though they are, will not have to be wholly met for a number of years. Broadly, we envisage three fairly distinctive stages. The first stage consists of the introduction of the family planning services, the non-contributory benefits, welfare benefits for children and the reorganisation and gradual expansion of the health services. These can be provided as soon as any necessary legislation has been passed and the administrative machinery is ready.

The second stage consists of the social insurance benefits for sickness, unemployment and fire disaster cover. This scheme cannot be brought into operation as quickly as the non-contributory benefits because it requires much more complicated administrative preparations. The legislation will also take more time to draft. An expanded employment bureau will be needed before unemployment benefit can be safely introduced; moreover, it would be most unwise to introduce sickness benefit before the plans for unemployment benefit are ready because of the heavy strain it would inevitably impose on the already overburdened Government Medical Service. In addition, a records office will have to be established, appropriate cards and stamps designed and printed, and staff trained to administer the scheme.

The third stage consists of the " Small Family Pension " and the contributory pension scheme. The costs of these schemes cannot be estimated until further actuarial and other information is available. The contributory scheme will be self-financing and should produce a surplus for investment in the early years.

Before detailing our figures, we make some general comments about the validity of the estimates. The cost of some benefits can be calculated within a fairly narrow margin of error. Provided all those eligible claim their benefit, there is no great difficulty in estimating the cost of providing immediately a three-child family benefit. In the case of other benefits eligibility can be affected and, indeed, is intended to be affected by the introduction of the scheme. For example, both the proposed maternity benefit and marriage grant are intended to encourage later marriages. The former is also aimed at encouraging the spacing of births at intervals of at least two years. It is obviously difficult to estimate the effects and the cost of these recommendations.

No less difficult is the task of calculating the costs of sickness and unemployment benefits. Claims for sickness benefit will depend not only on how many people satisfy the contribution conditions, and on how many people will be certified as sick by Government medical officers, but on how many sick people actually claim the benefit. This last factor will in turn depend on the individual's own standards of health and sickness, on his ability and willingness to undergo medical examination, on his confidence in the doctor, on his views about the value of sickness benefit, and a host of other imponderables.

As regards the cost of unemployment benefit, we have already explained in earlier chapters the difficulties of estimating the extent of involuntary unemployment. This is not peculiar to Mauritius; there are endless disputes today about the actual level of unemployment in Canada and the United States where great resources have been devoted to the question. But even if it were possible to produce an exact measure of involuntary unemployment in Mauritius in some recent year this would be no guide to the level of unemployment in the future. Unemployment is not an actuarial risk. All over the world forecasts of unemployment have proved wildly wrong. It should be added, however, that countries (including Britain) with bad histories of incorrect forecasts have not abandoned, and show no signs of abandoning, unemployment insurance.

We think it important to state these limitations on what we or any other advisers are able to do in estimating the costs of social insurance. If our estimates for the costs of sickness and unemployment benefit prove to be seriously in error, we at least will not be surprised. We hope the Legislative Council will not be surprised either. All over the world countries have to live with these uncertainties.

In saying all this, we do not wish to give the impression that we have not taken every possible care with the estimates we have made. We have investigated every conceivable source of information in Mauritius. We have compared our figures with those for other countries. We have discussed our conclusions with members of the Economic Survey Mission and with experts at the International Labour Office in Geneva. Inevitably, however, many of the figures we have used depend upon our judgment of a large number of variables.

The sources used include calculations from the 1952 census which have been projected forward, special tabulations of the data collected by Mr. Luce for his enquiry, and records of sickness experience in both the Railway and Public Works Departments. In addition, we have tried to check a number of our results by calculations made from a 1% sample of the cyclone relief registration scheme. During our second visit to Mauritius in March 1960, twelve school teachers helped us with the clerical work on this enquiry and we wish to thank them for their valuable assistance.

We estimate that the cost of the non-contributory benefits would be about Rs. 11 million in the financial year 1960/61. Detailed estimates for the separate benefits are given in Appendix F. If dried skimmed milk were issued to young children and shoes were issued to a third of primary school children the cost would be a further sum of over Rs. 800,000. If we allow Rs. 500,000 for administration, the total cost comes out at about Rs. 12·3 million. The introduction of these non-contributory benefits would give substantial relief to the Public Assistance Department. We estimate that a sum of about Rs. 3 million would be saved on this vote. The reduction of allowances for children in the income tax will substantially increase tax revenue. Thus, the new taxation which the Government will have to find if it implements the first stage of our proposals would amount to about Rs. 2 million. This is less than $1\frac{1}{2}\%$ of the national income.

In other words, 1½% more of the national income would have to be collected by the Government in taxes for distribution in the form of benefits in cash and in kind.

The cost of these non-contributory benefits may be expected to increase in years to come. The most substantial item, the family benefit, is, however, unlikely to become more expensive until after 1965 when the large number of girls born after the war reach child-bearing age, marry and have three children. The marriage benefit, which we estimate will cost Rs. 100,000 in 1960/61, could cost Rs. 500,000 in 1972 if no girls married before the age of 21. The maternity benefit could also increase greatly if marriages are postponed, as we hope they will be, and if births are spaced at something like two-year intervals. But increases of this kind in the cost of the marriage and maternity benefits would mean that fewer families would be claiming the family benefit. The cost of provisions for widows, widowers and orphans is unlikely to change greatly over the next few decades.

We estimate that the second stage, the introduction of social insurance, would involve expenditure (including administration) of nearly Rs. 5 million. This expenditure, apart from administrative costs, would, however, be financed by contributions. The Government would be relieved of expenditure on public assistance of about another million rupees. Thus, at this stage, the Government as distinct from the social insurance fund would have to find out of taxes less than Rs. 9 million more than at present.

Exact information is not available giving the total earnings upon which contributions will be payable but we estimate this figure at over Rs. 300 million. In fixing the level of contributions, we have had to take account of the fact that the costs of sickness benefit and industrial injury benefit may be expected to increase as long-term cases gradually become entitled to benefit. It is also prudent to allow some margin in view of the difficulty of making even approximate estimates and the advisability of building up a reserve fund. For these reasons we recommend that the contribution payable by all employees should be about 1¼% of wages and salaries. The costs of industrial injury and disease should fall wholly on employers. Accordingly, we recommend that the level of contribution payable by employers should be about 1½%.

We believe that these contributions are within the capacity to pay of both employees and employers. Other recommendations in our Report relieve employers of a number of substantial financial liabilities—in particular, the provision of hospital and medical services, of maternity benefits, and of the need for a number of *ex gratia* payments. In addition, we are substituting the cost of an industrial injury insurance scheme for the costs which they already bear for workmen's compensation. All these considerations could have been held to justify levying a much higher contribution on the employer than on the employee. The Meade Mission were, however, very anxious for reasons explained in their Report that we should keep to a minimum any increases in labour costs created by our proposals. It is for this reason that we have imposed such a low contribution on employers.

It would be wrong to compare the cost to the Government of our proposals with the expenditure of the Public Assistance Department on outdoor relief in the last year for which information is available; namely, Rs. 7 million for 1957/58. It would also be wrong to compare our estimates with expenditure on public assistance in the financial year 1959/60 which may well approach if not pass Rs. 10 million. What is critically important is that there has been a steady and apparently inexorable *trend* towards increasing expenditure on public assistance since the end of the Second World War.

As we have already emphasised, the cost of public assistance is now getting out of control. For reasons which we have attempted to analyse in Chapters 4 and 8, the system is increasingly incapable of meeting or preventing the rising tide of demands upon it—particularly the demands of rising unemployment which, fundamentally, are a consequence of rising population. The cost of our proposals should therefore be compared, not with past or present expenditures on assistance, but with the bill which can be anticipated in years to come if our proposals are not implemented, and if nothing is done to slow down the present alarming rate of population growth.

THE NEED FOR POPULATION CONTROL

We make no apology for stating over again in this concluding chapter the main facts about population growth. We have explained them at some length in Chapter 3 and Appendix B. We have burdened our Report with many technicalities to show the infinite care which has been taken to arrive at the facts. For those readers who want the conclusions presented in the simplest form we include a summary in this chapter.

In the thirty-year period ending in 1952 the population increased by 125,000 or 33%. Advances during this period in combating the evils of ignorance, poverty and malnutrition through health, education and social welfare policies in no way measured up to the challenge of this trend, nor took cognisance of its implications for the future. There could be no vision for the future nor, indeed, any sense of responsibility for the present so long as a system of taxation prevailed under which the poorest classes were more heavily taxed than the rich.*

In the ten year period 1947-57 the rate of population growth was phenomenal; numbers increased by 36%. This meant the addition of 158,000 people to a population of 436,000 in 1947. It is evident that this increase is not wholly attributable to the dramatic decline in mortality, especially among the young, in recent years. The birth rate is now over 25% higher than it was in the 1930's. Some of the reasons for these trends were discussed in the *Report of the Committee on Population* 1953-4† and by Mr. Brookfield in his analysis published in *Population Studies* in 1957.‡ We do not propose to attempt here any detailed explanation of the causes of one of the highest fertility rates in the world. We believe there are many contributory factors which, in combination, make for unrestrained fertility among the Mauritian people: strongly-held religious beliefs; an apathetic and fatalistic attitude to life nurtured by custom and a long history of suffering and hardship; early marriage and child-bearing; the low status of women and the lack of educational and occupational opportunities for girls and women; and an economic system by which a large proportion of the population subsist, seasonally and over the life cycle of the family, on irregular and unpredictable cash earnings. A system which quite literally engenders a "hand-to-mouth" pattern of daily life is not conducive to restraint in family-building habits. Such uncertainty and instability in the finances of the family do not encourage the belief that man has much control over his future. We have sought in our limited proposals for social insurance to inject some measure of income security as a partial corrective to the instabilities of the present wage system. But it is, we must emphasise, only a very limited and partial one.

The rapid decline in mortality, particularly in infancy and childhood, has contributed substantially to the growth of population. During the period 1944-48 the infant mortality rate was 155 per 1,000 live births. By 1958 it had fallen to 67.§ The campaign for the eradication of malaria and the absence of severe epidemics of dysentery and other infections have been major factors in the reduction of premature death in childhood.

It took Britain nearly thirty years to halve her infant death rate.

---

* In the early 1930's not less than 12% of the family income of the poorest classes went to Government revenue, while the charge on a man whose income was Rs. 50,000 per annum was only about 8% (*Report of Commission on the Financial Situation of Mauritius*, Cmd. 4034, 1932).
† *Sessional Paper No. 4 of* 1955.
‡ Vol. XI, No. 2, November 1957.
§ *Report on Mauritius*, 1958, p. 15.

This happened in Mauritius in less than five years. The rapidity of this change, in combination with the other factors of early marriage and unrestricted child-bearing, spells an alarmingly rapid rate of population growth in the future.

It would be quite wrong to assume, however, that more prevention of deaths necessarily means a fitter and healthier population. Medical science today can at least keep more people alive. It cannot by itself alone guarantee or bring about a healthier population. As we have noted elsewhere in this Report, there is much evidence of widespread malnutrition and general ill-health and incapacity in the population today—much of it concentrated in the large and poor families. Compared with the levels prevailing in many other countries mortality in some age groups and among the poorer classes is still excessive. Compared with the experience of Western countries, girl children still die in Mauritius at an abnormally higher rate than boy children—a reflection of the low status of women and of the disregard by men of women's social rights.

There is, indeed, ample scope for very substantial improvements in levels of health and for further reductions in mortality. Hence, many of our recommendations in this Report are aimed at preventing the onset of disabilities and chronic sickness and building healthier bodies in childhood and adolescence. This is not only sensible economics; the ethical foundation of medicine is to prevent suffering. The fact has to be faced, however, that the more successful medicine is in controlling the death rate the greater the problem becomes of controlling the birth rate.

In looking to the future, we have assumed, in two of our population projections, that mortality rates will continue to decline. The basis for this assumption is explained in Chapter 3 and Appendix B.

What this assumption of declining mortality implies can be simply illustrated. It means a gain in life expectancy at birth of $2\frac{1}{2}$ years every five years. Thus, the expectation of life at birth for males, for example, would rise from about 54 years in 1957 to about 66 years in 1982. In England and Wales the corresponding figure for males was 68 years in 1956-58.* We are only assuming, therefore, that in about 30 years' time the life expectancy in Mauritius will approximate to that obtaining today in England. It cannot be said that we are adopting assumptions which imply any startlingly rapid further falls in mortality in the future with their corollary of greatly improved levels of health. These assumptions are in line with those made on a similarly modest basis for Jamaica and other low-income and high fertility countries.†

* Abridged Life Table 1956-58 (*Registrar-General's Quarterly Review for England and Wales*, No. 442, June 1959).
† See, for example, Roberts, G. W., *The Population of Jamaica*, 1957, pp. 308-11.

Declining mortality is thus the first of our basic assumptions in Projections A and C. The second is that emigration and immigration will balance each other; in other words, that there will be no gain or loss from population movements to and from Mauritius. No other assumption can reasonably be made at the present time. The third assumption we have adopted (for Projection A only) is constant fertility. We have therefore applied the age-specific fertility rates for the years 1956-58 and have assumed that they will continue to operate.

Projection A, with these three assumptions of declining mortality, nil migration and constant fertility, forms the basis on which this Report is written and on which all our recommendations rest. In the light of all the known facts, and taking account of the experience of other countries and the best advice we could secure, we concluded that we should accept the estimates of future population growth which result from the application of these assumptions. The figures are set out in the tables in Chapter 3.

For purposes of comparison and illustration two other projections were worked out and the results are embodied in these tables. Projection B assumes constant mortality, nil migration and some decline in fertility. Projection C assumes declining mortality (on the same basis as Projection A), nil migration and rapidly declining fertility up to 1972. This particular projection was made as we wished to know what the hypothetical effects would be on the trend of population if, after some arbitrary date in the future, no Mauritian women had more than three children. The reason for this statistical exercise lies in our recommendations for a policy of popularising the three-child family. We therefore assumed for Projection C that the 1956-58 fertility rates would fall rapidly to levels in 1972 worked out on the basis that in that year and thereafter no women would have children in excess of three. This clearly implies a dramatic and rapid change in family building habits and in the acceptance of family planning. From 1972 onwards we assumed that fertility would remain constant at the level reached in 1972.

We now restate the actual population figures and their implications for the future which result from these exercises. We begin with our key Projection A. This shows that the 1957 population of 594,000 will grow by 357,000 to 951,000 in the 15 years to 1972. This means an *addition* to the population in 15 years much larger than that actually experienced in Mauritius over the past 100 years. In the ten years 1972-82 the increment will be larger still—414,000—giving a total population in 1982 of 1,365,000. This figure is, we should point out, about 300,000 higher than the projection for 1982 used in the Report of the Committee on Population 1953-4.

To project further in the future is a much more hazardous undertaking and we have not therefore burdened this Report with another complete set of tables. However, the calculations were made up to the end of the century on the assumptions explained in Chapter 3. The result is a total population by the year 2002 of 2,869,000. This implies a population density of over 4,000 people per square mile.

In making our recommendations which particularly concern the welfare of children and old people it was necessary for us to consider the future trend in numbers of these two dependent age groups.

In the five years 1952-57 the child population aged 0-14 rose by no less than 50,000—a remarkable increase of 24%. On the assumptions adopted for this projection the child population will increase to 641,000 by 1982—an addition of 381,000 children in 25 years. In other words, the number of children in the island will then be as large as the total population today.

The results of Projection C, which embodies the assumption of a transition to the three-child family, provide a very different picture. It is a far more balanced picture of a child population of 306,000 in 1982—less than half that implied by Projection A. This figure also shows an addition to the child population of only 46,000 in the 25 years—an increment smaller than that which actually took place between 1952 and 1957. If the assumptions which underlie these estimates for the future could be applied in practice; if family planning could spread in the next 12 years so that by 1972 the three-child family had become the popularly accepted family size, then Mauritius would avoid the disaster of unbearable population growth.

Briefly explained, these are the major implications which emerge from our estimates of the future trend of population. The assumptions adopted for Projection A represent, in our view, the most realistic ones that could be put forward in all the circumstances of today. They are based on the most careful statistical projections yet made on the demographic facts of Mauritius, and they rest on data furnished by the Central Statistical Office which is both excellent in quality and comprehensive in scope.

The prospects opened up by these projections are alarming; more alarming than any previous attempts to estimate the future growth of population. Frankly, they amount to economic, social and political disaster. We would be failing in our duty if we used any other word.

The economic implications are explained at length in the Meade Report. Already the national income of Mauritius is declining. What will the standard of living be like if the population more than doubles in the next 25 years? It is difficult to believe, even on the most optimistic view about future industrial development and capital investment, that the economy can stand the strain of another half a million inhabitants—let alone a further million or two million. Yet this is the prospect.

There is little scope, as the Meade Report emphasises, for the development of natural resources. This is one of the great limitations which distinguishes Mauritius from other countries facing similar problems of population growth. It is doubtful whether much encouragement can be drawn from the fact that there is no real peasant class in the island and very little true subsistence cultivation. Most Mauritians already draw all or the major part of their livelihood from wage labour in a cash economy. The prospect or possibility of the spread of family limitation in other countries as "peasant subsistence" shifts to wage and industrial labour hardly obtain in Mauritius.

To assume that the problem of over-population can be overcome by emigration is no more than wishful thinking. This is made abundantly clear in the Meade Report. Quite apart from the difficulty of finding countries willing to accept Mauritians on the scale and at the speed that would be necessary, there are the heavy costs of training and transport. It is expensive enough to provide education for those who will make their life in the island without the cost of endowing others with special skills in the hope that they will find somewhere in the world where those skills can be used.

By the most drastic action to develop existing industries and start new ones, it might be possible to stabilise the standard of living for a few more years. But if the growth of population is allowed to continue at its present rate, the trend of declining income per head which has shown itself in recent years will be resumed. It will gradually accelerate until even the present cost of the public services becomes an impossible strain on the community.

To maintain the present expenditure on public services as the population increases is to accept continually falling standards. If standards are to be maintained, a rapid growth in numbers—and especially in the child population—must by itself increase disproportionately the load on the public social services. The health, child welfare, education, housing and social security services will be confronted with demands which will soon outrun the resources available.*

As the economic depression deepens and spreads, an ever-increasing proportion of the population will require help from the social services. Three major factors, gathering force together and reacting on one another, will eventually represent an intolerable

---

* The impact of population growth on employment and the social services is treated in more detail in Part III of the *Report of the Committee on Population*, 1953-4 and in the Meade Report.

burden of destitution. More unemployment, under-employment and irregularity in earnings will lead to increasing demands on the Public Assistance Department. Secondly, and as a consequence of the growth of population and unemployment, a lower standard of living and inadequate diets for a substantial proportion of the population—and perhaps for more than half the children—can only result in more ill-health and disabling sickness. So far as we can see the medical services, already gravely inadequate, are likely to break down first under the strain. We are driven to this conclusion by the fact that all our major recommendations have had to take account of the existing shortage of doctors and medical facilities. The staff would soon be unable to contend with the dual demands for treatment and for sickness certification. The point would eventually be reached when the Government medical officers would be unable to co-operate with the Public Assistance Department.

The second department to collapse would be Public Assistance. Politically, it would be impossible to preserve the fiction of denying regular aid to able-bodied men. Administratively, it would be impossible to apply work tests or exhaustive examination of means. The flood gates would open. Monetary aid would flow to more and more applicants, both those destitute and those in full and part-time employment. Faced with bankruptcy, the Government or the Governor would have to withdraw the right to any aid. Then the island would be faced in turn with unrest, revolt, repression.

We are not alone in envisaging disaster for Mauritius. In his book *Modern Science and the Human Fertility Problem** Dr. R. L. Meier has drawn his own grim picture of what over-population could mean for Mauritius. He chose Mauritius as an indicator of what the prospects may be in other parts of the world. As a case study, it treats of the consequences of the present rapid growth of population in terms of famine, epidemic diseases and martial law. He foresees, as numbers continue to expand rapidly, more sickness and mortality, the growth of a large indigent population, and the establishment of camps for those without a place in the productive system. These camps, he suggests, will then become prisons for the surplus population.

> "Problems of petty theft and policing will probably lead to a demand by the independent residents of Mauritius that the camps be surrounded by barbed wire. The decay of the fabric in the tents will lead to the construction of barracks-type buildings. By that time it will not only feel like a prison, it will also *look* like a prison."
>
> "The chain of events can be traced somewhat farther. For the convenience of administrators, the population which speaks Hindi

* New York, 1959, especially pp. 53-63.

would very likely be separated from the Creole-speaking elements. Much smaller camps might be organised for the Chinese-speaking element and perhaps even for the immigrant natives of Rodrigues. If that were the case, at least four distinct 'indigent cultures' will be likely to develop. Each one, no doubt, would come to despise the others. Perhaps, to break the ennui, a kind of gang or guerilla warfare would break out between them. A decade or so of this will make it impossible to prevent general communal strife in Mauritius."

"No nation", writes Dr. Meier, "has yet really faced the problem of 'keeping people alive' in just the fashion that is likely to be encountered in overpopulated societies of the future, of which Mauritius is typical." He ends his study with the comment that "We cannot be optimistic and honest at the same time ".

A SUMMARY OF OUR PROPOSALS

We believe that the people of Mauritius can avoid the disaster which Dr. Meier so vividly describes. And in the process some modest improvements can be made to the social services. No one who has visited the homes of the poor and the sick can deny that such an improvement is needed. But we also see such an improvement as an integral part of a policy to restrain population growth. The implementation of our plan will require sacrifices. We have calculated earlier in this chapter that $1\frac{1}{2}\%$ more of the national income will need to be collected in taxes to be spent on the social security services. In addition, a further 1% will need to be collected in insurance contributions to be paid out in benefits. This burden on employers and employees and on the tax-payer is small compared to the alarming burdens which will fall upon them in the 1960's if the problem of overpopulation is ignored or shelved.

Our plan does not only depend upon the willingness of the population to make financial sacrifices. From the Government it calls for political courage of the first order, dynamic leadership and honest administration. From the people it demands tolerance and a high sense of moral conduct and national unity.

There are two steps which are essential prerequisites to our plan for improvements in the social security and health services. The first is the establishment of a nation-wide family planning service, and the second is the deliberate creation by the Government of a reasonably high level of employment.

We do not recommend the provision of the new range of benefits unless a family planning service is introduced. Nor do we recommend a family planning service unless it is accompanied by a series of benefits to support and strengthen family life. The two sets of proposals are essential to one another. We would plead that our recommendations should be accepted or rejected as a whole. They stand or fall together. We could not, therefore, approve any action, on political, religious or other grounds, which accepted only some of our proposals for legislation. In such circumstances we would prefer the whole of our Report to be rejected.

We take this stand, immoderate as it may seem, because we believe that it would not make sense to the people or have much hope of success if family planning were advocated on a massive scale unless, at the same time, such measures were accompanied by the most vigorous economic and social planning. The whole basis of the challenge to over-population must rest on this triple alliance of economic, social and family policies for the enlargement of welfare and the growth of freedom irrespective of colour, race or creed. That is one reason why we have dared to recommend a "Family Benefit" for all parents with three or more dependent children in all situations of earning and non-earning, health and sickness.

On certain conditions—and admittedly very stern conditions—the challenge of over-population could, in one generation, be largely overcome. Already certain countries—for example, Japan* and Puerto Rico—are showing the way. With its relatively small size, ease of communication, educational provision and other advantages, Mauritius could soon begin to rival them. It could set an example to the poorer countries of the world. It could make its own contribution towards solving the great problem of poverty.

We do not think that a purely negative approach to this question of family limitation would by itself have much appeal. It has to be seen and understood in the whole context of social and economic advance.

Thus we have attempted, in all our main recommendations for health, social security, and welfare, to do two things at one and the same time: to provide the basis for a healthier and more secure family life; and to encourage, in a series of integrated proposals, the desire for family planning, later marriage and smaller families. For purposes of illustration in this final chapter we summarise, therefore, some of our main recommendations and link them to our proposals for the development of a nation-wide campaign to popularise the three-child family.

---

* A massive birth control campaign developed in Japan from about 1949. In 1948 the birth rate stood at 34 per 1,000; by 1958 it had fallen to 18 per 1,000.

THE THREE-CHILD FAMILY

We recommend that a "Family Benefit" of Rs. 15 per month be paid to all families with three or more children under the age of 14, provided that the mother is over the age of 21 and that the head of the household was not liable to income tax in the previous year. With the introduction of this benefit, the present allowances for children, which may be interpreted as bounties for large families among the poor (under public assistance) and among the well-to-do (under income tax) should be abolished, except that the tax allowance should continue for a further five years in the case of certain children aged 11 and over.

No additional benefit would be paid for dependent children in excess of three. A statutory duty would be laid on public assistance officials to refer all married claimants, men and women, with four or more children, to the Health Service or other agency for advice and assistance on family planning.

To promote full and free discussion of these measures we recommend that every cinema and newspaper should be compelled to show at least one advertisement weekly which would aim (i) to popularise the three-child family, (ii) to explain the purposes of these social policy proposals and (iii) to provide information about family planning facilities. Such information should also be displayed on posters in all villages and printed on all social insurance and family benefit record cards and income tax forms.

Those married couples who have helped themselves and the community by restricting their families to fewer than three children should receive some recompense in old age. We have, therefore, suggested that in the future higher old age pensions of Rs. 37 per month should be paid to such couples.

LATER MARRIAGE

We consider that the time has come to abolish the distinction between men and women in respect to the minimum legal age for marriage under the Civil Status Ordinance. At present, this is 18 for men and 15 for women. We recommend that the age for women should be raised to 18*.

* In 1958 the Legislative Council of Fiji decided to make it illegal for girls to marry under the age of 16 and boys 18. Previously, the ages were 12 and 14. The new law, which applies to all races, comes into force in 1961. Even before 1958, however, there was some evidence for the Indian women in Fiji of later marriage and the later birth of first children. (McArthur, N., *Population Studies*, 1959, XII, No. 3, p. 202.)

To encourage later marriage, we have proposed that a Marriage Benefit of Rs. 50 be paid to the father in all cases of civil marriage where the bride and her future husband have attained the age of 21, provided that she has previously borne no children and that her father was not assessed to pay income tax in the previous year. The payment of this grant would be accompanied by the offer to the bride and bridegroom of advice on and assistance with family planning facilities.

We consider that the whole body of the law relating to marriage and inheritance should be examined by the Government as a matter of urgency. In our view, there is no alternative to bringing religious marriages into line with civil marriages. Unless this is done, our recommendations designed to encourage later marriage will break down.

THE SPACING OF CHILDREN

Our proposals for a Family Benefit and other allowances are designed not only to popularise the three-child family but to encourage the spacing of children, thus affording relief for mothers and a better start in life for the children. We have, therefore, recommended the payment of a Maternity Benefit of Rs. 20 per month for 12 weeks in the case of all maternities, provided that the woman is over 21, has not borne a child in the preceding 24 months, has less than three children alive and has attended an ante-natal clinic, and that her husband was not assessed to pay income tax in the previous year. This benefit would be drawn at the Maternity and Child Welfare Centres. Other maternity benefits payable under any civil service or other occupational schemes should be abolished with the introduction of this provision.

OTHER AID TO THE FAMILY

Our other proposals for the support of a healthier family life are set down in detail under the respective chapters; an improved and expanded Health Service; the introduction of social insurance and other benefits; the reform and improvement of public assistance; the development of measures of health education and social welfare; and the provision of school meals, milk for children under the age of six, and free or cheap shoes for all school children. These are all designed to strengthen family life, and to provide that in the future the children of Mauritius have a better start in life, free of the evils of malnutrition, disease, poverty and neglect.

HEALTH AND FAMILY PLANNING

To this end we recommend that the Health Service of Mauritius should provide at dispensaries, maternity centres, clinics, and hospitals free advice on and assistance with all modern methods of birth control. Private doctors should also be helped to offer similar facilities. The Government should bear the costs of such facilities as part of the budget for the Health Service. Ignorance about elementary sexual matters and family planning is—like ignorance about disease—a matter of health and for advisers on health. We therefore wish to see a family planning service provided as an integral part of the Health Service of Mauritius. Further recommendations on this matter are contained in Chapter 10.

As regards the fundamental question of individual conscience and religious beliefs we repeat what we had to say in Chapter 10:

"We are very conscious of the fact that in urging the need for a policy of family limitation we are challenging the attitudes and beliefs of a considerable section of the population. Nevertheless, we do so on the grounds that every man and woman should have the dignity of freedom to make decisions for themselves in obedience to conscience; a doctrine of society in which men and nations are bound to care for one another, and to help one another to alleviate the present suffering, and avert the threatened cataclysm, of over-population.

"While this knowledge and these services should be available to everyone in the island it would be illiberal to compel anyone to take advantage of them. We could not subscribe to any policy which entailed compulsion. Similarly, we would think it wrong if medical officers and others with religious scruples were not permitted to abstain from taking part in the provision of family planning facilities. The right of any individual on religious or any other ground to refuse to use these services or any particular method of family limitation must be safeguarded. The right of those who wish to know and who wish to use the services must equally be upheld. The tolerances and courtesies of a liberal society must be practised by all. The illiberalities of some must not thrive on the courtesies of others."

THE FINANCING OF HEALTH AND FAMILY PLANNING SCHEMES

The financial costs of developing and implementing a population policy on these lines will be heavy, particularly as it will call for a substantial expansion of Health Services. We would therefore propose that a consortium of Foundations be approached by the Government of Mauritius for a large-scale programme of aid covering at least a period of ten years. The total sum we have in mind for this period would be of the order of Rs. 200 million. We believe that such Foundations as Nuffield, Carnegie, Ford, Rockefeller and the Conservation Foundation should be given an opportunity of participating in this campaign to save Mauritius from the disaster of over-population, and to demonstrate that an alliance of social, economic and family planning can resolve the problems of population growth.

This demonstration project, covering the whole country, would provide many opportunities for social, biological and medical research on attitudes to family planning, the efficacy of different contraceptive practices, the scientific aspects of human fertility problems among different ethnic groups and so forth. Studies such as those undertaken in Jamaica (The Jamaica Family Life Project*), Japan†, India and other countries could be developed and carried much further in Mauritius. In particular, the hopes now being raised by scientific advances in the development of a simple, effective and low-cost oral contraceptive (chemical pill) might be tested in Mauritius. As progress is made in the laboratory more clinical trials will be necessary on the lines of the Puerto Rican "Field Experiment in Population Control".‡

THE SECOND STAGE — SOCIAL INSURANCE

Such is the first stage of our plan. The second stage—the introduction of social insurance—is no less essential. The provisions for sickness and unemployment have an important part to play in the alleviation of poverty and in building a stronger and more secure family life. The collection of insurance contributions, moreover, makes it possible to provide aid on a more discriminating basis. The responsibilities of the Public Assistance Department can thus be reduced to more manageable proportions.

But social insurance by itself is not a complete answer to the problem of abuse in the Public Assistance Department. While public assistance payments include allowances for children there will continue to be cases where those living on assistance have a higher level of living than those who are not. This is a further reason why

---

* Stycos, J. M., Back, K., and Mills, D. O., *A Preliminary Report on the Jamaica Family Life Project*, The Conservation Foundation, New York, 1957.
† Koya, Y., "Seven Years of a Family Planning Program in Three Typical Japanese Villages", *Millbank Memorial Fund Quarterly*, Oct. 1958, XXXIV, No. 4, and Taeuber, I. B., *The Population of Japan*, 1958.
‡ Stycos, J. M. and others, *Human Relations*, 1957, **10**, 315-333, and Hill, R., Stycos, J. M., and Back, K., *The Family and Population Control: A Puerto Rican Experiment in Social Change*, 1959.

we have recommended a universal family benefit. If social insurance were introduced without the non-contributory benefits, it would be very hard to resist the principle of paying children's allowances to those who are sick and unemployed. If the principle were conceded social insurance would be subject to abuse similar to that in public assistance. This is yet another reason why we plead for our proposals to be accepted or rejected as a whole.

Just as the prerequisite for the introduction of family benefits is a family planning service, the prerequisite for the success of social insurance is the deliberate creation of a reasonably high level of employment. There is a limit to the demands that can be met by a social insurance scheme. Any scheme, whether of social insurance or of social assistance, will be endangered if the level of unemployment becomes so high that an effective work test cannot be organised and applied.

The work test is the foundation stone upon which are built all our proposals in Chapters 5 and 8 for social insurance and the reform of public assistance. If aid is to be given to the unemployed, the genuinely unemployed must be separated from the work-shy. If we had not dared to recommend unemployment insurance, we would not have recommended a system of sickness benefit: the strain on the Government Medical Service would have been too great. And if we could not have counted on the work records provided by social insurance, we could not have drafted new regulations for public assistance. Thus, all our proposals in this field are interrelated: the whole structure depends upon the assumption that the work test can be made effective.

Unemployment benefit is not a solution to the problem of unemployment. It is merely a palliative which becomes more costly and less effective as the level of unemployment grows. There is only one solution to the problem of unemployment: that is the creation of jobs. The Meade Report makes many proposals for the extension of employment opportunities. If our Report is accepted, it becomes more important, not less important, to maintain as high a level of employment as is possible.

CONCLUSION

Our terms of reference, though liberally drawn, did not specifically request us to consider the problem of population growth. But, as will be seen from many chapters in this Report, we have been forced, again and again, to take account of present and future population trends. Questions of health and welfare cannot be viewed in isolation of changes in the size and composition of the population.

Measures to improve the standard of life of the people of Mauritius cannot ignore the fact that the problem of poverty in the island is dominated by the poverty of large families. For most families the low level of wages, the irregularity and instability of earnings and other factors to which we draw attention are accentuating a problem which policies of health and social welfare cannot—and should not—be expected to solve by themselves alone.

Nothing would have been easier for us than to have drawn up in general terms ambitious and progressive plans for comprehensive schemes of health, social security and welfare. They are certainly needed. Those who have opposed for long even moderate measures of social welfare for the poor and destitute would then have had a much larger target for criticism. But had we done so we should have evaded the fundamental issues. We might have added one more neglected report to the already long list of inquiries, investigations, committees and commissions that bulk so large in the documented social history of Mauritius in the past 50 years.*

It is a history of forgotten reports. As we have read these past reports, made our own enquiries, considered anew the intentions and recommendations of previous committees and commissions, and tried to find a way through conflicting principles of justice and welfare we have been struck by the gulf between promise and fulfilment. Much has been promised; little accomplished in relation to the nature and scale of the social problems that were identified and foreseen in the past.

When the Committee on Population appointed by the Governor of Mauritius were discussing many of these issues in 1953-4 they considered that the growth of population "will have been checked long before the population will have increased to one million."† The Committee, half of whom were Roman Catholics, thought that this check would result "either . . . from eventual voluntary acceptance of family limitation, or through a significant increase in mortality". It, therefore, entered a strong plea for mass education in birth control, not excluding the use of contraceptives. Only two members dissented from this recommendation, one essentially on "Socialist" grounds.‡ No case was argued, as no case can be argued, for more deaths of children and of parents of child-bearing ages.

It is now clear that the likelihood of the population of Mauritius reaching one million long before the end of the century is as certain as anything can be in the field of population forecasting. The prospect, indeed, if present trends continue is a population approaching three

---

* See list of reports in Appendix E.
† Sessional Paper No. 4 of 1955, p. 9.
‡ Brookfield, H. C., *op. cit.*, p. 112 and Sessional Paper No. 4 of 1955.

247

million by the end of the century. Developments in medicine will at least keep more Mauritians alive. The objectives of economic, social and family planning must henceforth be to prepare for an increase, to slow down the rate of growth with the aid of a massive birth control campaign, and eventually to stabilise the population at around one million.

It is the task of the outside adviser to sift the facts, analyse the problems and present alternatives to the elected representatives of the people. It is they who have to shoulder the responsibility for choosing a course of action. After intensive study of all aspects of the problems of Mauritius, we can see no alternative to the course of action we propose. No one in Mauritius would be spared the economic and political consequences of ignoring population growth. Our plan is one and indivisible. The problems we have described have been made worse by the neglect of the past. With every year of delay, the prospects of success with our plan or indeed any similar plan are diminished.

We do not reach these conclusions or make our many recommendations in the interests of a far-off posterity. We are concerned with the problems of today; with those who are sick because they are poor and who become poorer because they are sick. The children, as always, suffer most. That is why we believe that social planning and family planning are indivisible. To be effective, both require vision; a quality which we are confident is not lacking in the people of Mauritius.

APPENDIX A

List of Organisations and Individuals

(other than Ministers and Government Departments) who Submitted written or oral evidence, formally or informally, or who had general discussions with members of the Mission about the social problems of Mauritius

(a) ORGANISATIONS

Anglo-Mauritius Assurance Society Limited.

Arya Sabha Mauritius.

British Red Cross Society (Mauritius Branch).

Building Industry Workers' Union.

Comité National de la JOC-JOCF.

Confederation of Free Trade Unions of Mauritius.

Ex-Servicemen's Welfare Fund.

Government Medical and Dental Officers' Association.

Government Printing Workers' Union.

Government Teachers' Benevolent Fund.

Lotteries (H.M. Forces) Fund.

Mauritius Chamber of Agriculture.

Mauritius Family Welfare Association.

Mauritius Maternity and Child Welfare Society.

Mauritius Sailors' Home Society.

Mauritius Sugar Producers' Association.

Mauritius Trades Union Congress.

Mauritius Union Assurance Company Limited.

Primary Aided Teachers' Benevolent Association.

St. John Ambulance Association.

Secondary and Preparatory School Teachers' Union.

Société de St. Vincent de Paul.

Sugar Industry Labour Welfare Fund.

Sugar Industry Pension Fund.

Welfare of the Blind and Prevention of Blindness Society.

Widows' and Orphans' Pension Fund.

(b) INDIVIDUALS*

Mr. P. G. A. Anthony.

Mr. J. D. K. Appasamy.

Mr. P. d'Arifat.

Mr. M. Bhookun.

The Right Reverend the Lord Bishop of Mauritius.

The Right Reverend the Bishop of Port Louis.

The Honourable S. Bissoondoyal, M.L.C.

Mr. F. Bruneau.

The Reverend Father E. Dethise.

Mr. P. Ducler des Rauches.

Dr. G. Dufourmentel.

Dr. H. Ghoorah.

Mr. I. Kader.

Mr. R. Knight.

Dr. R. Lam-Po-Tang.

Dr. I. M. Mansoor and Mrs. Mansoor (Dr. Y. Singer).

The Reverend Mother Marie de l'Enfant Jésus, Superior Provincial of the Sisters of Our Lady of Good and Perpetual Succour.

Mr. W. L. Mayhew.

Mr. C. Moutia.

Mr. R. Naik.

Mr. C. Noël.

Mr. M. Panchoo.

Dr. D. A. Raman.

Mr. A. Ramdowar.

The Honourable R. Rey, M.L.C.

Mr. D. de Robillard.

Mr. E. de Robillard.

The Reverend Father H. Souchon.

Dr. the Honourable L. Teeluck, M.L.C., and Mrs. Teeluck.

---

* This list inevitably excludes a large number of other individuals with whom we had valuable conversations both in Mauritius and in London.

APPENDIX B

Population Estimates and Projections

by Edith Adams

I. INTRODUCTION

This appendix describes the technical aspects of the study of recent trends in the population of Mauritius and the methods followed in preparing the population projections which have been presented in Chapter 3. As background for the calculation of the projections, the study included certain adjustments to the base census data, and the bringing forward of these data to a current date. In addition, mortality and fertility trends were analysed on the basis of vital statistics and relevant census data so as to provide a foundation for assessing probable future courses of change. These problems are discussed in detail in the following pages.

Nature of the Data. The study was based primarily on statistics relating to sex, age and marital status characteristics of the population from the 1931, 1944 and 1952 censuses, birth statistics from 1871 to 1958, and death statistics classified by sex and age for the period from 1911 to 1958.* Data provided in the 1952 census on numbers of children ever born to women enumerated in the census were also utilised.

Vital registration is considered to be complete by Government authorities and, in fact, we did not find any evidence of marked under-registration of either births or deaths.† The vital statistics are tabulated according to date of registration rather than date of occurrence of the event. In the case of deaths, which by law have to be reported within 24 hours, this distinction may not be of any importance. In the case of births, however, up to 45 days is allowed for registration before a fine may be imposed. In addition, since 1925 the Ordinance regulating birth registration has called for persons in

---

* As stated in Chapter 3, census data are available for Mauritius as far back as the middle of the nineteenth century, but the results of censuses prior to 1931 have not been examined in any great detail for the present study. Likewise, vital statistics are available for earlier periods than have here been utilised. Apart from military movements, the net balance of migration during the period since 1931 has been negligible. The annual totals of arrivals and departures were sometimes substantial, but they generally showed fluctuations in the same direction and of nearly the same magnitudes. For purposes of the present study, it has been assumed that the factor of migration could be largely ignored.

† See section II-C on the under-enumeration of young children.

attendance at a birth to notify the nearest dispensary or sanitary office of the event, but this provision is not always complied with.*

II. ADJUSTMENTS TO CENSUS DATA

The types of adjustments made to the census data may be summarised under four principal headings: (1) additions for under-enumeration of young children; (2) additions necessitated by the absence at the time of the 1944 and 1952 censuses of men of military age who were serving overseas with the Pioneer Corps; (3) smoothing of the data to correct for digital preference in age reporting; and (4) adjustments to compensate for the over-statement of age on the part of older women. The latter two types of adjustments changed only the distribution of population by sex and age, while the first two affected total population size as well. Since the 1952 census data were to be used as a benchmark for the projections, they were subjected to especially careful scrutiny and adjustment. The 1931 and 1944 census data were also adjusted, though in some cases by less refined methods. The purpose of their adjustment was primarily to permit the computation of census survival ratios as a means of studying mortality.

A. *Pioneer Corps Adjustment*

The Mauritius Pioneer Corps was recruited shortly after 1939. Precise records of the numbers of men in each age group who were absent from the colony and serving in the Corps at the time of the 1944 and 1952 censuses are not available, but the total numbers involved are known within reasonable limits. It is also known that their ages ranged from 18 to 35 years.

By 1957 these men had virtually all returned to the island. Hence, it was desirable that they should be included in the base population used for preparing future estimates. Furthermore, by adjusting 1944 and 1952 census returns for their omissions, more accurate comparisons with 1931 data become possible.

The *de jure* population of Mauritius and dependencies at the 1952 census was 522,700, or just over 6,000 higher than the *de facto* population. Most of this difference was attributable to the Pioneer Corps. The island of Rodrigues, however, made a relatively large contribution to the Pioneer Corps, a fact which is clearly shown by the markedly unbalanced sex ratio and age structure of its population in 1952. In fact, more than 1,000 of the Pioneer Corps can be traced

---

* In a recent Government report it was stated that, on average, the lag in birth registration is probably only about three weeks. See *Natality and Fertility 1825-1955 (op. cit.)* p. 9.

to Rodrigues.* From migration data which include military movements, it is possible to deduce that approximately 5,000 men may have been absent from Mauritius at the time of the 1952 census.† A figure of about 5,000 is likewise confirmed by the military authorities.

Since no official records are available on the distribution of the Pioneer Corps by age groups, estimates were prepared on the basis of apparent deficits in the census totals for males in the military ages. For the age groups concerned, viz. 15-24 and 25-34, independent estimates for both males and females were derived by surviving corresponding births (that is, those occurring from 1917-27 and 1927-37) to 1952; this was done by deducting registered deaths in the appropriate ages. An alternative estimate for the age group 25-34 years in 1952 was derived by surviving to 1952 the corresponding cohorts enumerated at the 1931 census. Since these estimates are subject to various kinds of error, they could at best give only general guidance to the types of adjustment called for in the 1952 data. On the basis of the sex differentials in the comparisons of survived and enumerated populations, a total of 2,700 was added to males aged 15-24 and 1,400 to males aged 25-34. Later findings (see section III-A) suggested that these first adjustments were too high for the younger group and too low for the older group. The final adjustment adopted was 2,300 for the 15-24 group and 2,200 for the 25-34 group. The total adjustment thus amounted to 4,500—or somewhat lower than independently derived estimates of the size of the Pioneer Corps as a whole.

By similar methods, a first set of estimates were obtained for Pioneer Corps absences in 1944, and these were later adjusted as a result of evidence brought to light in the analysis of census survival ratios. The final adjustment came to a total of 6,000—about 3,100 constituting additions to the age group 15-24 and 2,900 to the group 25-34 years.‡

B. *Smoothing of the Age Distributions*

Digital preference in the reporting of ages at the census is present

---

* See Mauritius Central Statistical Office, *Census 1952*, Part I, p. 9. A total of 5,603 males and 7,072 females were enumerated in the General Group. It is stated that the low ratio of males to females is mostly due to the number of males on military service overseas, and that when adjustment is made for such absences, a sex ratio of 95 males per 100 females is obtained.
† From comparisions of total and civilian net migration figures derived from tables in the *Yearbook of Statistics*.
‡ This figure of 6,000 is considerably lower than the estimated number of men in the Pioneer Corps in mid-1944, according to the military authorities—about 8,500. However, some 2,000 British troops present in Mauritius, and enumerated in the census, partially compensated for absences of Mauritians.

to a marked degree in the statistics for Mauritius, as even a cursory examination of the tabulations by single years of age will indicate. At the young ages there is a strong preference for ages ending in the digits "2" and (to a lesser extent) "8", in addition to the customary preferences for ages ending in "0" and "5". Past middle age the concentration on ages ending in "0" becomes intensified.*

Combination of the data into five-year age groups, as required for the population projections, removes some of this bias, but since "0" has a greater attractive power than "5" a certain amount of distortion still remains. It has been suggested that, in such circumstances, combination of the data into ten-year groups beginning with ages ending in the digit "5" (i.e. 15-24, 25-34, etc.) may largely remove these errors.† We, therefore, started with the assumption that, except for those age groups requiring special adjustments (such as those affected by Pioneer Corps absences), the enumerated totals for ten-year groups as defined above were substantially correct.‡

Owing to the past variations which have occurred over short periods in the number of births, it did not appear feasible to attempt a further breakdown of these ten-year age groups by any technique which failed to take account of the corresponding number of births. To split the population into single years of age it was, therefore, assumed, as a first approximation, that the ratio of population aged x to births x years previous was a smooth function of x. The weighted average of these ratios [f(x)] was known for each ten-year age group. Assuming f(x) to be a quadratic function of x, we derived formulae in the usual manner to obtain first approximation estimates for the separate values of f(x) for each year of age, in terms of the average f(x) for the given ten-year age group and the two adjacent groups. These were only first approximations because (a) they ignored the weighting of the averages on which they were based; and (b) no mechanism had been incorporated in their derivation to ensure continuity at the boundaries between the groups. The first approximation survival ratios for single year cohorts were plotted and used as guides for drawing continuous curves of f(x) by visual means.

---

* Preference for digits "0", "5", "2" and "8", and increasing preference for digit "0" with advancing age, have been observed in census statistics for many countries. See Bachi, R., " The Tendency to Round off Age Returns: Measurement and Correction", *Bulletin of the International Statistical Institute*, Vol. XXXIII, Part 4, pp. 195-222, Calcutta, 1951.

† Carrier, N. H. and Farrag, A. M., "The Reduction of Errors in Census Populations for Statistically Underdeveloped Countries", *Population Studies*, Vol. XII, No. 3, March 1959, p. 247.

‡ The enumerated totals were actually increased slightly, since persons whose ages were not reported were distributed proportionally among the various age groups.

The values of f(x) read from these continuous graphs were finally adjusted to ensure that the sums of the products of births and survival ratios equalled the original total for the ten-year age group. The arbitrary character of this procedure was thus deliberately restricted, and in any event its use seemed justified by the limits of precision permitted by the data.

In this manner estimates by single years of age from 5 to 74 were obtained for 1952 and 1944. For 1931, the data were split into quinary age groups only by graphic interpolation. As might be expected, the smoothing process tended, in general, for all census dates, to increase the size of the groups starting with the last digit "5" and to lower those beginning with last digit "0".* The smoothed data for quinary age groups were checked for consistency, principally by examining the sex ratios for each group.† For 1952 the ratios appeared generally acceptable, except that a ratio of less than 100 was shown for the group 5-9.‡ A small transfer of 120 males from age group 10-14 to 5-9 and a similar transfer of females from age group 5-9 to 10-14 restored the sex ratios of 100·3 and 100·9 in the two groups, respectively, as shown by the enumerated figures.

For the remaining age groups, the sex ratio was found to rise with each successive age group, owing to the excess of female over male mortality, until the end of the child-bearing years; at the later ages it declined sharply with advancing years, as mortality fell much more heavily upon males. These changes in sex ratios over the age span are in accordance with general expectation and thus tend to confirm the adjustments applied independently to the two sexes. The sex ratios computed from the 1952 census data as finally adjusted are shown in a later table.

The pattern of sex ratios observed in the adjusted data for 1944 did not suggest any need for revision. For 1931, however, greater irregularities were noted, these being present in both the unadjusted and adjusted data.§ No adjustments were undertaken to improve

---

* There were some exceptions. For example, both for 1952 and 1931 the age group 5-9 was lowered and the group 10-14 raised in the adjustment process.

† On the application of sex-ratio tests see " Accuracy Tests for Census Age Distributions Tabulated in Five-Year and Ten-Year Groups", *The Population Bulletin of the United Nations*, No. 2, 1952. ST/SOA/Ser.N/2, New York, 1952, pp. 59-79.

‡ The birth cohort of which this group constituted the survivors had a low sex ratio; moreover, males of this cohort suffered excessive infant mortality according to registered death statistics.

§ In general, the sex ratios for the young adult ages from about 15 to 30 appear low. This finding might suggest the absence of some young men from the country, but Government authorities report no significant number of absences, and draftees were enlisted on a large scale only during World War II.

these ratios, since in any case the 1931 data did not figure to any great extent in the analyses concerned with our projections.

The adjusted 1952 census data by single years of age and the percentages they constitute of corresponding birth cohorts, are shown in Table B-I.*

Appendix B—Table 1. *Population by Sex and Single Years of Age and Percentages Surviving from Birth:* 1952.

Age	Males		Females	
	Number	Percentage surviving from birth	Number	Percentage surviving from birth
under 1	11,374	·9478	11,054	·9576
1	10,705	·9070	10,417	·9270
2	9,776	·8814	9,609	·8980
3	8,422	·8432	8,385	·8585
4	7,747	·8066	7,729	·8244
5	7,099	·7898	6,934	·7984
6	6,451	·7785	6,370	·7891
7	6,695	·7756	6,806	·7875
8	6,147	·7715	6,253	·7854
9	5,293	·7667	5,231	·7837
10	5,225	·7612	5,172	·7803
11	4,895	·7565	4,898	·7754
12	5,106	·7520	5,055	·7692
13	5,300	·7463	5,254	·7619
14	5,179	·7411	5,101	·7535
15	5,207	·7355	5,132	·7436
16	5,012	·7283	4,895	·7333
17	4,943	·7203	4,709	·7223
18	4,890	·7103	4,697	·7102
19	4,270	·7012	4,096	·6975
20	3,865	·6890	3,774	·6871
21	4,236	·6778	4,124	·6741
22	4,466	·6654	4,307	·6556
23	4,804	·6554	4,567	·6380
24	4,749	·6431	4,384	·6125
25	4,680	·6314	4,333	·6000
26	4,974	·6204	4,641	·5790
27	4,901	·6058	4,439	·5621
28	4,413	·5914	3,920	·5450
29	4,036	·5743	3,624	·5260
30	3,961	·5563	3,556	·5054
31	3,689	·5398	3,296	·4889
32	3,444	·5247	3,068	·4747
33	3,403	·5082	3,004	·4629
34	3,395	·4941	2,976	·4490
35	3,288	·4820	2,953	·4406
36	3,132	·4690	2,761	·4280

* Estimates of children 0-4 by single years of age were derived from data on registered births and deaths. No breakdown was estimated for the small group of persons aged 75 years and over.

Age	Males		Females	
	Number	Percentage surviving from birth	Number	Percentage surviving from birth
37	3,247	·4552	2,916	·4149
38	3,367	·4425	3,047	·4019
39	3,113	·4306	2,708	·3895
40	2,942	·4166	2,554	·3736
41	2,847	·4048	2,491	·3598
42	2,578	·3933	2,283	·3498
43	2,537	·3820	2,218	·3410
44	2,599	·3710	2,282	·3349
45	2,435	·3582	2,171	·3275
46	2,323	·3439	2,107	·3191
47	2,345	·3303	2,165	·3104
48	2,223	·3165	2,061	·3015
49	2,092	·3029	1,944	·2924
50	1,959	·2896	1,818	·2823
51	1,937	·2764	1,828	·2731
52	1,910	·2636	1,833	·2640
53	1,761	·2500	1,722	·2550
54	1,672	·2383	1,641	·2462
55	1,452	·2260	1,471	·2387
56	1,376	·2137	1,449	·2298
57	1,436	·2014	1,531	·2207
58	1,320	·1897	1,420	·2114
59	1,273	·1778	1,400	·2020
60	1,227	·1664	1,344	·1904
61	1,079	·1550	1,200	·1809
62	987	·1440	1,141	·1717
63	904	·1327	1,073	·1626
64	842	·1222	1,017	·1535
65	780	·1121	968	·1454
66	700	·1016	894	·1366
67	647	·0913	865	·1277
68	549	·0814	789	·1188
69	460	·0718	702	·1101
70	407	·0624	653	·1010
71	353	·0531	603	·0921
72	295	·0440	543	·0832
73	228	·0352	467	·0743
74	167	·0265	402	·0654
75 and over	1,126		2,152	
All ages	260,604		253,397	

C. *Adjustment for under-enumeration of young children*

Under-enumeration of young children is a problem common to all censuses—even to those carried out in countries with a long history of census-taking and a highly literate population. It is not surprising, therefore, that the test applied to the enumerated totals for the age group under 5 years of age revealed considerable deficits at each of the three censuses.

According to customary procedures, the numbers of children at certain ages believed to be free of errors of under-enumeration or digit preference were reverse-survived to test the adequacy of birth registration. For this purpose we used the adjusted numbers at ages 5-9 (that is, after smoothing to remove the distortions due to digital preference). Registered deaths were added to obtain an independent estimate of births during the period 5-10 years preceding the census date. This estimate, divided by the number of registered births, gave a "correction factor" for under-registration, which was assumed to apply also to the five-year period immediately preceding the census. The numbers of registered births during the latter period were then "corrected" for under-registration and survived to the census date by deducting registered deaths.* The results, compared with the numbers of children enumerated at ages 0-4 in the census, provided an estimate of under-enumeration.

Tables B-2 and B-3 show calculations of the "correction factors" for registered births and the estimated and enumerated groups aged 0-4 years at each census. It will be noted that the estimates of births obtained by reverse-survival of 5-9 year olds from the 1931 census were lower than the number of registered births, whereas correction factors of 1·028 and 1·007 for both sexes combined were obtained for 1944 and 1952 respectively.

Appendix B—Table 2. *Calculation of Birth Under-Registration in Periods Preceding Three Recent Censuses.*

	Smoothed estimate at ages 5-9 (1)	Related deaths (2)	Births by addition (3)	Registered births (4)	Correction factor col. 3÷col. 4 (5)
1931					
Males	27,612	9,888	37,500	37,718	·994
Females	26,528	9,598	36,126	37,032	·976
1944					
Males	26,298	9,442	35,740	34,914	1·024
Females	25,941	8,941	34,882	33,763	1·033
1952					
Males	31,685	9,452	41,137	40,778	1·009
Females	31,594	8,673	40,267	40,036	1·006

* It is probable that most infant deaths which escaped registration were likewise not registered as births. The amount of error introduced by correcting both for birth under-registration and for census under-enumeration by utilising registered deaths is thus not likely to be great.

Appendix B—Table 3. *Calculation of Under-Enumeration of Children aged under* 5 *Years in* 1931, 1944 *and* 1952.

	Registered births during 5 years preceding census	Births corrected for under-registration	Related deaths	Survivors aged 0-4 at census	Enumerated 0-4 at census *	Survivors minus enumerated
1931						
Males	35,088	35,088†	7,843	27,245	24,337	2,908
Females	34,162	34,162†	7,585	26,577	24,237	2,340
1944						
Males	34,997	35,976	6,663	29,313	25,496	3,817
Females	34,153	35,110	5,925	29,185	25,510	3,675
1952						
Males	54,487	54,869	6,763	48,106	43,824	4,282
Females	52,622	52,991	5,852	47,139	43,094	4,045

* Plus share of unknown ages.
† No correction made.

On the surface, this rather curious series of correction factors suggests a deterioration in birth registration between the 1920's and the 1930's, i.e. during periods 5-10 years before the 1931 and 1944 censuses. It is not inconceivable that such a deterioration might have taken place during the period of economic difficulties of the 1930's. On the other hand, distortions may have been introduced by the fact that birth statistics related to date of registration rather than occurrence.‡

On the basis of the findings of Table B-3 the following additions were made to the enumerated totals for ages 0-4 at the three censuses. The additions are further shown as percentages of the enumerated numbers of children.

	Enumerated 0-4 (*plus share of unknown ages*)	*Additions*	*Additions as per cent of enumerated*
1931	48,574	5,300	10·9
1944	51,006	7,500	14·7
1952	86,918	8,300	9·5

‡ The smoothing procedure which we adopted may have erred in reducing the size of the 5-9 year age group at the 1931 and 1952 censuses; this adjustment was essentially based on the numbers of births recorded for the years 1921-26 and 1942-47—both periods of rising fertility. A lag in registration during such periods would tend to understate the actual number of births. Unfortunately, the necessary data were not available to test the importance of a lag in birth registration. A special tabulation of births by date of occurrence and date of registration for the year 1958 suggests that the difference was negligible, but whether this is true for earlier periods is not known.

D. *Adjustment for over-statement of age*

From the analysis of census survival ratios, discussed in a later section, a tendency towards over-statement of age on the part of older women became apparent. This type of error, which has been encountered in many censuses,* showed up in the form of high survival ratios at the oldest ages, and lower ratios at the ages from about 45 on than would normally be expected. Surprisingly, the same type of error did not seem to be present to any marked degree in the statistics for males.

An adjustment was introduced to reduce this tendency in the 1952 data. Using survival ratios derived from appropriate United Nations model life tables (see Section III), we survived 1941 cohorts at the upper ages to 1951 to obtain "new" estimates. This procedure was begun with the group aged 65 and over in 1941, and was continued for successively younger five-year groups until the accumulated total of the new 1951 estimates approximated that of the original 1951 figures.† This point was reached at age 45. Finally, the adjusted 1951 data had to be brought forward one year to 1952. The revised 1952 data are shown in Table B-4, where they are compared with the data previously smoothed for digital preference but unadjusted for over-statement of age.

Appendix B—Table 4. Females Aged 45 Years and Over in 1952 Corrected for Over-statement of Age.

Age group	Smoothed but not adjusted for over-statement of age	Smoothed and adjusted for overstatement of age
45-49	9,756	10,448
50-54	8,181	8,842
55-59	7,023	7,271
60-64	5,904	5,775
65-69	4,522	4,218
70-74	3,143	2,668
75 and over	2,845	2,152
Total	41,374	41,374

---

* A tendency to exaggerate age at the older ages has been noted, for example, in the United States census statistics. See Spiegelmann, M., *Introduction to Demography*. Society of Actuaries, Chicago, 1955, pp. 48-50; and Jaffe, A., *Handbook of Statistical Methods for Demographers*. U.S. Bureau of the Census, Washington, 1951, pp. 91-92. Carrier and Farrag also found evidence of over-statement of age at the older ages in Egyptian census data. See Carrier, N. H. and Farrag, A. M., (*op. cit.*) pp. 263-264.

† The same procedure was applied in correcting for over-statement of age at death; it is illustrated in Table B-18.

While this procedure reduces the error arising from over-statement of age, it does not entirely remove it, since the 1941 data which were used as the basis for readjustment were no doubt also subject to some over-statement at the upper ages. Curiously, the 1941 data appeared to be less subject to this shortcoming, however, and the groups between 40 and 60 years, in particular, showed smooth patterns of survival from the corresponding cohorts in 1931.

The adjusted 1952 census data for all age groups are presented in Table B-5.

Appendix B—Table 5. Adjusted Population by Sex and Age: 1952.

Age group	Both sexes	Males	Females	Males per 1000 females
0- 4	95,218	48,024	47,194	101·8
5- 9	63,279	31,685	31,594	100·3
10-14	51,185	25,705	25,480	100·9
15-19	47,788	24,259	23,529	103·1
20-24	43,276	22,120	21,156	104·6
25-29	43,961	23,004	20,957	109·8
30-34	33,792	17,892	15,900	112·5
35-39	30,532	16,147	14,385	112·2
40-44	25,331	13,503	11,828	114·2
45-49	21,866	11,418	10,448	109·3
50-54	18,081	9,239	8,842	104·5
55-59	14,128	6,857	7,271	94·3
60-64	10,814	5,039	5,775	87·3
65-69	7,354	3,136	4,218	74·3
70-74	4,118	1,450	2,668	54·3
75 and over	3,278	1,126	2,152	52·3
All ages	514,001	260,604	253,397	102·8

III. MORTALITY TRENDS

The trend of the crude death rate in Mauritius has been traced over a long period in Chapter 3. To project the population into the future it was necessary to go beyond this analysis and study the pattern of mortality at different ages. To do this we had a choice of two different types of data: statistics of registered deaths and survival ratios computed from census statistics. The United Nations model life tables, described below, provided a means of readily comparing the mortalities at different ages deduced from these two sources.

A. *Census survival ratios*

The last three censuses of Mauritius were taken at irregular intervals, namely in 1931, 1944 and 1952. To compute conventional ten-year survival ratios it was necessary to have data at ten-year intervals, such as 1931, 1941 and 1951, or 1932, 1942 and 1952. Demographic factors in the past in Mauritius have not been very stable; marked annual variations in births have occurred, for instance, and it was therefore unsatisfactory to obtain estimates for the required years by a simple procedure of interpolation. Instead, the 1944 and 1952 populations were estimated in single years of age by a method which took account of the numbers of births in corresponding years.* The 1944 and 1952 populations were than reverse-survived to 1941 and 1951, respectively, by applying appropriate functions of official life tables for these dates.† The 1931 smoothed population, and the 1941 and 1951 reverse-survived populations, are shown in Table B-6 by sex and five-year age groups.

Next, for each five-year age group the proportion surviving to be ten years older at the next adjusted census date was computed. Thus, for example, the number of 25-29 year old males in 1951, divided by the number of 15-19 year old males in 1941, gives the survival ratio for 15-19 year olds. These survival ratios for 1931-41 and 1941-51 are given in columns 4 and 5 of Table B-6.

To assess the mortality levels at different ages indicated by these survival ratios, reference was made to the model life tables developed by the Population Branch of the United Nations. These model life tables were based on patterns of mortality variations by age observed in a study of more than 150 actual life tables for various countries extending over the period from 1900 to 1950.‡ The models cover the entire recorded range of mortality conditions in the world today, from very high to very low. They have been especially adapted for purposes of population projections to represent a time sequence.§ Thus, the 24 tables have been numbered at intervals of 5—from Level 0 (highest mortality) to Level 115 (lowest mortality), and in a situation of "normal" mortality decline, an advance of 5 mortality levels, i.e. from one model table to the next, can be assumed to occur during each successive five-year period of the projection.

In constructing these models, the United Nations staff took

* The method is described in Section II. Tabulations are given in single years of age in the census reports, but these are not reliable owing to digital preference.
† For example, the 1944 data in single years were combined into five-year groups 3-7, 8-12, 13-17, 18-22, etc., which correspond to the conventional groups 0-4, 5-9, 10-14, etc. at 1941. The survival ratios for these groups were computed from the 1944 official life table by the formula $\frac{_5L_{n+3}}{_5L_n}$

‡ United Nations, *Age and Sex Patterns of Mortality*. Model Life Tables for Under-developed Countries. ST/SOA/Ser.A/22, New York, 1955.
§ United Nations, *Methods for Population Projections by Sex and Age*, Manual III, Manuals on methods of estimating population. ST/SOA/Ser.A/25, New York, 1956. See particularly the Appendix.

account of the mortality declines which had been experienced by a number of countries for which adequate statistical data were available over a period of years in the present century.* Except for those countries where life expectancy was already fairly high at the outset of the period, an average annual gain of about 0·4 years was recorded in life expectancy at birth. Since there was reason to believe that future progress would take place at a somewhat more rapid rate than in the past 50 years, an annual gain of 0·5 years in life expectancy was assumed in the models.†

Among the life table functions shown in the U.N. models are the proportions of the populations in each five-year age group who may expect to survive for five years.‡ By multiplying the proportions for two successive five-year groups together, the proportion surviving for ten years is obtained; in this manner the models were adapted to the form of our data for Mauritius. By comparing the Mauritius survival ratios for each age group with the corresponding values obtained from the model life tables we could express the mortality at each age in terms of level numbers. The levels thus identified are shown in the final two columns of table B-6. In general, the numbers shown for the 1941-51 period are higher than those for the preceding decade, implying declining mortality, as would be expected. It may also be noted that, compared with average world patterns, mortality in Mauritius seems to have been relatively light at the young ages and relatively heavy at the older ages, especially among men.

Since the model life tables are based on average patterns, it could not be expected that the data for any particular country would precisely fit a particular model; nevertheless, divergences over a wide range of mortality conditions at different ages would cause the data to be suspect.§ The data for Mauritius reveal some inconsistencies and improbabilities. In fact, the use of census data to measure mortality is rendered virtually impossible for certain age groups, since unknown numbers of men were missing from two of the census

---

* The countries included 19 in Europe, five English-speaking countries of European settlement overseas, seven in Latin America and four in Asia. See United Nations, *Methods for Population Projections by Sex and Age* (*op. cit.*) p. 28.
† Actually, this is the assumption only where life expectancy at birth is less than 55 years. Beyond this point and until life expectancy of 65 years is reached, the rate of progress is assumed to accelerate slightly. Further gains beyond 65 years are assumed to take place at a considerably slower pace. See the United Nations study for further details.
‡ This is not the usual life table survival ratio p_x, which refers to the probability of surviving from exact age x to x + n, but it is rather a group survival ratio. It has been designated with the symbol P_x.
§ See Carrier, N. H. and Farrag, A. M., (*op. cit.*) p. 255, for an application of the United Nations model life tables to Egyptian data, and an assessment of tolerable deviations.

Appendix B—Table 6. Mortality Levels Implied by Recent Census Data.

Sex and age group	Census data adjusted to dates at 10-year intervals (first approximations)			10-year survival ratios		Corresponding mortality level of U.N. life tables	
	1931	1941	1951	1931-41	1941-51	1931-41	1941-51
	(1)	(2)	(3)	(4)	(5)	(6)	(7)
Males							
0- 4	27,237	28,392	44,502	·9080	·9072	50	49
5- 9	27,612	24,091	29,924	·9009	·9636	12	57
10-14	22,807	24,730	25,758	·8728	·9354	3	40
15-19	21,414	24,875	23,214	·8524	·8798	6	20
20-24	17,958	19,906	23,133	·8578	·8565	18	18
25-29	16,185	18,254	21,885	·8555	·8749	24	31
30-34	14,469	15,405	17,050	·8534	·8544	30	31
35-39	12,841	13,846	15,970	·8331	·8059	33	26
40-44	11,278	12,348	13,162	·7390	·7272	21	19
45-49	9,689	10,698	11,159	·6359	·6439	12	13
50-54	7,661	8,335	8,980	·5673	·5806	12	14
55-59	5,436	6,161	6,888	·4994	·4882	13	11
60-64		4,346	4,839		·3053		0
65-69	8,922	2,715	3,008	·2809	·2157	12	19
70-74		2,506	1,327				
75 and over			1,126				
Females							
0- 4	26,637	28,273	43,829	·8977	·9018	45	47
5- 9	26,528	23,511	29,902	·9080	·9481	20	45
10-14	22,125	23,912	25,497	·8454	·9136	0	30
15-19	20,539	24,088	22,291	·8068	·8422	0	9
20-24	17,338	18,704	21,847	·7965	·8268	3	13
25-29	15,327	16,571	20,288	·7994	·8518	11	26
30-34	13,137	13,810	15,464	·8102	·8282	19	23
35-39	11,907	12,252	14,115	·7900	·7701	18	14
40-44	10,297	10,643	11,438	·7586	·7565	18	17
45-49	8,675	9,406	9,435	·7318	·7590	20	26
50-54	7,082	7,811	8,051	·7012	·7381	25	35
55-59	5,030	6,348	7,139	·7068	·6983	46	44
60-64		4,966	5,765		·6230		53
65-69	10,408	3,555	4,433	·4106	·3634	49	70
70-74		4,274	3,094				
75 and over			2,845				

enumerations. Instead, the findings of implied mortality from the census ratios were useful in revising our original adjustments at these ages. The lower than average mortality for males aged 5-14 years in 1941, for example, suggested that our first approximation adjustments for Pioneer Corps absences in the age group 15-24 in 1952 were too high. Similarly, the higher than average mortality shown for the next age group among males indicated that the Pioneer Corps additions at ages 25-34 in 1952 had probably been too small. For the 1931-41 period, the suggested heavy mortality at ages 5-19 again may reflect to some extent the inadequacy of the Pioneer Corps adjustment at ages 18-32 in 1944.

Among females, the inconsistencies are more puzzling; most notably, the exceedingly low survival ratios for the age groups from 10-14 to 20-24 between 1931 and 1941, and for ages 15-19 and 20-24 between 1941 and 1951. In fact, the suggested mortality level for 10-19 year old girls during 1931-41 is higher than that recorded for any country known to have reasonably good statistics. It seems altogether more likely that these findings stem from deficiencies in either the 1931 or 1944 censuses—more probably the former.

As in the case of males, the ratios for females, when compared with the U.N. models, denote a relatively lower mortality at the early years of life than at later years. The levels of mortality indicated by the survival ratios at older ages—particularly for the 1941-51 period

Appendix B—Table 7. Mortality Levels for 1941-51 *Implied in Finally Adjusted Census Data.*

Sex and age group	Census data adjusted to dates at 10-year intervals (final estimate)		10-year survival ratios	Corresponding mortality level of UN life tables
	1941	1951	1941-51	
Males				
0- 4	28,392	44,555	·9060	49
5- 9	24,091	29,867	·9543	47
10-14	24,785	25,724	·9294	36
15-19	25,111	22,989	·8916	26
20-24	20,167	23,036	·8588	19
25-29	18,566	22,388	·8589	25
30-34	15,485	17,320	·8509	29
35-39	13,846	15,946	·8059	26
40-44	12,348	13,176	·7272	19
45-49	10,698	11,159	·6439	13
50-54	8,335	8,980	·5806	14
55-59	6,161	6,888	·4882	11
60-64	4,346	4,839	·3053	0
65-69	2,715	3,008		
70-74	} 2,506	1,327	} ·2157	} 19
75 and over		1,126		
Females				
0- 4	28,273	43,855	·9018	47
5- 9	23,511	29,903	·9473	44
10-14	23,912	25,498	·9136	30
15-19	24,088	22,272	·8441	10
20-24	18,704	21,847	·8246	12
25-29	16,571	20,333	·8504	26
30-34	13,810	15,423	·8358	25
35-39	12,252	14,092	·8326	28
40-44	10,643	11,543	·8099	29
45-49	9,406	10,201	·7778	30
50-54	7,811	8,620	·7155	29
55-59	6,348	7,316	·6456	32
60-64	4,966	5,589	·5207	29
65-69	3,555	4,098		
70-74	} 4,274	2,586	} ·2730	} 33
75 and over		2,131		

—strongly imply a tendency towards over-statement of age. For example, the proportion surviving from ages 65 and over in 1941 to ages 75 and over in 1951 is exceptionally high—corresponding to Level 70 on the U.N. scale. Relatively heavier mortality, indicated by lower level numbers, is implied for each successively younger group back to age 35 years. These are highly improbable findings, and were taken as evidence of a need to adjust the census data for over-statement of age. This adjustment is described in Section II-D above.

Table B-7 shows revised census survival ratios for the 1941-51 period resulting from further adjustments incorporated into the age structure on the basis of the findings of Table B-6. These final adjustments affected mainly men in the military ages and older women, although some minor changes are shown in other groups. With these adjustments, a smoother pattern of mortality change from age group to age group is obtained, although not all the inconsistencies have been eliminated. Our main purpose was to improve the most recent data, which were to be used as a base for the population projections, and hence it was not necessary to take the same care in studying and correcting for sources of error in the earlier data. The greatest single remaining irregularity in the 1952 data is the seemingly low number of women aged 25-34, which shows up in low survival ratios at ages 15-24. Whether some women in these age groups might have been omitted in the census enumeration or might have mis-stated their ages on a relatively large scale could not be determined. In the absence of an explanation for this discrepancy, no correction can be justifiably applied.

B. *Statistics on registered deaths*

The next step was to compare the mortality levels as indicated by the census survival ratios with those derived from statistics on registered deaths. This comparison was confined to the most recent inter-censal period, since official life tables are available only for 1944 and 1952. The q_x values of the two life tables were averaged for each five-year age group, and by comparing with the q_x values of the U.N. model life tables, the corresponding mortality levels were identified. These were then converted to the corresponding levels for P_x values (i.e. group survival ratios) by averaging the values for successive age groups.*

---

* To obtain P_x levels corresponding to 10 years' survival, we thus averaged the q_x levels for three successive age groups. For example, the P_x value shown for males aged 10-14 in col. 3 of Table B-8 is the average of 52, 44 and 40. To obtain the P_x level for the 0-4 age group, q_x levels for age 0 and ages 1-4 were first averaged, giving the latter appropriately more weight than the former. The average of q_x values for age groups 0-4, 5-9 and 10-14 was then computed.

Appendix B—Table 8. *Comparison of Mortality Levels Implied by Census Survival Ratios and Life Table Mortality Rates for a Recent Period.*

Sex and age group	Average of 1944 and 1952 life table q_x's	Corresponding mortality level of United Nations model life tables		Mortality level based on 1941-51 survival ratios
		(q_x)	(P_x)	(P_x)
	(1)	(2)	(3)	(4)
Males				
0	130·48*	65 ⎫	54 ⎫	49
1- 4	81·39	50 ⎭	⎭	
5- 9	20·82	58	51	47
10-14	16·48	52	45	36
15-19	29·82	44	39	26
20-24	45·59	40	35	19
25-29	55·40	33	31	25
30-34	64·40	31	28	29
35-39	78·37	28	24	26
40-44	105·30	24	20	19
45-49	140·86	20	17	13
50-54	182·81	17	13	14
55-59	240·65	13	10	11
60-64	308·07	10	7	0
65-69	396·97	6	9 ⎫	
70-74	505·45	6	19 ⎬	19
75-79	597·01	15	⎭	
80-84	675·01	37		
Females				
0	110·90*	66 ⎫	53 ⎫	47
1- 4	92·14	45 ⎭	⎭	
5- 9	21·90	56	47	44
10-14	17·88	53	37	30
15-19	41·00	33	28	10
20-24	63·17	25	28	12
25-29	68·63	27	31	26
30-34	69·31	31	33	25
35-39	69·94	34	34	28
40-44	75·29	34	33	29
45-49	88·20	34	31	30
50-54	113·37	31	28	29
55-59	155·04	27	26	32
60-64	211·33	26	26	29
65-69	283·93	26	33 ⎫	
70-74	393·06	26	43 ⎬	33
75-79	453·64	47	⎭	
80-84	577·08	55		

* Rates derived by relating infant deaths to births have here been substituted for the official rates which were based on central death rates and are thus less satisfactory.

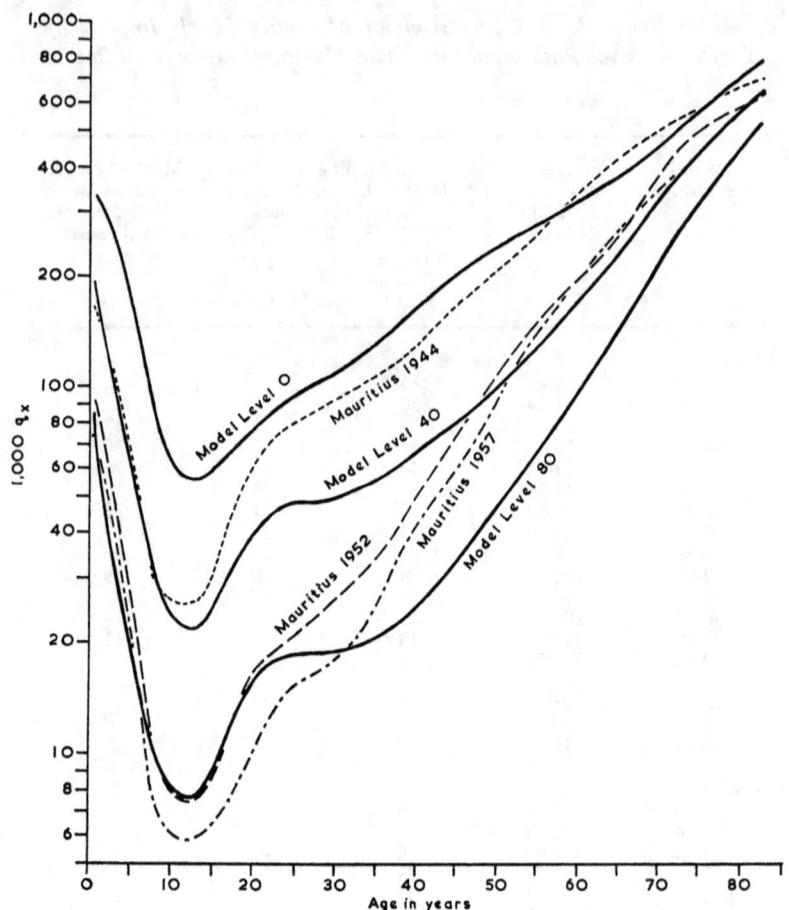

Fig. 3a. *Life-table mortality rates for MALES by age groups: Mauritius and selected United Nations models.*

The results, which confirm some of the hypotheses formulated on the basis of Table B-6 findings, are given in Table B-8. For males, with the exception of those age groups where the census comparison may still be adversely affected by an inadequate adjustment for omissions of military personnel, there is a remarkable degree of correspondence between the mortality levels derived by the two methods. This attests to the generally satisfactory quality of the statistics on registered deaths. At the youngest ages, the census survival ratios imply slightly higher mortality (about five level numbers lower on the U.N. scale) than do the vital statistics, thus

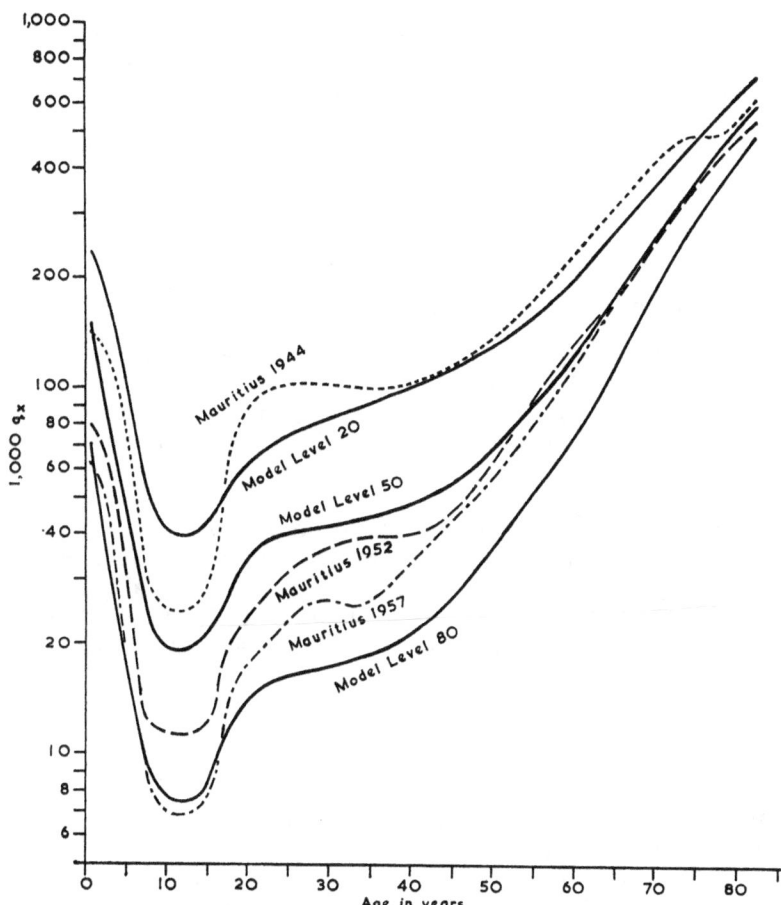

Fig. 3b. *Life-table mortality rates for FEMALES by age groups: Mauritius and selected United Nations Models.*

possibly suggesting some under-registration of deaths at these ages. The pattern of relatively high mortality at middle age and beyond is strikingly confirmed. These findings appear to provide clear evidence that mortality patterns among Mauritian males depart considerably from average world patterns as depicted in the U.N. model life tables. The extent to which this is so is readily seen in Figure 3a.

Among females, the pattern is somewhat different. On the basis of the vital statistics, fairly consistent mortality levels are observed from age group to age group. Apart from the youngest ages and the oldest ages (the latter showing some evidence of over-statement of age at death*) the mortality levels range only from about 26 to 37. The levels identified from census survival ratios show a less stable pattern owing to the apparent under-enumeration of the 25-34 year group at the latest census.

The conclusion to be drawn from these comparisons is that there is no evidence of gross under-registration of deaths, and that the death registration statistics, while perhaps under-stating mortality slightly at the younger ages, on the whole depict a reasonably sound pattern to use as the starting point for projecting future mortality trends.

C. *Post*-1952 *mortality trends*

Since the quality of the registered death statistics has been shown to be satisfactory, it was possible to use the post-census data from this source to bring the analysis of mortality trends up to the starting point for the population projection. An abridged life table was computed for the year 1957 by relating average annual deaths during the period 1956-58 to the estimated population by age and sex in 1957.† (See section V for the derivation of these population estimates). Some principal functions of this life table are shown in Table B-9. That a significant further improvement in mortality has taken place since the last census date is clearly demonstrated by the values for life expectancy at birth as computed from the successive life tables:

	1944	1952	1957
Males	32·2	49·8	54·0
Females	33·8	52·3	57·3

In contrast to the rapid advances made during this period, life expectancy for males is estimated to have increased by only about two years between 1931 and 1944. As pointed out in Chapter 3, the first major progress in mortality control did not occur until after the Second World War. The chief reasons for the dramatic achievements of the post-war period have been set out in the text.

From the q_x values of the three life tables, the corresponding mortality levels at each age were identified from the U.N. model life tables. The extremely high level of mortality still persisting in 1944, particularly among males above age 20 and among women in the peak child-bearing ages, can be seen in these figures (Table B-10). It is also evident that, when the big mortality decline took place, the greatest improvements were realised among adolescents and young

---

* The values were taken from official life tables and it is not known whether they incorporated any correction for over-statement of age.

† The data on registered deaths by age for females were adjusted to correct for an apparent over-statement of age at death.

Appendix B—Table 9. Some Functions of an Abridged Life Table for Mauritius: 1957.

Sex and age	Probability of surviving from age x to x+n	Probability of dying between age x and x+n	Survivors at exact age x	Years lived between age x and x+n
	$_np_x$	$_nq_x$	l_x	$_nL_x$
Males				
0-	·92431	·07569*	100,000	94,323†
1-	·95695	·04305	92,431	361,766
5-	·99183	·00817	88,452	440,452
10-	·99422	·00578	87,729	437,378
15-	·99193	·00807	87,222	434,350
20-	·98694	·01306	86,518	429,765
25-	·98359	·01641	85,388	423,440
30-	·97995	·02005	83,987	415,725
35-	·96686	·03314	82,303	404,695
40-	·95027	·04973	79,575	387,985
45-	·92437	·07563	75,618	363,790
50-	·88355	·11645	69,899	329,145
55-	·83234	·16766	61,759	282,910
60-	·77003	·22997	51,404	227,470
65-	·68325	·31675	39,583	166,570
70-	·61294	·38706	27,045	109,055
75-			16,577	92,656
Females				
0-	·93683	·06317*	100,000	95,262†
1-	·95187	·04813	93,683	365,712
5-	·99010	·00990	89,174	443,660
10-	·99302	·00698	88,291	439,915
15-	·98644	·01356	87,675	435,400
20-	·98015	·01985	86,486	428,140
25-	·97394	·02606	84,769	418,320
30-	·97463	·02537	82,560	407,560
35-	·97039	·02961	80,465	396,370
40-	·96175	·03825	78,082	382,940
45-	·95055	·04945	75,095	366,190
50-	·93246	·06754	71,382	344,860
55-	·90699	·09301	66,561	317,330
60-	·85516	·14484	60,370	279,990
65-	·79175	·20825	51,626	231,250
70-	·70915	·29085	40,875	174,655
75-			28,987	203,346

* Computed by relating infant deaths to births.
† By the formula $L_0 = ·25\, l_0 + ·75\, l_1$.

adults. For men aged 20-34, death-rates corresponding to Model Level 10 had been recorded around 1944; by 1952 the death-rates for this group approximated those of Levels 65-80, marking an exceptional rate of progress. Nearly the same remarkable improvements were shown among women at these ages. At infancy and early

Appendix B—Table 10. Mortality Levels Implied by Life Table Mortality Rates for Mauritius.

Sex and age group	Corresponding mortality level of United Nations model life tables (q_x)			Average annual change in mortality level	
	1944	1952	1957	1944-52	1952-57
Males					
0	51	77	82	+3·2	+1·0
-4	38	67	73	+3·6	+1·2
5- 9	42	80	87	+4·8	+1·4
10-14	37	81	88	+5·5	+1·4
15-19	21	80	93	+7·4	+2·6
20-24	12	79	89	+8·4	+2·0
25-29	9	71	84	+7·8	+2·6
30-34	9	65	79	+7·0	+2·8
35-39	11	56	65	+5·6	+1·8
40-44	11	48	57	+4·6	+1·8
45-49	7	40	49	+4·1	+1·8
50-54	5	35	40	+3·8	+1·0
55-59	0	32	34	+4·0	+0·4
60-64	Below 0	31	31	+3·9*	—
65-69	Below 0	26	27	+3·2*	+0·2
70-74	Below 0	18	38	+2·2*	+4·0
			Average:	+4·9	+1·6
Females					
0	52	78	82	+3·2	+0·8
-4	34	59	68	+3·1	+1·8
5- 9	43	74	80	+3·9	+1·2
10-14	40	69	81	+3·6	+2·4
15-19	11	64	75	+6·6	+2·2
20-24	Below 0	62	73	+7·8*	+2·2
25-29	6	57	67	+6·4	+2·0
30-34	14	55	70	+5·1	+3·0
35-39	19	56	68	+4·6	+2·4
40-44	19	58	68	+4·9	+2·0
45-49	19	56	66	+4·6	+2·0
50-54	18	52	66	+4·2	+2·8
55-59	14	46	60	+4·0	+2·8
60-64	9	49	56	+5·0	+1·4
65-69	5	52	50	+5·9	−0·4
70-74	4	50	51	+5·8	+0·2
			Average:	+4·9	+1·8

* The average annual change for these age groups is understated, since mortality in 1944 was higher than depicted in model level 0.

childhood, mortality was already at moderate levels by 1944, and the advances were therefore not quite so impressive.†

† Similar patterns of post-war mortality decline have been recorded in Ceylon, where malaria eradication was also the principal factor in bringing down the death-rate. The progress was most striking in the age groups between 10 and 30 years.

At the upper ages women seem to have benefited more than men from the improvements in health conditions. In fact, even in 1957 death-rates for men over 45 remained high by prevailing world standards.*

The average mortality gains recorded annually, defined in terms of U.N. model level numbers, amounted to about 1·7 levels during 1952-57, as compared with a very rapid gain of about five levels annually during the earlier period (Table B-10). Thus, even during the later period when the fall in the death-rate had tapered off, mortality was declining at a rate faster than the "normal" trend as defined for projection purposes in the U.N. models.

The past trend of mortality in Mauritius, which after a long period of only slight improvement has changed drastically in recent years, does not provide a useful basis for projecting the rate of decline likely to occur in the future. While the rapid rate of decline experienced since the war cannot long continue, it is nevertheless true that mortality still remains quite high at certain ages. Some further decline therefore seems probable. The method adopted for estimating future mortality trends for purposes of the population projections is described in Section VI-A.

IV. FERTILITY TRENDS

A. *Statistics on births by age of mother*

While trends in fertility as measured by the crude birth-rate or general fertility ratios can be studied over a long period in Mauritius, it is only recently that more refined data have become available. Since 1955 information relating to age of mother has been obtained on the birth registration form. Age-specific birth-rates computed from these

Appendix B—Table 11. *Age-specific Fertility Rates for Mauritius:* 1955-58†

(Births per 1,000 women in age group)

Age group‡	1955	1956	1957	1958
15-19	145·3	153·2	146·3	143·8
20-24	279·8	299·8	310·7	306·4
25-29	269·8	281·8	280·3	263·3
30-34	228·5	242·3	241·3	229·1
35-39	152·4	174·3	169·1	155·1
40-44	55·8	55·6	56·8	54·0

SOURCE: Recent issues of the *Yearbook of Statistics*
† For General and Indo-Mauritian population.
‡ Rates for ages below 15 and above 44 are here omitted.

* It will be seen that, beginning at age 30, a fall of approximately 10 levels, i.e. equivalent to two models, occurs with each successive age group. Beyond age 55 the disparity between mortality levels at successive age groups is not so great.

Appendix B—Table 12. *Age-specific Fertility Rates for Selected Countries*

(Births per 1,000 women in age group)

Age group*	Mauritius 1956-58	Ceylon 1956	Taiwan 1954	Singapore 1947	British Guiana 1954	Venezuela 1950	Guatemala 1950	Puerto Rico 1950	Trinidad & Tobago 1955	El Salvador 1950	Fiji 1955
15-19	144·3	71·0	47·5	101·1	165·5	NA	163·2	99·2	178·9	NA	109·5
20-24	299·0	289·4	263·2	314·1	323·3	276·4	285·7	279·7	321·4	296·0	280·8
25-29	289·3	323·9	334·1	333·8	288·4	277·5	298·2	260·3	276·8	320·2	271·1
30-34	239·3	221·7	291·8	269·7	214·2	217·3	258·5	200·0	201·2	249·4	180·4
35-39	169·7	173·5	218·2	196·3	125·7	144·7	197·1	143·1	129·3	146·0	141·2
40-44	54·6	39·3	104·4	83·3	43·0	52·4	86·9	53·1	40·5	58·4	59·3

NA = Not available.
SOURCE: Except for Mauritius and Ceylon, data are from the United Nations *Demographic Yearbook*. Ceylon rates from National Planning Council, *Population Projections for Ceylon 1956-1981*, Colombo, 1959, p. 32.
* Rates for ages below 15 and above 44 are here omitted.

data are shown in Table B-11.* These rates relate only to the General and Indo-Mauritian population who together constitute nearly 97% of the total.†

The time period for which these new data are available is too short to give any indication of trends. It will suffice to note that the levels of the rates are very high; in fact, if they were to continue in existence during the passage of a cohort of women through the child-bearing ages, these women would bear on average 5·7 children each. The numbers of female births related to age of mother for the year 1958 imply a gross reproduction rate of 2·97 and a net reproduction rate of 2·47.

It is also noteworthy that child-bearing begins at an early age in Mauritius. This may be seen very strikingly in Table B-12, where 1956-58 average fertility rates for Mauritius are compared with rates for some other countries. The early start to child-bearing is no doubt a reflection of the early marriages which are traditional in Indian culture. The same pattern is observed in other countries where Indians form a large part of the population, for example, in British Guiana, Trinidad and Tobago and Fiji. In these countries the peak period of child-bearing generally occurs at ages 20-24, whereas it is more often at ages 25-29 in other cultures.

As shown in Chapter 3, fertility in Mauritius has been characterised by marked annual fluctuations, and in recent decades has been sensitive to changes in economic conditions. With improvements in health and other post-war developments the birth-rate rose to

Appendix B—Table 13. *Derivation of Average Age-specific Fertility Rates for Mauritius:* 1956-58

Age group of women	Live births to General and Indo-Mauritian women 1956-58 (1)	Live births to all groups 1956-58‡ (2)	Estimated female population 1957×3 (3)	Age-specific fertility rates (births per 1,000 women) (4)
15-19 §	10,728	11,074	75,543	146·6
20-24	20,085	20,734	69,339	299·0
25-29	17,366	17,927	61,971	289·3
30-34	14,197	14,656	61,239	239·3
35-39	7,607	7,853	46,287	169·7
40-44 ‖	2,459	2,539	41,538	61·1
Total	72,442	74,783		

‡ Distribution in col. 1 applied to total.
§ Including also births to females under age 15.
‖ Including also births to females aged 45 and over.

* These rates are taken from the Mauritius *Yearbook of Statistics*. The current population estimates used as a base for computing these rates were calculated from 1952 census data and vital statistics for later years.
† Chinese births by age of mother are excluded from the published data.

higher levels. While part of this increase was only temporary, reflecting a post-war marriage boom, rates for 1956-58 may be relatively free of these temporary influences and may become stabilised. For the assumption of constant fertility at current rates to be used in one of our projections, we computed the average age-specific rates for 1956-58. These are shown in Table B-13. The distribution of live births by age of mother in the General and Indo-Mauritian population was assumed to apply to all births.* Total births by age of mother thus obtained were related to the estimated population at mid-year 1957 to derive age-specific rates. In computing the rates, the small number of births to mothers under age 15 were added to those occurring to women aged 15-19, and the small number to women over age 44 were added to the group 40-44.

B. *Census data on number of children born*

For the first time, in the 1952 census, data were collected on the number of children ever born to women. These data, which were tabulated separately for the major ethnic groups and by present age of women, are valuable in studying fertility differentials, since they are not subject to the shortcomings which have caused the comparisons of birth-rates for the different ethnic groups to be suspect (see Chapter 3). For our purposes, however, the data on number of children born to women were important mainly as an indication of the average fertility levels which had prevailed over a long period prior to 1952. They were utilised in setting out the fertility assumptions of two of our alternative projections.

The data purport to cover all women who had ever been married, whether legally or in religious ceremony only, or in the sense of living in a consensual union. In addition, single women who had given birth to children were theoretically included. Actually, the total numbers of women in the tabulation correspond very closely to the sums of women in marital status categories other than single, so that, in fact, very few unmarried mothers were included†. For convenience, the women included in these tabulations are here referred to as "ever-married" women.

---

* Unpublished tabulations of Chinese births by age of mother, which were received too late to incorporate in the projections, show a rather different distribution from that of the General and Indo-Mauritian groups—the average age of child-bearing being considerably higher. However, since the Chinese segment forms such a small part of the total, little error was introduced by assuming their births to be distributed in the same way as those of the rest of the population.

† There are slight discrepancies for various age groups; in some cases the totals exceed the numbers of "ever-married" women as shown in marital status tabulations, while for other age groups the reverse is true.

Table B-14 shows that, according to these data, the average size of family was 4·7 for all "ever-married" women 45 years of age and over, or 4·4 if all women regardless of marital status are included in the calculation. The figures for this age group, which are generally taken to represent completed fertility, are shown to be slightly lower than those for the preceding group aged 40-44.* Since child-bearing does not end for all women by age 44, a higher figure would normally be expected for the older women (in the absence of any trend toward rising fertility). It is very probable that the figures for the 45 and over group are deficient owing to memory factors, since older women are particularly liable to omit reporting births of children who died in infancy. Unfortunately, the tabulations provide no sub-divisions of the 45 and over age group, which would have been extremely useful in throwing further light on this question.†

The treatment of the group of "ever-married" women who did not report how many children they had given birth to deserves mention. It has been suggested that women who fail to reply to this question are very often those who have no children, but for reasons of social prestige are reluctant to admit it. In this event, the averages shown in cols. 4 and 6, which assume no children for the not reporting group, may be more accurate. In cols. 5 and 7, on the other hand, the not reporting group has in effect been distributed proportionally according to the replies of the others. It will be noted that the differences between the two columns are negligible for all groups except women aged 45 and over. In addition to a large "not-reported" category, the size of the group reporting no children was also relatively high for this age group. These are findings which suggested weaknesses in the data for older women and led us to distribute the group not reporting.

C. *Calculations of fertility rates for alternative projections*

The average completed size of family derived from the data on number of children ever born to women is thus not large compared with that which would be achieved given the continuance of present fertility rates (5·7 per woman). If fertility had remained fairly stable during a long period prior to 1952 it would be possible to estimate the effective age-specific fertility rates on the basis of the data on

---

* When the "not-reported" category is distributed, the average for these two age groups of "ever-married" women is nearly the same.

† It is possible that the permanent effects of the postponed marriages and births during the economic depression of the 1930's might have been proportionately greater for women aged 45-49 in 1952, as compared with those aged 40-44. The older groups were 25-29 at the height of the depression, and had less time remaining for the making up of postponed births. Moreover, the younger group was still in the child-bearing ages during the post-war period of high fertility. It is doubtful, however, whether these factors could have had a very great effect.

Appendix B—Table 14. Total and Ever-Married Females 10 years of Age and Over and Number of Children Born Alive to them: Census of 1952

Age group of women	Total women* (1)	Total women ever married (2)	Number of children born alive (3)	Average number of children per woman		Average number of children per ever-married woman	
				Including women not reporting number of children† (4)	Excluding women not reporting number of children‡ (5)	Including women not reporting number of children† (6)	Excluding women not reporting number of children‡ (7)
10-14	24,713	662	65	—	—	·10	·10
15-19	23,085	9,571	6,982	·30	·30	·73	·73
20-24	21,496	16,364	30,323	1·41	1·41	1·85	1·86
25-29	21,133	18,666	54,031	2·56	2·56	2·89	2·90
30-34	15,637	14,406	54,907	3·51	3·52	3·81	3·82
35-39	14,547	13,560	60,116	4·13	4·14	4·43	4·45
40-44	11,605	10,938	51,278	4·42	4·45	4·69	4·73
45 and over	41,278	38,575	170,914	4·14	4·38	4·43	4·71

SOURCE: Mauritius Central Statistical Office, *Census* 1952, Part II, pp. 35-37.
* These are unadjusted figures as enumerated in the census.
† In effect, the women not reporting number of children are assumed to have had none.
‡ Women not reporting number of children are assumed to have been distributed in the same way as those who did report.

numbers of children born to women.* Fertility levels were not, however, stable in Mauritius. Nevertheless, for lack of a better index, age-specific fertility rates were computed from these data for use in one of the alternative population projections which assumes a return to pre-1952 fertility levels.

To derive these rates, the average number of children per woman† was plotted for each five-year age group, and the dots joined in a smooth S-shaped curve. From the graph, values were read off at exact ages 10, 15, 20, 25, etc. Then, by differencing, estimates were obtained of the number of children born to women between these

Appendix B—Table 15. *Estimation of Age-specific Fertility Rates from Number of Children Ever Born to Women Enumerated at 1952 Census.*

Age of women in 1952	Average number of children per woman in age group‡	Average number of children per woman at exact age x (read from graph)	Number of children born per woman in age group x+5 (by differencing from col. 2)	Age-specific fertility rates annually per 1,000 women. $\frac{\text{col. 3}}{5} \times 1,000$
(1)	(2)	(3)	(4)
10-	—	—	·10	20
15-	·30	·10	·72	144
20-	1·41	·82	1·28	256
25-	2·56	2·10	·97	194
30-	3·52	3·07	·80	160
35-	4·14	3·87	·47	94
40-	4·45	4·34	·18	36
45-	4·53§	4·52	·02	4
50-		4·54		

‡ Women not reporting number of children were deducted from total before computing average.
§ Adjusted figure.

* T. E. Smith has done this for Malaya. See Smith, T. E., *Population Growth in Malaya*, London, 1952. On the assumption of constant age-specific rates, the difference between numbers of children reported for two successive age groups will tell the rate at which births occurred to women at ages approximately between the mid-points of these age groups.

† The averages were obtained by excluding the not reported group from the total. An adjusted figure was derived for the 45 and over group in view of the high proportion of this group which had reported "no" children (20%). It was assumed that the actual proportion who had had no children was the same for this age group as for the preceding age group, namely 16%; the number calculated as having been mis-classified in the "0" category were distributed proportionally among those who had reported one or more children. This revision, admittedly arbitrary, raised the average number of children to 4·53 for the 45 and over group.

ages, i.e. at 10-14, 15-19, 20-24, etc. (see Table B-15). As these rates (col. 3) cover a period of five years, they were divided by five to obtain the annual rates given in col. 4.

For the youngest age groups, the rates reflect the high fertility levels of the immediate post-war period. These rates are on a level with the current rates shown in Table B-13. Women now in the later child-bearing years, on the other hand, had a larger proportion of their total births during periods of lower fertility; hence, the rates computed for them by differencing from younger age groups appear rather low. It is of interest to note that, had the rates derived in Table B-15 been in effect in the year 1952, the total number of births resulting would have amounted to only about two-thirds the actual number occurring during that year.

In line with the proposals of the Mission to popularise the concept of the three-child family, it was considered desirable to demonstrate in one of the alternative projections the demographic consequences of the adoption of such a pattern. We therefore wished to derive a set of fertility rates based on the premise that after a certain date in the future women would cease to have births in excess of three. As a starting point for this calculation, we computed the distribution of women in each age group in 1952 according to the numbers of children they had borne*. On the assumption that the average values for the group were representative of the age at the exact mid-point of the group, i.e. age $12\frac{1}{2}$, $17\frac{1}{2}$, $22\frac{1}{2}$, etc., interpolations were made to obtain values for exact ages 15, 20, 25, etc. From these data we calculated the numbers of births of the 4th or higher orders occurring to women during their passage through a particular five-year age group. A total of 7·7 "excess" children was found per 100 women at age 20, 39·3 at age 25, etc. (Table B-16). Therefore, by differencing and dividing by five, the amounts to be subtracted from the annual age-specific birth-rates were obtained†. The results are shown in col. 2 of Table B-17.

This simplified procedure assumes that if the three-child family pattern were to be accepted by the population, women would not alter their family building habits until after they had borne three children. In actual practice, of course, they might begin child-bearing at a later age and allow a longer interval between births. It is likewise unrealistic to assume, as has been done here, that no

---

* For the group aged 45 and over the revised figures described above were substituted for the enumerated. Women not reporting number of children were deducted from the totals before computing the distribution in percentages. Single women were included in the "0" category.

† It was also necessary to multiply by 10 to put the age-specific rates on a per 1,000 basis.

woman would ever have more than three children. No doubt some women would have more than three children, while the proportions having only one or two might be higher than those assumed in these calculations. As stated in Chapter 3, these simplifications have been adopted for statistical convenience.

Appendix B—Table 16. *Distribution of Women at Specified Ages According to Number of Children Ever Born, and Calculation of Births of the Fourth and Higher Orders.*

(Based on data on number of children ever born to women enumerated at 1952 census)

Part A.

Number of children	Distribution of women in each age group according to number of children ever born							
	10-14 (12·5)	15-19 (17·5)	20-24 (22·5)	25-29 (27·5)	30-34 (32·5)	35-39 (37·5)	40-44 (42·5)	45 and over* (47·5)
0	99·8	78·8	38·4	22·3	17·1	16·3	16·3	16·3
1	0·2	14·4	19·5	12·8	9·8	9·2	9·6	10·4
2	—	5·3	19·6	15·8	11·5	9·9	9·3	9·5
3	—	1·2	12·8	16·8	13·2	10·0	9·6	8·9
4	—	0·3	6·3	14·3	13·5	11·0	9·8	8·5
5	—	—	2·3	9·9	11·9	10·4	8·7	8·5
6	—	—	0·7	4·7	9·2	9·7	8·5	7·7
7	—	—	0·3	2·1	6·6	7·8	7·4	7·1
8	—	—	0·1	0·7	3·7	6·1	6·1	6·4
9	—	—	—	0·4	1·9	4·3	5·1	5·2
10	—	—	—	0·1	0·9	2·5	3·9	4·3
11	—	—	—	0·1	0·4	1·3	2·5	2·6
12 or more	—	—	—	—	0·3	1·5	3·3	4·6
Total	100	100	100	100	100	100	100	100

Part B.

Number of children	Estimated distribution of women at exact age shown according to number of children ever born						
	15	20	25	30	35	40	45
0	89·3	58·6	30·3	19·7	16·7	16·3	16·3
1	7·3	16·9	16·2	11·3	9·4	9·4	10·0
2	2·6	12·4	17·7	13·7	10·7	9·6	9·4
3	0·6	7·0	14·8	15·0	11·6	9·8	9·2
4	0·2	3·3	10·3	13·9	12·4	10·4	9·1
5	—	1·2	6·1	10·9	11·1	9·5	8·6
6	—	0·4	2·7	6·9	9·4	9·1	8·1
7	—	0·2	1·2	4·3	7·2	7·6	7·3
8	—	—	0·4	2·2	4·9	6·1	6·3
9	—	—	0·2	1·2	3·1	4·7	5·1
10	—	—	0·1	0·5	1·7	3·2	4·1
11	—	—	—	0·3	0·9	1·9	2·6
12 or more†	—	—	—	0·1	0·9	2·4	3·9
Total	100	100	100	100	100	100	100
Children in excess of 3 per 100 women	0·2	7·7	39·3	98·6	161·9	205·0	226·5

* Adjusted figures.
† Assumed to be 12.

Appendix B—Table 17. *Derivation of Age-specific Fertility Rates on Assumption of Eliminating Births of Fourth and Higher Orders.*
(All rates are per 1,000 women)

Age group of women	Estimated births of 4th and higher orders occurring to women at specified ages*	Adjustment required to annual age-specific fertility rate†	Age-specific fertility rates derived from 1952 census data on number of children ever born to women	Age-specific fertility rates adjusted to eliminate births of 4th and higher orders
	(1)	(2)	(3)	(4)
10-14	2	—	20	20
15-19	75	− 15	144	129
20-24	316	− 63	256	193
25-29	593	−119	194	75
30-34	633	−127	160	33
35-39	431	− 86	94	8
40-44	215	− 43	36	—

* Obtained by differencing figures in last line of Table B-16.
† Column (1) divided by 5.

V. ESTIMATION OF 1957 POPULATION BASE

At the time this study was undertaken, vital statistics were available up to and including the year 1958. As a matter of convenience, mid-year 1957—a date exactly five years after the 1952 census—was adopted as the starting date for the population projections. The 1952 adjusted census population by sex and age was brought forward to 1957 by utilising the data on registered births and deaths, which had been found to be of sufficiently high quality for this purpose. The numbers of registered births during this period were used without adjustment.‡ It was assumed that births were distributed uniformly over the calendar year, so that for the period in question one-half of registered births for 1952 and one-half of those for 1957 were added to total births in the intervening years.

Registered deaths were tabulated for single years of age up to age 4, and by five-year groups from age 5 to 94 years. For ages 5 and above, the procedure followed in allocating registered deaths to particular cohorts was as follows. For any given five-year age group, the 1952 estimate was reduced by the number of registered deaths recorded at the same ages during the first half of the period plus those recorded

‡ It will be recalled that in estimating the extent of under-enumeration of young children at the 1952 census, a small correction was found to be required for under-registration of births (see Section II-C). The smallness of this correction factor (less than 1%) and the possibility of improved registration in recent years caused us to omit it for the 1952-57 period.

at the next higher age group during the second half of the period. Thus, for example, in surviving the group of males aged 10-14 years in 1952 we subtracted registered deaths at ages 10-14 for the period from mid-1952 to the end of 1954 and deaths at ages 15-19 for the period 1955 to mid-1957.*

Owing to the uneven distribution of deaths over the first years of life, a different procedure had to be adopted to obtain estimates for ages under 5. For this age range, single year cohorts were dealt with separately. It was assumed that two-thirds of deaths recorded during a given year at ages under 1 occurred to children born during the same year, and one-third to births of the previous year.† Similarly, three-fifths of deaths at age 1 were assumed to occur to children born during the preceding year, and two-fifths to those born during the next earlier year. From age 2 onwards, an even distribution of deaths between the two affected cohorts was assumed.

As a check on the adequacy of utilising registered deaths without adjustment to bring forward the 1952 census population, we calculated the implied five-year survival ratios for each sex-age group and compared them with the U.N. models. The mortality levels thus identified were generally acceptable for males, since they tended to confirm the pattern of mortality at different ages which had been observed in the census survival ratios. For females at the upper ages, however, there was seemingly clear evidence of over-statement of age at death. The mortality levels derived for females aged 30 and over are shown in col. 1 of Table B-18; they show a sharp drop in level number with increasing age.

The 1952 census data, it will be recalled, were adjusted for over-statement of age, but the registered deaths initially used in bringing forward the 1952 data to 1957 had not been so adjusted. The erratic values of col. 1 at the highest ages led us to correct the 1957 data. Accordingly, smoothed values of the model life table mortality levels shown in col. 2 were substituted for those in col. 1. Beginning with the oldest age group (70 and over in 1952) the corresponding P_x value from the model life table was used to obtain an estimate of survivors five years older in 1957. The same procedure was applied for successively younger age groups, and the new 1957 estimates were accumulated, beginning with the oldest age group. The process was halted at the point when the cumulated total approximated to that in the original estimate. This point was reached at age 35. The small

---

* Very similar results would have been obtained by the more usual procedure of totalling deaths for the five-year period and allocating to a particular age group in 1952 one-half of the deaths at that age group plus one-half at the next higher group. The procedure we used is, however, slightly more accurate.

† See United Nations, *Methods for Population Projections by Sex and Age* (*op. cit.*), p. 7.

Appendix B—Table 18. *Correction of 1957 Female Population for Over-statement of Age at Death.*

Age in 1952	U.N. model life tables mortality levels		Survival ratios corresponding to smoothed mortality levels (P_x values)	1952 adjusted population	Revised 1957 population (col. 3 × col. 4)	Revised 1957 population accumulated	Revised 1957 accumulated population adjusted to original total 35 years and over	Revised and adjusted 1957	Age in 1957
	Based on registered deaths 1952-57	Smoothed							
	(1)	(2)	(3)	(4)	(5)	(6)	(7)	(8)	
30-34	60-65	65	·9700	15,900	15,423	74,926	74,954	15,429	35-39
35-39	65	60	·9622	14,385	13,841	59,503	59,525	13,846	40-44
40-44	60	55	·9500	11,828	11,237	45,662	45,679	11,241	45-49
45-49	65	55	·9373	10,448	9,793	34,425	34,438	9,797	50-54
50-54	55-60	50	·9098	8,842	8,044	24,632	24,641	8,047	55-59
55-59	50	50	·8761	7,271	6,370	16,588	16,594	6,372	60-64
60-64	40-45	45	·8104	5,775	4,680	10,218	10,222	4,682	65-69
65-69	40	45	·7299	4,218	3,079	5,538	5,540	3,080	70-74
70 and over	25	45	·5102	4,820	2,459	2,459	2,460	2,460	75 and over

remaining difference between the revised and original totals for ages 35 and over was rateably distributed. The procedure and results are shown in Table B-18.

The 1957 population by sex and age derived by these methods was used as a base for computing the 1957 abridged life table described in Section III. It was also used as a base for the computation of certain fertility measures and it serves as the starting point for the projections which we now describe.

VI. THE POPULATION PROJECTIONS

A. *Mortality and fertility assumptions*

Our analysis of mortality trends showed that Mauritius has recently joined the group of countries with declining mortality, and pointed further to the likelihood of continued decline. While the leading pre-war cause of death—malaria—has now been eradicated, such diseases as hookworm, tuberculosis, anaemia, and dysentery still remain to be brought under complete control. Studies of the pattern of decline in other countries suggest that neither the past nor the current statistics of Mauritius are likely to furnish a reliable estimate of future mortality trends. The United Nations model life tables, which have been especially designed to reflect "normal" mortality decline, appeared to offer a more satisfactory basis for projecting future mortality changes in Mauritius.

Table B-10, presented earlier, shows the mortality levels of the model life tables which correspond most closely to values taken from the abridged Mauritius life table for 1957 for the various sex-age groups. These levels, which referred to 1957 q_x mortality rates, were converted into levels for P_x values and were then each increased by two-and-a-half (corresponding to a time period of two-and-a-half years) to approximate the mid-point of the first projection period—1957-62.* The levels thus obtained were rounded to the nearest number ending in digit "0" or "5", so that the survival ratios to be used in the projection could be read directly from the United Nations tables without requiring interpolation.† Five levels were added for each five-year projection period in the future, the equivalent of an increase of about two-and-a-half years in life expectancy at birth. The levels and the corresponding survival ratios which were used in Projections A and C for all dates are shown in Table B-19. For Projection B, mortality was assumed to remain constant,

---

* In addition, mortality levels for births and for the oldest age group, i.e. age 70 and over, were derived from the survival ratios implied in actual data for the 1952-57 period.

† Not all rounding was in the same direction, and the net effect is likely to have introduced less error than that inherent in the basic data.

Appendix B—Table 19. *Mortality Levels from United Nations Model Life Tables and Corresponding Survival Ratios used in Projections A and C for Mauritius.*

Sex and age group	1957-62 P_x level	1957-62 Survival ratio	1962-67 P_x level	1962-67 Survival ratio	1967-72 P_x level	1967-72 Survival ratio	1972-77 P_x level	1972-77 Survival ratio	1977-82 P_x level	1977-82 Survival ratio
Males										
Births	85	·9262	90	·9438	95	·9580	100	·9678	105	·9744
0- 4	90	·9818	95	·9867	100	·9908	105	·9936	110	·9954
5- 9	90	·9937	95	·9949	100	·9963	105	·9974	110	·9982
10-14	90	·9928	95	·9941	100	·9955	105	·9968	110	·9977
15-19	90	·9893	95	·9913	100	·9935	105	·9953	110	·9965
20-24	90	·9873	95	·9898	100	·9924	105	·9944	110	·9957
25-29	85	·9840	90	·9866	95	·9891	100	·9916	105	·9935
30-34	75	·9760	80	·9792	85	·9822	90	·9849	95	·9874
35-39	65	·9628	70	·9671	75	·9711	80	·9746	85	·9779
40-44	55	·9408	60	·9467	65	·9523	70	·9575	75	·9617
45-49	45	·9062	50	·9150	55	·9226	60	·9294	65	·9359
50-54	40	·8664	45	·8776	50	·8877	55	·8965	60	·9045
55-59	35	·8113	40	·8249	45	·8375	50	·8488	55	·8587
60-64	30	·7355	35	·7514	40	·7660	45	·7798	50	·7924
65-69	30	·6492	35	·6660	40	·6820	45	·6972	50	·7116
70 and over	30	·4506	35	·4640	40	·4770	45	·4892	50	·5009
Females										
Births	80	·9208	85	·9380	90	·9535	95	·9660	100	·9744
0- 4	80	·9731	85	·9791	90	·9844	95	·9892	100	·9925
5- 9	80	·9914	85	·9932	90	·9948	95	·9962	100	·9972
10-14	80	·9906	85	·9925	90	·9941	95	·9956	100	·9967
15-19	75	·9838	80	·9865	85	·9891	90	·9914	95	·9935
20-24	70	·9771	75	·9807	80	·9839	85	·9869	90	·9896
25-29	70	·9756	75	·9792	80	·9826	85	·9858	90	·9884
30-34	70	·9739	75	·9777	80	·9811	85	·9842	90	·9868
35-39	65	·9669	70	·9710	75	·9749	80	·9783	85	·9814
40-44	65	·9606	70	·9650	75	·9691	80	·9727	85	·9759
45-49	60	·9437	65	·9493	70	·9543	75	·9589	80	·9631
50-54	60	·9252	65	·9318	70	·9377	75	·9433	80	·9482
55-59	55	·8859	60	·8949	65	·9030	70	·9104	75	·9175
60-64	55	·8348	60	·8459	65	·8559	70	·8653	75	·8743

and thus the survival ratios shown for the 1957-62 period were applied throughout all projection periods.*

In the absence of voluntary family limitation on the part of a significant segment of the population, the continuance of fertility at a high level must be assumed. For Projection A, the average 1956-58 fertility rates, which exclude the peak fertility levels of the earlier post-war years, were used throughout the period to 1982. These are the rates derived in Table B-13. The Projection B fertility assumption, on the other hand, was based on family size data recorded in the 1952 census and thus reflects the average of fertility levels over some decades before 1952. If current fertility rates are still inflated by abnormal marriage patterns of the post-war years (see Chapter 3), it is conceivable that some fall may occur without a large-scale resort to family planning. Projection B attempts to define the lower limits of such a fertility decline. It was assumed that the lower birth-rates would be reached by 1967 and would remain constant thereafter to 1982. The fertility rates assumed to come into effect by 1967 in this Projection are those derived in Table B-15. Projection C, which has been included for illustrative purposes, assumes a drastic fall in fertility corresponding to the situation which would obtain if after 1972 no woman were to have more than three children (see Section IV-C). A systematic decline from present rates to these levels by 1972 has been assumed, with no further decline after 1972. In Table B-20 below the fertility rates used in the three projections are summarised.

B. *Method of projection*

The survival ratios for 1957-62 shown in Table B-19 were applied to the numbers in the corresponding sex-age groups in 1957 to determine how many might be expected to survive to be five years older in 1962. Similarly, the appropriate survival ratios were applied to obtain the estimates by sex and age for later dates.

In estimating births, the age-specific birth-rates were applied to the average numbers of women in the age group for the period concerned. For example, in estimating births for the 1957-62 period, the age-specific fertility rate for women aged 15-19 was multiplied by the mean of the numbers of women at these ages in 1957 and 1962. The results for all ages of mothers were summed and multiplied by five to give births during the quinquennial period. The total number of births thus derived was multiplied by a constant factor of ·5079— the proportion of male to total births registered during 1947-57— to obtain the estimated number of male births. This number was

---

* Thus, in this projection, an allowance was made for an improvement in mortality amounting to only two-and-a-half levels from that obtaining in 1957.

Appendix B—Table 20. *Age-specific Fertility Rates used in Population Projections for Mauritius.*

(Births per 1,000 women in age group)

Age group	1957-62	1962-67	1967-72	1972-77	1977-82
Projection A					
15-19	146·6				
20-24	299·0				
25-29	289·3	These rates assumed to remain constant			
30-34	239·3				
35-39	169·7				
40-44	61·1				
Projection B					
15-24	216·9	211·6	209·0	209·0	209·0
25-34	243·1	200·6	179·3	179·3	179·3
35-44	106·1	81·6	69·4	69·4	69·4
Projection C					
15-24	211·4	195·4	179·2	171·2	171·2
25-34	230·3	162·2	94·0	60·0	60·0
35-44	98·6	59·2	19·7	—	—

then multiplied by the survival ratio for male births to yield an estimate of boys aged 0-4 years in 1962; data for girls were treated similarly. The procedure is illustrated in Table B-21.

C. *Projection beyond* 1982

Although it is highly unrealistic to attempt to forecast populations at distant dates, Projections A and C were continued to the year 2002 solely to illustrate the cumulative long-term effects of a reduction in fertility. According to the assumptions adopted, mortality

Appendix B—Table 21. *Estimate of Births* 1957-62 *under Assumptions of Projection A*

(Illustration of method)

Age group	Female population			Age-specific fertility rates	Births
	1957	1962	Mean 1957-1962		
15-19	25,181	30,883	28,032	·1466	4,109
20-24	23,113	24,773	23,943	·2990	7,159
25-29	20,657	22,584	21,620	·2893	6,255
30-34	20,413	20,153	20,283	·2393	4,854
35-39	15,429	19,880	17,654	·1697	2,996
40-44	13,846	14,918	14,382	·0611	879

26,252 Total annual births
×5

131,260 Total births 1957-62
·5079 Estimated proportion of male births
66,667 Estimated male births
64,593 Estimated female births

would by 1982 reach a low level not unlike that of many Western countries at present, and therefore no further mortality decline was assumed during the remaining two decades to the end of the century. Likewise, no further changes in fertility were assumed during the period beyond 1982. The main results of these extended projections are given in Chapter 3.

D. *Summary of mortality and fertility indices implied in the projections*

The assumptions of declining mortality in Projections A and C would have the effect of raising life expectancy at birth to 64·7 years for males and to 68·2 years for females by 1982 (Table B-22). The corresponding figures for 1957 were 54·0 and 57·3 respectively. Thus, a gain of 0·4 years annually is implied—a rate of change similar to that found, on average, among the countries studied by the United Nations.

The crude birth- and death-rates implied in the three projections are shown in Table B-23.

It will be seen that even with assumptions of constant age-specific fertility rates (Projection A), the crude birth-rate would increase somewhat as a result of changing age structure, a normal feature of

Appendix B—Table 22. *Expectation of Life at Birth for Males and Females implied in Projections A and C*

Period	Males	Females
1957-62	56·2	58·1
1962-67	58·7	61·0
1967-72	61·1	63·7
1972-77	63·1	66·2
1977-82	64·7	68·2

Appendix B—Table 23. *Crude Birth- and Death-rates implied in the Population Projections.*

Period	Crude birth-rates			Crude death-rates		
--------	Projection A	Projection B	Projection C	Projection A	Projection B	Projection C
1957-62	40·9	38·9	37·4	11·0	10·9	10·8
1962-67	40·1	35·3	30·8	9·3	10·6	9·0
1967-72	41·1	35·5	26·0	7·9	10·6	7·8
1972-77	42·2	37·0	23·9	6·8	10·7	7·1
1977-82	42·5	37·3	23·8	5·8	10·6	6·7

population dynamics. The crude birth-rate of 35·5 implied in Projection B for 1967 is roughly representative of the average level which has been recorded in Mauritius over a long period in the past (see Chapter 3).* Projection C implies a drastic fall in the crude birth-rate—from its present level of about 40 to about 24 by 1972. Such a rapid rate of decline has seldom been achieved in any country.

E. *Comparisons with other projections*

The results of Projections A and B, which have been presented in full in the text of Chapter 3, are summarized in Table B-24 and compared with the various projections which had earlier been prepared for Mauritius by Mr. Brookfield and by the Colonial Office.†

Appendix B—Table 24. *Comparisons of various Population Projections for Mauritius:* 1957-82.

Year	Projection A of present study (constant fertility at 1956-58 levels, declining mortality)	Projection B of present study (moderately declining fertility, constant mortality at 1957-62 levels)	Brookfield projection (declining fertility and declining mortality)‡	Brookfield projection (constant fertility at 1955 levels; constant mortality at 1952 levels)§	Colonial Office projection (constant fertility and mortality at 1952 levels)§‖
1957	594,290	594,290	577,284	577,284	572,670
1962	690,195	683,763	631,770	632,812	649,474
1967	805,342	773,621	691,367	695,332	733,585
1972	950,948	876,301	759,314	768,014	828,249
1977	1,135,899	999,883	829,129	853,144	936,671
1982	1,365,487	1,142,381	897,799	947,476	1,065,525

Source: The Brookfield and Colonial Office projections appear in Brookfield, H. C., "Mauritius: Demographic Upsurge and Prospect" (*op. cit.*), p. 110.

‡ Fertility assumed to decline to reach by 1982 levels currently experienced in some European countries.

§ In addition to the difference in the level of the fertility rates used in these two projections, Brookfield's calculations start from a higher 1952 base, since he adjusted the census data for absences of Pioneer Corps and omissions of young children.

‖ This projection was intended merely as an illustration of method (See footnote † below).

* The average level shown throughout the period from the beginning of the century was about 36-37 per 1,000. As mentioned earlier, it is likely that there was some understatement in the 1952 census reports on numbers of children ever born, which formed the basis for the calculation of the fertility rates underlying Projection B. Moreover, these data incorporated some permanent fertility losses of the depression years.

† It must be noted that the population projection prepared by the Colonial Office was intended merely as a simplified example in methodology, and the assumptions incorporated in it were not necessarily considered to represent the most likely future trend of mortality and fertility. This purpose seems, on occasion, however, to have been misunderstood.

These earlier projections had 1952 as their starting date, and hence could take no cognizance of the recent trends in vital statistics, which reveal a continuation of the high rate of population growth. Our 1957 estimate, which takes account of registered births and deaths during the period following the 1952 census, is shown to be 17,000 above Brookfield's projected figure for that date. Moreover, there were certain important differences between the assumptions underlying our projections and those on which the earlier calculations had been based. None of the earlier projections assumed declining mortality and constant fertility—a particular combination of events which, on the basis of the more recent data available to us, seemed a likely possibility for the future course of population in Mauritius. Finally, there were some differences in the techniques of projection between our method and those used by the Colonial office and by Mr. Brookfield.*

The net result of these various differences is that by 1982 our Projection A shows a figure 300,000 in excess of the highest of the earlier projections (the Colonial Office projection which assumed the continuance of 1952 fertility and mortality levels). Even our Projection B, which incorporates a rather high mortality assumption (though not as high as those of the Colonial Office and Brookfield projections), and a moderate fertility assumption, gives somewhat higher totals than any of the earlier projections.

* Brookfield and the Colonial Office used somewhat simplified techniques, and it can now be seen that the errors introduced failed to compensate as much as might have been expected. In estimating births for the various projection periods, they applied age-specific fertility rates to the numbers of women in the age group at the beginning of the projection period, instead of the more accurate mean numbers for each period. When the population is growing at a rapid rate, as it is in Mauritius, such a method tends to consistently underestimate births. The survival ratios used in the Colonial Office and Brookfield projections were life-table p_x values, rather than group survival ratios. Thus, at the upper ages they are too high, while at ages 0-4 they are too low, reflecting the full force of infant mortality, which had already been taken into account in deriving the survival ratios for births. We have re-calculated Brookfield's projection based on declining fertility and declining mortality—retaining his base population figures for 1952 and his assumptions, but revising the two techniques outlined here. The result shows a 1982 population some 50,000 higher than his published figure. If his projection based on constant fertility and mortality were to be similarly revised, the difference would no doubt be greater, since this projection allows for a higher rate of population growth. For the methods used in the Brookfield and Colonial Office projections see Brookfield, H. C., "Mauritius: Demographic Upsurge and Prospect"(*op cit*), pp. 121-122; and *Report of the Committee on Population* (*op. cit.*), pp. 16-18.

APPENDIX C

Income Tax Statistics for Mauritius, 1957-58

by Tony Lynes, A.C.A.

The Income Tax Department sends an abstract of each tax assessment to the Central Statistical Office. These abstracts do not show the name of the taxpayer. They simply show the gross amount of his income grouped under various sources, any deductions made or allowances given in arriving at his chargeable income (on which tax is payable), and the amount of tax payable at each rate. Some of this information is analysed and published in summary form in the annual reports of the Income Tax Department. I am indebted to Mr. L. Honoré, Director of Statistics, and his staff for extracting certain further information from the statistical abstracts for the year of assessment 1957-58 (the last year for which sufficiently complete data were available) on which this appendix is based. The figures quoted here differ slightly from those given in the Annual Report of the Income Tax Department for 1957-58, because a number of additional assessments have been made since that Report was written.

The number of individuals assessed to Income Tax for 1957-58 was 7,081. Of these 6,670 were resident in Mauritius and its Dependencies, and 411 were non-resident. Table C-1 analyses the 6,670 resident taxpayers in gross income groups (gross income being income before making any deductions for tax allowances, interest payments, losses, etc.).

Appendix C—Table 1. Resident Taxpayers by Gross Income Groups.

Gross income Rs.	No. of taxpayers
5,000 and less	1,128
5,001 to 7,500	1,000
7,501 to 10,000	1,063
10,001 to 15,000	1,442
15,001 to 20,000	697
20,001 to 30,000	704
30,001 to 40,000	234
40,001 to 50,000	135
50,001 to 60,000	76
60,001 to 70,000	48
70,001 to 80,000	40
80,001 to 100,000	41
Over 100,000	62
	6,670

These gross incomes, after deducting relatively small amounts for interest paid, losses and investment and capital allowances, total rather more than Rs. 100 million, of which nearly half (just over Rs. 50 million) is absorbed by the various allowances and reliefs. Roughly one-third of the total allowances is accounted for by earned income relief (25% on the first Rs. 10,000 and 20% on the next Rs. 15,000*), and another third by the personal allowance of Rs. 2,500. The remaining third consists of allowances for dependants, life assurance premiums and contributions to superannuation schemes and widows' and orphans' pension funds:—

	Rupees
Wife (normally Rs. 2,000)	6,528,000
Children:	
At home (from Rs. 800 to Rs. 500 per child depending on number of eligible children)	5,229,400
Abroad (do.+Rs. 1,000)†	503,300
Dependent relatives (Rs. 500)	897,874
Life Assurance premiums	2,513,639
Superannuation contributions, etc.	774,255
	16,446,468

Table C-2 shows the proportion of taxpayers in each gross income group claiming each of these allowances.

Appendix C—Table 2. Proportion of Resident Taxpayers claiming Allowances, by Gross Income Groups.

Gross income Rs.	Percentage of taxpayers claiming each allowance					
	Wife	Children		Dependent relatives	Life assurance	Superannuation etc.
		At home	Abroad			
5,000 and less	1	2	—	13	2	24
5,001 to 7,500	14	9	—	28	6	25
7,501 to 10,000	52	36	1	32	11	33
10,001 to 15,000	70	62	3	28	21	35
15,001 to 20,000	75	63	3	34	33	35
20,001 to 30,000	78	58	9	26	43	33
30,001 to 40,000	80	60	12	34	50	25
40,001 to 50,000	77	59	10	27	54	19
50,001 to 60,000	79	62	11	30	58	28
60,001 to 70,000	77	44	10	35	60	8
70,001 to 80,000	82	67	10	17	72	12
80,001 to 100,000	93	56	15	34	83	20
Over 100,000	77	45	27	23	76	32
All taxpayers	49	39	3	27	21	30

* Increased to Rs. 25,000 in 1959-60.
† From 1959-60, an additional allowance of Rs. 2,500 is given for a child aged 16 or over studying abroad.

The proportion of taxpayers claiming these allowances in the lowest income groups is small, because in many cases the allowances are sufficient to reduce the *chargeable* income to nil, and the figures do not include these cases. Thus a married couple with no children and only earned income will pay no tax if their income does not exceed Rs. 6,000. The corresponding exemption limit for a couple with one child studying abroad is Rs. 8,400 (from 1959-60 this is raised to Rs. 11,625 if the child is aged 16 or over). It follows that taxpayers in the two lowest income groups, with gross incomes up to Rs. 7,500 a year, are for the most part single men or couples with no dependent children. At this income level, the allowances ensure that the man with a wife and children does not pay tax. However, they do not give any additional relief to the large family. It is not until we reach the Rs. 10,000-15,000 group that the full benefit of the allowances for a family of five or six children is obtained, and the further we move up the income scale the more these allowances are worth.

Table C-2 shows clearly that it is parents in the top income groups who send their children to be educated abroad. This allowance is claimed by over a quarter of those with incomes over Rs. 100,000, but by only 3% of those in the Rs. 10,000-20,000 groups. It cannot therefore be said that the allowance is very effective in enabling those who could not otherwise afford it to have their children educated abroad. The more generous allowance introduced in 1959-60 may prove more effective; on the other hand it may merely reduce still further the tax liability of the top income groups.

In view of the enormous encouragement the introduction of income tax is known to have given to sales of life assurance in Mauritius, it is not surprising to find that it is most popular among the well-to-do. Nevertheless, the regularity with which the proportion of taxpayers claiming relief for life assurance rises with income is quite remarkable.* It is in fact predictable economic behaviour, since the further one moves up the income scale the cheaper life assurance becomes. At the Rs. 100,000 income level and above, 75% or 80% of the premiums (at 1957-58 tax rates) are in effect paid by the Government.

The tendency for the proportion claiming an allowance for superannuation and widows' and orphans' pension contributions to decline above the Rs. 30,000 a year level is probably due to the fact that a considerable proportion of those claiming this allowance are civil servants.

After deducting all the allowances, we arrive at the *chargeable* incomes of the 6,670 resident taxpayers, on which tax is paid at the

* See also Table C-5.

appropriate rates. These chargeable incomes are analysed in Table C-3, which also shows the highest rate of tax paid by each group.

Appendix C—Table 3. Resident Taxpayers by Chargeable Income Groups.

Chargeable income Rs.	No. of taxpayers	Highest rate of tax %
5,000 and less	4,323	10
5,001 to 10,000	1,020	15
10,001 to 15,000	497	20
15,001 to 20,000	265	30
20,001 to 25,000	138	40
25,001 to 35,000	149	50
35,001 to 50,000	123	60
50,001 to 75,000	83	70
75,001 to 100,000	27	75
Over 100,000	45	80
	6,670	

The 4,323 taxpayers who only pay at the lowest rate of 10% include all the 2,128 with gross incomes not exceeding Rs. 7,500 (see Table C-1); all or nearly all of the 1,063 with gross incomes between Rs. 7,501 and Rs. 10,000 (since the personal allowance and earned income relief alone would reduce an earned income of Rs. 10,000 to a chargeable income of Rs. 5,000); and, presumably, the majority of the 1,442 with gross incomes between Rs. 10,001 and Rs. 15,000. It is, in other words, only those with really large incomes by Mauritian standards who pay tax at more than the minimum rate on any part of their income. A single man with no dependants and a salary of Rs. 10,000 a year pays only Rs. 500 in tax. In Britain, where his Rs. 10,000 salary (equivalent to £750) would not be greatly in excess of aveiage industrial earnings, he would have to pay £58 (Rs. 774) in tax and, in addition, £26 a year in National Insurance and National Health Service "tax-contribution".

Thus, although at the top end of the scale the marginal rate of tax (now 70%) is high, there would be considerable scope for increasing the rates at the lower end, if it were thought desirable to increase the total yield of the tax. Similarly, the number of taxpayers could be increased by making the allowances less generous.

Table C-4 shows the proportions of taxpayers at different levels of chargeable income who obtained their income from various

Appendix C—Table 4. Proportions of Resident Taxpayers by Chargeable Income Groups obtaining Income from various sources.

Total chargeable income	Number of taxpayers =100%	Percentage of taxpayers obtaining income from:						
		Employment	Self-employment	Dividends, interest etc.	Property (tax on annual value)	Rents etc.	Pensions, annuities etc.	Income from abroad	Other income
Rs.		%	%	%	%	%	%	%	%
5,000 and less	4,323	76	34	31	32	16	6	—	1
5,001–10,000	1,020	81	28	36	20	6	15	—	2
10,001–25,000	900	62	61	58	50	21	6	3	3
Over 25,000	427	72	78	86	69	20	4	9	7
All taxpayers	6,670	75	40	39	35	16	7	1	1

sources. The majority of taxpayers at all levels of income receive income from employment, though the proportions are somewhat lower above the Rs. 10,000 level. Self-employment, on the other hand, is much more common among those with chargeable incomes over Rs. 10,000. The same is true of dividends and income from property, which suggests that the distribution of income in Mauritius is closely correlated with capital holdings.

The total number of taxpayers receiving income from employment is 4,981, and a large proportion of them have other sources of income. As many as 1,921 (38%) have income in the form of dividends and interest, and 1,629 (33%) own property.

The information given in Table C-2 regarding the incidence of various allowances can be supplemented by an analysis of the allowances claimed by *chargeable* income groups. Thus, Table C-5 shows the amount of life assurance premiums for which allowances were claimed in each chargeable income group and the average amount claimed per taxpayer in each group.

Appendix C—Table 5. Life Assurance Allowances claimed by Resident Taxpayers, by Chargeable Income Groups.

Chargeable income Rs.	No. of taxpayers	Life Assurance premiums Rs.	Average per taxpayer Rs.
5,000 and less	4,323	272,835	63
5,001 to 10,000	1,020	248,199	243
10,001 to 15,000	497	238,954	481
15,001 to 20,000	265	193,405	730
20,001 to 25,000	138	128,334	930
25,001 to 35,000	149	256,261	1,720
35,001 to 50,000	123	325,877	2,649
50,001 to 75,000	83	312,415	3,764
75,001 to 100,000	27	148,674	5,506
Over 100,000	45	388,685	8,637
	6,670	Rs. 2,513,639	

If we assume (on the basis of Table C-2) that about 78%, or 35 out of the 45 taxpayers with chargeable income over Rs. 100,000 claim this allowance, the average premiums per head for these 35 are Rs. 11,105, on which the tax forgone is Rs. 8,884 (£666)—an astonishingly high figure. The total cost of this allowance in terms of tax forgone, deduced from Table C-5, was about Rs. 1,200,000 (£90,000) in 1957-58. From 1959-60, the cost would be somewhat reduced by the abolition of the 75% and 80% tax rates, but this is probably outweighed by the increase in premiums.

The allowances for contributions to superannuation schemes and widows' and orphans' pension funds cost about Rs. 160,000 for 1957-58. This figure is subject to the proviso mentioned in the next paragraph. Moreover, it represents only a small fraction of the cost of these schemes in terms of tax, since the greater part of the contributions are paid by employers and deducted from their taxable profits.

It is more difficult to estimate the cost of dependants' allowances, because we have no information as to the number of would-be taxpayers who escape tax altogether by claiming these allowances. This factor was of little importance in calculating the cost of the life assurance allowance, which is concentrated in the higher income groups. For the same reason, it is unlikely greatly to affect the cost of the allowance for children educated abroad. It does, however, represent a significant addition to the cost of the allowance for other children and dependent relatives—just how significant we have no means of estimating.

With this important proviso, we can arrive at a fairly reliable estimate of the cost of dependants' allowances* for 1957-58:—

	Rupees
Children: abroad	160,000
other	1,000,000
	1,160,000
Dependent relatives (including housekeepers)	150,000
	1,310,000

or £98,250. The additional Rs. 2,500 allowance for children studying abroad in 1959-60 would increase the cost of this allowance from the figure of Rs. 160,000 shown above to about Rs. 370,000 for the same number of children. As the number of full-time students in the U.K. alone (excluding G.C.E. and law students) appears to have risen from 264 in March 1958† to about 360 in October 1959,‡ it seems probable that the total cost of the allowance for 1959-60 will be in the region of Rs. 500,000.

* "Wife allowance" is omitted here because it is a "personal allowance" rather than a dependant's allowance. It could well be argued, however, that it should only be given on the wife's earnings.
† Sessional Paper No. 5 of 1959, *Report of the Ministerial Committee on Recruitment and Training*.
‡ Lists of students supplied by Mauritius Students' Unit in London.

APPENDIX D

Diet Sheet Submitted in Evidence by Mother Provincial of Bon Secours Convents

DIET FOR CHILDREN'S HOMES, YEAR 1960

(Showing food items with average weight served and price of same for one day: breakfast, lunch, tea, dinner)

Per Head

MILK, 40 centilitres	20 cs.
BREAD, 200 grms.	14 cs.
RICE, 250 grms.	15 cs.
LENTILS (or beans, etc.), 65 grms.	8 cs.
BUTTER (or margarine), 25 grms.	12 cs.
VEGETABLES, 250 grms.	26 cs.
SUGAR, 125 grms.	5 cs.
SPICES, TOMATOES, etc., 30 grms.	22 cs.
FRUIT (chiefly banana) or CAKE	5 cs.
TEA, 10 grms.	6 cs.
OIL, 30 grms.	$6\frac{1}{2}$ cs.
FISH, 250 grms., *only once a week* ($\div 7$ days)	10 cs.
MEAT, 200 grms., *only once a week* ($\div 7$ days)	12 cs.
SALT FISH, 5 *days in a week* (42 cs. $\div 7$ days)	6 cs.

Total: Rs. 1 · 68

Remark.

The diet is much the same for INFIRMARIES, except for less rice and more bread in some cases. HINDUS are served sardines or tinned fish instead of meat.

N.B.

Provision is not made in the above list for extra diets in case of illness; e.g. eggs, more milk, chocolate (cocoa) or Ovaltine served between breakfast and lunch, Custard or Sago, etc.

Fuel for cooking is not provided either.

(Signed) MOTHER Marie de l'Enfant Jésus
Superior Provincial
(SISTERS of Our Lady of
Good and Perpetual Succour).

22nd March 1960.

APPENDIX E

Official Enquiries into Social Conditions and Problems in Mauritius, 1910-1960

The following list of enquiries has been assembled to illustrate the extent to which the social problems of Mauritius have been investigated in the past 50 years. Although it is certainly incomplete, it is hoped that future investigators will find it of some value as a bibliography of official sources. A number of unpublished reports are listed, including three (marked *) of which we were unable to trace copies.

1921   Reports by Dr. A. Balfour on:—
  The Sanitation of Port Louis.
  Communicable Diseases in Port Louis.
  Sanitary Matters in the Districts of Moka and Pamplemousses.
  Sanitary Matters in the Districts of Rivière du Rempart and Flacq.
  The Sanitation of Beau Bassin, Rose Hill, Quatre Bornes, Phoenix, Vacoas and Curepipe.
  Sanitary Matters in Black River District and the Extra Urban Area of Plaines Wilhems.
  Sanitary Matters in the Districts of Grand Port and Savanne.
  Medical Matters in Mauritius.

*1929   Report of the Medical Commission.

1931   Report of the Poor Relief Enquiry Commission, and Dissenting Memorandum by Mr. G. M. D. Atchia.

1931   Report of the Commission on the Financial Situation of Mauritius (Cmd. 4034, 1932).

1935   Report of the Unemployment Committee.

1937   Report of the Commission of Enquiry into Unrest on Sugar Estates in Mauritius (1938).

1940   Report on the Condition of Indians in Mauritius, by S. Ridley. (New Delhi, 1941.)

1941   Report of the Social Insurance Committee, and Dissenting Memorandum by Dr. E. Millien.

1941   Report on Education in Mauritius, by W. E. F. Ward.

1943   Report of the Select Committee on the Ward Report on Education.

1943   Report on Labour Conditions in Ceylon, Mauritius and Malaya, by Major G. St. J. Orde Browne.

1944	Report on Health Conditions in Mauritius, by Dr. A. Rankine, M.C.
*1946 (?)	Report on the Management of "The Home", Beau Bassin, by a sub-committee of the Central Poor Law Board.
*1946 (?)	Survey of Poor Houses, by Mr. Magistrate Glover.
1947	Report on the Feeding in Infirmaries and Orphanages, by Miss J. C. Chettle.
1947	Report on Local Government in Mauritius, by J. B. Swinden.
1948	Report of the Mauritius Economic Commission, 1947-48.
1949	Report on the Project of Emigration from Mauritius to North Borneo, by R. C. Wilkinson.
1949	Employment Survey by the Labour Department.
1952	First Report of the Outdoor Relief Committee.
1953	Second Report of the Outdoor Relief Committee.
1953	Report of the Committee on a Health Insurance Scheme —Sessional Paper No. 4 of 1953.
1955	Report of the Fiscal Committee—Sessional Paper No. 5 of 1955.
1955	Report of the Committee on Population, 1953-54—Sessional Paper No. 4 of 1955.
1958	"A Plan for Mauritius": The Final Report of the Economic Planning Committee (the Five-Year Plan) —Sessional Paper No. 4 of 1958.
1958	Report on Employment, Unemployment, and Under-employment in the Colony in 1958, together with Report on an Investigation into the Wages and Conditions of Employment of Labourers and Artisans in the Sugar Industry, by R. W. Luce—Sessional Paper No. 7 of 1958.
1959	Report of the Ministerial Committee on Recruitment and Training—Sessional Paper No. 5 of 1959.
1959	Report of the Commission on the Purchasing Power of the Rupee in Mauritius—Sessional Paper No. 6 of 1959.

APPENDIX F

Estimated Cost of Social Insurance, Non-contributory and Welfare Benefits

Estimated annual cost
Rs.   Rs.

Phase I

Non-contributory benefits (Year 1960-61)

Family benefit	7,550,000	
Marriage benefit	100,000	
Maternity benefit	200,000	
Survivors' benefits:		
Childless widows' three-month benefit	50,000	
Widowed mothers' benefit	2,200,000	
Widowers with children	350,000	
Widow(er)s' children's allowances	200,000	
Guardians' and Orphans' allowances	300,000	
		10,950,000

Welfare benefits (Year 1960-61—see note)

Issue of dried skimmed milk to pre-school children	750,000	
Issue of shoes to a third of primary school children	100,000	
		850,000
		11,800,000
Administration		500,000
		12,300,000
Less saving on public assistance		3,000,000
		Rs. 9,300,000

NOTE:—The cost of a school meals service is not included in the above estimates owing to uncertainty as to the type of meal which could best be provided and the proportion of the cost which could be recovered from parents.

	Estimated annual cost
	Rs.

Phase II

Social Insurance Benefits

Sickness benefit	500,000
Unemployment benefit	3,400,000
Fire disaster benefit	100,000
Industrial injury benefit	200,000
	4,200,000
Administration	500,000
	4,700,000
Less saving on public assistance	1,000,000
	Rs 3,700,000

Phase III

No estimates have been made of the costs of a non-contributory "Small Family Pension" or of a graduated contributory pension scheme (see Chapters 5 and 12).

Index

Amis du Moulin à Poudre, 40
Anaemia, research on, 131
ATCHIA, MR. G., 70, 71

BALFOUR, DR. A., 165, 206
Barkly Asylum, 205-6
BENEDICT, DR. B., 130
Birth-rates, *see Population*
Blind, institutional care of the, 210
British Red Cross Society, 40
BROOKFIELD, MR. H. C., 42, 234, 247, 290

Calebasses Infirmary, 206-7, 213
Census, *see Population*
Central Prison, technical education in, 6
Charitable funds, 27-9
CHETTLE, MISS J. C., 209
Children:
  Adoption, 218
  Boarding out, 217
  Needs of, 131-3
  Of social security beneficiaries, 141-2
  Tax allowances for, 136-7, 180-1
Children's allowances to widows and widowers, 154
Children's homes:
  37, 205 et seq.
  Diet sheet, 299
CHRISTIANSEN, MR. E. W., 223
Civil service:
  Pensions, 21-2, 112
  Sick leave, 23-4
Civil Service Mutual Aid Association, 29-30
Colonisation and settlement, 2
Commission on the Financial Situation of Mauritius, 71
Compagnons Bâtisseurs, 40
Constitution, 8

Cost of proposals, 227-33, 302-3
Credit arrangements, 31-3
Credit Unions, 30-1
Cyclone damage, 9, 14-5

DANTIER, MISS E. L., 126, 138, 140
DARLOW, MISS M.:
  Appointment as Public Assistance Commissioner, 73, 74
  Darlow Report, The, 76, 77, 78, 145, 151, 152
Death-rates, *see Population*
de CHAZAL, DR. E. L., 166
de CHAZAL, MRS. L. M. D., 172
de CHAZAL, MR. MARC, 85, 86, 170
de ROBILLARD, MR. EDWIN, 31, 40
Disabled, non-residential training for, 124

Earnings:
  Ascertainment of, 148-9
  Disregards in calculating assistance payable, 78-9, 147-8
Education:
  Primary, 4
  Secondary, 4-5
Employment, survey of, 11-12
Ex-Servicemen's Welfare Fund, 27

Family allowances, 133-6
Family benefits, 135-6, 154, 232, 242, 243
Family planning, 36, 63, 186-7, 240-5
Family Welfare Association of Mauritius, 36, 186
Fertility, *see Population*
Fire disaster benefit, 106-7
Friendly societies, 29-30

General practitioner services, 35-6, 169-73, 192-8
Geographical and historical background, 1-9
Gross national product, 7

HAZAREESINGH, MR. K., appointment as Assistant Commissioner, 73
Health and family planning services, financing of, 244-5
Health Insurance Committee, 171-3
Health services:
33-7, 161-204
Ambulances, 189
Charges for services, 199-202, 229
Clinique Mauricienne, 35
Cost of improvements, 288-9, 244-5
Dental services, 168, 198-9
Dispensary services, 168, 174
District hospitals, need for, 188
Doctors' residences, provision of, 195-6
Drugs, distribution of, 35, 176-7, 198
Estate medical services, 4, 34, 164-5, 189-92
Family doctor service, 192-8
Family planning service, 36, 63, 186-7, 240-5
Future plans, 168-9
General Medical Council, proposed, 175
General Nursing Council, proposed, 176
General practitioner services, 35-6, 169-73, 192-8
Historical background, 161-4
Hookworm infestation, 185
Hospitals, 34-5, 167, 188-9, 196, 200-2
Infirmaries, responsibility for, 218
Maternity and child welfare services, 36, 166, 168, 184-5
Medical students, 180-3
Mental defectives, hospital and training centre, 188-9, 218-9

Ministerial Committee, 172-3
National Health Service of Mauritius, 201
Nursing staff, training, 167, 197
Panel practice, 169-73, 192-3
Private clinics, 29, 34-5, 202
Public health services, 33, 185
Recommendations, summary, 202-4
Recruitment of doctors, 178-83
Rehabilitation of disabled, 124, 218
School medical service, 36-7, 168
Shortage of doctors and nurses, 174, 178-83, 191, 195
Social Insurance Committee, 169-71
Unethical practices, 174-8
HEIN, MR. RAYMOND, 85, 86, 170
HONORÉ, MR. L., 292
Hookworm infestation, 141, 185
Hospitals, 34-5, 167, 188-9, 196, 200-2
Housing, 6-7

Income tax statistics, 292-8
Indian indentured labourers, 2
Industrial injuries and diseases, 17, 114-24
Infirmaries, 37, 205 et seq.
Institutional care:
37-8, 205 et seq.
Amis du Moulin à Poudre, 223
Blind persons, 210, 223-4
Boarding out of children, 217-8
Calebasses Infirmary, administration by Government, 207
Children's officer, 217-8
Classification of inmates, 212-3, 215, 219-20
Food, 209-10, 214-5, 221-2, 299
Historical background, 205-10
Lady Visiting Officer, appointment of, 208
Latrines, 214, 221
Non-denominational institutions, proposed, 219-21

Overcrowding, 213, 221
Poor Relief Enquiry Commission (1929), 206-7
Privacy, lack of, 213-4
Public Assistance Department grant, 206, 209-10, 211, 221-2
Recommendations, summary, 224-5
Rehabilitation centre, plans for building, 218
Religious denominations, 207-8, 211, 213, 219
Staff, 210, 216, 222-3
Survey of institutions, 211-3
Voluntary work, 223
Work done by inmates, 208, 214
International Voluntary Service, 40

Languages, 2
Leper Hospital, 223
Life Assurance allowances, 19-21
Local government, 8-9
Loïs Lagesse Residential and Training Centre, 37-8, 210, 223
Lotteries (H.M. Forces) Fund, 28
LUCE, MR. R. W., 3, 11-12, 231

Malaria, eradication of, 2, 46-7
Marriage benefit, 130, 232, 243
Maternity and child welfare services, 36, 166, 168, 169, 185-6
Maternity and Child Welfare Society, 36, 166
Maternity benefit, 130-1, 243
Mauritius Agricultural Bank, housing loans, 6
Meade Report, 226, 238, 246
Medical services, *see Health services*
MEIER, DR. R. L., 239
MILLIEN, DR. C. E., 85, 86, 169, 170, 172
Mortality, *see Population*
Muslim Orphanage, 207

National Assistance Board, proposed establishment of, 157-9
Non-contributory benefits, cost of, 144, 229, 231, 302

Official enquiries into social conditions and problems, 1910-1960, 300-1
Old age pensions, 4, 17, 88-9, 107
O'MALLEY, SIR EDWARD, 70
Orphanages, 37, 205, et seq.
Orphans' benefit, 142
Outdoor Relief, *see Public Assistance*

Pension schemes:
  Civil service, 21-2, 112
  Old age and blind pensions, 4, 17, 29, 88-9
  Small family pension benefit, 107-8, 111·
  Sugar Industry Pension Fund, 24-5, 112
  Town Boards and Municipality, 23
  Wage related pensions, 108-12
  War pensions, 18
  Widows and Orphans Pension Fund, 22
Pioneer Corps, 252-3
Poor Law, *see Public Assistance*
Poor Law Ordinance, 1902, 67-8
Poor Relief Enquiry Commission, 70-1
Population:
  42-66, 233-40
  Adjustments to census data, 252-61
  Age structure, 54-5, 59-62, 237
  Birth-rates, 46, 47-51, 234, 289-90
  Census data, 45, 51-2, 54, 252-66 274-7
  Committee on Population (1953-54), 42, 236
  Comparison with other countries, 47, 55, 62, 235, 274, 276
  Composition, 3, 43
  Control, need for, 15, 42, 59, 63, 233-40
  Death-rates, 46, 47-50, 234-5, 289
  Density, 47, 237
  Emigration, 63, 236, 238

Fertility assumptions, 57-8, 236, 287
Fertility trends, 47-51, 54, 57-8, 273-82
Growth, 2, 10, 43-7, 59-62, 233-4
Immigration, 2, 45-6, 236
Marriage, 50-4
Mortality assumptions, 56-7, 58, 235-7, 285-7
Mortality trends, 45, 47-9, 56-7, 234-5, 261-72
Projections, 55-6, 59-66, 235-7, 285-91
Three-child family, 58, 61, 66, 107, 135, 236-7, 242, 279-82
United Nations model life tables, 261 et seq.
Vital registration, 47, 251-2, 258-9, 266-70, 273-5, 282-3

Post-natal services, 138-40, 185-6
Pre-school children, provision of milk for, 137-40
Private pension schemes, 26, 110, 112
Public Assistance:
  18-9, 67-84, 145-60
  Administration 18, 75-6, 155-9
  Advisory Committees, 18, 69-70, 73-6, 79, 155-6
  Ascertainment of earnings, 148-9
  Assessment of needs, 76-80
  Burden of work falling on Government medical officers, 35, 79-80
  Children's allowances, 84, 132, 153-4
  Cost, 8, 13-4, 19, 68-71, 74-5, 231-3
  Cyclone relief, 15
  Discretionary allowances, 155
  Disregarded earnings, 78-9, 147-8
  Historical background, 67-75
  Liable relatives, 80, 151-2
  National Assistance Board, proposed, 157-9
  Normal earnings, 145-7, 149
  Office building programme, 75
  Payment by the Post Office, 157
  Poor Relief Enquiry Commission, 70-71
  Present scale of relief, 19, 77-9
  Proposed scale of relief, 152-5
  Recommendations of Mauritius Royal Commission (1909), 68-70
  Recommendations, summary, 159-60
  Rent allowance, 153
  Selection and training of officers, 156
  Sickness claims, 10-11, 35, 81, 148
  Unemployment relief, 71-3, 80-2
  Wage stop, 78, 154-5
  Work record cards, 82-3
  Work test, 82, 150-1
Public health, 33, 185
Public revenue, 7-8
Public works, 105-6

RANKINE, DR. A., 165
READ, LADY, 166
Red Cross Society, British, 40
Religions, 3
Rents, 153
Repas des Pauvres, 40

St. John Ambulance Association, 40
Scholarships, 5, 180-2
School meals and milk service, 37, 125-6, 133, 140
School medical service, 36-7, 186
Shoes, provision of free to schoolchildren, 141
Sickness insurance, 90-103
Slaves, introduction and freeing of, 2
Small family pension benefit, 107-8, 111
Social Insurance:
  85-113, 245-6
  Children's allowances, 141-2
  Contributions, 86-7, 89-90, 93-4, 95-7, 101, 109
  Cost of benefits, 90, 230-2
  Duration of benefits, 102-3
  Earlier enquiries, 85-90

Employment bureaux, 104
Fire disaster benefit, 106-7
Industrial injuries, 122-4
Introduction of scheme, 229-30
Ministerial Committee, 89-90
Occupational provisions, 110, 111-2
Pensions, contributory, 85-7, 108-12
Qualifying conditions, 100-6
Rates of benefit, 86, 90, 98-100, 106-7, 110-1
Self-employed persons, 94-5, 110
Sickness insurance, 90-103
Social Insurance Committee, 85-7, 169-71
Unemployment insurance, 85, 87, 90-106, 246
Waiting periods, 102-3
Widows' pensions, 110-1
Work records, 92-3
Work test, 103-6
Social Welfare Department, 38-9
Society of St. Vincent de Paul, 40
Sugar industry:
2, 3, 9-10, 13
End of year bonus, 25-6
Estate medical services, 4, 34, 164-5, 189-92
Sugar Industry Pension Fund, 24-5

Sugar Industry Labour Welfare Fund:
36, 37, 38-40
Housing activities, 7
Survivor's benefit, 127-30

Tax allowances:
19, 292-8
For children, 136-7, 180-1
Tea crop, development of, 2
Technical education, 5-6
Tobacco crop, development of, 2
Trade union funds, 30
Tuberculosis, allowances in cases of, 154

Unemployment, 10-13, 72-3, 80-1, 90-1
Unemployment insurance, 85, 87, 90-106, 246

Voluntary organisations, 40-1

War pensions, 18
Welfare of the Blind and Prevention of Blindness Society, 29, 210
Widows and Orphans Pension Fund, 22
Work test, 103-6
Workmen's compensation, 4, 17-8, 114, et seq.

For Product Safety Concerns and Information please contact our EU representative GPSR@taylorandfrancis.com
Taylor & Francis Verlag GmbH, Kaufingerstraße 24, 80331 München, Germany

www.ingramcontent.com/pod-product-compliance
Lightning Source LLC
Chambersburg PA
CBHW051628230426
43669CB00013B/2226